Transitional Justice and the Criminal Responsibility of Judges

AF755166

This collective volume delves into the criminal responsibility of judges under authoritarian regimes, with case studies from Germany, Argentina, and Chile, examining their involvement in criminal human rights abuses and failures to protect victims from such crimes.

Through comparative analysis, this volume offers insights into the legal and doctrinal challenges of prosecuting judicial involvement in crimes such as murder ('judicial murder'), kidnapping, unlawful detention, and torture. Bridging a gap in transitional justice and international criminal law literature, it focuses on the rarely explored criminal responsibility of judges beyond judicial misconduct. In doing so, it provides readers with a deeper understanding of judicial roles in authoritarian regimes and the complex legal standards involved in prosecuting such cases. It also informs the ongoing discourse on judicial accountability and the potential legal implications for judges in contemporary contexts.

Transitional Justice and the Criminal Responsibility of Judges is ideal for students, scholars, and civil servants or practitioners working in the domestic or the international criminal justice system.

Claudia Cárdenas is Associate Professor in the Department of Criminal Sciences at the Faculty of Law of the Universidad de Chile.

Jaime Couso is Professor in the Department of Criminal Law and Dean of the Faculty of Law at Universidad Diego Portales (Chile).

Florian Jeßberger is Professor at Humboldt-Universität zu Berlin (Germany), where he holds the Chair in Criminal Law, Criminal Procedure, International Criminal Law, and Modern Legal History.

Milan Kuhli is Professor and Vice Dean for Academic Affairs of the Faculty of Law at Universität Hamburg (Germany), where he holds the Chair in Criminal Law and Criminal Procedure, including its International and Historical Context.

Directions and Developments in Criminal Justice and Law

www.routledge.com/Directions-and-Developments-in-Criminal-Justice-and-Law/book-series/DDCJL

The ways in which crime is constructed in society is of time-honored interest to criminologists across the globe. The ever-changing landscape of what is criminal and what is not affects scholars and policymakers in their approach to the body of law defining prohibited conduct, how that law evolves, and the modes by which it is administered. Rule of law cannot exist without a transparent legal system, strong enforcement structures, and an independent judiciary to protect against the arbitrary use of power. Critical consideration of the mechanisms through which societies attempt to make the rule of law a reality is essential to understanding and developing effectual criminal justice systems. The *Directions and Developments in Criminal Justice and Law* series offers the best research on criminal justice and law around the world, offering original insights on a broadly defined range of socio-legal topics in law, criminal procedure, courts, justice, legislation, and jurisprudence. With an eye toward using innovative and advanced methodologies, series monographs offer solid social science scholarship illuminating issues and trends in law, crime, and justice. Books in this series will appeal to criminologists, sociologists, and other social scientists, as well as policymakers, legal researchers, and practitioners.

17. **The Political Economy of Plea Bargaining**
    Robert Schehr

18. **Wrongful Convictions and the Criminalization of Innocence**
    International Perspectives on Contributing Factors, Models of Exoneration and Case Studies
    Edited by Kathryn M. Campbell, Barak Ariel, Anat Horovitz and Irwin Cotler

19. **Transitional Justice and the Criminal Responsibility of Judges**
    Edited by Claudia Cárdenas, Jaime Couso, Florian Jeßberger and Milan Kuhli

Transitional Justice and the Criminal Responsibility of Judges

Edited by Claudia Cárdenas, Jaime Couso, Florian Jeßberger and Milan Kuhli

In Collaboration with Cath Collins

Routledge
Taylor & Francis Group
LONDON AND NEW YORK

First published 2025
by Routledge
4 Park Square, Milton Park, Abingdon, Oxon OX14 4RN

and by Routledge
605 Third Avenue, New York, NY 10158

Routledge is an imprint of the Taylor & Francis Group, an informa business

© 2025 selection and editorial matter, Claudia Cárdenas, Jaime Couso, Florian Jeßberger and Milan Kuhli; individual chapters, the contributors

The right of Claudia Cárdenas, Jaime Couso, Florian Jeßberger and Milan Kuhli to be identified as the authors of the editorial material, and of the authors for their individual chapters, has been asserted in accordance with sections 77 and 78 of the Copyright, Designs and Patents Act 1988.

All rights reserved. No part of this book may be reprinted or reproduced or utilised in any form or by any electronic, mechanical, or other means, now known or hereafter invented, including photocopying and recording, or in any information storage or retrieval system, without permission in writing from the publishers.

Trademark notice: Product or corporate names may be trademarks or registered trademarks, and are used only for identification and explanation without intent to infringe.

British Library Cataloguing-in-Publication Data
A catalogue record for this book is available from the British Library

ISBN: 9781032746043 (hbk)
ISBN: 9781032746081 (pbk)
ISBN: 9781003470069 (ebk)

DOI: 10.4324/9781003470069

Typeset in Times New Roman
by Newgen Publishing UK

Contents

Contributors

Markus Abraham is based at the University of Hamburg (Chair of Prof. Jochen Bung) and at time of writing was interim Professor of Criminal Law and Criminal Procedural Law at the University of Freiburg. He holds first degrees in law and in philosophy, and his doctoral thesis in law, in the area of theory of punishment, is entitled 'Norm, Sanction, Faith: The Significance of Pain and Punishment Today' (2018). Abraham is presently working on the question of omission and the duty to rescue.

Daniela Accatino holds a first degree in Legal and Social Sciences from Universidad de Chile (1996), and qualified as a lawyer in 1997. She holds a PhD in Law from the University of Granada, Spain (2006), and in 1999 joined the Faculty of the Law School of the Universidad Austral de Chile, where she is currently Dean of Law. Her main areas of research are transitional justice; legal reasoning; evidence theory; theory of norms and legal reasoning; proof and constitutionalism; and judicial activism and the constitutional state. She is the author of numerous scientific publications in the area of her area of expertise.

Claudia Cárdenas is Associate Professor of the Department of Criminal Sciences at the Faculty of Law of the Universidad de Chile, having served as Department Director between 2021 and 2023. She holds LLM and Doctor Iuris degrees from Humboldt-Universität zu Berlin, and a first degree in Legal and Social Sciences from the Universidad de Chile. She is a former Director of the Graduate School (2016–2017) and the Human Rights Center (2014–2016) of the Faculty of Law of the Universidad de Chile, and of the Legal and Political Science Group at Chile's National Fund for Scientific and Technological Development (FONDECYT) (2015–2016). Her academic work involves undergraduate and postgraduate teaching, research, and outreach, while her research publications are mainly related to international and transnational criminal law and human rights.

Alejandra Castillo Ara is a lawyer with a first degree in Legal Sciences from the Universidad Adolfo Ibáñez, Santiago de Chile. She holds LLM and Doctor Iuris degrees from the Albert-Ludwigs-Universität in Freiburg, Germany. She is currently Professor of Criminal Law at Chile's Universidad Diego Portales, where she directs the Department of Criminal and Criminal Procedural Law. She has published several articles and books on the topic of mistake of law, including *Normbefolgungsunfähigkeit im Strafrecht* (Duncker & Humblot 2019).

Nancy Combs is the Ernest W. Goodrich Professor of Law, Robert E. and Elizabeth S. Scott Research Professor, and Director of the Human Security Law Center at William & Mary Law School, in Virginia, USA. She specializes in issues of international criminal justice and has authored two books (Cambridge University Press and Stanford University Press) along with dozens of law review articles.

Kai Cornelius is Professor of Criminal Law at Universität Hamburg. He received his doctorate from Universität Heidelberg, Germany, in 2005 for a dissertation with a legal-historical background. In 2014, he completed the habilitation procedure at Universität Heidelberg and now he holds the Chair of Criminal Law with International Criminal Law at Universität Hamburg. In 2023, he was also appointed as a Judge at the Hanseatic Higher Regional Court in Hamburg.

Jaime Couso is Professor and Dean of Law at Universidad Diego Portales, Chile. He holds a Doctor of Laws degree from the Universidad de Sevilla, Spain, and has been a Postdoctoral Fellow of the Alexander von Humboldt Foundation at the Humboldt Universität zu Berlin, Germany, a Fulbright Postdoctoral Fellow at the University of California at Berkeley, USA, and a Magdalene Schoch Fellow at Germany's Universität Hamburg. He was lead researcher on the project 'Criminal Responsibility for Human Rights Violations Committed in the Exercise of Judicial Functions', funded by Chile's National Agency for Research and Development, 'ANID'.

Julia Geneuss is Professor of Criminal Law, Criminal Procedure and International Criminal Law at Universität Potsdam, Germany. She obtained her higher Habilitation degree from the Universität Hamburg, and her Doctorate from Humboldt-Universität zu Berlin, both in Germany. She holds a Master of Laws Degree in International Legal Studies from the New York University School of Law, and is co-chair of the editorial committee of the *Journal of International Criminal Justice* (Oxford University Press). Her research focuses on international – in particular, German international – criminal law, as well as European and transnational criminal law.

Héctor Hernández Basualto is Professor of Criminal Law and Research Coordinator at the Universidad Diego Portales, Santiago de Chile. He holds a first degree in law from the Pontificia Universidad Católica de Chile, and LLM and doctoral degrees from the Universität Freiburg, Germany. He was a Postdoctoral Fellow of the Alexander von Humboldt Foundation at the Universities of Bonn, München and Köln, Germany.

Florian Jeßberger is Professor at Humboldt-Universität zu Berlin (Germany), where he holds the Chair in Criminal Law, Criminal Procedure, International Criminal Law, and Modern Legal History. He has been a Visiting Professor, inter alia, at Columbia Law School (USA), and the Universities of Haifa (Israel), and Ferrara (Italy). His teaching and research interests are centered on international and comparative criminal law and modern legal history. A Co-Editor-in-Chief of the *Journal of International Criminal Justice* (Oxford University Press) he has published widely in those areas and is, inter alia, a co-author, of *Principles of International Criminal Law* (4th edn, Oxford University Press, 2020 with G. Werle). and a co-editor of *Why Punish Perpetrators of Mass Atrocities?* (Cambridge University Press, 2020, with J. Geneuss), *Domesticating International Criminal Law* (Routledge, 2023, with C. Meloni and M. Crippa), and *International Criminal Law – A Counter-Hegemonic Project?* (Asser Press/Springer, 2023; with L. Steinl and K. Mehta).

Milan Kuhli is Professor of Law at Universität Hamburg (Germany), where he holds the Chair in Criminal Law and Criminal Procedure (including its International and Historical Context), and is Vice Dean for Academic Affairs at the Law Faculty. In addition, he is a Judge of the Hamburg Higher Regional Court. His teaching and research interests are in criminal law, criminal procedure, and modern legal history. His recent publications include *Geschichte des Strafrechts* (Nomos, 2025), *Normentheorie und Digitalisierung* (Nomos, 2023, co-ed. with F. Rostalski), *Vielfalt im Recht* (Duncker & Humblot, 2022, co-ed. with M. Schmidt), and *Korruption – Demokratie – Strafrecht. Ein Rechtsvergleich zwischen Brasilien und Deutschland* (Mohr Siebeck, 2022, co-ed. with F. Jeßberger et al.).

Fernando Londoño M. is Full Professor of Criminal Law at Universidad Diego Portales Law School, Santiago, Chile. He holds a PhD from the Università degli Studi di Ferrara, Italy (2008) and a Bachelor of Laws degree from the Universidad de Chile (2001). He held a Postdoctoral Fellowship awarded by the Fundación Carolina (Madrid, UAM, 2017), and in 2019 was invited to join the Doctoral Faculty of the *Dottorato in Scienze Giuridiche* at the Università degli Studi di Milano, Italy. He has held visiting professorships by invitation at the Universidad Autónoma de Madrid, Spain (2019) and the Università degli Studi di Milano (2022). Prof. Londoño's scholarship deals mainly with white collar crime and the legal theory of crime.

Rocío Lorca is Associate Professor and Research Director at Universidad de Chile Law School. She was a Hauser Global Scholar at the New York University School of Law (New York University, USA, 2022–2023). She holds a law degree from the University of Chile ('07), an LLM ('10), and a JSD ('15) from New York University. Her research and publications focus on the philosophy of punishment, particularly the relationship between criminal justice and other spheres of justice, such as economic and political justice. She is currently working on a revision of the concept of impunity.

Juan Pablo Mañalich R. is Professor at the Law Faculty of the Universidad de Chile, where he served as Director of the Department of Criminal Law between

2017 and 2021. He has held research fellowships from the German Academic Exchange Service and the Alexander von Humboldt Foundation, and has been a visiting professor at the University of Puerto Rico and the Universidad Autónoma de Madrid, Spain. He is the author of nine books and more than a hundred articles and book chapters, mainly addressing philosophical, theoretical and doctrinal problems of both the general and the special parts of criminal law.

Antonio Martins is Professor of Criminal Law at the Universidade do Estado do Rio de Janeiro, Brazil, and Professor of Criminal Law and Criminology at Brazil's Universidade Federal do Rio de Janeiro. He holds higher (LLM and Doctor Iuris) degrees from the Goethe-Universität, Frankfurt am Main, Germany.

Omar Palermo is Professor of Criminal Law at the Universidad Nacional de Cuyo, Mendoza, Argentina, and a judge of the Supreme Court of Justice of Mendoza, Argentina. He holds a PhD in law from Pompeu Fabra University, Barcelona, Spain, and was a postdoctoral researcher at the University of Freiburg, Germany, funded by the Alexander von Humboldt Foundation (2018–2021). He previously served as Attorney General to the Federal Court of Appeals of Mendoza, and is a former coordinating prosecutor of the regional Prosecutor's Office for Crimes against Humanity, under whose auspices the 'Mendoza megacase', involving judges and prosecutors of the Argentine dictatorship era, was pursued.

Luis E. Rojas A. received his doctorate from the Albert-Ludwigs-Universität Freiburg, Germany, with a thesis on fraud against the State ('*Haushaltsuntreue*'). He was a Postdoctoral Fellow of the Alexander von Humboldt Foundation, and Lecturer in Criminal Law at the Law Faculty of Chile's Universidad Alberto Hurtado, and is currently Professor in the Department of Criminal Sciences of the Universidad de Chile.

Elies van Sliedregt is Chair of Criminal Law & Procedure at the Law School of Tilburg University in the Netherlands. She was previously Professor of International Criminal Law at Leeds University, UK, and Dean of the Law School at the Vrije Universiteit in Amsterdam (2011–2015). Prior to this she held posts at the Universities of Leiden, and Utrecht, in the Netherlands. She is a Fellow of McLaughlin College, York University (Toronto, Canada), a Trustee at the British Institute of International and Comparative Law (BIICL) and a member of the Royal Netherlands Academy of Arts and Sciences, 'KNAW'.

Francesco Viganò has been Professor of Criminal Law at Università Bocconi, Milan, Italy, since 2016, concurrently serving as a judge on the Italian Constitutional Court (a position to which he appointed by the President of the Republic on February 2018, for a nine-year term). He previously occupied the Chair in Criminal Law at the Università degli Studi, Milan, and was Secretary General of the Société Internationale de Défense Sociale (2012–2018). He was co-founder of the legal journal "Diritto penale contemporaneo – Rivista trimestrale" (www.penalecontemporaneo.it/rivista-trimestrale), and has authored, co-authored, or co-edited 14 books, including a monograph (2021) on the proportionality of penalties. His research currently focuses on human rights and criminal law, constitutional criminal law, and medical law.

Moritz Vormbaum is Professor of Criminal Law, Criminal Procedure and International Criminal Law at Universität Münster, Germany. Prior to taking up this post he was Senior Researcher at Humboldt-Universität zu Berlin, as well as Coordinator and Lecturer at the South African-German Centre for Transnational Criminal Justice.

Gerhard Werle was Director of the African-German Network on Transitional Criminal Justice, and is Professor Emeritus at Humboldt-Universität zu Berlin, Germany, where he held the Chair in German and International Criminal Law, Criminal Procedure and Modern Legal History from 1993 to 2020. He has authored and edited dozens of books in the field of international criminal law and transitional justice, such as *Justiz-Strafrecht und polizeiliche Verbrechensbekämpfung im Dritten Reich* (De Gruyter 1989), *Die strafrechtliche Aufarbeitung von DDR-Unrecht* (2nd edn, De Gruyter 2020 co-authored with K. Marxen and M. Vormbaum), and *Principles of International Criminal Law* (4th edn, Oxford University Press, 2020, co-authored with F. Jeßberger).

Javier Wilenmann is Professor of Criminal Law and Director of the Centro de Investigación en Derecho y Sociedad at Chile's Universidad Adolfo Ibáñez. He received his PhD from the Albert-Ludwig-Universität Freiburg, Germany, and his law degree at the Universidad de Chile. His research deals with institutional behavior in the field of criminal justice, and with doctrinal work on criminal law.

Preface

This volume addresses a largely neglected aspect of transitional justice: the criminal responsibility of judges for their activity under authoritarian or totalitarian rule, and their involvement in crimes under international law.

The issue, its political relevance, and the complex theoretical and doctrinal questions that it raises, led the editors to convene leading experts to make contributions to this collective volume, which deals with relevant cases and cross-cutting topics. The experts gathered for this purpose include scholars with a background in transitional justice and international and comparative criminal law. They represent different legal systems and traditions including those of Chile, Argentina, Brazil, Germany, the Netherlands, Italy, and the United States.

Early drafts of the chapters were presented at a conference in Santiago de Chile in June 2023. The conference was hosted by Universidad de Chile and Universidad Diego Portales, and was convened by the editors of this volume jointly with Professor Juan Pablo Mañalich.

The result of this enterprise is an unprecedented volume that offers a comparison of the different patterns of judicial involvement in the crimes of a dictatorship that are discernible in the cases under study. The book also sheds light on how different legal systems have dealt with the phenomenon, identifying commonalities and relevant differences and evaluating the conditions under which criminal liability of judges could be asserted.

We are indebted to Professor Cath Collins, who provided invaluable support by language editing the volume. Julius Bayón, Luca Hauffe Charlotte Kallien, Dr. Hannah Ofterdinger, Micael Soares-Kamprad, and Hannah Welling helped with the copyediting of the manuscript. We are also grateful to Universität Hamburg, Universidad de Chile, Universidad Diego Portales, and Humboldt-Universität zu Berlin for providing funding for both the originating conference and this volume. Morwenna Scott, Commissioning Editor at Routledge, did an excellent job throughout the production process.

Santiago, Berlin, and Hamburg
June 2024
Claudia Cárdenas, Jaime Couso,
Florian Jeßberger, and Milan Kuhli

Abbreviations

Abl./KR Dtl. – Amtsblatt des Kontrollrates in Deutschland/Official gazette of the Control Council in Germany
AC – Appeal Cases
ACHR – American Convention on Human Rights
ADPCP – Anuario de Derecho Penal y Ciencias Penales
Advoc Q – The Advocates' Quarterly
AIDP/IAPL – International Review of Penal Law
AJIL – American Journal of International Law
Ala – Alabama Reports
Alberta L Rev – Alberta Law Review
All ER – All England Law Reports
ALR – Administrative Law Review
ALR – American Law Reports
Alternative L J – Alternative Law Journal
ARSP – Archiv für Rechts- und Sozialphilosophie
Art. – Artikel/article
BeckRS – Beck-Rechtsprechung
BeZG – Bezirksgericht/District Court
BGBl. – Bundesgesetzblatt/Federal Law Gazette
BGH – Bundesgerichtshof/German Federal Court of Justice
BGH GS – Großer Senat des Bundesgerichtshof/Joint Senate of the German Federal Supreme Court of Justice
BGHSt – Entscheidungen des Bundesgerichtshofes in Strafsachen/Recent Case Law of the German Federal Court of Justice in Criminal Law
BJCLCJ – Bergen Journal of Criminal Law & Criminal Justice
BT – Besonderer Teil
BT-Drs. – Bundestagdrucksachen; Documents of the German Bundestag
BVerfG – Bundesverfassungsgericht; German Federal Constitutional Court
Case W Rsrv L Rev – Case Western Reserve Law Review
Case W. Res. J. Int'l L. – Case Western Reserve Journal of International Law
Cato J – Cato Journal
CCL – Control Council Law

Cf. – compare
Chs. – chapters
CLP – current legal problems
CNI – Central Nacional de Informaciones/National Information Centre
CNPPT – Comisión Nacional sobre Prisión Política y Tortura/National Commission on Political Imprisonment and Torture
CNVR – Comisión Nacional de Verdad y Reconciliación/Chilean National Commission on Truth and Reconciliation
Colum. L. Rev. – Columbia Law Review
Cons – consideration
CSCL – Corte Suprema de Justicia de Chile
DINA – Dirección de Inteligencia Nacional; National Intelligence Directorate
DJZ – Deutsche Juristen-Zeitung
DOAJ – Anuario de Derechos Humanos
DtZ – Deutsch-Deutsche Rechts-Zeitschrift
Duke L J – Duke Law Journal
ECCC – Extraordinary Chambers in the Courts of Cambodia
ECHR – European Convention on Human Rights
EGStGB – *Einführungsgesetz zum Strafgesetzbuch*/Introductory Act to the German Criminal Code
EJIL – European Journal of International Law
ELR – Erasmus Law Review
F2d – Federal Reporter, Second Series
FRJ – Fraudulent res judicata
GA – Goltdammer's Archiv für Strafrecht
GDR – German Democratic Republic
GLJ – German Law Journal
HHRJ – Harvard Human Rights Journal
Harv L Rev – Harvard Law Review
HCA – High Court of Australia
IACtHR – Inter-American Court of Human Rights
Ibid – ibidem
ICC – International Criminal Court
ICL – International Criminal Law
ICRC – International Committee of the Red Cross
ICTR – International Criminal Tribunal for Rwanda
ICTY – International Criminal Tribunal for the former Yugoslavia
IJTJ – The International Journal of Transitional Justice
ILC – International Law Commission
IMT – International Military Tribunal
IMTFE – International Military Tribunal for the Far East
InDret – Indret: Revista para el Análisis del Derecho
IP – Ius et Praxis
JA – Juristische Arbeitsblätter
JCLC – Journal of Criminal Law and Criminology

JICJ – Journal of International Criminal Justice
JIPIT – Journal of International Political Theory
JOB – Judicial Officers Bulletin
JuS – Juristische Schulung
JZ – JuristenZeitung
KJ – Kritische Justiz
KritV – Kritische Vierteljahresschrift für Gesetzgebung und Rechtswissenschaft
L&S – Langage et Société
LALS – Latin American Legal Studies
LaP – Law and Philosophy
Law Soc Rev – Law and Society Review
LG – Landgericht/District Court
LJIL – Leiden Journal of International Law
LRTWC – Law Reports of Trials of War Criminals
LSI – Law & Social Inquiry
MLR – Missouri Law Review
Neb – Nebraska Reports
New Zealand L Rev – New Zealand Law Review
NJ – Neue Justiz
NJLP – Netherlands Journal of Legal Philosophy
NJW – Neue Juristische Wochenschrift
NMT – Nuremberg Military Tribunal
NStZ – Neue Zeitschrift für Strafrecht
NStZ-RR – Neue Zeitschrift für Strafrecht-Rechtsprechungs-Report
NSWLR – New South Wales Law Reports
NWU L Rev – Northwestern University Law Review
NYU L Rev – New York University Law Review
NZLR – New Zealand Law Reports
OGHSt – Amtliche Sammlung der Entscheidungen des Obersten Gerichtshofes für die Britische Zone/Official collection of the judgments and decisions of the Surpreme Court of the British zone
OTP – Office of the Prosecutor (at the International Criminal Court)
Oxf J Leg Stud – Oxford Journal of Legal Studies
Polít. crim. – Política Criminal
Punishm Soc – Punishment & Society
QB – Queens Bench
QBD – Queens Bench Division
RChD – Revista Chilena de Derecho
REJ – Revista de Estudios de la Justicia
Rev. derecho penal criminol. – Revista Derecho Penal y Criminología
Rev. derecho (Valdivia) – Revista de Derecho (Valdivia)
Rev. mex. cienc. polít. soc. – Revista mexicana de ciencias políticas y sociales
Revista JCS – Revista de Derecho y Jurisprudencia y Ciencias Sociales.
RGBl. – Reichsgesetzblatt/Imperial Law Gazette
RIDPP – Rivista Italiana di Diritto e Procedura Penale

RIS – Revista internacional de sociología
RStGB – Reichsstrafgesetzbuch/Criminal Code of the German Empire
RW – Rechtswissenschaft – Zeitschrift für rechtswissenschaftliche Forschung
S Carolina L Rev – South Carolina Law Review
San Diego L Rev – San Diego Law Review
SBZ – Sowjetische Besatzungszone/Soviet zone of occupation
SCOTUS – Supreme Court of the United States
SCSL – Special Court for Sierra Leone
SJZ – Süddeutsche Juristen-Zeitung
SMU L Rev – Southern Methodist University Law Review
StA – Staatsanwaltschaft/German public prosecution
State Ct J – State Court Journal
StGB – *Strafgesetzbuch*/German Criminal Code
Temp L Rev – Temple Law Review
Mod. L. Rev. – The Modern Law Review
Touro L Rev – Touro Law Review
U Balt L Rev – University of Baltimore Law Review
UK – United Kingdom
UNB L J – University of New Brunswick Law Journal
Univ. Chic. Law Rev. – University of Chicago Law Review
UNWCC – UN War Crime Commission
US – United States (of America)
Va L Rev – Virginia Law Review
Vanderbilt j. transnatl. Law – Vanderbilt Journal of Transnational Law
VIZ – Zeitschrift für Vermögens- und Immobilienrecht
ZaöRV – Zeitschrift für ausländisches öffentliches Recht und Völkerrecht
ZAP-Ost – Zeitschrift für die Anwaltspraxis-Ost
ZIS – Zeitschrift für internationale Strafrechtsdogmatik
ZJS – Zeitschrift für das juristische Studium
ZStW – Zeitschrift für die gesamte Strafrechtswissenschaft

Introduction

Jaime Couso and Florian Jeßberger

This book deals with the criminal responsibility of judges for their activities under authoritarian or totalitarian rule. It does so in a historical and comparative perspective, taking as its starting point the precedents offered by German and South American dictatorships and highlighting the global significance of the topic for scholarship in transitional justice and international criminal law. Establishing criminal responsibility for murder, torture, and unlawful detention committed or assisted through exercise of a judicial role – or, indeed, through failure to exercise such a role – poses highly complex legal and political questions. These often surface in contexts where transitional or post-transitional criminal prosecutions are being pursued or considered, in post-authoritarian or post-conflict settings.

The prosecution of actors other than military and political leaders or personnel has been somewhat neglected, in scholarship as in practice, since the 'renaissance' of international criminal law and the emergence of transitional justice as a distinct line of scholarship in the 1990s. Only recently has the issue of responsibility of judicial actors been propelled into the forefront of transitional justice scholarship due to several court proceedings in Argentina,[1] and to some extent in Chile,[2] building on previous case law from the post-World War II period. This explains why these precise settings are among the case studies by way of which this volume provides further treatment of the topic.

By comprehensively analyzing these recent developments and the substantive and procedural law questions that underlie them, the present volume aims to make a contribution to scholarly discourse on this matter by providing the wherewithal for a historical and comparative foundation. That the present topic cannot be reduced to a matter of mere legal history, nor treated as of importance only to South America or to Germany, is amply demonstrated by contemporaneous efforts to hold accountable judges from Iran, Russia, Turkey, and elsewhere for involvement in what may amount to international crimes.

1 From Nuremberg to Mendoza

The most prominent precedent dealt with in this volume dates back to what is usually referred to as the 'Justice Case', heard before a US Military Tribunal in

Nuremberg after World War II. Famously, during that case, the expression 'judicial murder' was used by the prosecution as a rationale for charging some defendants. The term was applied to killings that resulted from death sentences those defendants had handed down in application of aberrant criminal provisions, or in the context of blatantly unfair trials. As the Tribunal famously explained, "The dagger of the assassin was concealed beneath the robe of the jurist".[3] Since the Justice Case there have been other instances of criminal prosecutions and convictions, whether for judicial murder or for what might, in the same vein, be referred to as 'judicial torture' and 'judicial unlawful detention', perpetrated in dictatorial contexts. A feature common to all of the extant examples is that the defendants were found guilty not – or not only – of 'judicial perversion of justice', but also of the criminal consequences resulting from it. That is, they were treated as though they themselves had perpetrated the ensuing killings, torture, and kidnappings; and indeed the guilty verdicts that were handed down asserted that they did.

Seventy years later, and thousands of miles away from Nuremberg, in 2017 four former Argentine judges and public prosecutors were sentenced to life imprisonment as one result of a large-scale criminal prosecution, known as the '*megacausa*', carried out in the Argentine city of Mendoza. The grounds for the convictions were that the four had deliberately failed to prosecute secret police agents who had arrested, tortured, and eventually murdered several political dissidents; despite having had a legal duty to do so, and to protect victims whose deaths – it was asserted – they could have prevented. The decision set a historical precedent for South American transitional justice, entailing some political – and arguably legal – consequences for other countries. These include Chile, whose Supreme Court had granted the 2013 extradition of one of the four defendants to Argentina after finding the charges outstanding against him in Mendoza to also be punishable as murder under Chilean criminal law.

Over the course of the seven decades that separated Nuremberg from Mendoza, Germany once again saw judges were convicted of judicial murder, both in socialist East Germany (the German Democratic Republic, GDR) and in the reunified Federal Republic after 1990. First, GDR courts convicted dozens of Nazi judges and prosecutors for wartime actions similar to those the 'Justice Case' had dealt with. Later (after 1990) a handful of GDR judges were in turn convicted over some of the custodial sentences and death sentences they had handed down against Nazi war criminals. This second tier of prosecutions took as its basis the unfairness of the prosecutions and trials to which the former Nazi collaborators had been subjected in the GDR.

2 Between Immunity and Responsibility

The theoretical and doctrinal foundations of the decisions discussed here, by which judges were convicted of murder, kidnapping, or torture, are by no means settled matters. 'Show trials' present a relatively straightforward example, but in several other instances too, there has been criminal prosecution and trial of prosecutors and judges who acted on the basis of unjust, but applicable, laws to deliver or uphold unfair convictions with consequences including imprisonment or even death. Moreover, judicial or prosecutorial failure to prevent killings, tortures, and kidnappings committed by state agents during dictatorships are absolutely not simple cases of criminal liability of the respective prosecutors or judges as perpetrators or aiders and abetters of these crimes.

In fact, this is a matter about which legal traditions tend to diverge. The Anglo-American legal tradition seems to abide by the principle of judicial immunity, at least where there is an actual exercise of jurisdiction. Accordingly, judges face, at most, the risk of being held liable for judicial misconduct. By contrast, other traditions – German criminal law among them – find it less difficult to ascribe criminal liability for killings or unlawful detentions, so long as the judge's decision can also be considered to have constituted judicial 'perversion of justice' (*Rechtsbeugung* (Germ.); *prevaricación* (Sp.)). Under such circumstances a defendant will be convicted for judicial perversion of justice in addition to – not instead of – murder or unlawful detention. In 2017, the Argentine court that heard the Mendoza '*megacausa*' case rejected a defense argument based on the first of the traditions characterized above: the defense had alleged that when judges, by omission, fail to prevent a killing, they do not commit murder but, at most, the crime of judicial dereliction of duty (an omissive variant of judicial misconduct). In its ruling, the Court instead seems to have favored the German tradition, just as the Chilean Supreme Court had done in its extradition ruling.

Criminal liability of judges and prosecutors for murder, torture, and unlawful detention also raises complicated issues of causality, mens rea, and modes of liability, especially in cases of failure to prevent these crimes. Asserting such liability could pose questions related to the weak or absent causal link between the justice officer's conduct and the result of the crime, depending on prevailing patterns of judicial involvement in criminal repression in each historical case. Thus, for example, factors such as the degree of proximity between courts and agents ordering or directly perpetrating a dictatorial regime's crimes, and/or the level of legal formality of the proceedings, would have to be considered.

Criminal intent or – more broadly – mens rea requirements could moreover be difficult to prove if justice system officers were not certain what would happen to detainees; were unaware of their actual power to intervene, or were afraid of the consequences of such an intervention for their personal safety, to a degree that would affect their capacity to act willingly. Finally, if judicial immunity is rejected, a defense of mistake of law could be raised if the defendant is not to be blamed for having mistakenly assumed that they were bound by law to prosecute and convict.

3 Novelty of This Research in the Field

Relatively little scholarly work has been done on this issue.[4] While previous works do exist, their main contributions are in identifying patterns of judicial involvement with authoritarian repression, and reflecting on the limited, but in some contexts nonetheless real, margin of action that courts might enjoy if seeking to use their power to prevent human rights violations.

The present volume offers a fresh analysis of all major legal issues specifically related to criminal responsibility for judicial involvement in murder, unlawful detention, and torture. It is also innovative in comparing the already well-known examples of the Nuremberg 'Justice Case', East German prosecutions of former Nazis, and reunified German prosecutions of East German judges and prosecutors, with more recent cases not previously discussed in legal scholarly literature in English (namely, Argentina's 2017 *megacausa* ruling, and recent rulings in Chile invalidating verdicts of dictatorship-era courts-martial).

In so doing, as mentioned above, the volume fills a gap in transitional justice and international criminal law scholarship by comprehensively analyzing these developments, and the underlying substantive and procedural law issues, for the first time.

4 Structure of This Volume

The structure of the volume reflects the aims and ambitions set out above. Immediately following this introduction (written by two of the editors, Couso and Jeßberger), Part I of the book presents case studies carefully selected for relevance. These deal, in turn, with the Nazi period in Germany; the East German Socialist regime; the 1976–1983 Argentine military dictatorship; and the Pinochet dictatorship in Chile. The chapters that make up this part are by Jeßberger and Kuhli (the Nazi era's 'NS-*Justizunrecht*'), Cornelius ('Waldheim Trials'), Werle and Vormbaum (East Germany's 'SED'-dictatorship), Palermo (the Mendoza '*Megacausa*'), Couso (the Pinochet dictatorship), and Accatino (self-representations by Chilean judges). Together, they offer a legal-historical account of the main precedents that case studies offer. Beginning with the Nuremberg 'Justice Case', which ushered in the contemporary history of criminal prosecution of 'judicial murder', the part goes on to study the re-emergence of this same issue that was brought about by the post-1990 prosecution, in democratic Germany, of judges from the former GDR. Next, it traces the beginnings of the 'internationalization' of this new chapter of transitional justice. This is exemplified first through the '*megacausa*' prosecutions in Argentina, and then by recent events in Chile. These include the invalidation of the historical decisions of dictatorship-era courts martial and the convictions of some of their members, along with demonstrable change in the attitude of the Chilean Supreme Court regarding its own historical responsibility for atrocities. Notwithstanding fundamental differences between the various German and South American settings and periods discussed in this part, 'dictatorship' is used across Part I as an umbrella term to denote the authoritarian or totalitarian rule under which the grave human rights violations at issue here took place. Germany, Argentina, and Chile have after all each faced – albeit in distinct historical circumstances and to a differing degree – the challenges entailed by (efforts to) hold judges or members of military tribunals responsible for crimes committed through the exercise of jurisdiction, or indeed through a failure to duly exercise it. Any reader concerned with this topic cannot but wish to learn more about these particular case studies, as they are the first to emerge after the half-century of oblivion that followed the Nuremberg

'Justice Case'. It was, precisely, in the three countries that are our focus in Part I that criminal prosecution of judges experienced a renaissance, built moreover on a moral rationale and doctrinal foundations akin to those that had led, five decades earlier, to the conviction of Germany's Nazi jurists. The fact that each of the three contemporaneous case studies has been relatively well researched in its own right (providing a solid point of departure for our specific interests) further strengthens our analytical framework, as does the fact that we are dealing with three countries that have a shared understanding of the foundations of criminal liability.

In its subsequent parts and their component chapters, the volume groups together three sets of studies on crosscutting topics.

Part II embarks upon identification and analysis of some of the complex theoretical and legal-doctrinal issues raised by the prosecutions and trials studied in Part I. In particular, it deals with factors that could limit the possibility of a conviction: judicial immunity, *res judicata*, and the 'blocking effect' of convictions for malfeasance. This part contains chapters by Combs (on an Anglo-American approach to judicial immunity), Wilenmann (judicial immunity in South America), Abraham (invalidation of judicial decisions in cases of farcical prosecutions), Mañalich (fraudulent *res judicata* and impunity in Chile), and Cárdenas (invalidation, under international law, of judicial decisions based on 'show trials'). As this part shows, while judicial immunity tends to be a strong defense in the common law tradition, the 'blocking effect' is a German device that for decades prevented German courts from convicting judges. By contrast, in South America *res judicata* was not allowed to impede courts in countries including Chile invalidating courts martial decisions and convicting some of their members. This came about owing, in part, to an important ruling by the Inter-American Court of Human Rights (introducing the doctrine now commonly known as 'fraudulent' *res judicata*).

Part III, in turn, features chapters by Martins (a normative approach to mistake of law as a defense in cases of judicial abuse of office), Castillo (a comparative approach to mistake of law as a defense for judges of rogue regimes), Viganò (judicial murder, torture and unlawful detention under Italian law), and Rojas (on the relationship between judicial perversion of justice and judicial participation in crimes against humanity). It continues the analysis of issues raised by the case studies at the level of criminal law doctrine. These include, first, to what extent a judge's reliance on the validity of the law applicable at the time can be raised as a defense, where such law is contrary to basic standards of human rights and justice; and second, whether it is sound to impute the consequences of judicial misconduct – killings, tortures, kidnappings – to the justice officer responsible for that misconduct.

The analysis of the legal-doctrinal issues raised by the historical precedents studied in the volume concludes with Part IV, which contains chapters by Hernández (responsibility of judges for their failure to prevent atrocities under Chilean criminal law), van Sliedregt (modes of responsibility applicable to jurists or judges from the perspective of international criminal law), Londoño (judges' responsibility for participation in a criminal association from a comparative perspective), Lorca (judges as criminal associates under international law, with a focus on the Chilean case), and Geneuss (participation of judges in a criminal or terrorist association under German law). Even if justice officers are to be held liable for the consequences of their misconduct, some important questions remain as to the mode of liability that best fits their participation. This part accordingly examines whether such officers can be considered principals or just accomplices in relation to ensuing murders, tortures, and unlawful detentions. It further considers whether active intervention – such as unjustly condemning a victim to death – should be required, or whether omissive behavior suffices (e.g. failure to repeal an unjust conviction or to prevent active perpetration of the crimes by a third party). Prosecution of judges as either members of a criminal association or external accomplices of it is explored as an alternative, arguably easier, charge.

The volume ends with a brief summary and conclusion written by two of its editors (Cárdenas and Kuhli).

We conclude this introduction with one final note regarding terminology, an issue which every comparative (legal) study must, to a greater or lesser extent, confront. Legal terms often defy simple translation, since they carry their own 'thick' meaning and are loaded with intent and inference beyond the superficially plain meaning of the words that make them up. It is of course the preserve of each and every author of the chapters that follow to explain the specific meaning(s) they attach to any particular term or concept within the context of the individual topic or chapter concerned. Nonetheless, we think it helpful to offer the reader some preliminary orientation here regarding a number of the key words and concepts that appear frequently in the rest of this volume. This is not intended in any way to detract from the self-evident fact – which many chapters explicitly address – that these same terms may have their own specific meaning(s) across different jurisdictions.

- ***Judicial murder*** – as used in this volume, the term does not refer to a particular offence or mode of liability, but, in a broad sense, to the death of a person, when that death was unlawfully ordered or determined by any person invested with, or claiming to have, judicial or prosecutorial jurisdiction. This unlawfulness may derive either from the absence of genuine exercise of judicial or prosecutorial jurisdiction, or from serious procedural or substantive defects in the criminal law.
- ***Show trials** and **farcical prosecution*** – as used in this volume, the terms 'show trial', 'sham trial', or 'farcical prosecution' are used to denote a fraudulent imitation of a real criminal prosecution or trial, used as a cover-up or pretext for the illegitimate imposition of a punishment that had been decided before the initiation of the prosecution or trial. It can lead to judicial murder, where the outcome is a sentence of capital punishment.
- ***Judicial perversion of justice*** (*Rechtsbeugung* (Germ.); *prevaricación judicial* (Sp.)) – in what follows, the term refers to a criminal offence consisting of willful bending of the law by a judge or prosecutor. The offence presupposes that there has been an actual exercise of judicial or prosecutorial jurisdiction, but with a flawed application of substantive or procedural law. In the context

of authoritarian rule, judicial perversion of justice in criminal matters can lead to the unjust imposition of a death sentence or prison sentence. In most legal systems, however, provided that the judge or prosecutor is genuinely exercising jurisdiction they will not, as a general rule, later face attempts to hold them responsible for (judicial) murder or unlawful detention. Instead, they may find themselves accused of the lesser crime of perversion of justice, judicial misconduct, or malfeasance in office. Exceptions to this general rule can however be found: some legal systems allow, and have seen, conviction of a judge or prosecutor for (judicial) murder, unlawful detention, or other regular crimes. This may be without requiring any special conditions beyond (indirect) intervention in the crimes through the exercise of jurisdiction – as in the case of the Argentine judges and prosecutors convicted in the so-called *megacausa* – or only if the (arguably stringent) requirements for judicial perversion of justice are simultaneously met (this latter is the case in Germany: see discussion of the 'blocking effect', *Sperrwirkung*).

- ***Judicial immunity*** – this volume deploys this term to refer to a legal safeguard that judges and prosecutors enjoy, which prevents them from facing criminal responsibility for judicial acts (i.e., for a genuine exercise of judicial or prosecutorial jurisdiction) even if the outcome turns out to be unlawful. This legal safeguard, which aims to protect judicial independence, takes different forms in different jurisdictions, and may have a broader or narrower reach in each. It may prevent a judge or prosecutor from facing any criminal charges at all (absolute immunity); or may allow (for example) a criminal charge for bending the law or malfeasance in office, while ruling out prosecution for the unlawful death or detention of the convicted person (relative immunity). It can be virtually invincible, as is the case in the United States, or it can be susceptible to challenge, as in Germany (where, following what is often termed the 'Radbruch formula', it may be set aside if the judge has purposely bent the law, and the conviction was based on an unbearably unjust application of the law).[5] Jurisdictions also exist where no such immunity is granted in any form, as in the case of many South American jurisdictions: here, however, there are usually special procedural safeguards in place which in some manner shield judges from politically instrumentalized prosecution.

Notes

1 See Argentina's Judges' Trial, by the Tribunal Oral en lo Criminal Federal No 1 de Mendoza; Judgment of 20 September 2017, Sentence N° 1718 Autos Nr. 076-M 2689; cf. also Chapter 4.

2 See Chile's 'Fundo El Toro' case, by Instructing magistrate Judge Álvaro Mesa Latorre, Judgment of 26 September 2019, Rol No 10.819 and Judgment of 10 February 2021, Rol No 10.819; cf. also Chapter 5.

3 *United States v. Josef Altstötter et al* (1947).

4 Perhaps the most comprehensive work in the field, and still relatively recent, is Hans Petter Graver's legal-comparative volume *Judges Against Justice: On Judges When the*

Rule of Law Is Under Attack (Heidelberg: Springer, 2015). This text addresses many of the legal issues raised by judicial complicity with atrocities at an exploratory level, thereby contributing to setting an agenda for further research that could deepen analysis on specific questions. Earlier works focus on selected historical cases, such as David Dyzenhaus' *Judging the Judges, Judging Ourselves: Truth, Reconciliation and the Apartheid Legal Order* (Oxford: Hart Publishing, 1998), or offer a comparative political science analysis of the role of courts in dictatorships, such as Tom Ginsburg and Tamir Moustafa's edited volume *Rule by Law. The Politics of Courts in Authoritarian Regimes* (Cambridge: Cambridge University Press, 2008). Additionally, some works not available in English offer a deeper insight into the relevant legal issues in specific historical cases, such as Juan Pablo Bohoslavsky's *¿Usted también, doctor?: Complicidad de jueces, fiscales y abogados durante la dictadura* (Buenos Aires: Siglo Veintiuno Editores, 2015) or Ingo Müller's *Furchtbare Juristen. Die unbewältigte Vergangenheit der deutschen Justiz* (Berlin: Verlag Klaus Bitterman, 2015).

5 Radbruch, 'Gesetzliches Unrecht und übergesetzliches Recht' (1946) 1 *SJZ* 105, 105 et seq.

Bibliography

Alexy R, *The Argument from Injustice. A Reply to Legal Positivism* (Oxford University Press 2002).

Barros R, 'Courts Out of Context: Authoritarian Sources of Judicial Failure in Chile (1973-1990) and Argentina (1976-1983)' in Tom Ginsburg/Tamir Moustafa (eds), *Rule of Law. The Politics of Courts in Authoritarian Regimes* (Cambridge University Press 2008).

Couso J, 'From Nuremberg to Mendoza: Judicial Murder and Its *Aufarbeitung*' in Florian Jeßberger/others (eds.), *Strafrecht und Systemunrecht* (Mohr Siebeck 2022).

Dyzenhaus D, *Judging the Judges, Judging Ourselves: Truth, Reconciliation and the Apartheid Legal Order* (Hart Publishing 1998).

Eisert W, *Die Waldheimer Prozesse* (Springer-Verlag 1993).

Feinman J/Cohen R S, 'Suing Judges: History and Theory' (1980) 31 *South Carolina Law Rev* 201.

Graver H P, *Judges Against Justice. On Judges When the Rule of Law Is Under Attack* (Springer-Verlag 2015).

Hilbink, L, *Judges beyond Politics in Democracy and Dictatorship: Lessons from Chile* (Cambridge University Press, 2007).

Hohoff U, *An den Grenzen des Rechtsbeugungstatbestandes – Eine Studie zu den Strafverfahren gegen DDR-Juristen* (Berlin-Verlag Spitz 2001).

Lischka J, *Umgang mit Unrecht – Die Aufhebung von während der NS- und DDR-Zeit ergangenen strafrechtlichen Unrechtsurteilen* (Dr. Kovač 2021).

Marxen K/Werle G, *Strafjustiz und DDR-Unrecht. Dokumentation, vol 5: Rechtsbeugung* (De Gruyter 2007).

Marxen K/Werle G/Vormbaum M, *Die strafrechtliche Aufarbeitung von DDR-Unrecht* (2nd edn, De Gruyter 2020).

Morgenstern F, *Cosa juzgada fraudulenta* (BdeF 2015).

Müller I, *Furchtbare Juristen. Die unbewältigte Vergangenheit der deutschen Justiz* (Edition Tiamat 2020).

Olowofoyeku A A, *Suing Judges: A Study of Judicial Immunity* (Oxford University Press 1993).

Ostendorf H/ter Veen H, *Das "Nürnberger Juristenurteil". Eine kommentierte Dokumentation* (Campus 1985).
Radbruch G, 'Gesetzliches Unrecht und übergesetzliches Recht' (1946) 1 *Süddeutsche Juristen-Zeitung* 105.
Reicher H, 'Evading Responsibility for Crimes against Humanity: Murderous Lawyers at Nuremberg' in Alan E Steinweis/Robert D Rachlin (eds), *The Law in Nazi Germany: Ideology, Opportunism, and the Perversion of Justice* (Berghahn 2013).
Reisinger Coracini A/Tallgren I, 'Article 20 Ne bis in idem' in Kai Ambos (ed), *Rome Statute of the International Criminal Court. Article-by-Article Commentary* (4th edn, Beck-Hart-Nomos 2022).
Rüter C F, *DDR-Justiz und NS-Verbrechen, Band 14 Die Verfahren Nr. 2001–2088, Waldheimverfahren* (De Gruyter Saur 2009).
Shaman J M, 'Judicial Immunity from Civil and Criminal Liability' (1990) 27 *San Diego L Rev* 1.
Spendel G, *Rechtsbeugung durch Rechtsprechung* (De Gruyter 1984).
van Sliedregt E, *Individual Criminal Responsibility in International Law* (Oxford University Press 2012).
Vormbaum T, *Der strafrechtliche Schutz des Strafurteils* (Duncker & Humblot 1987).
Werle G, *Justiz-Strafrecht und polizeiliche Verbrechensbekämpfung im Dritten Reich* (De Gruyter 1989).
Werle G/Jeßberger F, *Principles of International Criminal Law* (4th edn, Oxford University Press 2020).
Withöft B, *Die Todesurteile der Waldheimer Prozesse* (2nd edn, Universität Wien 2014).

Part I

Case Studies

Germany, Argentina, and Chile

1 Settling Accounts for Nazi-era Judicial Injustice (*NS-Justizunrecht*) before Allied and (West-)German Courts

Charting New Territories and Failed Opportunities*

Florian Jeßberger and Milan Kuhli

1.1 Introduction

This chapter deals with the criminal responsibility of judges for their involvement in crimes during Nazi rule in Germany. Therefore, as we shall see, it engages with a pioneering and groundbreaking set of case law, produced by different courts and tribunals judging on different legal bases and – most noteworthy – coming to different legal findings. The chapter forms part of the analysis and discussion of the case of Germany in this volume, and is complemented by Cornelius, Werle & Vormbaum on East Germany.

After presenting a brief overview of the administration of justice between 1933 and 1945 in Germany (see Section 1.2), the chapter sheds light on the various ways judges were involved in activities that may amount to crimes (under domestic or international law). It also develops a typology of judicial injustice (*Justizunrecht*) in Nazi Germany (see Section 1.3). In its next, main part, the chapter goes on to address efforts to establish criminal responsibility for these judicial acts before Allied and (West-)German courts and tribunals in post-Second World War Germany. Specifically, this main section (Section 1.4) starts by presenting and discussing two relevant examples, both of which applied specific legislation on crimes against humanity and rejected the common law principle of judicial immunity. These are, first, the seminal 'Justice Case', heard before a US Military Tribunal sitting at Nuremberg, and, second, the respective case law of the Supreme Court for the British Zone (see Section 1.4.1). Section 1.4.2 then turns to the jurisprudence of the courts in the Federal Republic of Germany. These, unlike the US Military Tribunal and the Supreme Court for the British Zone, not only applied general German criminal law but also established a 'judges privilege' (*Richterprivileg*), which ultimately resulted in almost complete impunity. The chapter concludes, in Section 1.5, with a brief critical reflection on what remained for decades a hidden chapter of transitional justice in Germany.

DOI: 10.4324/9781003470069-2

1.2 The Nazi Judicial System at a Glance

It is problematic, when focusing on crimes committed by the judiciary, to speak of *the* Nazi criminal justice system. Rather, it is necessary to take a differentiated view that distinguishes various courts and cases.[1] In particular, a distinction must be drawn between regular criminal courts, on the one hand, and specially created tribunals, on the other. While regular courts were responsible for the prosecution of 'ordinary' crimes, special tribunals were used to deal with political delinquency.[2] One obvious and notorious example of the latter is the infamous People's Court (*Volksgerichtshof*), which was responsible, inter alia, for the adjudication of offenses against the state.[3] This Court was established in 1934 because the Nazi leadership had found the Reich Court of Justice (*Reichsgericht*) to be too lenient in specific cases.[4] Alongside the People's Court, the category of specially created tribunals also included what were referred to as 'special courts' (*Sondergerichte*). Criminal proceedings before these courts were governed by special rules of criminal procedure, e.g., abbreviated limits for summons, which predominantly operated to the detriment of the accused.[5]

1.3 Typology of Judicial Crimes between 1933 and 1945

For the period between 1933 and 1945, different types of 'judicial crimes' can be identified. We may distinguish three types. The first one relates to criminal proceedings in which illegitimate criminal legislation was applied and enforced. One such highly illegitimate and discriminatory law was, for instance, the "Law for the Protection of German Blood and German Honor" (*Blutschutzgesetz*) of 1935, which criminalized intermarriages between Jews and non-Jews.[6] Other illegitimate laws included those that provided for the death penalty for minor acts, often on a discriminatory and racist basis. The second type refers to proceedings conducted with flagrant disregard for the procedural rights of the accused.[7] One example concerns the summary executions that were carried out in the last days of the war.[8] Here, the predominant question is to what extent the entities handing down such 'judgments' were judicial courts at all.[9] Our third type relates to judicial excesses, i.e., to cases in which judges pronounced sentences that were in violation of Nazi laws. The notorious Oswald Rothaug is an example of a judge of this type. Rothaug was a judge at the Special Court of Nuremberg, where he blatantly expressed his antisemitism,[10] and where he seems to have issued judgments that were harsher even than underlying Nazi laws allowed.[11] According to Safferling and Luber (2017), one of these verdicts was so severe as to have even caused astonishment in Roland Freisler, the infamous President of the People's Court. Rothaug was one of the defendants in the post-1945 Nuremberg Trials,[12] where he was convicted for crimes against humanity and sentenced to life imprisonment.[13] Rothaug's judicial practice was characterized by extensive interpretation of the law and the use of analogies that were probably illegal even on the basis of Nazi law. The US Military Tribunal noted that[14]:

> By his manner and methods [Rothaug] made his court an instrumentality of terror and won the fear and hatred of the population. From the evidence of his closest associates as well as his victims, we find that Oswald Rothaug represented in Germany the personification of the secret Nazi intrigue and cruelty. He was and is a sadistic and evil man. Under any civilized judicial system he could have been impeached and removed from office or convicted of malfeasance in office on account of the scheming malevolence with which he administered injustice.

1.4 Prosecution and Punishment of Nazi Judges

After 1945, the question arose as to whether, and under what circumstances, judges could be held criminally responsible for the acts outlined above. Not only did their prosecution meet obstacles in post-war German society; it was also considered legally problematic. Could a judge who acted in accordance with the legal requirements of the Nazi regime be punished for this compliant behavior?

Between 1945 and 1949, Germany was under occupation by the former Allied powers.[15] Against the backdrop of the emerging Cold War, the Allies were soon unable to agree on a common strategy on how to deal with Germany going forward. The year 1949 saw the founding of two states: the Federal Republic of Germany (*Bundesrepublik Deutschland*, henceforth 'West Germany') and the German Democratic Republic (*Deutsche Demokratische Republik*, henceforth GDR or 'East Germany').[16]

This historical setting allowed for a unique diversification of judicial actors, each facing a moreover unprecedented task: the investigation, prosecution, and eventual punishment – or not – of the very same set of historical facts. These circumstances turned the German experience into a unique laboratory, one reason why this is such an informative case to study in more detail.[17] The chapter will now take a closer look at three of the aforementioned judicial actors, namely, a US Military Tribunal, the Supreme Court for the British Zone, and the West German courts (particularly, the Federal Court of Justice (*Bundesgerichtshof*)).

1.4.1 Allied Tribunals

After the International Military Tribunal at Nuremberg had completed its work concerning the major war criminals, the Allies' commitment to joint prosecution of the Nazi leadership came to a standstill.[18] Thereafter, the prosecution of so-called secondary major war criminals (*Zweitrangige Hauptkriegsverbrecher*)[19] was instead carried out separately by each of the four Allied powers. The history of those subsequent Allied prosecutions offers two extremes: one is the seminal and widely known Justice trial, while the other is the largely forgotten case law produced by the Supreme Court for the British Zone. Their common legal basis was formed by Control Council Law No. 10 (CCL 10),[20] whose Article II(1)(c) provided that the following acts – as crimes against humanity – are "recognised as a crime":

> Atrocities and offenses, including but not limited to murder, extermination, enslavement, deportation, imprisonment, torture, rape, or other inhumane acts committed against any civilian population, or persecutions on political, racial or religious grounds whether or not in violation of the domestic laws of the country where perpetrated.

Art. II Paragraph (2) meanwhile explains that:

> Any person without regard to nationality or the capacity in which he acted, is deemed to have committed a crime as defined in paragraph 1 of this Article, if he was (a) a principal or (b) was an accessory to the commission of any such crime or ordered or abetted the same or (c) took a consenting part therein or (d) was connected with plans or enterprises involving its commission or (e) was a member of any organization or group connected with the commission of any such crime [...].

1.4.1.1 US Military Tribunal III (Nuremberg): The Justice Case

The seminal Justice Case (*United States of America v. Josef Altstötter et al.*) was one of the twelve Nuremberg follow-up trials (Case No. 3). The trial opened in early 1947, before US Military Tribunal III. Its verdict was delivered on 3 and 4 December 1947. Sixteen jurists were in the dock, including prosecutors, justice ministry officials, and former judges of the People's Court and the Special Court. The highest-ranking defendant was Franz Schlegelberger, a former undersecretary of state in the Reich Ministry of Justice; the most prominent Nazi jurists (Freisler, Thierack, and Bumke) were already dead.

Interestingly, the defendants were charged not for individual acts but for their participation in state crime. This prosecution strategy required, as a first step, establishing the criminal character of the Nazi legal system per se or certain sub-areas of it. A second step had to be the examination of the extent to which each individual defendant had consciously participated in or contributed to the system or sub-area in question. Accordingly, the major arguments made by the Tribunal in the judgment were twofold: first, the Nazi legal system constituted, per se, a criminal institution (making participation in it punishable under CCL No. 10); second, there is no judicial immunity.

The Tribunal identified seven areas of legislative and judicial acts, each of which was examined to determine whether the acts constituted crimes under international law: Cases in which the extreme penalty was imposed may in large measure be classified in the following groups:

1 Cases against habitual criminals.
2 Cases of looting in the devastated areas of Germany; committed after air raids and under cover of blackout.
3 Crimes against the war economy – rationing, hoarding, and the like.

4 Crimes amounting to an undermining of the defensive strength of the nation; defeatist remarks, criticisms of Hitler, and the like.
5 Crimes of treason and high treason.
6 Crimes of various types committed by Poles, Jews, and other foreigners.
7 Crimes committed under the Nacht und Nebel program and similar procedures.[21]

The Tribunal then drew an important distinction:

> We merely hold that under the particular facts of this case we cannot convict any defendant merely because of the fact, without more, that laws of the first four types were passed or enforced. [...] A different situation is presented when we consider the cases which fall within types 5, 6, and 7.[22]

The Tribunal followed the prosecution in firstly establishing that the Nazi legal system was to be considered per se a criminal institution, such that participation in it was punishable under Control Council Law No. 10:

> The very essence of the prosecution case is that the laws, the Hitlerian decrees and the Draconic, corrupt, and perverted Nazi judicial system themselves constituted the substance of war crimes and crimes against humanity and that participation in the enactment and enforcement of them amounts to complicity in crime. [...]
>
> No defendant is specifically charged in the indictment with the murder or abuse of any particular person. If he were, the indictment would, no doubt, name the alleged victim. [...]
>
> The dagger of the assassin was concealed beneath the robe of the jurist.[23]

According to CCL 10 Art. II para. 1 (c), it was not possible to invoke the defense that the action was in accordance with the law in force at the time of the crime. In the opinion of the Tribunal, this rule did not constitute a violation of the prohibition of retroactivity since CCL 10 was, in the Tribunal's view, merely a codification of principles of international law that were already recognized at the time of the crime.

> The defendants claim protection under the principle nullum crimen sine lege, though they withheld from others the benefit of that rule during the Hitler regime. Obviously the principle in question constitutes no limitation upon the power or right of the Tribunal to punish acts which can properly be held to have been violations of international law when committed. [...]
>
> It would be sheer absurdity to suggest that the ex post facto rule, as known to constitutional states, could be applied to a treaty, a custom, or a common law decision of an international tribunal, or to the international acquiescence which follows the event. To have attempted to apply the ex post facto principle to

judicial decisions of common international law would have been to strangle that law at birth.

As mentioned above, a key issue was the question of judicial immunity. As a concept, this was familiar to the US judges. The Tribunal explained:

> In view of the conclusive proof of the sinister influences which were in constant interplay between Hitler, his ministers, the Ministry of Justice, the Party, the Gestapo, and the courts, we see no merit in the suggestion that Nazi judges are entitled to the benefit of the Anglo-American doctrine of judicial immunity. The doctrine that judges are not personally liable for their judicial actions is based on the concept of an independent judiciary administering impartial justice.
>
> Furthermore, it has never prevented the prosecution of a judge for malfeasance in office. If the evidence cited supra does not demonstrate the utter destruction of judicial independence and impartiality, then we "never writ nor no man ever proved." The function of the Nazi courts was judicial only in a limited sense. They more closely resembled administrative tribunals acting under directives from above in a quasi-judicial manner.[24]

The Tribunal rejected the two major arguments of the defense, namely, the claim that the defendants had no knowledge of systematic persecution and extermination and the contention that the defendants had simply remained in their position to prevent "worse things" from happening. The Tribunal explained:

> This Tribunal is not so gullible as to believe these defendants so stupid that they did not know what was going on. [...]
>
> The pattern and plan of racial persecution has been made clear. General knowledge of the broad outlines thereof in all its immensity has been brought home to the defendants. The remaining question is whether or not the evidence proves beyond a reasonable doubt in the case of the individual defendants that they each consciously participated in the plan or took a consenting part therein.[25]

And went on:

> That their program of racial extermination under the guise of law failed to attain the proportions which were reached by the pogroms, deportations, and mass murders by the police is cold comfort to the survivors of the "judicial" process and constitutes a poor excuse before this Tribunal. The prostitution of a judicial system for the accomplishment of criminal ends involves an element of evil to the State which is not found in frank atrocities which do not sully judicial robes.[26]

The Tribunal also rejected the defense's argument that the accused had only applied existing law. The rejection was mainly based on referring to the explicit provision in CCL No. 10.

Ultimately, the Tribunal convicted all of the defendants but four, sentencing those who were found guilty to either life sentences or long terms of imprisonment. The convictions were for having perverted the system into one by way of which international crimes were committed under the pretext of the application of the law. It should be noted, however, that the Tribunal did *not* deal with the jurisprudence created by Nazi Germany's regular courts but with the practices of the specially created tribunals mentioned above (Section 1.2).

Reactions to the judgment in Germany were either hostile or indifferent. Among the German population, the judgment was received with some criticism (viewed negatively as 'victors' justice'): the general understanding was that the judges had performed 'normal legal activities'. It is also interesting to note that the judgment was largely ignored by the (West-)German judiciary and within academia until the 1990s. It has been argued that the "explosive verdict disappeared into the poison cupboard of German law faculties".[27] It is, indeed, telling that the complete German language version of the verdict was published for the first time as late as 1996.[28] So the verdict had only a very limited signaling effect, if at all.

1.4.1.2 The Supreme Court for the British Zone

It is worth recalling that the Supreme Court for the British Zone was not a 'proper' Allied Tribunal within the meaning of the IMT or the Nuremberg US Military Tribunals, these former being presided over by international – or, in the latter case, US-American – judges. Rather, the Supreme Court, although established by the British Military Government, was created for a limited period (1948–50) and with limited territorial jurisdiction. Its function was to bridge the jurisdiction of the now-defunct *Reichsgericht*, on the one hand, and the yet-to-be-established *Bundesgerichtshof* of West Germany, on the other, by serving as a court of last resort in regular criminal and civil proceedings. Its judges were German jurists who had opposed the Nazi regime and had accordingly been in exile or had themselves been persecuted. They were appointed by the British Military Government. The Court had jurisdiction for appeals against the verdicts of the regional courts in criminal cases. Like the US Military Tribunals before it, the Supreme Court applied Control Council Law No. 10. This fact, together with the fact that the judges were appointed by the British Military Government, allows us to regard the Supreme Court as an Allied Court for the purposes of this chapter. There were no similar courts in Germany's other occupied zones.

The Court rendered four judgments that are relevant to our concerns. Interestingly – and, as we shall see, contrary to the finding of the Supreme Court – all defendants were ultimately acquitted, in all cases, either as the result of a retrial or via a later decision of the Federal Court of Justice. This makes the Supreme Court a very much isolated voice.

The Supreme Court held that the crime of perversion of justice (*Rechtsbeugung*) requires indirect intent only (*dolus eventualis*), whereas the (subordinated) regional courts had found that direct intent (*dolus directus*) was necessary. And it was the regional court's position, which was later adopted by the Federal Supreme Court (Bundesgerichtshof) up to 1994 – we will come back to this issue in Section 1.4.2.

In addition, the Supreme Court held that the crime of perversion of justice does *not* have any 'blocking effect' (*Sperrwirkung*) with regard to the application of the offences spelt out in CCL No. 10. So a judge could be punished for crimes under Control Council Law No. 10, even if the elements of the crime of perversion of justice were not fulfilled. The Court explained:

> [T]hat numerous courts, above all the "Volksgerichtshof" and many special courts, handled criminal law in a way which led to the fact that the law, instead of atoning for wrongs committed, became more and more a means of terrorist oppression.
>
> In some cases, punishment was meted out for acts that, according to general opinion, were not worthy of punishment at all; in other cases, punishment was meted out for conduct that was in itself worthy of punishment, and which no longer bore any humanly tolerable relation to the event.
>
> The victims of this handling of the law, which violated the principles of humanity, were so numerous that it was not a matter of individual cases but of a mass phenomenon, i.e., a case which should be covered by the provision of Art. II 1 c CCL 10.[29]

The Court noted:

> The question whether a criminal judge could commit a crime against humanity by a sentence that was cruel in its severity was answered in the negative by the jury court on the grounds that, in the interest of the judge's independence and personal inviolability, his prosecution under criminal law pursuant to § 336 StGB [i.e. the offence of judicial perversion of justice] was limited to the case of intentional bending of the law, but that there was no bending of the law as a matter of fact if the sentence imposed was within the statutory penalty range. To answer the question in the affirmative would mean the end of any independent administration of justice.
>
> This position is legally erroneous. [...] The idea of wanting to heal the dependence of the administration of criminal justice in the Nazi era, in particular its dependence on Nazi ideology and Nazi direction of justice, by leaving unpunished an inhumanity of a judge's decision born of it, is completely untenable. On the contrary, its punishment is intended to underscore and guarantee the restoration of a judiciary that judges only according to law and justice, independent of the influence of political power holders, and thus justifies the necessary public trust in judicial independence. [...]

> If, at a time when violence and arbitrariness dominated public life, judges [...] abused this system to commit inhumanities, this was one of the most dangerous and intolerable forms of this type of crime.
>
> It would be incomprehensible to exempt precisely such judges from being labeled and punished as inhumanity criminals because they were judges and should have judged independently. From the CCL 10, such a restriction cannot be inferred in any way.[30]

And further:

> CCL 10 requires [...] everyone to choose to uphold the principles of humanity when a state law or its handling offered him the opportunity to violate them. There is no apparent reason why the judge alone should be exempt. [...]
>
> In principle, therefore, the possibility must be affirmed that an adjudicating judge was guilty of the crime against humanity without at the same time realizing the elements of the crime of intentional perversion of justice under German criminal law.[31]

Therefore, the Supreme Court applied Control Council Law No. 10, in particular Art. II par. 1 (c), without regard to Nazi law in force at the time. With regard to the interpretation of the elements of crimes against humanity, and specifically with a view on cases of an intolerable disproportion between guilt and punishment, the Court found that:

> To accept a criminal punishment from the state, not because this punishment is deserved by one's own guilt, but because the state has found here a first-best object to deter others from the same deed by the example of an inexorable treatment, is intolerable degradation of the victim to a mere means for an end [...].
>
> If this happens with severe damaging effect for the victim and from a system of an existing tyranny, then at the same time the supra-personal value of humanitas and as its guardian and bearer humanity itself is attacked, thus the objective facts of the crime against humanity according to the CCL 10 are fulfilled to that extent.[32]

As a result, the Supreme Court constitutes a clear counterpoint to the jurisprudence of the regional courts in the postwar period; the principles it developed could have been a starting point for the further punishment of Nazi-era judicial crimes by the courts of the Federal Republic. As we will see below, however, this was not the case.

1.4.2 (West-)German Courts

As we have seen, in Nuremberg the US judges had, with recourse to international law, rejected the so-called judges privilege. However, this privilege was being prominently discussed in German jurisprudence at the time, namely by the German legal philosopher Gustav Radbruch. In his essay "Statutory Lawlessness and Supra-Statutory Law" (*Gesetzliches Unrecht und übergesetzliches Recht*), published in 1946, Radbruch did not only substantiate what would come to be known as the 'Radbruch formula'. He also commented on the criminal liability of Nazi judges who had imposed death sentences on the basis of Nazi laws.[33] Radbruch stated:

> The culpability of judges for homicide presupposes the simultaneous determination that they have perverted the law, since the independent judge's decision can be an object of punishment only if he has violated the very principle that his independence was intended to serve, the principle of submission to the statute, that is, to the law.[34]

On the basis of this privilege, the question of whether a judge had fulfilled the prerequisites for the crime of judicial perversion of justice (*Rechtsbeugung*) became the bottleneck for sanctioning judicial crimes. Since criminal liability thus also depended on the intent to break the law, the question of how to deal with fanatical judges inevitably had to be asked. One could argue that a fanatical Nazi judge – a judge who was blinded by National Socialism – actually had no intent to break the law. With recourse to the judges privilege postulated by Radbruch, such an assumption had to lead to the conclusion that fanatical Nazi judges must not be convicted for their actions.[35]

The question of whether Radbruch's idea of a judges privilege is convincing has to date remained open. It is true that today there is some evidence to suggest that a judge in a constitutional state can indeed only dispense justice without being influenced if he or she does not perceive themselves as being exposed to the permanent danger of being prosecuted for having imposed a sentence. The extension of this same principle to the National Socialist judiciary can, however, be countered by pointing out that this quite simply was not an independent judicial system.[36] In any event, something else is noteworthy at this point: according to analysis by Thomas Vormbaum, there is some evidence that judges privilege, as postulated by Radbruch, was established on an ad hoc basis – i.e., without historical precedent – after the end of the Third Reich.[37] Seen in this light, the first beneficiaries of this privilege were thus the very judges who had acted between 1933 and 1945.

When the first proceedings against Nazi judges were conducted, German jurisprudence had, in principle, two legal bases at its disposal. The first was the Criminal Code (*Strafgesetzbuch – StGB*), and the second was Control Council Law No. 10, whose use by the German courts had been authorized by the Allies (although it was finally repealed, in 1956).[38] After some wavering, the (West) German judiciary based its jurisprudence on Nazi judicial crimes on judges privilege.[39] This resulted in only a handful of Nazi judges being convicted in West Germany prior to 1990,[40] in contrast to the German Democratic Republic's convictions of over 140 Nazi judges and prosecutors in the same period.[41] It should be noted nonetheless that many of these GDR judgments were handed down under conditions that were contrary to the rule of law.[42]

In the mid-1990s, something remarkable occurred in the German judiciary. The Federal Court of Justice, which had in the preceding decades made a significant contribution to the *lack* of prosecution of Nazi judges, made the rare move of issuing a public apology. In 1995, they issued a verdict containing the following statement:

> Judges of the Nazi judiciary who had passed death sentences were [...] not held accountable by the Federal German judiciary [...]. In the fact that this did not happen lies a momentous failure of federal German criminal justice.[43]

The admission appears as part of the published statement of reasoning in a verdict dealing with the matter of a GDR judge's possible perversion of justice through his participation in death sentences. As in other proceedings in the 1990s,[44] in this case, the judge's actions were found to have constituted judicial perversion of justice.[45]

An observer may take the different ways in which members of the National Socialist judiciary and the GDR judiciary were dealt with under criminal law as evidence that West German post-war judges acted in a biased manner.[46] In fact, there is no room for a judges privilege wherever judicial activity is only an outer shell that serves as a cover for an oppressive regime. Those who do not judge, but only order execution, have to answer like any other citizen without privileges.[47]

1.5 Conclusion

Post-war efforts in Germany to settle accounts for Nazi-era judicial injustice – *NS-Justizunrecht* – were pathbreaking. For the first time, *Justizunrecht* was made systematically subject to judicial scrutiny. The various courts and tribunals involved – the US judges in the landmark Justice Case, the judges of the Supreme Court for the British Zone, and the judges of the West German Federal Court of Justice – each positioned themselves quite differently. Beyond the obvious differences – whereby, for instance, some courts held Nazi-era judges responsible for crimes against humanity, whereas others re-integrated them into the judicial system, even praising the 'heroic attitude' of some – our brief analysis unearthed fundamentally different underlying views and approaches. These differences are in evidence in regard to, inter alia, the legal basis for charging (national or international law) and the exact legal framing of charges. Divergence can also be seen regarding the scope of judicial scrutiny (limitation to specially created courts versus general judicial oversight), whether or not there is judicial immunity ('judicial exceptionalism'), and whether the crime of judicial perversion of justice has or should have a 'blocking effect' or not. What is common to all the efforts is that they received very little attention, or none at all, from fellow jurists engaged in legal scholarship.

How can we explain the differences? One explanation refers to court personnel, contrasting a court staffed by dissident, or anyway non-Nazi, judges versus one with continuity of membership. Another has to do with the prevailing social climate in Germany, where the dominant sentiment moved rapidly, after the end of the war, toward *Schlussstrichmentalität*, a desire to draw a line under the Nazi past. It is also interesting to note the learning curve evinced in the changing position of the (West-)German judiciary. However, many further issues are unresolved, such as whether the Military Tribunal's focus, in the Justice Case, on members of specially created courts should be taken to imply an exoneration of the judges of regular courts. These and other questions remain open to discussion.

Notes

* The author Jeßberger thanks Antonia Vehrkamp for her assistance in collecting the materials for this paper.

1 For details regarding the *Volksgerichtshof*, see Vormbaum/Bohlander, *A Modern History of German Criminal Law* (2014) 201.

2 For details, Hoefer, 'The Nazi Penal System' (1944–45) 35 *JCLC* 385.

3 RGBl. 1934 I, 345; see Köpke, *Der Volksgerichtshof: Im Namen des Volkes? Eine Analyse im Kontext der Neuordnung der Justiz im nationalsozialistischen Deutschland* (2011) 27.

4 Vormbaum/Bohlander (2014) (n 1) 181.

5 Rüping/Jerouschek, *Grundriss der Strafrechtsgeschichte* (2011), para 290.

6 RGBl. 1935 I, 1146.

7 See Ostendorf/ter Veen, *Das 'Nürnberger Juristenurteil' Eine kommentierte Dokumentation* (1985) 18.

8 See Müller, *Furchtbare Juristen. Die unbewältigte Vergangenheit der deutschen Justiz* (2020) 362 et seq; Bästlein, 'Der Nürnberger Juristenprozeß und seine Rezeption in Deutschland' in Peschel-Gutzeit, L M (ed) 33.

9 See Ostendorf/ter Veen (1985) (n 7) 60.

10 Luber, *Strafverteidigung im Nürnberger Juristenprozess am Beispiel des Angeklagten Oswald Rothaug* (2018) 93.

11 For example, in the *Katzenberger* case, see Safferling/Luber, ' "Der Tempel der deutschen Justiz muss wieder eingeweiht werden" – Der Nürnberger Juristenprozess nach 70 Jahren' (2017) 43 *JA* 881, 885.

12 Safferling/Luber (2017) (n 11) 884 et seq.

13 Although the sentence was later commuted to 20 years of imprisonment, Rothaug was released from prison in 1956.

14 NMT, Judgment of 4 December 1947, 3 Trials of War Criminals Before the Nuremberg Military Tribunals Under Control Council Law No. 10, *USA v. Altstötter* (hereinafter Justice Trial) 1156.

15 See Epkenhans, *Geschichte Deutschlands. Von 1648 bis heute* (2011) 111.

16 See Kuhli, 'Grundzüge der Strafrechtsgeschichte. Vom 18. Jahrhundert bis zur Gegenwart – Teil 1' (2021) 13 *ZJS* 21, 26.

17 See in addition – for East-German courts – Cornelius in this Volume.

18 See Vormbaum/Bohlander (2014) (n 1) 214.

19 Wesel, *Rechtsgeschichte der Bundesrepublik Deutschland. Von der Besatzungszeit bis zur Gegenwart* (2001) 22.

20 The English and German versions of the Control Council Law No. 10 are printed in Werle/Jeßberger, *Principles of International Criminal Law* (2020) 857 et seq. It should be noted that the crime of perversion of justice was not part of CCL10 (but of German criminal law). The same holds true for the offense of malfeasance in (public) office

(which can be found in many domestic systems; it was part of German criminal law only until 1943).

21 Justice Trial (n 14) 1025.

22 Justice Trial (n 14) 1027.

23 Justice Trial (n 14) 984 et seq.

24 Justice Trial (n 14) 1024 et seq.

25 Justice Trial (n 14) 1081.

26 Rejoinder of the court in respect to the defendant Schlegelberger, Justice Trial (n 14) 1086.

27 See Weinke, *Die Nürnberger Prozesse* (2015) 72.

28 See Peschel-Gutzeit (ed).

29 OGHSt 2, 23, 43 ('Müller'). This and all following translations by the authors. [OGHSt is the official collection of the judgments and decisions of the Supreme Court (*Amtliche Sammlung der Entscheidungen des Obersten Gerichtshofes für die Britische Zone*).

30 OGHSt 1, 217, 227 et seq ('Buea').

31 OGHSt 2, 272 et seq ('Brumshagen'), cited after Pöpken, *Vergangenheitspolitik durch Strafrecht. Der Oberste Gerichtshof der Britischen Zone und die Ahndung von Verbrechen gegen die Menschlichkeit* (2021) 5.

32 OGHSt 1, 217, 220 ('Buea'), cited after Ohlenroth, *Der Oberste Gerichtshof für die Britische Zone und die Aufarbeitung von NS-Unrecht* (2020) 195.

33 Radbruch, 'Gesetzliches Unrecht und übergesetzliches Recht' (1946) 1 *SJZ* 105, 105 et seq.

34 Radbruch G, *Statutory Lawlessness and Supra-Statutory Law* (1946) 108. The original German wording is: 'Die Strafbarkeit der Richter wegen Tötung setzt die gleichzeitige Feststellung einer von ihnen begangenen Rechtsbeugung [...] voraus. Denn das Urteil des unabhängigen Richters darf Gegenstand einer Bestrafung nur dann sein, wenn er gerade den Grundsatz, dem jene Unabhängigkeit zu dienen bestimmt war, die Unterworfenheit unter das Gesetz, d.h. unter das Recht, verletzt hätte'. Translation by Paulson/Paulson (2006) 26 *Oxf J Leg Stud* 1.

35 See Müller (2020) (n 8) 361 et seq.

36 See Ostendorf, 'Der "Nürnberger Juristenprozess" und seine Auswirkungen auf eine internationale Strafgerichtsbarkeit' in Ostendorf/Danker (eds) 134; Ostendorf/ter Veen (1985) (n 7) 59 et seq.

37 Vormbaum/Bohlander (2014) (n 1) 220.

38 See Luber, *Strafverteidigung im Nürnberger Juristenprozess am Beispiel des Angeklagten Oswald Rothaug* (2018) 319, 321.

39 See in detail Wassermann, 'Fall 3: Der Nürnberger Juristenprozeß' in Ueberschär G R (ed) (2008) 99, 106 et seq; Ostendorf/ter Veen (1985) (n 7) 60; Luber (38) 321.

40 See in detail Rottleuthner, 'Das Nürnberger Juristenurteil und seine Rezeption in Deutschland – Ost und West' (1997) 51 *NJ* 617, 622; Bästlein (8) 33.

41 See in detail Ostendorf (2003) (n 36) 125 et seq; Rottleuthner (1997) (n 40) 622 et seq. See also Cornelius in this volume.

42 See Ostendorf (2003) (n 36) 125 et seq.

43 Translation by the authors; the original German wording is: 'Richter der NS-Justiz, die Todesurteile gefällt hatten, [wurden] [...] von der bundesdeutschen Justiz nicht zur Verantwortung gezogen [...]. Darin, daß dies nicht geschehen ist, liegt ein folgenschweres Versagen bundesdeutscher Strafjustiz', BGH, Judgment of 16 November 1995, 5 StR 747/94, (1996) 49 *NJW* 863 et seq.

44 See Marxen/Werle/Vormbaum, *Die strafrechtliche Aufarbeitung von DDR-Unrecht* (2020) 52.
45 BGH, Judgment of 16 November 1995, 5 StR 747/94, (1996) 49 *NJW* 863.
46 Luber (2018) (n 38) 336.
47 Ostendorf/ter Veen (1985) (n 7) 60.

Bibliography

Bästlein K, 'Der Nürnberger Juristenprozeß und seine Rezeption in Deutschland' in Peschel-Gutzeit, L M (ed), *Das Nürnberger Juristen-Urteil von 1947. Historischer Zusammenhang und aktuelle Bezüge* (Nomos 1996) 9.
Epkenhans M, *Geschichte Deutschlands. Von 1648 bis heute* (UTB 2011).
Hoefer F, 'The Nazi Penal System' (1944–45) 35 *Journal of Criminal Law and Criminology* 385.
Köpke D, *Der Volksgerichtshof: Im Namen des Volkes? Eine Analyse im Kontext der Neuordnung der Justiz im nationalsozialistischen Deutschland* (Diplomica 2011).
Kuhli M, 'Grundzüge der Strafrechtsgeschichte. Vom 18. Jahrhundert bis zur Gegenwart – Teil 1' (2021) 13 *Zeitschrift für das juristische Studium* 21.
Luber M, *Strafverteidigung im Nürnberger Juristenprozess am Beispiel des Angeklagten Oswald Rothaug* (Duncker & Humblot 2018).
Marxen K/Werle G/Vormbaum M, *Die strafrechtliche Aufarbeitung von DDR-Unrecht* (2nd edn, De Gruyter 2020).
Müller I, *Furchtbare Juristen. Die unbewältigte Vergangenheit der deutschen Justiz* (Edition Tiamat, 2020).
Ohlenroth J, *Der Oberste Gerichtshof für die Britische Zone und die Aufarbeitung von NS-Unrecht* (Mohr Siebeck 2020).
Ostendorf H, 'Der "Nürnberger Juristenprozess" und seine Auswirkungen auf eine internationale Strafgerichtsbarkeit' in Ostendorf H/Danker U (eds), *Die NS-Strafjustiz und ihre Nachwirkungen* (Nomos 2003) 125.
Ostendorf H/ter Veen H, *Das 'Nürnberger Juristenurteil' Eine kommentierte Dokumentation* (Campus 1985).
Peschel-Gutzeit L M (ed), *Das Nürnberger Juristen-Urteil von 1947. Historischer Zusammenhang und aktuelle Bezüge* (Nomos 1996).
Pöpken C, *Vergangenheitspolitik durch Strafrecht. Der Oberste Gerichtshof der Britischen Zone und die Ahndung von Verbrechen gegen die Menschlichkeit* (Nomos 2021).
Radbruch G, 'Gesetzliches Unrecht und übergesetzliches Recht' (1946) 1 *Süddeutsche Juristen-Zeitung* 105.
Radbruch G, 'Statutory Lawlessness and Supra-Statutory Law' (1946). Translated by Paulson B L/Paulson S L (2006) 26 *Oxford Journal of Legal Studies* 1.
Rottleuthner H, 'Das Nürnberger Juristenurteil und seine Rezeption in Deutschland – Ost und West' (1997) 51 *Neue Justiz* 617.
Rüping H/Jerouschek G, *Grundriss der Strafrechtsgeschichte* (6th edn, C.H. Beck 2011).
Safferling C/Luber M, ' "Der Tempel der deutschen Justiz muss wieder eingeweiht werden" – Der Nürnberger Juristenprozess nach 70 Jahren' (2017) 43 *Juristische Ausbildung* 881.
Vormbaum T/Bohlander M (ed), *A Modern History of German Criminal Law. Translated by Margaret Hiley* (Springer 2014).

Wassermann R, 'Fall 3: Der Nürnberger Juristenprozeß' in Ueberschär G R (ed), *Der Nationalsozialismus vor Gericht. Die alliierten Prozesse gegen Kriegsverbrecher und Soldaten 1943–1952* (3rd edn, Fischer 2008) 99.
Weinke A, *Die Nürnberger Prozesse* (2nd edn, C.H. Beck 2015).
Werle G/Jeßberger F, *Principles of International Criminal Law* (4th edn, Oxford University Press 2020).
Wesel U, *Rechtsgeschichte der Bundesrepublik Deutschland. Von der Besatzungszeit bis zur Gegenwart* (2nd edn, C.H. Beck 2001).

2 Malfeasance in Office as a Crime in the Context of Dictatorships

The Example of Judicial Perversion of Justice in the East German Waldheim Trials

Kai Cornelius

> Such a complete disregard for the ideas of justice and humanity as characterises the image of Nazi justice did not exist in the [East German Socialist] judiciary (with the possible exception of the "Waldheim trials").[1]

What were the Waldheim trials? Why are they an obvious example to turn to when discussing abuse of office, and why have they been selected as the central topic of the present chapter? The Waldheim trials are fertile terrain for a comparative view of subsequent reappraisals of judicial abuse of office (perversion of justice – *Rechtsbeugung*) after the German Nazi and socialist dictatorships. In what follows, I will first discuss the Waldheim Trials in general and then focus on their legal reappraisal in post-1990 Germany. The chapter goes on to address differences in post-reunification jurisprudence surrounding past Nazi injustice and injustice committed by the East German socialist regime in the GDR.[2]

2.1 The Waldheim Trials

2.1.1 Background

From 1948 onward, Soviet occupation policy in Germany was strategically oriented toward the formation of a state within the borders of the Soviet zone of occupation.[3] This policy also involved the handover to the new East German socialist republic of the Soviet 'special camps'.[4] These camps were established in former Nazi concentration camps but operated with concepts and methods shaped by Soviet forced labor camp (The GULAG) experiences.[5] The objective was to facilitate the disappearance of political opponents.[6] In 1950, some 3,400–3,500 former inmates of these camps were handed over to the new East German Ministry of the Interior for judicial sentencing.[7] This sentencing took place via the Waldheim Trials: chambers of the Chemnitz Regional Court in the small town of Waldheim were commandeered to act as 'special purpose courts of exception'.[8] The legal basis was Directive No. 38 of the Allied Control Council,[9] entitled 'The Arrest and Punishment of War Criminals, Nazis, and Militarists and the Internment, Control,

DOI: 10.4324/9781003470069-3

and Surveillance of Potentially Dangerous Germans', dated 12 October 1946.[10] Proceedings were conducted in secret, with the exception of ten public show trials.[11]

2.1.2 Proceedings against Nazis and War Criminals

In practice only a small proportion of the Waldheim trials were directed against Nazis and war criminals.[12] Those affected also included some jurists (like lawyers, prosecutors, and judges).[13] The original verdicts show that at least 13 former judges were sentenced in Waldheim.[14] Additional sources also reveal further proceedings, some against judicial figures.[15]

These proceedings did not conform to rule of law principles. There was no independent collection of evidence; indictments were presented as evidence exclusively for the duration of the trial but were not made available to the public; and verdicts were based solely on excerpts from Soviet arrest records.[16] With the limited and partial exception of the ten show trials, no witnesses were called and no defense was provided. No individual proof of guilt was sought or given:[17] verdicts were often passed solely based on membership in a fascist organization.[18]

The sentences handed down by the Waldheim judges for war crimes or crimes against humanity always cited as their basis Control Council Law No. 10 of 20 December 1945, in conjunction with Control Council Directive No. 38, and with Order No. 201 of the Soviet Military Administration in Germany (SMAD), issued in 1947 as a 'denazification' order. There was no reference to the special function of the sentenced persons as former judges.[19] This is all the more remarkable since Control Council Directive No. 38 contained a special provision for persons who "unlawfully interfered in the administration of justice in the service of National Socialism" or who "politically abused their office as judge or public prosecutor" (Section II, Article III, A, II, Clause 4).[20] This provision did not, however, apply to the most serious category of major offenders. It applied only to a second tier of 'incriminated persons' for whom the maximum sentence contemplated was ten years' imprisonment. To be able to sentence former judges who stood trial in Waldheim to harsher sentences, they had to be classified in the category of major offenders.[21]

2.1.3 The Waldheim Judges

The Waldheim proceedings were conducted by 37 career judges, 29 lay judges, and 18 public prosecutors. All were ruling (Socialist) party members, each with only short periods of legal training. They had been designated for the task by an ad hoc Party executive commission.[22] Twelve of them had lived experience of Nazi-era persecution, having been inmates of Nazi prisons or concentration camps. Two had themselves previously served time in the Waldheim penitentiary.[23] It should be emphasized that at the outset of the trials, those charged with conducting them were fully under the impression that their task would exclusively involve judging former Nazis and war criminals.

For security reasons, Waldheim judges and prosecutors were closely monitored by the party apparatus. Anyone deemed politically 'weak' was weeded out. Party functionaries acted as 'judges behind the judges', furnishing them with 'political advice'.[24]

2.2 Legal Reassessment of the Waldheim Trials after Reunification

2.2.1 Determination of Violation of the Rule of Law and Compensation

After German reunification in 1990, the Waldheim trials were made subject to judicial review by the courts. As early as 1991, the Dresden District Court ruled that the Waldheim sentences had been contrary to the rule of law.[25] The process of coming to terms with the East German socialist past also included the granting of compensation for the maintenance of dependents of those who had been sentenced to death in the Waldheim Trials. As the Federal Constitutional Court explained, the purpose of the Criminal Law Compensation Act,[26] "which is to remedy as far as possible the injustice caused by the criminal judgments of the courts of the former GDR, can only be achieved if those entitled to maintenance can also be awarded compensation after the death of the convicted person".[27] In this respect, Section 1(2) of the 1999 Criminal Rehabilitation Act also stipulated that "the decisions of the Regional Court of Chemnitz, Waldheim Branch, from 1950 ('Waldheim Trials') are incompatible with the fundamental principles of a free constitutional order".[28]

2.2.2 Trials of the Waldheim Judges

In addition, several proceedings for perversion of justice were conducted against former Waldheim judges after reunification.[29] Helbig, for example, has pointed out that six or seven surviving former Waldheim judges were sentenced in the 1990s (most of them receiving suspended sentences of around two years' probation).[30]

Those subjected to these proceedings included, for example, Otto Jürgens, who was an associate judge at seven Waldheim trials.[31] Jürgens, a skilled carpenter and member of the Communist Party, received fast-track training to become a so-called 'people's judge', subsequently (after 1950) continuing to practice as a public prosecutor in Halle.[32] In 1993, he was sentenced by the Leipzig Regional Court to two years' imprisonment (suspended) for obstruction of justice, concurrent with deprivation of liberty. The sentence also included a fine of 6,000 marks, to be paid to a victims' relatives' association (the *Bund der stalinistisch Verfolgten*, Association of People Persecuted by Stalinism).[33] In his closing remarks, Jürgens, who had himself been arrested and tortured by the Gestapo in 1933, said: "The Nazi criminals who were sentenced at Waldheim more than deserved their punishment".[34]

Irmgard Jendretzky was sentenced to four years' imprisonment for obstruction of justice in 12 cases, five of them concurrently with manslaughter, one of them concurrently with attempted manslaughter, and six of them concurrently with deprivation of liberty.[35] Ilse Kühne,[36] who had been a 31-year-old judge at the time of the Waldheim proceedings, was also prosecuted.[37] Otto Fuchs, served with an indictment in 1992, committed suicide before his scheduled trial could take place at the Leipzig Regional Court.[38] Fuchs, who had chaired one of the criminal chambers at Waldheim, left a suicide note bearing eloquent witness to his belief that he had done no wrong. It read:

> I assure you that in my criminal chamber we only sentenced war criminals, and I am sure that we do not have to be ashamed of any verdict. However, all signs point to turning everything into its opposite, branding me as a criminal in a show trial. (...) Today, after a long period of Nazi crimes, everyone – no matter how heavily burdened – believes themselves to have been completely innocent. This repression went and goes so far that [even] Auschwitz is presented as a lie.[39]

2.2.3 Legal Issues Arising

The post-1990 reappraisal of the systemic injustice of the East German socialist regime, injustice of which the 'Waldheim Trials' were probably the clearest judicial expression, inevitably had points of contact with the parallel process of post-hoc coming to terms with Nazi systemic injustice. Thus, the proceedings instituted in the reunified Federal Republic against the Waldheim judges raised legal questions that had already played a role in proceedings against Nazi judges for perversion of justice. The initial question was whether the original Waldheim proceedings should be considered judicial proceedings at all. This was in light of the opening of the scope of application of the crime of perversion of justice. Alternatively, it was proposed that they were "merely legally disguised murder, merely sentences expressing arbitrary power, dressed up in the form of a verdict, following the orders of a principal".[40]

2.2.3.1 Requirements for a Procedure to be Deemed Judicial (Reappraisal of Nazi-era Injustice)

Federal German jurisdiction had already had to deal with this question in the Huppenkothen-Thorbeck proceedings against a high-ranking Nazi prosecutor and judge, respectively. The proceedings concerned, inter alia, the part played by both men in a court martial held in April 1945 at the Flossenbürg concentration camp, which handed down death sentences against Wilhelm Canaris, Dietrich Bonhoeffer, and others for their alleged part in the Wolf's Lair assassination attempt on Hitler. While the first-instance ruling in the post-war prosecution of Huppenkothen and Thorbeck still maintained that the court martial had had a 'judicial façade', the Federal Court of Justice (FCJ) made it clear in its first appeal ruling, in 1952, that the court martial should not be considered judicial in nature. In the FCJ's view, even if all the legal provisions in force at the time had been observed, this had only been done in order to conceal the true purpose of the proceedings.[41] The Court's reasoning ran thus: it is part of the

> indispensable character of a judge's decision [...] that it is made by judges independently of orders, as a decision of their untrammelled legal conscience, on the basis of a procedure designed to inquire into the truth, and to ascertain and determine guilt or innocence and the degree of guilt; so that on the result of these proceedings alone depends the verdict to be rendered by the judges according to their conscience.[42]

This is not the case, continued the FCJ, when a proceeding "only preserves a 'judicial façade', that is, one that only outwardly and in appearance observes the rules governing judicial proceedings".[43] Since the proceedings were subsequently referred back, the FCJ had to deal with the matter on two more occasions. Its third, definitive appeal decision completely reversed its own initial 1952 verdict, citing in particular an ostensible lack of proof as to the allegedly farcical nature of the original court martial proceedings "in particular as regards the internal factual aspect".[44] This verdict heralded a development that would ultimately prove fatal for attempts to come to terms with Nazi injustice through criminal prosecution: henceforth, for former judges to be tried over past judicial actions, there would be a requirement that the accused could be shown to have possessed 'sure knowledge' of the illegality of his or her actions.[45]

2.2.3.2 Reappraisal of East German Socialist Regime Injustice

The post-reunification reappraisal of East German regime injustice provided an opportunity for Federal Germany to critically examine its previous postwar reappraisal of Nazi injustice and further develop case law in this regard. For instance, in a 16 November 1995 ruling, the FCJ stated that Nazi injustice had been incomparably more serious than GDR injustice.[46] The same court chambers pointed out, in another decision, that no error exempting the judge from criminal liability could be considered if a judge "speaks 'law', due to reasons of state, in a way that obviously exceeds the limits derived from fundamental unbreakable legal principles known to him".[47]

2.3 Summary

The discussion above leads us to conclude that evaluation of the Waldheim trials does not turn so much on the question of legal injustice per se but on the question of disregard of the law in force in the GDR at that time. Such disregard, which in Waldheim ultimately became systematic, particularly affected the rights of the accused.

Involvement or immersion in a system of injustice cannot in itself be sufficient to allow the judge who administers the law in such a system to go unpunished. The concrete circumstances surrounding this immersion (such as pressure, coercion, disadvantages in the event of refusal, etc.) can only have the effect of reducing the degree of guilt or punishment that is deserved. Such a position – admitting mitigation, but not immunity – means setting aside the attribution of independence and freedom from instruction that was originally demanded if Nazi injustice was to be dealt with in ways that included the pursuit of individual criminal liability. Independence and freedom from instruction are now no longer a prerequisite for a finding that a particular court or judge (according to the provision) was guilty of perversion of justice.[48] In consequence, Nazi or East German regime judges could in principle also see their act subsumed under the offence of perversion of justice. An exception is when their participation was in sham proceedings that do not fulfill the minimum requirements to be afforded the status of a 'court' (such as Nazi stand court proceedings). With regard to those sham proceedings, other offences could apply directly (cf. §§ 211 et seqq of the German Criminal Code), since in this eventuality the so-called judges' privilege does not apply.[49] This privilege means that a judge cannot be charged with another criminal offense in connection with his or her judicial activity if no perversion of justice is found.[50]

Nevertheless, it is clear from reappraisal of the judicial injustices committed under both German dictatorships of the twentieth century that the offence of perversion of justice is intended to protect against abuse of justice by *individual* judges, but not against the *systematic* abuse of justice by the entire state. It should not be forgotten, however, that such state-level judicial injustice can be addressed through means other than criminal law. Such means may include, for example, rehabilitation and reparation of victims of these systems of injustice.

Notes

1 This is a translation by the author of the following quote: BGH, Judgment of 16 November 1995, 5 StR 747/94, (1996) 49 *NJW* 857: "Eine so vollständige Mißachtung der Ideen von Gerechtigkeit und Menschlichkeit, wie sie das Bild der NS-Justiz prägt, hat es in der DDR-Justiz (vielleicht abgesehen von Verfahren in den 'Waldheim-Prozessen') nicht gegeben".

2 'German Democratic Republic' in the original, DDR (Deutsche Demokratische Republik), headed by the Socialist Unity Party of Germany, SED (Sozialistische Einheitspartei Deutschlands).

3 The zone known as the Sowjetische Besatzungszone (SBZ). See Possekel, 'Entscheidungsblockaden mit massenhafter Todesfolge (November 1946–August 1948)' in Mironenko et al (eds) 73, 83.

4 Internment camps set up toward the end of the war by the Soviet Military Administration in Germany, SMAD; also known as 'silence camps' because their inmates were kept in almost total isolation from the outside world. See Otto, 'Die Waldheimer Prozesse' in Mironenko et al (eds) 533, 536; Possekel (1998) (n 3).

5 Bonwetsch, 'Der GULag – das Vorbild für die Speziallager in der SBZ' in Reif-Spirek/Ritscher (eds) 62; Cornelius, *Vom spurlosen Verschwindenlassen* (2006) 116 et seqq.

6 Erler, *Tätigkeit sowjetischer Militärtribunale in Deutschland* (1998) 210.

7 On the basis of Order No. 0022, issued on 6 January1950 by Soviet Interior Minister Colonel General Kruglov. See Haritonow, 'Zur Geschichte des Speziallagers Nr. 4 (3) in Bautzen' in Mironenko et al (eds) 331, 345 with reference to GARF, f 9409, op 1, d 41, 25; see also Prieß, 'Die Speziallager des NKVD Nr. 7 (Nr. 1) Sachsenhausen' in Mironenko et al (eds) 380, 408; Otto (1998) (n 4) 537.

8 BezG Dresden, Judgment of 1 November 1991, BSK (1) 118/91, (1992) 3 *DtZ* 91 et seqq.

9 The body that governed Allied occupation zones in Germany and Austria after the end of the Second World War. It was composed of the Soviet Union, the United Kingdom, the United States, and France.
10 A directive intended to implement the 'denazification' called for in the 1945 Potsdam Agreement.
11 Werkentin, 'Die Waldheimer Prozesse (1950)' in Groenewold et al (eds) 1, 3.
12 Maiwald, 'Rechtsbeugung im SED-Staat' (1993) 46 *NJW* 1881, 1885; Wassermann, 'Zur Anwendung der sogenannten Radbruchschen Formel auf Unrechtsurteile der DDR-Justiz' (1992) 14 *NJW* 878.
13 Estimated numbers in this regard vary. According to Otto (1998) (n 4) 549, there were at least 164 lawyers among the defendants. Werkentin (2012) (n 11) 3, estimates a total of around 130 judges, prosecutors, and lawyers.
14 Rüter, *DDR-Justiz und NS-Verbrechen, Band 14 Die Verfahren Nr. 2001–2088, Waldheimverfahren* (2009) proceedings against Walter Karl Max Teu. (magistrate – sentenced to life) file No 2025 reprinted 137 et seqq, Felix Erich Le. (Judge at the Dresden Higher Regional Court – sentenced to 25 years). No 2038 reprinted 205 et seqq, August Eberhard Johannes M. (Judge at the Dresden Field Court – sentenced to death, pardoned to life imprisonment) No 2040 reprinted 215 et seqq, Wilhelm Fritz Osk. (war court councillor – sentenced to 25 years) No 2042 reprinted 227 et seqq, Werner Paul Zie. (*Oberkriegsgerichtsrat* and *Oberrichter* – sentenced to death, commuted to life imprisonment) No 2048 printed 225 et seqq, Alfred Erhard Vol. (Amtsgerichtsrat – sentenced to life) No 2051 printed 273 et seqq, Walter Karl Sch. (*Oberstabsrichter* – sentenced to death, executed) No 2061 printed 327 et seqq, Martin Tre. (*Amtsgerichtsrat* – sentenced to 18 years imprisonment) No 2067 reprinted 359 et seqq, Horst Friedrich Rec. (*Kriegsgerichtsrat* and *Oberstabsrichter* – sentenced to death penalty, executed) No 2069 reprinted 367 et seqq, Hans-Ullrich Walter Rot. (Judge at the Imperial War Court – sentenced to life imprisonment) No 2070 reprinted 375 et seqq, Helmuth Otto Wilhelm Kut. (Oberkriegsgerichtsrat – sentenced to life imprisonment) No 2077 reprinted 417 et seqq, Paul Fritz Franz Vo. (Senate President of the Reich Court – sentenced to 20 years) No 2082 reprinted 469 et seqq, Hans Hugo Richard Teu. (District Court Director – sentenced to 18 years) No 2086 reprinted 501 et seqq.
15 According to Withöft, *Die Todesurteile der Waldheimer Prozesse* (2nd edn, Universität Wien 2014) 38 et seqq, Alfred Herzog and Rudolf Niejahr were also sentenced to death. Niejahr had been the presiding judge of a special court in Pomerania. According to Marxen et al (eds), *Strafjustiz und DDR-Unrecht, Band 5/2. Teilband: Rechtsbeugung* (De Gruyter 2007), 791 et seqq, Paul L. (war council member) and Johannes M. (military tribunal judge) were also sentenced.
16 Werkentin, 'Scheinjustiz in der frühen DDR' (1991) 24 *KJ* 333, 340.
17 Otto (1998) (n 4) 550.
18 Werkentin (1991) (n 16) 337. Cf. on the most diverse violations of Criminal Code and Code of Criminal Procedure regulations in force in East Germany at the time, see LG Leipzig, Judgment of 1 September 1993, 1 Ks 04 Js 1807/91, (1994) 48 *NJ*, 111 et seqq.
19 See the judgments provided in Rüter (2009) (n 14). On the legal basis of the Waldheim Trials, see Withöft (2014) (n 11) 20 et seqq.
20 ABl/KR Dtl. 1946 Nr, 11 (31 October 1946) 184.
21 Withöft (2014) (n 15) 37.
22 Werkentin (1991) (n 11) 4 et seq; Otto (1998) (n 4) 539.
23 Otto (1998) (n 4) 546.
24 Werkentin (1991) (n 11) 6; Werkentin (1991) (n 16) 339.

25 BezG Dresden, Judgment of 1 November 1991, BSK (1) 118/91, (1992) 3 *DtZ* 91 et seqq.
26 Gesetz über die Entschädigung bei Strafverfolgungsmaßnahmen.
27 BVerfG, Judgment of 19 November 1992, BvR 1793/94, (2000) 10 *VIZ* 307. These proceedings concerned the surviving dependants of Chief Staff Judge Walter S., who was sentenced to death at the Waldheim trials and subsequently executed.
28 Criminal Rehabilitation Act, version published on 17 December 1999 (BGBl. I 2664). Most recently amended by Article 12 of the Act of 2 June 2021 (BGBl. I 1387).
29 Werkentin (1991) (n 11) 12.
30 Helbig, 'Waldheim-Prozesse: Die juristische Aufarbeitung von DDR-Justizverbrechen' (2006) *Betrifft JUSTIZ* 312, 315. Helbig was the presiding judge of the competent criminal division of the Leipzig Regional Court.
31 Otto (1998) (n 4) 553.
32 Helbig (2006) (n 30) 312.
33 LG Leipzig, Judgment of 1 September 1993, 1 Ks 04 Js 1807/91, (1994) 48 *NJ* 111 et seqq.
34 Gerhard Feldbauer, ' "Wende"-Zeiten in der DDR'.
35 LG Leipzig, Judgment of 28 November 1997, 1 Ks 825 Js 21999/94, in Marxen et al (n 15) 795 et seqq. The appeal against this decision was rejected by the BGH, Judgment of 18 February 1999, 5 StR 236/98, (1999) 49 *NJ* 327 et seq later confirmed by the BVerfG, Judgment of 13 April 1999, 2 BvR 562/99, BeckRS 1999, 30054636.
36 See Marxen et. al. (2007) (n 15) 881 note 27.
37 Proceedings: BGH, Judgment of 13 August 1997, 3 StR 158/97, BGHR StGB § 46 Abs 1 Strafhöhe 12 (Gründe) confirming LG Leipzig, Judgment of 29 July 1996, 1 Ks 20 Js 5115/93 825 Js 21994/94.
38 Helbig (2006) (n 30) 312.
39 Reprinted in Feldbauer (2020) (n 34), author's translation.
40 Werkentin (1991) (n 11) 13.
41 Seliger, 'Die Prozesse gegen Walther Huppenkothen und Otto Thorbeck 1950–1956' in Groenewold (eds) 1, 13.
42 BGH, Judgment of 12 February 1952, 1 StR 658/51, BeckRS 1952, 30384879.
43 BGH, Judgment of 12 February 1952, 1 StR 658/51, BeckRS 1952, 30384879.
44 BGH, Judgment of 19 June 1956, 1 StR 50/56, (1996) 16 *NStZ* 485, 487; the 'internal factual aspect' refers to intent (mens rea).
45 Seliger, 'Die Prozesse gegen Walther Huppenkothen und Otto Thorbeck 1950–1956' in Groenewold (eds) (n 41) 1, 15.
46 See the citation in BGH (1995) (n 1).
47 BGH, Judgment of 15 September 1995, 5 StR 713/94, (1995) 48 *NJW* 3324.
48 Uebele, '§ 339 Rechtsbeugung' in Erb (eds), *Münchener Kommentar zum Strafgesetzbuch* para 9; Hilgendorf, '§ 339' in Hilgendorf (eds), *Leipziger Kommentar zum Strafgesetzbuch* para 16 with further references.
49 Uebele (2022) (n 48) § 339 para 9.
50 Vormbaum, 'Die rechtliche Transformation Deutschlands nach dem Zweiten Weltkrieg' in Muñoz Conde/Vormbaum (eds) 183, 192.

Bibliography

Bonwetsch B, 'Der GULag – das Vorbild für die Speziallager in der SBZ' in Reif-Spirek P/Ritscher B (eds), *Speziallager in der SBZ – Gedenkstätten mit doppelter Vergangenheit* (Links 1999) 62.

Cornelius K, *Vom spurlosen Verschwindenlassen zur Benachrichtigungspflicht bei Festnahmen* (Berliner Wissenschaftsverlag 2006).

Erler P, *Tätigkeit sowjetischer Militärtribunale in Deutschland* (De Gruyter 1998).

Feldbauer G., '*"Wende"-Zeiten in der DDR*' (blog). www.schattenblick.de/infopool/geist/meinung/gmsp0021.html (accessed 18 December 2023).

Haritonow A, 'Zur Geschichte des Speziallagers Nr. 4 (3) in Bautzen' in Mironenko S et al (eds), *Sowjetische Speziallager in Deutschland 1945 bis 1950, Band 1: Studien und Berichte* (De Gruyter 1998) 331.

Helbig W, 'Waldheim-Prozesse: Die juristische Aufarbeitung von DDR-Justizverbrechen' (2006) 86 *Betrifft JUSTIZ* 312.

Hilgendorf E, '§§ 331–358' in Hilgendorf E et al (eds), *Leipziger Kommentar zum Strafgesetzbuch, vol 19* (13th edn, De Gruyter 2024).

Maiwald M, 'Rechtsbeugung im SED-Staat' (1993) 46 *Neue Juristische Wochenschrift* 1881.

Marxen K et al, *Strafjustiz und DDR-Unrecht, Band 5/2. Teilband: Rechtsbeugung* (De Gruyter 2007).

Otto W, 'Die Waldheimer Prozesse' in Mironenko S et al (eds), Sowjetische Speziallager in Deutschland 1945 bis 1950, Band 1: Studien und Berichte (De Gruyter 1998) 533.

Possekel R, 'Entscheidungsblockaden mit massenhafter Todesfolge (November 1946–August 1948)' in Mironenko S et al (eds), *Sowjetische Speziallager in Deutschland 1945 bis 1950, Band 2: Sowjetische Dokumente zur Lagerpolitik* (De Gruyter 1998) 73.

Possekel R, 'Speziallager in Deutschland – Filiale der GULAG (August 1948 – April 1950)' in Mironenko S et al (eds), *Sowjetische Speziallager in Deutschland 1945 bis 1950, Band 2: Sowjetische Dokumente zur Lagerpolitik* (De Gruyter 1998) 87.

Prieß L, 'Die Speziallager des NKVD Nr. 7 (Nr. 1) Sachsenhausen' in Mironenko S et al (eds), *Sowjetische Speziallager in Deutschland 1945 bis 1950* (Akademie Verlag 1998) 380.

Rüter C F, *DDR-Justiz und NS-Verbrechen, Band 14 Die Verfahren Nr. 2001–2088, Waldheimverfahren* (De Gruyter Saur 2009).

Seliger H, 'Die Prozesse gegen Walther Huppenkothen und Otto Thorbeck 1950–1956' in Groenewold K et al (eds), *Lexikon der Politischen Strafprozesse* (Stiftung Kurt Groenewold 2012) 1.

Uebele M, '§§ 298–358' in Erb V et al (eds), *Münchner Kommentar zum Strafgesetzbuch, vol 6* (4th edn, CH Beck 2022).

Vormbaum T, 'Die rechtliche Transformation Deutschlands nach dem Zweiten Weltkrieg' in Muñoz Conde F/Vormbaum T (eds), *Transformation von Diktaturen in Demokratien und Aufarbeitung der Vergangenheit* (De Gruyter 2010) 183.

Wassermann R, 'Zur Anwendung der sogenannten Radbruchschen Formel auf Unrechtsurteile der DDR-Justiz' (1992) 14 *Neue Juristische Wochenschrift* 878.

Werkentin F, 'Die Waldheimer Prozesse (1950)' in Groenewold K et al (eds), *Lexikon der Politischen Strafprozesse* (Stiftung Kurt Groenewold 2012) 1.

Werkentin F, 'Scheinjustiz in der frühen DDR' (1991) 24 *Kritische Justiz* 333.

Withöft B, *Die Todesurteile der Waldheimer Prozesse* (2nd edn, Universität Wien 2014).

3 Prosecuting State Criminality after German Unification

Judging the Judges[1]

Gerhard Werle and Moritz Vormbaum

3.1 Legal Reckoning rather than Revolutionary Accounting

There was no revolutionary accounting for the crimes of the East German regime in 1989. From the beginning, the peaceful revolution guided the punishment of East German crimes in the direction of legal process. Initial steps towards legal accountability were taken by the East German legal system itself following the fall of the communist regime. After unification, Germany's federal justice system took on this task and extended it to other manifestations of East German state criminality.

Our research project at Humboldt-Universität zu Berlin followed this process from the beginning. We had access to all relevant trial documents, particularly indictments and judgments. In this chapter, we will refer to the results of this project, which was initiated in 1994 by Klaus Marxen and Gerhard Werle and in which Moritz Vormbaum has taken an active part in recent years. On the basis of extensive data from over 700 criminal trials, we can paint a complete picture of the process of legal reckoning that is the subject of this chapter.

Legal accountability for the SED [*Sozialistische Einheitspartei Deutschlands*/ Socialist Unity Party of Germany] regime extended to a wide variety of areas that may be mentioned, at least briefly. They included ten categories of offenses: violence on the internal German border, electoral fraud, perversion of justice – our main subject – denunciations (i.e., reporting someone to the authorities), activities of the Ministry of State Security, mistreatment of prisoners, doping of sport competitors, abuse of office, corruption and related economic crimes, and finally, espionage.

3.1.1 What Law Applies?

Where criminal law is concerned, the first question lawyers asked was which law to apply. While East German criminal law applied when the acts were committed, Article 8 of the Unification Treaty made the criminal law of former West Germany binding on the new states, the so-called accession zone (*Beitrittsgebiet*), after 3 October 1990.

Upon unification, East German law went out of force. However, punishment exclusively under the new German laws could not be reconciled with the

DOI: 10.4324/9781003470069-4

prohibition on retroactivity. Therefore, lawmakers required that Section 2 of the criminal code of the Federal Republic be applied to all offenses committed prior to accession. Section 2 provided that the law in force at the time of the commission of the crime was to be applied in principle but added the following: If the law in force upon completion of the crime (in this case, East German law) changed before the judgment (in this case, through the introduction of West German law), the more lenient law should apply.

3.1.2 'Two-Key Approach'

Under this rule, the legislature equated the replacement of East German criminal law with West German criminal law to a change in national law between the completion of the crime and the judgment. In prosecuting East German crimes, the law most favorable to the perpetrator would be dispositive at trial (the so-called most favorable principle). A 'two-key approach' was therefore used: Only if both 'keys', East and West German law, fit the case could the door to punishment be 'unlocked'.

For the courts, this required a nuanced test.[2] The first step was to establish whether a crime had been committed under East German law. If this were not the case, there would be no criminal liability. Otherwise, the second step would be to subsume the relevant acts under the criminal law of the Federal Republic.

3.1.3 Continuity of Crime

If both keys fit, a third question was raised of so-called continuity of crime between the old and new norms. It was necessary to establish that the new norm (lex posterior) – that is, the relevant crime under the law of the Federal Republic – was not only 'formally' able to subsume the crime, but that the relevant act also corresponded substantively to the types of crimes defined in East German law at the time of commission. Only if this was the case could violations of the prohibition on retroactive punishment be avoided.[3] For individual rights such as life or health, this legal step was unproblematic. But for offenses connected to national political bodies or institutions, it could cause considerable difficulty, in particular for the perversion of justice on which we are focusing.[4] If continuity of the type of crime was found, the court then determined the more lenient punishment overall.[5]

3.2 Patterns of Judicial Involvement

Before we address the prosecution of East German judges and prosecutors under the principles set out above, we would like to describe the East German justice system and its place in the dictatorship's repressive apparatus.

3.2.1 The East German Justice System

Most important to the functioning of the East German criminal justice system were central guiding organs that were expected to ensure the 'partiality' (*Parteilichkeit*) of criminal law – that is, to apply the law in the spirit of the party's policies. What this guidance meant was succinctly summarized by the former East German judge and Minister of Justice Hilde Benjamin:

> Correct guidance means always examining the activities of the organs of justice from the point of view: Does it serve the building of socialism? Correct guidance means exposing the ideological roots of false ideas that harm the building of socialism. It means bringing about changes in mistaken procedures by the organs of justice and in the consciousness of the staff, and it means educating cadres in the spirit of the working class world view, of dialectical and historical materialism.[6]

One of the central guiding organs was the East German Supreme Court, the task of which was to guarantee the legal unity. Its opportunities to do so were at first limited by the law of 8 December 1949 governing its establishment. The Supreme Court was only a court of first instance in state security matters and a court of cassation. However, the dissolution of the federal structure and the disappearance of state supreme courts from the court landscape in 1952 gave the national Supreme Court broad opportunities to control the judiciary. It was integrated into the court hierarchy and given extensive instruments of control, such as the authority to issue binding guidelines for lower courts. The Supreme Court itself sometimes called its chambers 'state-political leadership organs'.

A second judicial guidance organ was the Chief Prosecutor's Office. This office was already granted effective instruments of control upon its establishment. Under Section 10 of the Law on the Supreme Court and the Chief Prosecutor of 1949, it was authorized to issue instructions to all other prosecutors, and was thus the central prosecutorial supervisory body. In addition, it had broad discretion in personnel matters and was empowered to change prosecutorial structures. As it had the right to take over cases from subordinate prosecutors' offices and bring them before the Supreme Court as political proceedings, the Chief Prosecutor's Office played an important role in the judicial system, especially because judges as a rule took their cues from the prosecutor's indictment.

The relatively independent, central status of the prosecutor's office was expanded in later years, although its relationship to the political leadership was generally ambivalent throughout East Germany's history. Furthermore, the prosecutor's so-called supervision of legality did not extend to cases of misconduct by party functionaries.

The third central judicial guidance organ was the Justice Ministry, which, according to its official description, dealt, among other things, with the direction, monitoring, and analysis of district and county courts, the choice of lay assessors, and the processing of clemency petitions.

Finally, political leaders influenced the judiciary in a variety of ways. The Politburo or the Central Committee's Department of State and Legal Matters could intercede directly in the courts' activities and require a politically desirable result. The Prosecutor's Office maintained close contacts with the political leadership during important criminal cases. Indeed, a Politburo resolution on 26 August 1952 stated, "The State Prosecutor General's Office is obliged to report to the Politburo before the occurrence of important trials".

According to a study by Johannes Raschka, in later years little direct influence was exercised on the outcome of political trials, in contrast to the judicial practice in the early years of the East German state. One can interpret this as a sign that the careful choice of judicial personnel and years of indoctrination of the judiciary had borne fruit. In addition, political influence was not limited to specific interventions; it permeated the entire judicial system, down to the local level, for example, in the staffing of judicial bodies, admission to legal studies, and the content of university education.

Historically significant facts about the East German judicial system can be found in many German federal court decisions after 1990. They indicate that the German judiciary came to essentially the same conclusions as this text.[7] The courts found, for example, that law in East Germany functioned to 'exercise the state power of the working class'. In the process, it was 'firmly integrated into the unified system of power'. The following are examples of cases dealt with by the justice system of the Federal Republic after 1990 that vividly illustrate how the East German justice system served as a 'lever for the political leadership' (as it was termed in the ruling party's jargon).

3.2.2 Waldheim Trials

Many charges of perversion of justice concerned the Waldheim trials, held from April to July 1950, which were convened to try real and supposed Nazi criminals. Special criminal panels had been established in the Chemnitz State Court for this purpose and were active at Waldheim. The trials violated the defendants' procedural rights and were heavily influenced by the SED. The substantive bases for the judgments were Control Council Law No. 10 (20 December 1945)[8] and Control Council Directive No. 38 (12 October 1946).[9] The Waldheim trials led to the conviction of 3,324 prisoners; 32 were sentenced to death.[10] In many cases, trials lasted only a few minutes. The rights of the defendants were grossly violated. After unification, a number of former staff were found guilty of participating in these trials. They were generally sentenced to prison terms with probation,[11] although former East German judge Irmgard Jendretzky received four years without probation.[12]

3.2.3 'Operation Rose'

Operation Rose, in 1953, involved the prosecution of owners of hotels, pensions, and similar businesses on the coast of the Baltic Sea and the expropriation of their property.[13] The legal basis for these measures was the Economic Crime Decree of 20 October 1948.[14] The allegations were essentially that the owners of these hotels and pensions had bought and used rationed goods without ration cards, kept food intended for their guests for themselves, evaded taxes, and maintained contact with 'American imperialist intelligence centers' in West Berlin and West Germany. In the course of the operation, 711 businesses were searched, 527 investigations initiated, and 442 people taken into investigative custody. Four hundred and eight people were convicted; 440 hotels and pensions, as well as 181 restaurants, apartments, and other businesses, were confiscated.[15] The trials were held before chambers of the Bützow district court created especially for this purpose.

The post-unification indictments by the Schwerin prosecutor's office, directed at a prosecutor who had taken part in the operation, involved nine cases concerning 15 former defendants – one case in which a monetary fine had been imposed, four cases of imprisonment from four to ten months, and nine cases of aggravated imprisonment (*Zuchthaus*) from five months to five years. In most cases, all of the defendants' property had been confiscated, although some cases had been limited to the expropriation of a single business.

The former prosecutors charged with perversion of justice after unification were accused of having drafted the indictments and requested that the arrest warrants be upheld. The Rostock regional court convicted the former prosecutor of perversion of justice, in some cases in conjunction with deprivation of liberty.[16] The Federal Court of Justice, however, affirmed only the charge of accessory to perversion of justice, changing the guilty verdict to reflect that decision, and set aside the sentence.[17]

3.2.4 Other Political Trials

The above-mentioned trials provide two examples of large-scale manipulation of the justice system by political leaders. Political trials were an everyday occurrence in East Germany. Over the years, various legal bases were developed for political trials. In East Germany's early days, which were heavily influenced by Stalinist ideology, dissident activities such as distributing pamphlets and collecting information for western entities were considered "boycott agitation and peace-threatening propaganda"; they were prosecuted and sometimes punished with the death penalty. Those who took part in the mass protests against the regime on 17 June 1953 were convicted of 'breach of the peace'. After the Wall was built in 1961, the political leadership began to utilize court-ordered 'residency restrictions' to keep dissidents away from border areas. Before 1968, the Criminal Code of the German Reich and various Acts covering economic crimes, political crimes, as well as some areas of the General Part were applied. Starting in 1968, political trials were based on the East German criminal code, which was adopted in that year and contained various types of offenses that could be used against dissidents. In East Germany's final years, many people were tried for filing applications to emigrate in order to protest the regime, rather than with the intent of actually leaving the country. The East German justice system considered this a violation of Section 214 of the criminal code, 'interference with state or societal activity'.

3.2.5 Procedures in Other Areas of Law

In addition to criminal trials, after 1990 the German courts dealt with matters in other areas of law, such as labor and family law. They also examined situations in which trials had not been held, even when there was clear evidence (for example, East German prosecutors' refusal to investigate electoral fraud).

3.3 Legal Rationale and Doctrines for Prosecuting Jurists

3.3.1 Introduction

After unification, the German justice system initiated numerous criminal proceedings against East German legal personnel for perversion of justice. Criminal proceedings were primarily begun against judges and prosecutors who were directly involved in decisions at the time. They represented the largest group charged with the commission of systemic crimes in East Germany.[18] The charges were generally perpetration of perversion of justice, sometimes in conjunction with deprivation of liberty or homicide. Members of the Justice Ministry and the Ministry of State Security were also prosecuted for participating in (inciting and abetting) these offenses. The factual basis for the criminal charges of incitement and abetting was the pressure brought to bear on judges and prosecutors through instructions, orientation laws, and guidelines.

A few indictments were aimed at people external to the justice system who had not been involved in deciding concrete cases. They were accused of exercising influence on judges' decisions through general directives; the charge in such cases was incitement to perversion of justice. No lay assessors were indicted for contributing to penal judgments.

3.3.2 Facts

The facts established by the courts involved, first of all, the past trials that were the basis for the charge of perversion of justice, and second of all, the East German justice system itself, in which those trials were embedded and which were relevant to judging the criminal activity.

Among the issues the prosecutions dealt with were the Waldheim trials, sabotage, economic crimes, boycott agitation, and anti-peace propaganda. Most political trials were held under the East German criminal code of 12 January 1968. Two hundred fifty-three of the total of 374 indictments we examined for perversion of justice – that is, around 67% – involved trials under that criminal code.

We will now address the many legal problems with prosecuting perversion of justice. In a number of leading cases, the Federal Court of Justice developed a uniform jurisprudence that prosecutors and lower courts followed.

3.3.3 Two-Key Approach and Continuity of Crime

The starting point for these legal considerations was the two-key approach, that is, the act's criminality under both East German law (Section 244 of the East German criminal code) and the law of the Federal Republic (Section 339 of the criminal code). In addition, there was a third requirement: that the crime of perversion of justice under East German law and the corresponding crime in the legal system of reunited Germany at heart protect the same legal interest (so-called continuity of crime). Given the politicization of the East German justice system, this presumption required particular justification, as it meant recognizing the substantive legitimacy of East German law. The Federal Court of Justice argued as follows: the criminalization of perversion of justice under the law of the Federal Republic served to protect the independent, unbiased administration of justice. The justice system in East Germany was never de facto independent, but it also served to regulate social coexistence. In principle, even in East Germany, the goal of adjudication was to resolve conflicts peacefully and punish misdeeds. It was guided by the effort to reach neutral, fair decisions.[19] Human rights violations as a result of court judgments were to be seen as abuses of judges' decision-making power in individual cases.[20] Given this more or less neutral adjudicative practice, despite the outside pressures brought to bear, it was therefore possible to compare the protected legal interests in both legal orders.[21]

Judicial justifications for continuity of crime, in contrast, referred to citizens' individual interests. From this perspective, the crime of perversion of justice under both Federal Republic and East German law exercised a reflexive effect to protect citizens subject to the law. These citizens had to be protected from ways of applying the law that contradicted the national legal order.[22] In this sense, the two offenses delineated crimes identical in type and value.

Both these lines of argument have been criticized in the literature. The question has been raised whether Section 244 of the East German criminal code can really be compared to Section 339 of the Federal Republic's criminal code, given the very different justice systems in each state. The incorporation of the East German justice system into a political system based around the ruling party and judges' lack of independence has been more strongly emphasized.[23]

Some have also asked whether East German courts, in individual cases, fulfilled the necessary minimum conditions to fall under the crime of perversion of justice.[24] In fact, however, to apply the Federal Republic's law on perversion of justice, it is not necessary for judges to actually be independent and not subject to instruction; even judges in totalitarian regimes can be perpetrators of perversion of justice.[25]

A judge's decision does not fulfill the requirements for perversion of justice if "a tribunal can no longer be considered a 'court', its procedures 'legal procedures', or its decisions 'judgments'".[26] In such a case, these are distinguished from mistaken or invalid judgments and are considered so-called nonjudgments, lacking the quality of law.[27] An example of these would be the judicial acts of the Nazi People's Court after Roland Freisler became its president in August 1942,[28] as well as the summary courts martial in the final days of World War Two.[29]

The quality of the courts in the Waldheim trials has been discussed with an eye to the judicial performance of East German courts.[30] The post-unification Leipzig Regional Court determined that the 1950 Waldheim courts did meet the minimum requirements of a court, even though the decisions they reached could be considered arbitrary.[31] In response, some scholars have argued that these were 'non-judgments' and therefore the crime of perversion of justice does not apply.[32] The consequence of this view, however, is not necessarily impunity. Instead, criminal liability can be found independently of perversion of justice through other offenses such as deprivation of liberty or homicide. This leaves no room for the so-called judges' privilege, under which, if no perversion of justice is found, a judge cannot be charged with any other crime related to his or her judicial acts.[33]

3.3.4 Limiting Criminal Liability to Arbitrary Acts

It therefore makes sense to presume criminal liability for perversion of justice whenever there has been an unlawful decision as defined by Section 244 of the East German criminal code and perversion of justice under Section 339 of the Federal Republic's criminal code. However, the Federal Court of Justice has greatly narrowed the scope of criminal liability, "aside from individual excesses, to cases in which the unlawfulness of the decision was so obvious, and the rights of others, particularly their human rights, were so grossly violated that the decision could be described as an arbitrary act".[34] Thus a gross violation of human rights is required, as for other types of offense.

In its legal reasoning, the Federal Court of Justice distinguished between cases of criminal prosecution and those in which perpetrators were not prosecuted in order to achieve a politically desirable goal.[35]

For prosecutions, the Federal Court of Justice described three types of cases in which East German judges and prosecutors could be held criminally liable under the principles discussed above:

> Cases in which, by going beyond the actual wording of the law or exploiting its vagueness in applying it, the scope of offenses were stretched to such an extent that their punishment, particularly by imprisonment, can be considered obviously unjust; also cases in which the sentence imposed was unacceptably disproportionate to the act involved, so that the sentence necessarily appears to be seriously unjust and a gross violation of human rights, even in contravention of the provisions of East German criminal law; further, gross violations of human rights in the means by which trials, specifically criminal trials, were carried out, in which prosecution and sentencing did not in any way serve the attainment of justice, but only the elimination of a political opponent or a particular social group.[36]

In cases of deliberate non-prosecutions, which by their nature could not lead to direct violations of human rights, the Court found it dispositive whether the illegality of the decision was so obvious that it could readily be considered an arbitrary act.[37] This could be presumed if the severity of the non-prosecuted act was equivalent to a human rights violation. Otherwise, the main issue was the degree of the breach of duty represented by the act.[38]

In explaining its restriction of criminal liability to arbitrary acts, the Federal Court of Justice referred first of all to what it considered 'restrictions inherent in the concept of perversion of justice'.[39] The crime of perversion of justice, in this view, was only meant to punish fundamental violations of the administration of justice.[40] The Federal Republic's definition of perversion of justice already recognized that the crime could be committed only by officeholders who departed from law and justice intentionally and in grave fashion.[41] Second, the restrictions on the offense with regard to judges and prosecutors followed from the fact that the behavior involved took place in a different legal system.[42] More extensive punishment would violate the basic principle of guilt in criminal law, as well as the prohibition on retroactivity inherent in the rule of law, in particular Article 103 (2) of the Basic Law (*Grundgesetz*) of the Federal Republic of Germany.[43]

These Federal Court of Justice decisions clearly limited the scope of the crime of perversion of justice and concentrated it on cases involving gross violations of human rights. Such limitations were not at all discernable in the text of the law, leading to criticism of this reasoning in the literature.

Some scholars have rejected the limitations on criminal liability developed by the Federal Court of Justice. Criticism begins with the Court's doctrinal starting point, limiting the scope of the Federal Republic's crime of perversion of justice to intentional and grave offenses.[44] Such restrictions on the crime, in this view, do not conform to the wording of that law.[45] There has also been criticism of the limitation on criminal liability for East German judges and prosecutors to arbitrary acts involving obvious and gross violations of human rights.[46] In this argument, neither the Federal Republic's nor East Germany's law on perversion of justice required a particularly grave injury to those affected by the decision.[47] In fact, the Unification Treaty's terms require – in addition to fulfillment of the elements of the crime – only an illegal decision as defined under Section 244 of the East German criminal code and perversion of justice as defined under Section 339 of the Federal Republic's criminal code.

3.3.5 Application of East German Law

A central problem in trials of East German perversion of justice was the interpretation of unlawful decisions.[48] It implicated the meaning of the East German concept of law: What was 'law' in East Germany?

The Federal Court of Justice took a positivist approach. In assessing unlawfulness, East Germany's written law was considered effective law within the meaning of Section 244 of the East German criminal code.[49] Thus, the Court found that a decision was not unlawful if the judge's or prosecutor's actions were supported by the text of the law. Laws were to be interpreted according to the interpretive methods of East Germany, not the Federal Republic.[50] There was no doctrine in East Germany under which law was created merely at the discretion of the holder of state power.[51] Rules without the quality of law could not be grounds for criminal liability, nor could they limit it. Decisions and guidelines by the highest court with binding legal effect were only to be respected to the extent they remained within the bounds of the law's text.[52] However, the elementary requirements of justice and protection of international human rights also applied in East Germany.[53] Therefore, the Federal Court of Justice considered it possible, in principle, to justify finding a decision unlawful because it violated higher-ranking law.[54] Still, cases in which East German laws would not be respected because they violated core rights had to remain rare exceptions for the sake of legal certainty.[55]

The Federal Court of Justice did not find such an exception for perversion of justice. It did not consider even the laws on political crimes in East Germany to be invalid. The incompatibility of these laws with human rights, especially restrictions on travel and the freedoms of opinion, assembly, and association, did not go so far, in the Court's opinion, as to attain the degree of unacceptability that would allow a presumption that it was nonbinding, in the spirit of the Radbruch formula.[56] In individual cases, the applicability of human rights norms in East Germany might have required the country to limit its use of criminal laws.[57] Still, this human-rights-friendly interpretation of East German law was an exception in the Federal Court's jurisprudence.

The concept of law developed by the Federal Court of Justice has been criticized in the literature for failing to take account of the law as it was applied in East Germany in practice.[58] In the East German legal system, systemic state crimes, including decisions by East German judicial personnel, were not prosecuted. The East German state did not merely apply fundamentally correct law in a malign spirit; it in fact shaped law in this way.[59] Therefore, the critics argued, the retroactive punishment of East German judges and prosecutors violated the prohibition of retroactivity in Article 103(2) of the Basic Law.[60]

A strong objection to the above view, and to the Court's interpretation of East German law, is also found in the literature. Here, some scholars argue that the East German law to be applied must be interpreted according to rule-of-law standards.[61] Any decisions that violated the rule of law were therefore also unlawful under East German perversion of justice laws. There is no violation of the prohibition on retroactivity, as changes in the interpretation of laws are not included in the protective scope of that prohibition.[62]

The Federal Court of Justice limited the scope of liability considerably with its idea that East German laws were to be treated as valid and that the particular features of the East German justice system were to be taken into account in interpreting norms, as well as in restricting the criminal liability of East German judges and prosecutors to arbitrary acts. This is expressed in the number of investigations that were terminated, as well as acquittals and decisions not to initiate prosecutions.[63] The jurisprudence of the Federal Court of Justice required the trial judges to examine every single East German decision on the basis of often vague East German laws. However, the point at which decisions could be considered arbitrary was not easy to determine.[64]

Cases concerned with a lack of proportionality between offenses and sentences were particularly relevant. Judges were generally only assumed to be liable for perversion of justice if they had imposed disproportionately long prison terms or the death penalty.[65] In the opinion of the Federal Court of Justice, such punishments must always be considered gross violations of human rights.

The Federal Constitutional Court affirmed the jurisprudence of the Federal Court of Justice on the criminal liability of East German judges and prosecutors.[66] It refused to take up a constitutional complaint by an East German judge against her conviction for perversion of justice. The Constitutional Court did not consider the interpretation and application of the East German law on perversion of justice to be a violation of the prohibition on retroactivity in Article 103(2) of the Basic Law. The fact that the East German judge's decisions at times conformed to East German state practice was irrelevant to the question of whether the prohibition on retroactivity had been violated. According to the Court, the prohibition on retroactivity did not apply if the state practice behind the law's implementation grossly violated generally recognized international human rights norms.[67] The Court included among these generally recognized international human rights norms, in addition to protection of life and bodily integrity, the right to personal freedom and protection from cruel and inhuman punishment.[68] In the group of cases heard by the Federal Court of Justice involving prosecution and overbroadening of crimes and the imposition of grossly unjust sentences, said the Constitutional Court, unacceptable human rights violations had been at issue; here the East German judges concerned could not fall back on the protection of expectations principle found in Article 103(2) of the Basic Law.[69]

3.3.6 Subjective Element

The Federal Court of Justice's decisions included few discussions of the subjective element of the East German law on perversion of justice. The Court offered no definition of the direct intent requirement in Section 244 of the East German criminal code. Apparently, the Court tacitly based the concept of intent on Federal Republic legal doctrine; that is, knowledge and desire to carry out the offense.[70] In the process of determining intent, the perpetrator's knowledge was as a rule presumed, with the justification that the offense was obviously a gross violation of human rights.[71]

The Federal Court of Justice provided differing answers to the question of whether East German criminal law recognized mistakes of law and whether this could therefore preclude intent. The starting point for its jurisprudence, however, was consistent. The Court thought it possible that a judge or prosecutor might recognize the unlawfulness of their decision but believe it to be 'correct' because of their integration into an unjust system.[72] In one judgment, the Court found that this belief was irrelevant under East German law.[73] In another decision, the Court, without considering East German law, did not address whether the belief that one was acting legally could be seen as a mistake of law; in any case, said the Court, this mistake "was neither unavoidable nor ever appropriate to change the sentencing range".[74] This line of argument was criticized for not taking sufficient account of East German criminal law.[75] According to East German criminal law doctrine, in this view, a consciousness of illegality (though this term is only used in the doctrine of the Federal Republic) was an element of intent.[76] Without such a consciousness of illegality, it would not be possible, under East German law, to prosecute for an intentional offense.

3.3.7 Modes of Participation

The judges who participated in the decisions in question were all viewed as perpetrators of a perversion of justice. In the case of prosecutors, the Federal

Court of Justice considered them perpetrators of a perversion of justice only for official acts in investigations – for example, applications for arrest warrants or indictments.[77] Prosecutors who appeared at trial could only be charged as accessories, as responsibility for the trial was transferred to the court.[78]

3.3.8 Statute of Limitations

The statute of limitations for perversion of justice in East Germany began on 3 October 1990. Because the acts involved had not been prosecuted, due to the express or implied will of the East German state and party leadership, for political or other reasons not compatible with essential principles of a state governed by the rule of law, the statute of limitations did not run from 11 October 1949 to 2 October 1990. In principle, this meant that it ended after five years, on 2 October 1995.[79] However, the third statute of limitations law extended this period to 2 October 2000. The statute of limitations for perversion of justice expired permanently on that date.[80]

3.3.9 Sentencing

In determining the legal basis for sentencing, the courts started with the principle of strict alternativity. This provided that the sentence was to be calculated using both Federal Republic and East German law and then determined according to the more lenient law.

The fact that East German judges' and prosecutors' offenses were connected with the system was taken into account in sentencing in two ways. First of all, it acted to mitigate punishment because the perpetrators had been integrated into the East German system and were subject to heavy pressure.[81] The Court found that it was much more difficult for members of the East German justice system to uphold the law than to succumb to massive outside pressures.[82] Secondly, the frequent suspension of sentences under Federal Republic law in these cases was considered justified because this group of defendants was considered to possess a favorable social prognosis.[83] Recidivism for perversion of justice was unlikely since the judges and prosecutors were no longer part of the justice system. It was also unlikely, in the Court's view, that they would commit other offenses.[84] It is noteworthy that the Court also considered, in mitigation of sentencing, the fact that the Federal Republic had failed to prosecute Nazi judicial crimes.[85] It argued that, given this history, harsher punishments would be perceived as unjust by the defendants – especially as the Federal Republic had only recently changed its jurisprudence on perversion of justice by members of the Nazi judiciary, thereby making it possible to punish East German judges and prosecutors.[86]

3.4 Assessment

3.4.1 Two Routes in Prosecuting East German State Criminality

Two primary routes have been used in the post-1990 Federal Republic for prosecuting State-sponsored East German crimes: Punishment of gross violations of human rights and continuity of prosecution. For perversion of justice, the first route was relevant, although the punishment of gross violations of human rights is not a limitation found in the definition of the crime of perversion of justice. Many charges in this area had to be dismissed. As a result, prosecutions concentrated on convictions by East German courts that were amounting to gross violations of human rights and resulted in the imposition of the death penalty or long prison sentences.

3.4.2 The Right Signal

The punishment of gross violations of human rights by the Federal Republic's justice system sends the right signal, both domestically and internationally. Through these prosecutions, the awareness that a 'culture of impunity' makes the repetition of gross human rights violations more likely has once again gained the endorsement of state practice. Prosecution of perversion of justice confirms the validity of basic human rights norms even in the face of arbitrary judicial behavior and helps to individualize responsibility for collective injustice. It is also important to recognize and investigate the history of injustice; the trials for perversion of justice contributed to this recognition in the judicial system. The decisions precisely document the use of arbitrary political trials, especially in the case of the Waldheim trials.

Despite some plausible objections, the focus on cases of perversion of justice that contain gross violations of human rights was a positive development. In our opinion, the comparatively lenient sentences were appropriate and refute the mistaken accusation of victors' justice. Instead, the differentiated sentencing indicates an effort to do justice to individual responsibility within a dictatorial system of injustice.

3.4.3 Human-Rights-Friendly Interpretation of East German Law

We see a certain weakness in the picture painted by the Federal Republic's judiciary of the role of the East German judiciary. The idea of a human-rights-friendly interpretation of East German law distorts and downplays the reality of the SED dictatorship. The systematic persecutions of political opponents, including by the judiciary, have been portrayed as 'exceptions' and 'excesses', while the justice system in general has been classed as 'normal'. In our view, this is an incorrect portrayal that obscures the fact that the justice system as a whole was a tool of the ruling party. There was no place in East German legal practice for a human-rights-friendly interpretation against the will of the political leadership.

3.4.4 'Victors' Justice'?

Post-1990 prosecution of East German injustice was controversial in public debate at the time. Criticism was not limited to the weaknesses discussed here and other partial aspects. Instead, the whole process of dealing with the East German past through criminal justice was criticized in principle.

The accusation of 'victors' justice', in its most robust form, argues that the (West German) victors were judging the (East German) vanquished. They wanted revenge, not justice. The verdicts were not legal decisions but exercises of power. The (West German) victors' judges did not have the authority to sit in judgment over the (East German) vanquished.

The accusation of 'victors' justice' has been fully refuted by the findings we have presented. Let us first consider the cases of intermediate criminal liability in which no human rights violations were committed. These involved mainly the offenses of abuse of office, corruption, and electoral fraud. Given the relatively less serious nature of the offenses, the accusation of victors' justice might prima facie appear not entirely misplaced. However, it was the East German population that clearly manifested its desire for prosecution following the fall of Communism. It was the democratic forces in East Germany that wanted to put an end to the criminal privileges hitherto enjoyed by the East German leadership. The East German prosecutors' offices initiated energetic efforts to this end in the interlude between the fall of the Berlin Wall, in November 1989, and unification in October 1990. These facts speak for themselves, and many of those who were prosecuted later would probably not have gotten off as lightly in the courts of post-Communist East Germany as they did in the Federal Republic.

As far as the gross human rights violations committed in East Germany are concerned, here too, post-Communist East Germany had already taken steps towards prosecution. However, a prosecutorial focus in this area only developed following unification. Prosecution gained legitimacy through the seriousness of the offenses. Prosecution is the normal, fair state response to gross violations of human rights and is also preferred by international law. The fact that the East German regime's legal practice had been the diametrical opposite of this could not protect those responsible from subsequent prosecution. In fact, the post-unification courts declared offenses that violate elementary human rights to be unlawful and punishable. This was the case regardless of East German domestic legality and legal practice.

At the same time, the post-1990 courts regularly imposed relatively mild punishments. Former East German border guards, for example, almost all received probation for intentional homicide. Harsher penalties were imposed only on members of the state or military leadership and on perpetrators of excesses. But even here, the harshest penalty imposed, ten years' imprisonment, was well under the maximum sentence for homicide. Characterizing this sentencing practice as an expression of 'victors' justice' is simply wrong. The accusation of 'victors' justice' is also refuted by the many decisions in which applying the principles of the rule of law led to an early end to the proceedings. The most spectacular example was the dismissal of the case against Erich Honecker.[87]

Invoking 'victors' justice' is a denial of facts, one which moreover downplays the actual injustices that occurred under the East German dictatorship.

3.5 Conclusion

In our view, holding judges accountable after dictatorship is necessary. Simply integrating judges and prosecutors into a new democratic system is not enough.

Justice requires clarifying the role of the judiciary in the past dictatorship; the facts surrounding that role must be established, and those responsible must be named. A society can only learn what mistakes to avoid in the future by confronting the full truth about its past.

The conclusion of our chapter is a clear affirmation of the importance of prosecuting the legal accomplices to dictatorship. Trying judges and prosecutors is mandatory if they participated in gross violations of human rights.

Notes

1 The authors would like to thank Belinda Cooper for the translation of the German text and for her substantive contributions in the process.

2 Fundamental to the relevant understanding of the regulatory technique of Art. 315 EGStGB BGH, Judgment of 3 November 1992, 5 StR 370/92, BGHSt 39, 1, 6 et seqq, reprinted in Marxen/Werle, *Strafjustiz und DDR-Unrecht. Dokumentation, vol 2: Gewalttaten an der deutsch-deutschen Grenze* (2002), 135; to differing opinions in the literature, which were, of course, hardly compatible with the wording and system of the law, see the overview at Tröndle/Fischer, Strafgesetzbuch: StGB – mit Nebengesetzen, preliminary remark § 3 para 46.

3 Fundamental to the requirement of continuity of injustice BGH GS, Decision of 10 July 1975, GSSt 1/75, BGHSt 26, 167, 172 et seq; in the context of coming to terms with GDR injustice, BGH, Judgment of 26 November 1992, 3 StR 319/92, BGHSt 39, 54, 67 et seqq, reprinted in Marxen/Werle, *Strafjustiz und DDR-Unrecht. Dokumentation, vol 1: Wahlfälschung* (2000) 217.

4 For details on this, as well as other problems of the application of law, see Marxen/Werle/Vormbaum, *Die strafrechtliche Aufarbeitung von DDR-Unrecht* (2020) 8 et seqq. In terms of structure, the BGH was not uniform. While he proceeded in the order described in the case of electoral fraud (Marxen/Werle/Vormbaum, *Die strafrechtliche Aufarbeitung von DDR*-Unrecht) 47, the examination of the continuity of injustice of the offense of obstruction of justice (Marxen/Werle/Vormbaum, *Die strafrechtliche Aufarbeitung von DDR-Unrecht*) 76 was carried out abstractly before entering into factual considerations.

5 Exceptions to this procedure were made in accordance with Art. 315 para 4 EGStGB in the rare case that the criminal law of the Federal Republic had already applied to offenses committed in the GDR before the accession took effect.

6 Benjamin, 'Vom IV. zum V. Parteitag der Sozialistischen Einheitspartei Deutschlands' (1958) *NJ* 437, 438. For more information on the GDR judiciary see Vormbaum, *Das Strafrecht der Deutschen Demokratischen Republik* (2015).

7 Evidence at Marxen/Werle/Vormbaum (2020) (n 4).

8 Official Gazette of the Control Council in Germany No 3, 1946, 50 et seqq.

9 Official Gazette of the Control Council in Germany No 11, 1946, 184 et seqq.

10 On the Waldheim trials, see Eisert, *Die Waldheimer Prozesse* (1993); Fricke, *Zur Menschen- und Grundrechtssituation politischer Gefangener in der DDR* (1990), 205 et seqq as well as the findings of LG Leipzig, Judgment of 1 September 1993, 1 Ks 04 Js 1807/91 (1994) 48 *NJ* 111 and BezG Dresden, Decision of 28 October 1991, BSK (1) 231/91 (1992) 12 *NStZ* 137.

11 LG Leipzig, Judgment of 1 September 1993, 1 Ks 04 Js 1807/91 (1994) 48 *NJ* 111 confirmed by BGH, Decision of 10 August 1994, 3 StR 252/94 (1994) 48 *NJ* 456; LG Leipzig, Judgment of 7 November 1994, 9 Ks 20 Js 17/92; LG Leipzig, Judgment of 18 July 1996, 1 Ks 20 Js 5115/93, confirmed by BGH, Judgment of 13 August 1997, 3 StR 158/97.

12 LG Leipzig, Judgment of 28 November 1997, 1 Ks 835 Js 21999/94, reprinted in Marxen/Werle, *Strafjustiz und DDR-Unrecht. Dokumentation, vol 5: Rechtsbeugung* (2007) 795; BGH, Decision of 18 February 1999, 5 StR 236/98 (Rejection of the appeal), reprinted in Marxen/Werle (2007) (n 12) 883; The high sentence results from the fact that her case involved five counts of obstruction of justice combined with manslaughter.

13 For the Rose campaign, see Behlert, 'Die Staatsanwaltschaft' in Bundesministerium der Justiz (ed), *Im Namen des Volkes? Über die Justiz im Staat der SED* (1994) 85 et seqq; Müller, *Die Lenkung der Strafjustiz durch die SED-Staats- und Parteiführung der DDR am Beispiel der Aktion Rose* (1995) 17 et seqq; Werkentin, *Politische Strafjustiz in der Ära Ulbricht* (1995) 59 et seqq.

14 Government Gazette for Mecklenburg No 25 1948, 165 et seqq.

15 StA Schwerin, Indictment without date, 191 Js 21263/93, 12 et seqq.

16 LG Rostock, Judgment of 23 June 1997, III KLs 4/95, reprinted in Marxen/Werle (2007) (n 12) 519.

17 BGH, Judgment of 9 July 1998, 4 StR 599/97, reprinted in Marxen/Werle (2007) (n 12) 559.

18 See Marxen/Werle/Vormbaum (2020) (n 4) 253.

19 BGH, Judgment of 13 December 1993, 5 StR 76/93, BGHSt 40, 30, 39, reprinted in Marxen/Werle (2007) (n 12) 21.

20 Marxen/Werle (2007) (n 12) 21.

21 Marxen/Werle (2007) (n 12) 21.

22 BGH, Judgment of 6 October 1994, 4 StR 23/94, BGHSt 40, 272, 275, reprinted in Marxen/Werle (2007) (n 12) 165; Roggemann, 'Richterstrafbarkeit und Wechsel der Rechtsordnung' (1994) 49 *JZ* 769, 773; Bemmann, 'Zu aktuellen Problemen der Rechtsbeugung' (1995) 50 *JZ* 123, 124.

23 Roggemann (1994) (n 22), 769, 773; doubting the premise of the BGH also Willnow, 'Die Rechtsprechung des 5. (Berliner) Strafsenats des Bundesgerichtshofs zur strafrechtlichen Bewältigung der mit der deutschen Vereinigung verbundenen Probleme' (1997) *JR* 265 n 110.

24 The continuity of injustice merely involves an abstract comparison of legal interests, which the Federal Court of Justice – as described above – undertakes on the basis of a generalized view of the judicial system.

25 Hilgendorf, '§ 339: Rechtsbeugung' in Jähnke et al (eds), *Leipziger Kommentar zu Strafgesetzbuch*, para 16; Heger, '§ 339 StGB: Rechtsbeugung' in Lackner et al (eds), *Strafgesetzbuch: StGB – Kommentar*, para 2.

26 Hilgendorf (2009) (n 25) para 147.

27 Hilgendorf (2009) (n 25) para 148.

28 This is the accusation of the StA at the LG Berlin against Paul Reimers of 6 September 1984, 3 P (K) Js 6/97, 209; likewise Rüping, 'Strafjustiz im Führerstaat' (1984) 131 *GA* 297, 304 et seq.

29 Hilgendorf (2009) (n 25) para 147.

30 On the Waldheim trials, see Marxen/Werle/Vormbaum (2020) (n 4) 54 et seq. The judicial quality of the GDR courts could also be doubtful in individual cases if a court, whether due to non-judicial influences or "autonomous" decisions, had already decided on the conviction and the exact sentence before the main hearing.

31 LG Leipzig, Judgment of 1 September 1993, 1 Ks 04 Js 1807/91 (1994) 48 *NJ* 111, 114; confirmed by BGH, Decision of 10 August 1994, 3 StR 252/94 (1994) 48 *NJ* 456.

32 Wassermann, 'Zur Anwendung der sogenannten Radbruchschen Formel auf Unrechtsurteile der DDR-Justiz' (1992) 45 *NJW* 878, 879.

33 For an in-depth examination of the issues involved, see Hohoff, *An den Grenzen des Rechtsbeugungstatbestandes – Eine Studie zu den Strafverfahren gegen DDR-Juristen* (2001).

34 BGH, Judgment of 13 December 1993, 5 StR 76/93, BGHSt 40, 30, 41, reprinted in Marxen/Werle (2007) (n 12) 21; BGH, Judgment of 15 September 1995, 5 StR 713/94, BGHSt 41, 247, 253, reprinted in Marxen/Werle (2007) (n 12) 321.

35 This differentiation was explicitly emphasized by the Federal Court of Justice in a decision on the non-prosecution of charges of falsification of local elections of 7 May 1989, see BGH, Judgment of 21 August 1997, 5 StR 652/96 (1998) 51 *NJW* 248, 249 et seq, reprinted in Marxen/Werle (2007) (n 12) 1007.

36 BGH, Judgment of 13 Decembert 1993, 5 StR 76/93, BGHSt 40, 30, 42 et seq, reprinted in Marxen/Werle (2007) (n 12) 21; BGH, Judgment of 15 September 1995, 5 StR 713/94, BGHSt 41, 247, 254, reprinted in Marxen/Werle (2007) (n 12) 321; according to the Federal Court of Justice, these case groups are not exhaustive, see BGH, Judgment of 21 August 1997, 5 StR 652/96 (1998) 51 *NJW* 248, 250, reprinted in Marxen/Werle (2007) (n 12) 1007.

37 BGH, Judgment of 21 August 1997, 5 StR 652/96 (1998) 51 *NJW* 248, 250, reprinted in Marxen/Werle (2007) (n 12) 1007 with reference to BGH, Judgment of 9 May 1994, 5 StR 354/93, BGHSt 40, 169, 181.

38 BGH, Judgment of 21 August 1997, 5 StR 652/96 (1998) 51 *NJW* 248, 250, reprinted in Marxen/Werle (2007) (n 12) 1007.

39 BGH, Judgment of 15 September 1995, 5 StR 713/94, BGHSt 41, 247, 253, reprinted in Marxen/Werle (2007) (n 12) 321, 324.

40 BGH, Judgment of 15 September 1995, 5 StR 713/94, BGHSt 41, 247, 251, reprinted in Marxen/Werle (2007) (n 12) 321.

41 BGH, Judgment of 15 September 1995, 5 StR 713/94, BGHSt 41, 247, 251, reprinted in Marxen and Werle (2007) (n 12) 321; BGH, Judgment of 13 December 1993, 5 StR 76/93, BGHSt 40, 30, 40; BGH, Judgment of 6 October 1994, 4 StR 23/94, BGHSt 40, 272, 283; the BGH has already developed these principles for § 339 StGB independently of the question of the criminal liability of judges and public prosecutors in the GDR; see BGH, Judgment of 23 May 1984, 3 StR 102/84, BGHSt 32, 357, 363 et seq; BGH, Judgment of 29 July 1986, 1 StR 330/86, BGHSt 34, 146, 149; BGH, Judgment of 29 October 1992, 4 StR 353/92, BGHSt 38, 381, 383.

42 BGH, Judgment of 15 September 1995, 5 StR 713/94, BGHSt 41, 247, 253, reprinted in Marxen and Werle (2007) (n 12) 321.

43 Marxen and Werle (2007) (n 12) 321.

44 Kraut, *Rechtsbeugung? Die Justiz der DDR auf dem Prüfstand des Rechtsstaates* (Beck 1997) 133 et seq; Seebode, 'Rechtsbeugung und Rechtsbruch' (1994) *JR* 1, 3; Schulz, 'Rechtsbeugung und Missbrauch staatlicher Macht' (1995) 15 *StV* 206, 209.

45 Seebode (1995) (n 44) 1, 3.

46 Hohmann, 'Zur Rechtsbeugung durch DDR-Staatsanwälte' (1995) 49 *NJ* 128, 131; Kraut (1997) (n 44) 133 et seq; Spendel, 'Rechtsbeugung und Justiz' (1995) 50 *JZ* 375, 378 et seq.

47 Hohmann (1995) (n 46) 128, 131; Hirsch, *Rechtsstaatliches Strafrecht und staatlich gesteuertes Unrecht* (1996) 24; Kraut (1997) (n 46) 133 et seq; Spendel (1995) (n 46) 375, 378 et seq.

48 Section 244 East German criminal code.

49 BGH, Judgment of 15 September 1995, 5 StR 713/94, BGHSt 41, 247, 256, reprinted in Marxen and Werle (2007) (n 12) 321.

50 BGH, Judgment of 13 December 1993, 5 StR 76/93, BGHSt 40, 30, 41, reprinted in Marxen and Werle (2007) (n 12) 21.
51 BGH, Judgment of 15 September 1995, 5 StR 713/94, BGHSt 41, 247, 256, reprinted in Marxen and Werle (2007) (n 12) 321.
52 BGH, Judgment of 15 September 1995, 5 StR 713/94, BGHSt 41, 247, 261, reprinted in Marxen and Werle (2007) (n 12) 321.
53 BGH, Judgment of 15 September 1995, 5 StR 713/94, BGHSt 41, 247, 257, reprinted in Marxen and Werle (2007) (n 12) 321; BGH, Judgment of 15 November 1995, 3 StR 527/94 (1996) 7 *DtZ* 92, 93.
54 BGH, Judgment of 15 September 1995, 5 StR 713/94, BGHSt 41, 247, 256 et seqq, reprinted in Marxen and Werle (2007) (n 12) 321; BGH, Judgment of 6 October 1994, 4 StR 23/94, BGHSt 40, 272, 276, reprinted in Marxen and Werle (2007) (n 12) 165.
55 BGH, Judgment of 15 September 1995, 5 StR 713/94, BGHSt 41, 247, 257, reprinted in Marxen and Werle (2007) (n 12) 321; BGH, Judgment of 15 November 1995, 3 StR 527/94 (1996) 7 *DtZ* 92, 93.
56 BGH, Judgment of 15 September 1995, 5 StR 713/94, BGHSt 41, 247, 257, reprinted in Marxen and Werle (2007) (n 12) 321.
57 BGH, Judgment of 15 November 1995, 3 StR 527/94 (1996) 7 *DtZ* 92, 95; BGH, Judgment of 30 November 1995, 4 StR 777/94 (1996) 16 *NStZ-RR* 65, 68; BGH, Judgment of 15 September 1995, 5 StR 642/94, copy of the Judgment 32 (insofar not published), reprinted in Marxen and Werle (2007) (n 12) 237.
58 Dencker, 'Vergangenheitsbewältigung durch Strafrecht? Lehren aus der Justizgeschichte der Bundesrepublik' (1990) 73 *KritV* 299, 303; Schlink, 'Rechtsstaat und revolutionäre Gerechtigkeit' (1994) 48 *NJ* 433, 435.
59 See Jakobs, 'Untaten des Staates – Unrecht im Staat. Strafe für die Tötungen an der Grenze der ehemaligen DDR?' (1994) 141 *GA* 1, 9.
60 See Buchholz, 'Rechtsbeugung durch DDR-Richter und -Staatsanwälte' (1996) *ZAP-Ost* 219, 226 et seq; Schlink (1994) (n 58) 433, 435.
61 Bemmann (1995) (n 22) 123, 126; Spendel (1995) (n 46) 375, 378.
62 Bemmann (1995) (n 22) 123, 126.
63 See Marxen/Werle/Vormbaum (2020) (n 4) 260 et seqq, 263 et seqq.
64 See in this respect the detailed compilation of BGH case law at Willnow (1997) (n 23), 265, 266 et seqq.
65 This is also the analysis of Willnow (1997) (n 23) 265, 266 et seqq.
66 BVerfG, Decision of 7 April 1998, 2 BvR 2560/95 (1998) 51 *NJW* 2585, reprinted in Marxen and Werle (2007) (n 12) 265.
67 BVerfG, Decision of 7 April 1998, 2 BvR 2560/95 (1998) 51 *NJW* 2585, reprinted in Marxen and Werle (2007) (n 12) 265.
68 BVerfG, Decision of 7 April 1998, 2 BvR 2560/95 (1998) 51 *NJW* 2585, copy of the Decision 13 (insofar not published), reprinted in Marxen and Werle (2007) (n 12) 265.
69 BVerfG, Decision of 7 April 1998, 2 BvR 2560/95 (1998) 51 *NJW* 2585, copy of the Decision, 14, reprinted in Marxen and Werle (2007) (n 12) 265.
70 Sternberg-Lieben/Schuster, '§ 15 StGB: Vorsätzliches und fahrlässiges Handeln' in Schönke/Schröder (eds), *Strafgesetzbuch: StGB – Kommentar*, para 9 with further evidence.
71 BGH, Judgment of 15 September 1995, 5 StR 713/94, BGHSt 41, 247, 276, reprinted in Marxen and Werle (2007) (n 12) 321; BGH, Judgment of 16 November 1995, 5 StR 747/94, BGHSt 41, 317, 337, reprinted in Marxen and Werle (2007) (n 12) 457; BGH, Judgment of 15 November 1995, 3 StR 527/94 (1996) 7 *DtZ* 92, 94. Confirmed by

BVerfG, Decision of 7 April 1998, 2 BvR 2560/95, copy of the Decision 18 et seq, reprinted in Marxen and Werle (2007) (n 12) 265.

72 BGH, Judgment of 16 November 1995, 5 StR 747/94, BGHSt 41, 317, 339, reprinted in Marxen and Werle (2007) (n 12) 457.

73 BGH, Judgment of 15 September 1995, 5 StR 713/94, BGHSt 41, 247, 277, reprinted in Marxen and Werle (2007) (n 12) 321.

74 BGH, Judgment of 16 November 1995, 5 StR 747/94, BGHSt 41, 317, 340, reprinted in Marxen and Werle (2007) (n 12) 457.

75 Hohoff, 'Vorsatz und "Unrechtsbewusstsein" im Strafrecht der DDR als Problem aktueller Rechtsanwendung' (1997) 8 *DtZ* 308, 313.

76 Hohoff (1997) (n 75) 308, 312; likewise Amelung, 'Strafbarkeit von "Mauerschützen" – BGH, *NJW* 1993, 141' (1993) 33 *JuS* 637, 643; Gropp, 'Naturrecht oder Rückwirkungsverbot? – Zur Strafbarkeit der Berliner "Mauerschützen"' (1996) 50 *NJ* 393, 397.

77 BGH, Judgment of 15 September 1995, 5 StR 713/94, BGHSt 41, 247, 249 et seq, reprinted in Marxen and Werle (2007) (n 12) 321.

78 BGH, Judgment of 15 September 1995, 5 StR 713/94, BGHSt 41, 247, 250, reprinted in Marxen and Werle (2007) (n 12) 321. Incitement could not be considered because it could not be ruled out that the sentencing judges had already decided on the offence before the prosecutor's final motion; see Willnow (1997) (n 23) 265 para 114.

79 Section 78 para 3 no 4 StGB.

80 Sections 78c para 3 sentence 2, 78 para 3 no 4 StGB.

81 In this respect, only exemplary BGH, Judgment of 16 November 1995, 5 StR 747/94, BGHSt 41, 317, 341 et seq, reprinted in Marxen and Werle (2007) (n 12) 457; LG Berlin, Judgment of 21 April 1994 (520) 76 Js 681/92 KLs (68/92), copy of the Judgment 129 et seq, reprinted in Marxen and Werle (2007) (n 12) 177; LG Dresden, Judgment of 28 February 1994, 5 Kls 82 Js 13837/92, copy of the Judgment, 271 et seq; LG Erfurt, Judgment of 5 July 1994, 510 Js 463/90 – 1 Ks, copy of the Judgment, 181 et seq; LG Magdeburg, Judgment of 15 February 1994, 23 KLs 11/91, copy of the Judgment, 1060. This had an effect, among other things, on the assumption of a less serious case of manslaughter – which may have been realized in addition to the violation of the law.

82 BGH, Judgment of 16 November 1995, 5 StR 747/94, BGHSt 41, 317, 341, reprinted in Marxen and Werle (2007) (n 12) 457.

83 LG Berlin, Judgment of 21 April 1994 (520) 76 Js 681/92 KLs (68/92), copy of the Judgment 131 et seq, reprinted in Marxen and Werle (2007) (n 12) 177; LG Dresden, Judgment of 28 February 1994, 5 Kls 82 Js 13837/92, copy of the Judgment 272 et seq; LG Frankfurt/Oder, Judgment of 4 September 1996, 25 Ks 7/95, copy of the Judgment 119 et seq; LG Erfurt, Judgment of 5 July 1994, 510 Js 463/90-1 Ks, copy of the Judgment 185 et seq.

84 LG Dresden, Judgment of 28 February 1994, 5 Kls 82 Js 13837/92, copy of the Judgment 273; LG Frankfurt/Oder, Judgment of 4 September 1996, 25 Ks 7/95, copy of the Judgment 120.

85 S. Jeßberger/Kuhli in this anthology.

86 BGH, Judgment of 16 November 1995, 5 StR 747/94, BGHSt 41, 317, 343, reprinted in Marxen and Werle (2007) (n 12) 457; likewise LG Frankfurt/Oder, Judgment of 4 September 1996, 25 Ks 7/95, copy of the Judgment 118. Both decisions deal with death sentences.

87 Honecker, the most powerful figure in the East German regime until just before its fall in November 1989, was put on trial in Berlin in November 1992 in connection with border

killings. The case against him was, however, abandoned in January 1993 on health grounds (other co-defendants were later found guilty).

Bibliography

Amelung K, 'Strafbarkeit von "Mauerschützen" – BGH, *NJW* 1993, 141' (1993) 33 *Juristische Schulung* 637.

Behlert W, 'Die Staatsanwaltschaft' in Bundesministerium der Justiz (ed), *Im Namen des Volkes? Über die Justiz im Staat der SED* (Forum 1994).

Bemmann G, 'Zu aktuellen Problemen der Rechtsbeugung' (1995) 50 *Juristenzeitung* 123.

Benjamin H, 'Vom IV. zum V. Parteitag der Sozialistischen Einheitspartei Deutschlands' (1958) 12 *Neue Justiz* 437.

Buchholz E, 'Rechtsbeugung durch DDR-Richter und -Staatsanwälte' (1996) *Zeitschrift für die Anwaltspraxis-Ost* 219.

Dencker F, 'Vergangenheitsbewältigung durch Strafrecht? Lehren aus der Justizgeschichte der Bundesrepublik' (1990) 73 *Kritische Vierteljahresschrift für Gesetzgebung und Rechtswissenschaft* 299.

Eisert W, *Die Waldheimer Prozesse* (Springer-Verlag 1993).

Fricke K-W, *Zur Menschen- und Grundrechtssituation politischer Gefangener in der DDR* (Verl. Wissenschaft und Politik 1990).

Gropp W, 'Naturrecht oder Rückwirkungsverbot? – Zur Strafbarkeit der Berliner "Mauerschützen"' (1996) 50 *Neue Justiz* 393.

Heger M, '§ 339 StGB: Rechtsbeugung' in Lackner K et al (eds), *Strafgesetzbuch: StGB – Kommentar* (30th edn, CH Beck 2023).

Hilgendorf E, '§ 339: Rechtsbeugung' in Jähnke B/Laufhütte H/Odersky W (eds), *Leipziger Kommentar zu Strafgesetzbuch, vol 13 (§§ 331–358)* (12th edn, De Gruyter 2009).

Hirsch H J, *Rechtsstaatliches Strafrecht und staatlich gesteuertes Unrecht* (Westdeutscher Verlag 1996).

Hohmann O, 'Zur Rechtsbeugung durch DDR-Staatsanwälte' (1995) 49 *Neue Justiz* 128.

Hohmann O, 'Die strafrechtliche Bewältigung der Rechtsanwendung durch Richter und Staatsanwälte der DDR – Aktuelle Probleme der Rechtsbeugung' (1996) 7 *Deutsch-Deutsche Rechts-Zeitschrift* 230.

Hohoff U, 'Vorsatz und "Unrechtsbewusstsein" im Strafrecht der DDR als Problem aktueller Rechtsanwendung' (1997) 8 *Deutsch-Deutsche Rechts-Zeitschrift* 308.

Hohoff U, *An den Grenzen des Rechtsbeugungstatbestandes – Eine Studie zu den Strafverfahren gegen DDR-Juristen* (Berlin-Verlag Spitz 2001).

Jakobs G, 'Untaten des Staates – Unrecht im Staat. Strafe für die Tötungen an der Grenze der ehemaligen DDR?' (1994) 141 *Goltdammer's Archiv für Strafrecht* 1.

Knabe H, *Die Täter sind unter uns. Über das Schönreden der SED-Diktatur* (3rd edn, List 2009).

Kraut G M, *Rechtsbeugung? Die Justiz der DDR auf dem Prüfstand des Rechtsstaates* (Beck 1997).

Lüderssen K, 'Entkriminalisierung durch Politisierung' (1997) 52 *Juristenzeitung* 525.

Marxen K/Werle G, *Strafjustiz und DDR-Unrecht. Dokumentation, vol 1: Wahlfälschung* (De Gruyter 2000).

Marxen K/Werle G, *Strafjustiz und DDR-Unrecht. Dokumentation, vol 2: Gewalttaten an der deutsch-deutschen Grenze* (De Gruyter 2002).

Marxen K/Werle G, *Strafjustiz und DDR-Unrecht. Dokumentation, vol 5: Rechtsbeugung* (De Gruyter 2007).
Marxen K/Werle G/Vormbaum M, *Die strafrechtliche Aufarbeitung von DDR-Unrecht* (2nd edn, De Gruyter 2020).
Müller K, *Die Lenkung der Strafjustiz durch die SED-Staats- und Parteiführung der DDR am Beispiel der Aktion Rose* (Lang 1995).
Pawlik M, 'Das Recht im Unrechtsstaat' (1994) 25 *Rechtstheorie* 101.
Raschka J, *Justizpolitik im SED-Staat* (Böhlau 2000).
Roggemann H, 'Richterstrafbarkeit und Wechsel der Rechtsordnung' (1994) 49 *Juristenzeitung* 769.
Rüping H, 'Strafjustiz im Führerstaat' (1984) 131 *Goltdammer's Archiv für Strafrecht* 297.
Schlink B, 'Rechtsstaat und revolutionäre Gerechtigkeit' (1994) 48 *Neue Justiz* 433.
Schulz L, 'Rechtsbeugung und Missbrauch staatlicher Macht' (1995) 15 *Strafverteidiger* 206.
Seebode M, 'Rechtsbeugung und Rechtsbruch' (1994) 70 *Juristische Rundschau* 1.
Spendel G, 'Rechtsbeugung und Justiz' (1995) 50 *Juristenzeitung* 375.
Sternberg-Lieben D/Schuster F, '§ 15 StGB: Vorsätzliches und fahrlässiges Handeln' in Schönke A/Schröder H (eds), *Strafgesetzbuch: StGB – Kommentar* (30th edn, CH Beck 2019).
Tröndle H/Fischer T, *Strafgesetzbuch: StGB – mit Nebengesetzen* (54th edn, CH Beck 2007).
Vormbaum M, *Das Strafrecht der Deutschen Demokratischen Republik* (Mohr Siebeck 2015).
Vormbaum T, 'Zur strafrechtlichen Verantwortlichkeit vonn DDR-Richtern wegen Rechtsbeugung' (1993) 47 *Neue Justiz* 212.
Wassermann R, 'Zur Anwendung der sogenannten Radbruchschen Formel auf Unrechtsurteile der DDR-Justiz' (1992) 45 *Neue Juristische Wochenschrift* 878.
Werkentin F, *Politische Strafjustiz in der Ära Ulbricht* (Links 1995).
Willnow G, 'Die Rechtsprechung des 5. (Berliner) Strafsenats des Bundesgerichtshofs zur strafrechtlichen Bewältigung der mit der deutschen Vereinigung verbundenen Probleme' (1997) *Juristische Rundschau* 221.

4 Dictatorship and Judicial Complicity

The Case of Argentina

Omar Palermo

4.1 Introduction

In 2017, the so-called oral mega-trial (*megajuicio* or *megacausa oral*) was held in the city of Mendoza, Argentina. The trial resulted in former judges and prosecutors who held office during Argentina's most recent civil-military dictatorship (1976–1983) being sentenced to life imprisonment for the systematic omission of investigation of crimes against humanity that came to their attention. The court considered that, by means of the overt and generalized nature of the omission to pursue investigations, the former judges and prosecutors had guaranteed impunity for those acts. They were accordingly sentenced to life imprisonment as primary accomplices of the crimes whose investigation they had failed to pursue. The present chapter reviews the dogmatic correctness of this reasoning and offers systematic arguments in its favor.

During Argentina's civil-military[1] dictatorship of 1976–1983, prosecutors and judges became aware of crimes against humanity but did not investigate their perpetration. It is indisputable that these omissions constituted crimes against the administration of justice,[2] since the aforementioned authorities were guarantors of the promotion of such investigations. The challenging question here is therefore whether the systematic breach of these duties to promote judicial investigation (guarantors' duties, resulting from an institutional position) can be considered as aiding and abetting, by omission, those same crimes against humanity. As is well known, in the aforementioned trial – also commonly referred to as Argentina's 'Judges' Trial' – the former judges and prosecutors were sentenced to life imprisonment as necessary accomplices to the crimes they did not investigate. The repeated omission of investigation was considered to have constituted a way of ensuring impunity for those crimes.

For this reason, the trial court considered that the former judges and prosecutors who had systematically failed to investigate the very serious facts of which they had been made aware had provided indispensable collaboration. This consisted of the judiciary's failure to obstruct the plan of repression against the civilian population. By way of example, former prosecutor Otilio Romano, who had failed to investigate a single one of the numerous aggravated homicides committed within his jurisdiction, was sentenced to life imprisonment as a primary participant in

DOI: 10.4324/9781003470069-5

thirty-three of those aggravated murders, treated moreover as separate, not concurrent, offenses. The court understood that Otilio Romano's repeated omissions of investigation had had the purpose of guaranteeing impunity for those acts.[3]

In this chapter, I offer arguments in favor of this outcome, a solution for which I advocated as a prosecutor for crimes against humanity from the very outset of the investigation that culminated in the 2017 convictions. In order to do so, I first present some general considerations about the complicity of the judiciary with the dictatorship (section two). Next, in section three, I set out the theoretical assumptions that formed the basis of case analysis and address the systematic consequences that proceed from the application of that theoretical model to the determination of the individual responsibilities of the judges of the Argentine dictatorship. Finally, section four outlines some conclusions.

4.2 The Judiciary's Double Standard During the Dictatorship

The complicity of the judiciary with the state terrorism implemented under Argentina's most recent civil-military dictatorship constitutes possibly the greatest denial of justice in Argentine history. During those years, the civilian population was the victim of the fiercest and bloodiest, generalized and systematic attack in living memory. The crimes perpetrated include homicides, enforced disappearances, illegal deprivation of liberty, torture, humiliation, and the rape of men and women – including pregnant women, illegally detained, who were later disappeared and whose children were illegally appropriated. Judges and prosecutors became aware of these very serious facts through habeas corpus writs and other complaints filed by victims' relatives, who turned to the judiciary as the last bastion of the state that they could trust. However, the judiciary limited itself to formally processing complaints and writs. It went through the motions, shelving thousands of cases after only perfunctory processing, without carrying out a single serious investigation of the very grave facts that were reported. Quite simply, the judiciary did not pursue a single investigation of these crimes.

At the same time, and before the self-same courts, the opposite situation prevailed in proceedings in which victims of political persecution were being investigated for infringements of Law No. 20.840, known as the 'Anti-Subversion Act'.[4] Such proceedings advanced rapidly: political prisoners against whom charges had been brought were routinely convicted, with their protestations that their 'confessions' had been obtained through torture and harassment studiously ignored. This state of affairs demonstrates the axiomatic nature of the double standard practiced by the dictatorship-era judiciary. The harshest possible face was turned against victims of politically motivated persecution, while impunity was guaranteed to those responsible for very serious crimes committed in pursuit of state terrorism. Those responsible for this double standard are not guiltless: it is a sign of the evident judicial complicity that favored the state terrorism of those years. This leniency over one aspect of the past must have repercussions for determining individual responsibilities of those judges and prosecutors who, out of conviction, fear, or convenience, silenced victims' pain and tolerated acts of repression. The next section considers the theoretical foundations that were drawn on in determining this responsibility.

4.3 Theoretical Assumptions Used to Justify the Complicity of Judges and Prosecutors: The Theory of Quantitative Accessoriness

Some methodological clarifications are required as to the theoretical foundations of the initial accusation, which served as the starting point for convicting former judges and prosecutors of the Argentine dictatorship. On the one hand, it must be clarified that this indictment departs from the restrictive concept of perpetrator[5] whereby it is maintained that there is a qualitative difference between perpetrators and accomplices. According to this restrictive conception, the perpetrator is the one who executes the act, while accomplices are those who intervene in the previous phase. The accusation in the Mendoza *megacausa* was instead drawn up based on the theory of quantitative accessoriness,[6] a theory proposed by a small but highly qualified sector of German doctrinal scholars,[7] and which has had an important influence in the Spanish[8] and Latin American[9] literatures. This theory draws a distinction based on quantities of intervention. Deploying this theoretical model in the service of cases over judicial responsibility for the crimes of the dictatorship requires one to take, in turn, several systematic steps. While purely didactic in nature, these steps are fundamental to a holistic analysis of the problems of imputation posed by these cases. Accordingly, it must first of all be determined what kind of duties – negative or positive – were breached by the former judges and prosecutors. This requires explaining the theoretical importance of the distinction between breach of positive and negative duties, both of which can be breached either by action or by omission (section 3.1, below). Secondly, and bearing in mind that in most crimes against humanity what is infringed is a negative duty not to harm, it is necessary to determine who was part of the group of persons that committed these acts and whether the former judges of the dictatorship are among them. For this purpose, a distinction must be made between two key categories: *accessory conduct* and *prohibition of return*. A behavior is *accessory* when it is meant to be continued by others, so that the intervening party is not only responsible for his or her contribution but also for what happens next. The opposite of accessoriness is the prohibition of return; here, we think of contributions as being socially appropriate, in the sense that they are not continued by others. Where this latter situation obtains, the imputation cannot reach back to the first person, whose contribution is merely causal. It is therefore necessary to establish whether judges' behavior during dictatorship is accessory to the behavior of the armed or security forces or is distanced from it (below, section 3.2). Third, reference will be made to the particularities of participation by omission and its possible application to the situation of dictatorship-era judges and prosecutors (section 3.3). Fourth, the social importance of the contributions of each of the accomplices must be measured. It must be established whether the greatest weight of each contribution was felt in the preparatory phase, during the execution, or after the execution. The extent of this contribution will in turn serve as a basis for determining the degree of imputation: the intervening party will be perpetrator, instigator, or accomplice according to the importance of his or her contribution to the total act (section 3.4). Finally, reference will be made to the link between the concept of accessoriness and the subjective requirements of the conduct.

It should be noted that this methodological option in no way implies the development of an ad hoc doctrine, created exclusively to be applied to cases such as the one at hand[10]. Indeed, German criminal theory cannot be treated as a menu of theories from which the interpreter selects in order to support a decision that in reality has been taken intuitively beforehand. To avoid such unwarranted 'cherry picking', jurisprudence that adopts a particular theory ought always to do so while also considering the respective methodological context within which the theory was developed.[11] Otherwise the resolution of the case may not only be haphazard, but also arbitrary.[12]

4.3.1 The Distinction Between Positive and Negative Duties

The criminal liability of a person acting as an individual is based on the infringement of a duty, not on the mere malicious causing of harm. The same is not, however, true of crimes that imply an infringement of a positive duty. In these, the determining factor is not control over the act, but rather it is the infringement of an extra-criminal institutional duty by a person who has the special quality of perpetrator required by the offence type (*intraneus*). In such offences, the specially obliged person is liable as a perpetrator irrespective of whether he or she personally carries out the crime (perpetrator's contribution); collaborates with a third party who materially carries it out (accomplice's contribution); or fails to prevent a third party from carrying out the crime (omission). In all these cases, the *intraneus* is always liable as a perpetrator.[13]

Within the ambit of these specified crimes, the decisive factor is not that the perpetrator has control over the harmful event, but rather that he or she has breached a duty; in this case, a negative duty. Where duties are negative, the decisive factor is not to improve the personal space or sphere of action of the other but rather to abstain from worsening it.[14] The duty consists of not harming the other person's autonomy, i.e., respecting him or her as a person by 'leaving him or her alone'.[15] Negative duties, like positive ones, can be breached by action or omission.[16]

Most of the crimes committed by former judges and prosecutors during the dictatorship were actions that implied a breach of their positive duties as public officials. Indeed, to the extent that, despite having the special capacity of perpetrator required by the type, they did not promote criminal investigation of criminal acts that came to their knowledge (art. 274 of the Argentine Criminal Code),[17] or did not stop – inter alia – unlawful mass deprivations of liberty that they were duty bound to prevent (art. 143 inc. 6 of the Argentine Criminal Code), they must be considered perpetrators of these crimes.

Now, while it is true that the judges and prosecutors of the dictatorship were guarantors of the carrying out of those investigations, it is no less true that they were not guarantors of the avoidance of the crimes. In other words, the fact that a judge did not investigate a crime of homicide clearly does not imply, without further conditions, that this judge was the perpetrator or accomplice of the homicide that was not investigated.[18] However, the drastic and persistent way in which the judges of the dictatorship violated their institutional duties transformed the generalized omission of investigation of these facts into a systematic way of guaranteeing impunity for them. If this is so, not only did the dictatorship-era judiciary violate its positive duties, but its omissive contribution also had the effect of favoring the commission of the acts that went uninvestigated.[19] The disappearances of persons and aggravated homicides committed during the dictatorship constitute breaches of negative duties to which the former magistrates contributed by guaranteeing impunity. This implies that judges and prosecutors were also part of the group that committed these extremely serious acts.

4.3.2 'Joint Competence' in Case of Intervention of Several Persons: The Role of Judges in Collective Breach of Duty

To assert that the guarantee of impunity offered by the dictatorship-era judiciary had the effect of favoring the crimes against humanity that were committed requires proving that the armed forces, security forces, and judiciary formed a 'collective person'. This is so because what underlies the reciprocal imputation of contributions in cases where several persons are involved in a crime is the 'joint competence' of the intervening parties. Indeed, in the same way that in the case of an individual act of a person, the decisive factor is not the intentional causing of damage but the infringement of a duty, in the case of intervention by several persons, the decisive factor is not the co-causation of the injury but the 'collective infringement of a duty'.[20] This includes both those who act, on the horizontal plane, during the execution and those who, on the vertical plane, intervene in the previous phase.

That the judiciary has membership in the group that committed crimes against humanity during the Argentine dictatorship does not seem to be seriously under debate, since Argentina's 'terrorist state' had prosecutors and judges who suspended, dismissed, or simply ignored complaints received in hundreds of cases, thus guaranteeing total impunity for those responsible for these extremely serious acts. In other words, those who devised and prepared the widespread attack on the civilian population; those who ordered the commission of these crimes and then executed them; and those who silenced the facts instead of investigating them, together formed a 'collective person' whose members must answer for the crimes committed. It is immaterial whether the contributions took the form of an action or an omission, as long as they have the meaning of making those facts possible.[21]

Through failing to carry out serious investigations, the former judges of the dictatorship era not only violated their duties as public officials but also provided the guarantee of impunity that was necessary in order for the widespread plan of human rights violations to be carried out. The omissive contribution of the judicial branch had the effect of making these events possible. There is, therefore, joint competence between former judges and prosecutors and the rest of the intervening parties. The fact that the judicial branch was part of the collectivity that committed several acts whose impunity it guaranteed means that judges and prosecutors, to a greater or lesser extent, also killed, tortured, and disappeared the victims. All the intervening parties that constitute the collective conduct the act through the hand of the executor.[22] The distribution of tasks means that the criminal result becomes the work of all those who intervened, not only in the execution phase but also in the previous phase.[23]

4.3.3 Participation by Omission, in Crimes of Commission

From what has been said so far, it should be clear that the decisive distinction is not the one between action and omission but the one between negative and positive duties. If this is accepted, participation by omission in crimes of commission offers no particularities. First of all, we must ask whether the omission has the meaning of adaptation to or encouragement of the criminal conduct or whether, on the contrary, it is a neutral omission that does not have the meaning of being continued by the other accomplices. In short, in the case of omission also, the relevant distinction is between accessory conduct and prohibition of return. Second, when the omission expresses the sense of adaptation to the behaviour of the executor, it is necessary to determine the social weight of the omissive contribution.[24] Consequently, the intervening-party-by-omission may be a perpetrator, co-perpetrator, instigator, or accomplice according to the quantitative weight of his or her contribution.[25]

The general and systematic omission practiced by dictatorship-era judges and prosecutors, which ensured impunity for illegal repression, can in no way be a neutral omission when it is a contribution that consists of a violation of the duties of a public official. Furthermore, the omissive contribution of the former judges had the purpose of making possible the acts committed by the security forces, so it is an omission that integrates the former judges and prosecutors into the group of responsible accomplices. Thus, it only remains to establish the extent of their contribution in order to determine whether the judicial omission has sufficient weight for dictatorship-era judges to be considered co-perpetrators or accomplices of the acts whose impunity they guaranteed.

Moreover, the fact that the contribution of the former magistrates was by omission does not mean that the judges were guarantors, in commission by omission, of avoiding the acts carried out by the security forces. The judges and prosecutors were guarantors of carrying out a serious investigation into the acts committed during the dictatorship, but they were not guarantors of the avoidance of the crimes they did not investigate.[26] References to the saving power of the judges, or to the idea that investigations would have put an end to the clandestine nature of repression, are therefore not decisive in determining what charges apply. The judges and prosecutors of the dictatorship are not perpetrators by omission in a crime of commission. They are, rather, an omissive intervening party in the crime of commission perpetrated by the armed and security forces, since by not systematically investigating, they joined in the plan of repression and thus participated in the acts that they had the duty to investigate.[27] To the extent to which they contributed, they are responsible for the deaths, disappearances, and other crimes that were silenced, whether or not they had the possibility of preventing them.

4.3.4 Quantitative Distinction between Perpetrators and Accomplices

It has been concluded so far that the judges of the dictatorship period, by systematically failing to investigate the facts of which they became aware,[28] became part of the collective of all those who in one way or another were involved in the crimes against humanity committed during those years. It has also been said that, as a consequence of the distribution of tasks among those involved, the act belongs to everyone, not only to those who carried it out. How does this theoretical schema distinguish between perpetrators and accomplices? In crimes of infringement of a positive duty, insofar as the perpetrator can only be the one who has the special quality required by the type of crime, the difference can only be qualitative. In the area of negative relationships, on the other hand, the distinction is quantitative. It is the social weight of the contribution that distinguishes the perpetrator from the accomplice: the perpetrator is the one who has the power to configure that which is characteristic of the act, while the accomplice only deals with what is accessory.[29]

The fact that the judiciary cannot be distanced from the collectivity that was responsible for the preparation and execution of crimes against humanity implies that prosecutors and judges also committed those crimes through the hand of the executors. Now, although the judges are in some way part of this group, it cannot be denied that their contribution cannot be the same as that of the main shapers of the repressive plan or that of the perpetrators themselves. Indeed, in a complex organizational structure such as the one behind a terrorist state, high-level military commanders are the true 'lords of the fact', even if they were not the executors.[30] There seems to be no doubt that those who determined not only whether, but also how, the repressive plan of the dictatorship should be carried out were the major shapers of the facts. There is therefore little scope for holding them accountable other than as co-perpetrators of those crimes, due to the weight of their contribution in the phase before the execution.

The executors must also be held accountable as co-perpetrators, even though in general they were subordinates of the security forces, often with little decision-making power. This imputation of co-perpetration has nothing to do with the idea of the restrictive concept of perpetration, which considers the perpetrator to be the one who executes the act and the accomplice to be the one who intervenes in the previous phase. In the previous phase, as well, one can be both a co-perpetrator and an accomplice in the execution. In the case of crimes against humanity, the execution itself has such a determinant weight that the perpetrators must answer as co-perpetrators, even if they have occupied a marginal place in the hierarchy of the armed forces or the police. The execution of a homicide is generally a co-perpetrator's contribution, even if the person who intervened in the previous phase has more responsibility due to being, for example, the head of a terrorist state. Both the leader of the gang and the subordinate who carried out the act must answer as co-perpetrators.

As for determining the extent of the contribution of judges and prosecutors, it is clear that they did not shape the plan of repression since they did not intervene in its conception, did not give the orders for the acts to be carried out, and did not take part in their execution. Consequently, the complicit silence with which the intervening judges or prosecutors guaranteed impunity for repression must be sanctioned with the punishment prescribed for accomplices.

The Argentine Criminal Code distinguishes between two forms of criminal participation, primary and secondary. The necessary accomplice, termed the 'primary participant' in Argentine law, is the person who provides the perpetrator with assistance or co-operation without which the crime could not have been committed (art. 45 of the Argentine Criminal Code). The secondary accomplice – or participant – on the other hand, is the one who co-operates with the execution of the act or provides the perpetrator with assistance guaranteeing a prior promise (art. 46 of the Argentine Criminal Code).

In the Mendoza case, in the formal request for a preliminary investigation – which is the action with which criminal proceedings were initiated – the prosecution put forward the charge of crimes against the administration of justice and, as an alternative charge, the hypothesis of secondary participation in the homicides and other crimes that were committed. The relevant part of the request argued that the purpose of the rule regarding accessories is "to avoid creating an expectation in the offender that he will have subsequent help, because this expectation constitutes a psychological support that creates incentives to commit a crime".[31] Well, the judiciary offered this psychological support by not investigating the facts, which amounted to a "gesture to the military authorities, suggesting that they could count on the guarantee of impunity offered by the judiciary". Accordingly, we understood that, although the judges' omissions took place after the fact, their systematic nature constituted a form of adaptation to the uninvestigated facts. It was subsequent assistance based on, at least, an earlier tacit promise. Our understanding at that stage of the proceedings was that this should be classified as, at the very minimum, secondary participation in the uninvestigated crimes. The central argument of our hypothesis of complicity was that a prolonged and systematic cover-up must cease to be seen only as subsequent aiding and abetting and must come to acquire the meaning of at least a tacit favoring of the facts.

The subsequent progress of the prosecution determined that the weight of those contributions was even greater. In fact, during the course of the trial, the prosecution – without my presence – extended the indictment to all the former judges and prosecutors charged, considering them necessary accomplices in the crimes that had not been investigated. It was considered that the judiciary, by guaranteeing impunity for crimes against humanity committed within its jurisdiction, had offered as a contribution a scarce asset that only the judges of that jurisdiction could provide. Based on this accusation, the defendants were sentenced to life imprisonment as necessary accomplices to the crimes whose impunity was ensured by the judges of the dictatorship.

4.3.5 Limited Accessoriness?

The model of criminal intervention whose main outline (only) has been sketched out here implies abandoning the principle of limited accessoriness in criminal liability. The fact that the interveners form a collective that transforms them all, to a greater or lesser extent, into executors does not mean that accessoriness requires malicious collaboration in a malicious wrongful act of the perpetrator. Indeed, the fact that a conduct is accessory does not mean that a common agreement among the interveners is required. Rather, a binding distribution of tasks is sufficient, in which each contribution has the sense of being assembled or continued by others. Thus, the contribution must be interpreted as a form of adaptation to the fact.

In short, the existence of personal links among the intervening party, based on the need for intentional convergence, is not a prerequisite for punishable participation. Nor is it necessary for perpetrators and accomplices to know each other or to know of the other's contribution. In complex organizational structures, it is perfectly possible to differentiate the areas of competence of the individuals responsible, determining quotas of responsibility on that basis. The binding division of tasks is independent of the subjective aspect of the act. Although, in order to be considered implicated, the persons involved must be persons who have full capacity for the attribution of culpability, each of them is liable for his or her own intent or recklessness.

All in all, the fact that there was an objective distribution of tasks only means that the omissive contribution of the judges and prosecutors of the dictatorship had as its end goal to favor the systematic plan of repression. That is why they were sentenced as accomplices. Nevertheless, it is not necessary to prove an express agreement whereby the authorities responsible for repression negotiated impunity. For a behavior to be accessory, it is not indispensable for judges and the military to have been in one another's pockets. It is sufficient that there was self-evidently a division of tasks, within which the judiciary played the important role of not pursuing any investigation during the dictatorship, thereby guaranteeing impunity for those acts. Consequently, in my view, sentencing the highest authorities of the nation's judicial branch as necessary accomplices was correctly justified.

4.4 Conclusions

Some of the main theses that I have presented here were questioned by Hector Hernández Basualto in the international colloquium that served as the basis for the present volume. My respected Chilean colleague maintained that there would be no difficulty holding judges responsible as accomplices if it could be proven that they had made an agreement with the perpetrators of the crimes. In the absence of evidence of such an agreement, he considers that one would instead need to resort to the dogmatics of the position of guarantor in order to demonstrate that judges were duty-bound to prevent these crimes. He considered that such a view would nonetheless be difficult to sustain, not least because the perpetrators were not hierarchically subordinate to the power of the judges. He also pointed out that in the Mendoza 'mega-case' verdict it is doubtful that the judges had any real power to prevent the crimes, and that therefore, at least in regard to this point, one might argue for invoking the principle of *in dubio pro reo*. In short, while for Hernández Basualto the Mendoza verdict is emphatic in exposing the judges' grave failure to fulfill their duty to investigate, he finds it less convincing in verifying that they had both a 'duty' and the 'power' to impede the commission of the acts they failed to judge.

For various reasons, I do not share these criticisms. It has already been said here that accessory liability does not require there to have been a common agreement between participants.[32] It is probable that there was no express agreement between the judges and the perpetrators. This does not, however, constitute an obstacle to the charge of complicity: even if the hierarchical superiors of the dictatorship's organized apparatus of power did not negotiate impunity for repression, it is quite clear that the creation of such impunity was the purpose of the judiciary's contribution. Not only is it not necessary that perpetrators should be shown to have actively required the contribution that the judges made, but there can (also) be complicity even if the perpetrators did not know about the participants' contributions or were not counting on their collaboration.[33]

Certainly, although an express pact is not a prerequisite for indictment, accredited evidence of such a pact would at least reinforce the thesis that judges were accomplices in the acts that they failed to investigate. What has been accredited, however, is that there was at least a *tacit* pact of impunity. Indeed, the fact that not a single serious investigation was opened into even such major crimes as mass sentencing of victims of politically motivated persecution is at the very least redolent of an unspoken agreement by which impunity for repression was guaranteed. In short, although participation does not require an express pact among the intervening parties, in the Mendoza 'mega-case' the existence of a tacit pact was demonstrated, making judicial complicity with the Argentine dictatorship even more evident.

As to criticisms of the use of the figure of guarantor, I think I have made it clear here that judges were not duty bound to prevent the crimes that were brought to their attention: it is not the task of judicial officers to prevent the acts that they must then prosecute. In general terms, their duty as guarantors is circumscribed exclusively to their duties to promote the investigation of those facts.[34] It is therefore irrelevant whether the judges had any real material power to save, as in most cases they were not the guarantors of the prevention of such acts. Now, judicial complicity is founded not on judges' supposed position as guarantors but on their adaptation to the plan of repression, expressed through failing to systematically and selectively prosecute those crimes committed by the dictatorship that were brought to their attention through habeas corpus writs or criminal complaints. In isolation, a breach by judges and prosecutors of the duty to investigate could be considered an autonomous crime of ex post-facto omission. However, a general and systematic cover-up ceases to be just an isolated crime of omission and instead becomes a form of punishable participation.[35]

This omissive complicity is possible even in those cases in which the participant is not the guarantor of the avoidance of the result. Roxin upholds the punishability of omissive intervention when this operates to positively favor the act of a third party. This occurs

> when the subject, in consideration of the planned crime, omits an action which he was prepared to carry out outside of the commission of the crime and which would have objectively prevented or hindered the commission of the crime. On the other hand, the person who omits an action that would have prevented or hindered the result, which he would not have carried out in any case, even though he knew that the crime had been committed, goes unpunished. To put it briefly: whoever, to make a crime possible, abandons the resolution to act which has already been taken, is guilty of participation; whoever does not make the effort to counteract a crime, goes unpunished.[36]

The question that remains to be resolved is whether judicial inaction should be understood as a crime of omission or as complicity in the form of 'positive encouragement of the act'.

The investigation of crimes that come to the attention of magistrates is not only something that judges or prosecutors are 'willing to carry out'; rather, it forms part of their duties as public officials. However, the systematic sentencing of political prisoners during the dictatorship shows that judges' and prosecutors' absolute 'unwillingness to investigate the facts' only applied to cases of crimes against humanity committed by the security forces. This generalized and selective abstention from criminal investigations cannot be interpreted as anything other than a priori guarantee of impunity for these acts. Such behavior constitutes a form of facilitating or favoring the commission of uninvestigated crimes. In conclusion, we are dealing with a form of punishable participation and not with simple crimes of omission. Determining the exact weight of this contribution and how far it should influence what individual sanctions must apply is perhaps the only aspect of this thesis that remains subject to discussion.

Notes

1 This term is widely used in Argentina and more broadly in Latin America, in the context of the transitional justice debate, to emphasize the fact that dictatorial regimes led by the military, and the atrocities committed to sustain them, counted on the systematic collaboration and complicity of civilian sectors, including judges.

2 More precisely, the crime of breaching the duty to prosecute and punish, set down in Art. 274 of the Argentine Criminal Code (Código Penal de la Nación Argentina). This was the determination reached in the Judges' Trial by the Tribunal Oral en lo Criminal Federal No 1 de Mendoza; Judgment of 20 September 2017, Sentence No 1718 Autos Nr. 076-M 2689.

3 Romano's conviction also included other crimes. In fact, the former prosecutor was convicted as a primary participant in the following crimes: abusive deprivation of liberty aggravated by violence and threats (nine counts); abusive deprivation of liberty aggravated by violence and threats and lasting more than one month (five counts); infliction of torments aggravated by the victim's condition of political persecution (thirty-eight

counts); illegal breaking and entering (one count); and as the author of the crime of failing to comply with the duty to prosecute and suppress criminals (one count). In the same trial, on similar charges, former judges Luis Francisco Miret, Rolando Evaristo Carrizo, and Guillermo Petra Recabarren were each also sentenced to life imprisonment. The sentence of the Federal Oral Court was confirmed by the Federal Chamber of Cassation, whose decision was appealed before the Supreme Court of Justice of the Nation. Otilio Romano and Luis Francisco Miret died while the appeals were being processed.

4 This law enabled people to be arrested on ideological grounds where there had been what was described as an attempt to alter the 'constitutional order and social peace'. It also criminalized trade union conflicts when strikes were declared illegal and created penalties for journalists or those in charge of the media who publicized actions or images linked to 'subversion'.

5 See Renzikowski, *Restriktiver Täterbegriff und fahrlässige Beteiligung* (1997) 13 et seqq.

6 I have put forward this thesis in Palermo, *Das eigene Unrecht der Teilnahme an einer fremden Tat* (2020); also in Palermo, 'El delito de participación. Un análisis crítico' in Lopéz et al (eds).

7 The quantitative theory of accessoriness put forward in the accusation follows, in broad outline, Günther Jakobs's thesis; see Jakobs 21/1; Jakobs, 'Beteiligung' in Doling (ed) 561 et seqq; Jakobs, *Theorie der Beteiligung* (2014) 2 et seqq. See also his followers. Lesch, 'Intervención delictiva e imputación objetiva' (1995) 48 (3) *Anuario de derecho penal y ciencias penales* 911 et seqq and Pawlik, *La libertad institucionalizada. Estudios de filosofía jurídica y Derecho Penal* (2010) 134 et seqq.

8 See Sánchez-Vera Gómez-Trelles, 'Intervención omisiva, posición de garante y prohibición de sobrevaloración del aporte' (1996) 48 (1) *ADPCP.* A very similar approach, with some nuances, can be found in Planas, *La participación en el delito. Fundamento y límites* (2003). Also Feijóo Sánchez 'Autoría y participación en organizaciones complejas' (2008) in Feijóo Sánchez (ed) 3 et seqq.

9 In Chile this thesis is propounded by Van Weezel *Curso de Derecho Penal. Parte General* (2023) 2, II, VII. In Peru, García, *Derecho Penal. Parte General* (2012) 702 et seqq.

10 This concern is shared by Mañalich 'Intervención "organizada" en el hecho punible: Esbozo de un modelo diferenciador' in Couso/Werle (eds).

11 Schünemann, *Consideraciones críticas sobre la situación espiritual de la ciencia jurídico-penal alemana* (1996) 48 et seqq.

12 Gimbernant, *¿Tiene un futuro la dogmática juridicopenal?* (1990) 140 et seqq.

13 Roxin, *Täterschaft und Tatherrschaft* (2022) 525 et seqq.

14 Jakobs, 'Tatherrschaftsdämmerung: ein Beitrag zur normativierung rechtlicher Begriffe' in Jakobs/Cancio Meliá (eds) 195 et seqq; Pawlik likewise distinguishes between respect competences and improvement competences.

15 Pawlik, *Das Unrecht des Bürgers* (2012) 2/A/III/2.

16 Pawlik, *Das Unrecht des Bürgers* (2012) (n 15), 2/A/I.

17 Pawlik, *Das Unrecht des Bürgers* (2012) (n 15).

18 For the preclusive or 'blocking' effect of the crime of miscarriage of justice (*Sperrwirkung* theory), see Couso/Perret, 'Responsabilidad penal por intervención en crímenes de dictaduras en el ejercicio de funciones judiciales. Estudio exploratorio del caso chileno y perspectiva comparada' (2023) 36 *Polít. crim.* 908 et seqq; also, Couso,' Responsabilidad penal por la intervención en crímenes de la dictadura en el ejercicio de roles judiciales. Perspectivas comparadas para una exploración en Chile', 497 et seqq. and chapters by Rojas and by Wilenman in this volume.

19 Roxin, *Autoría y dominio del hecho en Derecho Penal* (2016) 457 et seqq.

20 Jakobs, 'Tatherrschaftsdämmerung: ein Beitrag zur normativierung rechtlicher Begriffe' in Jakobs/Cancio Meliá (eds) 175 et seqq.
21 Jakobs, 'Beteiligung' in Doling (ed) 36 et seqq.
22 Dencker, *Kausalität und Gesamttat* (1996) 142 et seqq. propounds the thesis of a 'total fact'. A similar position is taken by Frister, 'Zum Strafgrund von Mittäterschaft und Teilnahme' in Degener/Heghmanns (eds).
23 This implies that both perpetrator and accomplices fulfill the legal type. See Jakobs (2003) (n 7) 11 et seqq. The opposite view is taken by Sancinetti. *Ilícito personal y participación* (1997) 68 and Renzikowski (1997) (n 5) 131 et seqq.
24 A more exhaustive development of this idea can be found in Bermejo/Palermo, 'Die strafrechtlichte Verantwortung des Compliance Officers wegen Beteligung an einer Straftat' in Kuhlen et al (eds) 71 et seqq.
25 Jakobs (2014) (n 7) 50 et seqq. This thesis is also put forward by Vachelli, *Intervención delictiva. Significado y función del principio de accesoriedad* (2020) 80 et seqq.
26 Otherwise, they would be perpetrators. See Roxin (2016) (n 19) 442 et seqq.
27 Roxin (2016) (n 19) 459.
28 Couso, 'From Nuremberg to Mendoza: Judicial Murder and Its Aufarbeitung' in Jeβberger et al (eds) 57–58.
29 Jakobs (2000) (n 14) 175 et seqq. For a review of quantitative theories, Orcozco López Beteiligung an organisatorischen Machtapparaten (2018) 237 et seqq.
30 In this line Jakobs (2014) (n 7) 50 et seqq.
31 Extract from the Requerimiento de Instrucción (prosecutor's formal request for a preliminary examination) in the Mendoza megacausa, on file with the author. Author's translation.
32 Clearly in this sense, Jakobs, *La imputación objetiva en Derecho Penal* (1996) 91–92.
33 Jakobs, *Derecho Penal. Parte General. Fundamentos y teoría de la* imputación (1997) 22/42 '[…] the perpetrator does not need to know about the complicity, and even less must needs have given rise to it' (author's translation).
34 For another opinion, Peralta, 'Sobre la responsabilidad de los jueces por la omisión de tramitar habeas corpus en la última dictadura argentina' in Ambos/Malarino et al (eds) 114–123. According to this author, the judges were in a position of guarantor regarding what was done by the security forces. However, he considers this to have been a weak or second-order position of guarantor, with the members of the security forces holding the position of guarantor in the strong sense. For this reason, Peralta proposes the secondary accomplice penalty for judges. This thesis cannot be shared, however. If judges were part of the group that committed the acts, they must respond as primary or secondary perpetrators or participants, depending on the weight of their contribution. On the other hand, in the absence of a joint organization, if judges are in a position of guarantor with respect to the avoidance of the result, they must respond as unitary perpetrators in commission by omission. Punishment as a secondary participant for a judge who is considered to be in a position of guarantor is not possible, as a matter of *lege lata,* and does not seem dogmatically convincing.
35 Thus, Jakobs (1997) (n 5) 22/40 "if it is the promise of a cover-up that makes the perpetrator willing to commit the crime, this promise constitutes complicity in the crime" (author's translation).
36 Roxin (2022) (n 13) 525 passim Roxin (2016) (n 19) 467.

Bibliography

Bermejo M/Palermo O, 'Die strafrechtlichte Verantwortung des Compliance Officers wegen Beteligung an einer Straftat' in L Kuhlen et al (eds), *Compliance und Strafrecht* (C.F. Müller 2012) 71.

Couso J, 'Responsabilidad penal por la intervención en crímenes de la dictadura en el ejercicio de roles judiciales. Perspectivas comparadas para una exploración en Chile' in J Couso et al (eds), *Justicia criminal y dogmática penal en la era de los Derechos Humanos. Estudios en homenaje a Jorge Mera Figueroa* (Thomson Reuters 2021) 497.

Couso J, 'From Nuremberg to Mendoza: Judicial Murder and Its *Aufarbeitung*' in F Jeßberger et al (eds), *Strafrecht und Systemunrecht. Festschrift für Gerhard Werle zum 70. Geburstag* (Mohr Siebeck 2022) 57.

Couso J/Perret S, 'Responsabilidad penal por intervención en crímenes de dictaduras en el ejercicio de funciones judiciales. Estudio exploratorio del caso chileno y perspectiva comparada' (2023) 18 (36) *Política Criminal* 904.

Dencker F, *Kausalität und Gesamttat* (Duncker & Humblot 1996).

Feijóo Sánchez B, 'Autoría y participación en organizaciones complejas' in B. Feijóo Sánchez (ed), *Cuestiones actuales de Derecho Penal Económico* (BdeF 2009) 191.

Frister H, 'Zum Strafgrund von Mittäterschaft und Teilnahme' in W. Degener/M. Heghmanns (eds), *Festschrift für Friedrich Dencker zum 70. Geburstag* (Mohr Siebeck 2012).

García Cavero P, *Derecho Penal. Parte General* (3rd edn, Ideas 2022).

Gimbernat Ordeig E, *¿Tiene un futuro la dogmática jurídicopenal?* (3rd edn, Tecnos, 1990).

Jakobs G, *Strafrecht Allgemeiner Teil. Die Grundlagen und die Zurechnungslehre* (2nd edn, De Gruyter 1991).

Jakobs G, *Derecho Penal. Parte General. Fundamentos y teoría de la imputación* (2nd edn, Marcial Ponst 1997).

Jakobs G, *La imputación objetiva en Derecho Penal* (trans. Canció Meliá, Universidad Externado 1996).

Jakobs G, *Theorie der Beteiligung* (Mohr Siebeck 2014).

Jakobs G, 'Beteiligung' in D Dölling (ed), *Jus Humanum. Grundlagen des Rechts und Strafrecht. Festschrift für Ernst-Joachim Lamp* (Duncker & Humboldt 2003) 561.

Jakobs G, 'Tatherrschaftsdämmerung: ein Beitrag zur normativierung rechtlicher Begriffe' in G Jakobs/M Cancio Meliá (eds), *El sistema funcionalista del Derecho penal* (Grijley 2000) 195.

Lesch H, 'Intervención delictiva e imputación objetiva' (1995) 48 (3) *Anuario de derecho penal y ciencias penales* 911.

Mañalich J P, 'Intervención "organizada" en el hecho punible: Esbozo de un modelo diferenciador' in J Couso/G Werle (eds), *Intervención delictiva en contextos organizados* (Tirant lo Blanch 2017) 23.

Milton Peralta J, 'Sobre la responsabilidad de los jueces por la omisión de tramitar habeas corpus en la última dictadura argentina' in K Ambos/E Malarino et al. (eds), *Responsabilidad jurídico-penal de civiles en delitos de lesa humanidad* (Hammurabi 2022) 114.

Orozco López H, *Beteiligung an organisatorischen Machtapparaten* (Mohr Siebeck 2018).

Palermo O, 'Das eigene Unrecht der Teilnahme an einer fremden Tat?' in E Hilgendorf et al (eds), *Brücken Bauen. Festschrift für Mercelo Sancinetti zum 70. Geburstag* (Duncker & Humboldt 2020).

Palermo O, 'El delito de participación. Un análisis crítico' in H D Orozco López et al (eds), *Libro homenaje a Alfonso Reyes Echandía en el nonagésimo aniversario de su nacimiento* (Uniandes 2022) 721.
Pawlik M, *La libertad institucionalizada. Estudios de filosofía jurídica y Derecho Penal* (trans. Enrique Bacigalupo, Marcial Pons 2010).
Pawlik M, *Das Unrecht des Bürgers* (Mohr Siebeck 2012).
Renzikowski J, *Restriktiver Täterbegriff und fahrlässige Beteiligung* (Mohr Siebeck 1997).
Robles Planas R, *La participación en el delito. Fundamento y límites* (Marcial Pons 2003).
Roxin C, *Täterschaft und Tatherrschaft* (11th edn, De Gruyter 2022).
Roxin C, *Autoría y dominio del hecho en Derecho Penal* (7th edn, trans. by Cuello Contreras of the 9th edn, Marcial Pons 2016).
Sánchez-Vera Gómez-Trelles J, 'Intervención omisiva, posición de garante y prohibición de sobrevaloración del aporte' (1995) 48 (1) *Anuario de derecho penal y ciencias penales* 187.
Sancinetti M, *Ilícito personal y participación* (Ad Hoc 1997).
Schünemann B, *Consideraciones críticas sobre la situación espiritual de la ciencia jurídico-penal alemana* (trans. Canció Meliá, Universidad Externado 1996).
Vacchelli E, *Intervención delictiva. Significado y función del principio de accesoriedad* (Atelier 2020).
Van Weezel A, *Curso de Derecho Penal. Parte General* (Ediciones UC 2023).

5 Judicial Murder in Chile

Patterns, Cases, and Doctrines for Prosecuting Jurists[1]

Jaime Couso

5.1 Introduction

In those few national legal systems that have prosecuted judicial officials for homicides, kidnappings, or torture that occurred during dictatorships or authoritarian regimes, prosecution has only taken place in exceptional cases.[2] These cases involve serious unlawfulness in judicial conduct, featuring at least one of the following defects: (1) extraordinary situations where it is doubtful whether there was ever a genuine exercise of jurisdiction, which we can call 'show trials', or (2) serious procedural or substantive criminal law defects arising in the course of what was, in principle, a genuine exercise of jurisdiction.

Once it has been established that there has been a defect in the conduct of a judicial officer that reaches the required level of unlawfulness, the imputation of homicides and kidnappings takes place in different ways. The alternatives depend on whether the defects came about during a show trial or by means of a genuine, but seriously flawed, exercise of jurisdiction. In the former case, the conduct of the judicial authority who participates in a set-up – typically, a court martial – designed to disguise as a jurisdictional act, something that is actually a summary execution, can be qualified without the need for much dogmatic elaboration as co-perpetration, instigation, or perpetration-by-means of homicide. The conduct might also be classifiable as aiding or abetting or, as a final alternative, accessorial liability after the fact if its role in the set-up is decided after the summary execution has already taken place. In the second scenario, where there was a real exercise of jurisdiction, the aspects of the prosecutor's or judge's conduct that are criminal consist of the decision to charge or convict victims for crimes that are later punished with death sentences or prison terms. They may also consist of issuing requests or orders for arrest or preventive detention. Omissions have occasionally also been imputed, although they have generally been treated as active behaviors (such as not abandoning a criminal action, not reversing an unlawful conviction, or failing to prosecute the active perpetrators).[3]

Following the scheme of analysis set out above, this chapter examines cases and patterns of conduct of Chilean judges during the country's 1973–1990 dictatorship that can be considered potentially relevant as homicide or kidnapping. For the sake of expediency, and making use of its symbolic charge, the label 'judicial murder'[4]

DOI: 10.4324/9781003470069-6

will be used as a common denominator except where specific reference is made to cases of kidnappings, illegal detention, or false imprisonment.

5.2 The Threshold of Unlawfulness in Judicial Murder in Chile

5.2.1 Show Trials

Probably the most paradigmatic hypothesis of the perversion of the judicial function is that of the show trial, well known in German legal doctrine under the term *Scheinverfahren*.[5] Show trials are associated with the perpetration of homicides in contexts where the exercise of the judicial function is only apparent. This type of defect is difficult to detect by a simple review of the sentences of Chile's dictatorship-era courts martial, which generally appear to have been handed down in accordance with the prevailing legality in force at the time. It is, however, possible to identify a group of particularly serious cases in which the process and its outcome deviate so blatantly from legality that they can hardly be considered lawful. This occurred, for example, when sentences were passed after the summary execution of the victim had already taken place. It also happened in cases where the ruling was not the result of a true trial or process of deliberation undertaken by a court but was rather a mere act of approval or ratification of an execution previously decided on by the military prosecutor.[6] Although these are two different phenomena, in each case the victim was deprived of any trial, with the sentence being a mere fiction or façade of a legality that never existed in fact.[7]

One example of such a situation that appears in Chile's official 1991 truth commission report relates to the execution of five detainees in the northern town of Pisagua. The men were supposedly convicted by a court martial, of which there is, however, no record except for a vague reference in a military pronouncement of October 1973.[8] The truth commission report notes that according to the testimony of several other detainees at the same camp, the five victims were never even informed of the constitution of a court martial. Nor, of course, were they provided with defense lawyers to represent them before it.[9] Another similar case concerned two uniformed police officers attached to the Algarrobo Police Station. The men were allegedly sentenced to death by court martial and were executed the day after their arrest. However, no record was ever made of the constitution or operation of the court martial, nor of the evidence on which the conviction was based.[10]

A further example of a show trial is the court martial to which six people in the district of Fresia were subjected. They had been arrested by soldiers and uniformed police on the ranch known as the 'Fundo El Toro'. The detainees were subsequently sentenced to death for their part in the crimes of treason and illegal possession of weapons.[11] According to subsequent testimony by witnesses and the defense lawyer, however, the order to arrange a firing squad to execute the victims was given even before the court martial was held. According to the defense lawyer, there was 'a preconceived determination to give the appearance of a formal process, without granting the defendants a real and effective opportunity to defend themselves'.[12] This testimony was later collected and validated as evidence by investigative magistrate Judge Álvaro Mesa, who first indicted and then sentenced the two surviving members of the court martial for six counts of aggravated homicide.[13]

As can be seen from this examination of defects in the courts martial held during the dictatorship, they amount to a gross *ex post facto* simulation of a proceeding that never took place. There is therefore no need for a special examination of the high level of unlawfulness required to impute the crimes to (pseudo)judges. There was no actual exercise of judicial functions, not even formally. Indictments against these judges or prosecutors would therefore have to take place in ways already familiar in contexts where criminal responsibility for human rights violations is attributed: co-perpetration, perpetration-by-means, etc. This seems to be the understanding of the Court of Appeals of Santiago, in a judgment pronounced in August 2020, holding that:

> [I]t is only possible to consider the deaths of the aforementioned victims as homicide in the terms provided in Article 391 N° 5 [sic] of the Criminal Code, since the only possible conclusion is that the decision to order each of them to be shot, creating the appearance of the carrying out of a judicial resolution emanating from a supposed court martial, reveals the existence of a previously conceived plan to proceed to kill people who were [otherwise in the process of] being subjected to a regular judicial proceeding, carried out before a Prosecutor's Office.[14]

5.2.2 Serious Procedural or Substantive Defects of Law in Situations Where There Is Genuine Exercise of Jurisdiction

Moving on from show trials, we may instead consider the actions of courts martial that did actually take place during the dictatorship and did exercise jurisdiction. Here it is common to find a perverse application of the law that reaches the threshold of unlawfulness required to impute the status of murders or kidnappings to judges' decisions.

In the 'Fundo El Toro' case mentioned above, the court martial judgment constituted a flagrant violation of the principle of non-retroactivity, as contemplated in Article 11 of the Constitution of the time. In practice, in order to impose the death penalty, the court martial found it necessary to apply two provisions of Decree Law No. 5 – which came into force on 22 September 1973 – to acts that had taken place some days previously (namely, between 15 and 20 September). This flaw was brought to the attention of the members of the court martial by the detainees' defense lawyer and even by the military auditor, Carlos Ebensperger. The members of the court martial, however, ignored this claim, and the auditor was later removed from his post on the alleged grounds of 'treason, professional ineptitude, and lack of military courage'.[15]

Other examples of serious defects include convictions handed down without any evidence or where the only evidence was the confession of the accused, obtained by torture. The seriousness of this defect is evident in pronouncements by the Inter-American Court of Human Rights (IACtHR), first, and the Chilean Supreme

Court, later, declaring court martial judgments to be null. In 2015, the IACtHR ordered the State of Chile to review convictions that had been handed down by dictatorship-era courts martial. The Supreme Court subsequently invalidated several such sentences, affirming the victims' innocence since their convictions had been based on confessions obtained under torture.[16]

Equally serious flaws can be seen in the convictions that various courts martial handed down for political crimes of conscience. For example, Decree Law No. 77 of 8 October 1973 outlawed and dissolved political parties that promoted 'Marxist doctrines', establishing various criminal offenses related to membership in such parties or to meeting and organizing for the purpose of propagating their ideologies. Convictions for these offenses were then handed down. For example, a court martial in Valparaíso imposed prison sentences of up to five years and one day on activists of the Movimiento de Izquierda Revolucionaria, MIR, who had engaged in clandestine organizing.[17] Their purpose had been to oppose the ruling military Junta by spreading anti-regime propaganda through pamphlets, graffiti, etc.[18]

Finally, other vices of a similar nature can be found in some court martial decisions that imposed sentences of greater severity than were contemplated by law, in flagrant violation of the rules of sentencing.[19]

5.3 Patterns of Judicial Involvement and Legal Subsumption in the Crimes of Homicide, Kidnapping, and Illegal Deprivation of Liberty

5.3.1 Patterns Under the Chilean Dictatorship

The presence of flaws in the administration of justice gives rise to a possible additional liability under the heading of malfeasance in office or judicial misconduct. This could open the door to consideration of the specific judicial conduct at issue under the heading of homicide, kidnapping, and/or illegal deprivation of liberty.

The ways in which these crimes can be imputed to particular judicial conduct, and the legal requisites for so doing, vary according to the particular pattern of legal and judicial involvement in atrocities. Analyzing the cases of Argentina and Chile, Barros has identified four such patterns:

1. Extrajuridical repression, carried out by state agents acting covertly without any legal cause, exceptional authorization, or adherence to judicial or administrative formalities. This may entail, inter alia, unauthorized detention, torture, disappearance, and execution.
2. Administrative repression, including detention authorized under a state of siege, which may have some legal foundation but departs from the rule of law, e.g., because it was carried out without trials and convictions.
3. Summary (quasi-)judicial repression, where there is some semblance of trial proceedings but the rule of law is flouted through the application of retroactive, secret, or unclear laws, limitation of the right to a defense, or the application of dubious standards of evidence.

4. Legal repression for political offenses, using regular judicial mechanisms but with what Barros terms a 'draconian' application of the law.[20]

Each of these patterns offers diverse opportunities for criminal prosecution while at the same time creating different obstacles to it. In the first case, extrajuridical repression, what is done has a blatantly unlawful character even according to the standards of formal legality of the dictatorial regime. This leaves any judge who took part in the repression, or at a minimum condoned or facilitated its misdeeds, little or no room for any defense based on having applied existing law. Factual or evidentiary difficulties might arise, however, for instance, concerning the (hypothetical) causal relationship between a judge's condoning or promotion of clandestine repression, on the one hand, and the deaths, torture, or kidnappings that were the empirical result, on the other. Evidence of criminal intent to kill, torture, or kidnap, on the part of a judge who 'just' did not prevent these crimes, might also be elusive. These difficulties could prove insurmountable for holding judges to account. They might also affect judicial liability for administrative repression, though perhaps to a lesser degree.[21]

When it comes to legal repression actively carried out by prosecutors and judges themselves, causality and intent are easy to establish. Lines of defense based on the application of the existing law at the time could, however, stand in the way of holding such defendants liable for their judicial decisions. Liability for summary (quasi-)judicial repression has in practice faced similar obstacles, notwithstanding its weaker legal basis. The only exceptions have tended to be cases where lower-level members of extraordinary tribunals or courts martial have been held to account, leaving judges from higher ordinary courts free of any charges despite having also condoned the misdeeds or turned a blind eye to them.

All things considered, the only relatively easy scenario for accountability seems to be one where enthusiastic, true-believer judges have either exercised summary (quasi)-judicial repression or have willingly co-operated with direct perpetrators of extrajuridical or administrative repression.

5.3.2 Judicial Murder in Chile

5.3.2.1 Cases of Active Judicial Contribution to Crimes

In the case of the Chilean dictatorship, it is easy to discern patterns of legal or summary (quasi)judicial repression if one considers the role played by the military justice system, particularly the so-called wartime justice system, in the months immediately following the military coup. This role actively contributed to murder and/or false imprisonment.

Turning once again, for example, to the 'Fundo El Toro' case mentioned above, the six victims were handed over to the wartime Military Prosecutor's Office after their initial detention, interrogation, and torture. Together with other civilians, they were subjected to a court martial that exhibited the serious defects described above. The court-martial convicted them to death, a sentence that was duly carried out on

19 October 1973, at 9.00 a.m., at Chilean Air Force facilities located in the Chamiza sector of the city of Puerto Montt. The six victims all died on the spot.[22] This is why resolutions issued by present-day investigative magistrate Álvaro Mesa, referenced above, are categorical in concluding that the court-martial indulged in an act that 'can only be classed ... as homicide' when it rejected the representations made by the defense lawyer and the military auditor, thereby 'approving the death penalty for the accused without making any objection'. More precisely, concluded Judge Mesa, this was aggravated homicide as set out and duly sanctioned in Article 391, no. 1 (first circumstance) of the Chilean Criminal Code in force at the time of the acts. Judge Mesa also classified the incident as a crime against humanity.[23]

However, in another case from October 1973, the present-day Court of Appeals of Santiago seems to have felt the need to deny that a court martial was ever actually carried out. This incident, the killing of twelve people in the city of Valdivia, was part of an operation led by the infamous Caravan of Death (Caravana de la Muerte).[24] The Court of Appeals of Santiago appears to have deemed it necessary, in order to convict for murder, to reject the notion of an actual court martial having taken place, to avoid its existence being used on the defendant's behalf:

> Insofar as a court-martial that legally justified the death of the victims has been ruled out, it can only be concluded that this defendant, although he did not participate in the group of people who, under Arellano Stark's command,[25] travelled around the country taking part in events of the kind that are the subject of these proceedings, collaborated with them, as he contributed, through his actions, to giving the appearance of legality to an act that had none; namely, the execution of the aforementioned persons.[26]

This shows that a defense based on the application of existing law at the time can indeed stand in the way of liability for summary (quasi-)judicial repression unless the threshold of serious unlawfulness of the judicial conduct is met.

Let us now consider so-called peacetime military justice, i.e., justice as administered not by courts martial but by ordinary military courts after the coup of 11 September 1973. The potentially relevant behavior of members of these latter courts concerns their involvement in post-coup prosecutions of events that occurred before it. In one such case, eight inhabitants of the town of Llanquihue were sentenced to five years and one day in prison for having allegedly participated in a February 1973 attack on a police station. The attackers employed stones and fists, rather than firearms, and the guilty verdicts later handed down followed proceedings where no evidence was produced as to the participation of four of the men who were convicted. Indeed, the final decision attributed the attack generically to a 'mob', 'rabble', or 'crowd'; and considered participation to have been proven in the case of only four of the eight defendants – moreover, without clearly specifying the conduct of even those four.[27]

A second example from the ordinary military justice system concerns the conviction of a person accused of being one of various protestors who fired shots during a violent August 1972 demonstration, at which a uniformed police officer was shot dead. Six years later – i.e., during the dictatorship – the defendant was sentenced to 15 years in prison for the crimes of homicide in a quarrel, mistreatment of a police officer, and attempted homicide.[28] In accordance with the penalties established by law for these crimes at the time of the events, the sentence tariff should have been in the range of five to ten years, at most. If Criminal Code Article 75 – applicable to the commission of several offenses in one single act – had been invoked, the maximum resulting sentence would have been five years. Even if that provision had been ignored, the sentence should at the very outside have had a ceiling of nine years and six months' imprisonment. Even that total would have been at the very outer edges of prevailing legality, as it is the simple arithmetical sum of the maximum penalties applicable to each of the counts that were invoked. Calculating the sentence in this way would have involved ignoring Art 75, in favor of application of the general rule of Art. 74. The excess portion of the sentence – in this case, up to 10 years of deprivation of liberty – could well qualify as false imprisonment were it to be considered that the qualifying requirements of unlawfulness indicated above had been met.

Outside of the military justice system, it is more difficult to attribute criminal responsibility to judges for active intervention in homicides, kidnappings, or false imprisonment. Supreme Court judges, at least, could, however, have been charged with accessorial liability after the fact. This would have applied to occasions when they had actively prevented or, at a minimum, obstructed the actions of other courts in cases where those actions had tended to pursue the criminal responsibility of members of the security forces or to adopt measures that could have prevented the death of persons illegally detained on irregular or clandestine premises. Such seems to be the case, for example, in relation to sanctions imposed by the Supreme Court on Judge Carlos Cerda in 1986. Judge Cerda was disciplined in order to prevent him from investigating the so-called 'Case of the Thirteen', involving the 1976 kidnapping and enforced disappearance of 13 people, most of them Communist Party members.[29]

Furthermore, although there is not enough of an evidence base for a detailed analysis, it is possible to surmise that Supreme Court conduct of this type carried such weight as regards judicial discipline that it could eventually form the basis for attribution of more serious responsibility. Indeed, one might attempt to link these disciplinary actions exercised by the highest court with further, perhaps subtler, dissuasive actions adopted by the same court in the months that followed. If these actions were directed at first-instance judges (i.e., investigative magistrates) or at members of courts of appeal, the latter might have accordingly felt pressurized into failing to provide effective protection to persons detained by security agencies. Where such persons were later killed, the responsibility of the members of the Supreme Court who obliged other judges to omit due protection for victims could be deemed to constitute active instigation to homicide by omission. Moreover, such conduct could even qualify as active perpetration-by-means if the judges who were obliged to abstain from adopting the appropriate measures acted under conditions that exculpated them and if the mental requirements of these particular modes of intervention were deemed to be satisfied.

5.3.2.2 Cases of Passive Judicial Contribution to Crimes

Beyond the cases of active involvement in crimes discussed above, Chilean judges could also potentially be held responsible for homicides or kidnappings, in the exercise of their judicial function, if the requirements of commission by omission are met. This would be in relation to crimes whose active perpetrators were agents of the Chilean Armed Forces or its secretive intelligence agencies,[30] but which were condoned by judges.

However, while judicial passivity in the face of the dictatorship's atrocities was pervasive, most of the relevant cases raise often-insuperable problems that are inherent to the attribution of criminal responsibility to justice system officials in contexts of *extrajuridical* and *administrative* repression (Barros's first and second categories, as discussed above). As we have seen, these problems include, especially, the difficulty of establishing the (hypothetical) causal relation between a judge's condonation or favor, subsequent deaths, torture, or kidnappings, and the existence of criminal intent as to the relevant offense.

That said, a recent conviction upheld by the Chilean Supreme Court opens the door for holding military justice system personnel liable, at least, for omitting to prosecute or report extrajudicial repression. In a case over the 1973 kidnapping and killing of two men – prominent singer-songwriter and Communist activist Víctor Jara and former national prisons chief Littré Quiroga – the Supreme Court held that the defendant had made himself liable as an accessory after the fact to murder and kidnapping.[31] The defendant, at the time a military prosecutor, had interrogated Quiroga and realized that he had been subjected to torture. Shortly afterward, he had received autopsy reports on the extrajudicial killings of both victims. His failure to either prosecute the perpetrators or report the crimes to other judicial authorities made him liable, in the eyes of the present-day Supreme Court, as an accessory after the fact.

In the field of the ordinary justice system, meanwhile, a potentially relevant constellation of circumstances is provided by the systematic omission by the Courts of Appeal and the Supreme Court of efficacious responses to thousands of habeas corpus writs (*recursos de amparo*). The writs were filed by individuals and human rights organizations seeking to prevent the death or disappearance of persons who had already been detained by the dictatorship's security agencies. In effect the courts' response violated the principle of 'immediacy': under the law in force at the time, the courts were duty bound to rule on such writs within a 24-hour deadline. To fail to do so was grossly dilatory and evasive, to the point of suggesting or amounting to connivance with the illegal acts committed by the authorities of the day.

Particularly illustrative of this type of omission is the 'Case of the Thirteen', referred to above. Over the course of a 21-day period in November and December 1976, each of the 13 victims was 'arrested' on the streets of Chile's capital city, in plain view of passersby. In the days following the disappearances, victims' friends and relatives filed several habeas corpus writs before the Court of Appeals of Santiago. These writs, if elevated on appeal, also went before the Supreme Court. Both courts systematically refrained from exercising their regular powers, which included the ability to set deadlines and subpoena the administrative authorities or to inspect the clandestine detention centers named in the writs. Thus, the courts failed to provide the victims with protection that might – although no one can be certain – have prevented their subsequent deaths or disappearances.[32] It is admittedly debatable whether this possibility is sufficient to meet the requirement of hypothetical causality or objective imputation that is necessary for affirming omissive perpetration. It may well be less debatable, however, to characterize the behavior as at least satisfying the requirements of aiding and abetting by omission. This latter is, after all, imputable to a guarantor who fails to at least hamper an active perpetrator from committing crimes when he or she should have done so.

Omissions can moreover also occur in the context of complaints filed in criminal courts over incidents of kidnapping. A particularly shocking case involves omissive behavior that a Church-linked human rights lawyer attributed to a judge from the Sixth Criminal Court of Santiago. A total of three Communist Party activists were kidnapped off the streets by plainclothes police agents on 28 and 29 March 1985, in two incidents that took place in broad daylight and in front of numerous witnesses. Some hours after the second kidnapping, a lawyer from the Vicaría de la Solidaridad[33] filed a criminal complaint before a magistrate. The writ aimed to obtain the men's release, so as to pre-empt their probable disappearances and/or deaths. According to the lawyer, although the judge received him in person, he rejected the complaint because it did not identify the exact offenders.[34] In a race against time, the lawyer returned hours later with precise information as to where the abductees were being held. This information would have allowed the institutional affiliation of the offenders to be deduced, as it was a city-center building belonging to the uniformed police force (Carabineros). According to the lawyer's account, the judge nonetheless refused to go to the named site, an action that could have saved the men's lives. In the event, some hours later, the detainees' bodies were found abandoned on waste ground. Their throats had been slit, after having been tortured in the police precinct indicated by the human rights lawyer.[35]

From a legal-doctrinal perspective, it would be challenging, though not impossible, to impute criminal responsibility for homicide and kidnapping in these examples. The bar would be even lower if the imputation were to be for omissive aiding and abetting,[36] against judges who had both the competence and the legal duty to act to protect victims' life and liberty. As to the mental element, a combination of three conditions should be sufficient: knowledge of the circumstances upon which the duty to act was founded, plus knowledge of the danger of death that threatened the victims, and the possibility of intervening to (at a minimum) hamper this possibly homicidal action. Each of these conditions is plausible given the reported facts. Defense strategies based on alleged duress are, however, conceivable and could also be plausible, at least if made by trial judges officiating in settings that presented a foreseeable danger to their safety (rather than solely to their career prospects).

Notes

1 This chapter has been prepared under the auspices of Regular Fondecyt Project No. 1181825, 'Criminal Responsibility for Human Rights Violations Committed in the Exercise of Judicial Functions', of which the author is the lead researcher. The chapter reflects findings also discussed in Couso, 'From Nuremberg to Mendoza: Judicial Murder and Its *Aufarbeitung*' in Jeßberger et al (eds) 49–59, and Couso/Perret, 'Responsabilidad penal por intervención en crímenes de dictaduras en el ejercicio de funciones judiciales. Estudio exploratorio del caso chileno y perspectiva comparada' (2023) 18 (36) *Polít. Crim.* https://politcrim.com/edicion-abierta-open-issue/ (accessed 29 December 2023). The author acknowledges and thanks Sabrina Perret, co-author of the latter article, as well as the research assistants Romina Villarroel and Mario Catalán, who carried out the search for and selection of the cases analyzed.
2 See Graver, *Judges against Justice. On Judges When the Rule of Law Is under Attack* (2015) 166.
3 See Couso (2022) (n 1) 51–58.
4 The label was famously used by Telford Taylor, Chief Prosecutor before the US Military Tribunal in Nuremberg that convicted several former German judges in the so-called Justice Trial of 1947. See Reicher, 'Evading Responsibility for Crimes against Humanity: Murderous Lawyers at Nuremberg' in Steinweis et al (eds) 140.
5 See Spendel, '§ 339' in Jähnke et al (eds), *Leipziger Kommentar zum Strafgesetzbuch* para 131.
6 Spendel, '§ 339' in Jähnke et al (eds), *Leipziger Kommentar zum Strafgesetzbuch* para 131.
7 This was highlighted by the report of Chile's first truth commission, the Comisión Nacional de Verdad y Reconciliación (CNVR), which maintains that it is possible to presume that several death sentences attributed to courts martial actually make reference to trials that never took place. CNVR, Informe de la Comisión Nacional de Verdad y Reconciliación (1991), Tomo 1 Vol. I, 83.
8 CNVR (1991) (n 7), Bando No 82 of 11 October 1973.
9 CNVR (1991) (n 7) 75–76.
10 CNVR (1991) (n 7) 84.
11 Consejo de Guerra de Puerto Montt, Judgment of 17 October 1973, Rol No 11-73.
12 Instructing magistrate Judge Álvaro Mesa Latorre, Judgment of 26 September 2019, Rol No 10.819 cons 1 G and Judgment of 10 February 2021, Rol No 10.819 cons 1 G. Translations from domestic Chilean court verdicts are the author's, here and throughout.
13 ibid.
14 Court of Appeals Santiago, Judgment of 6 August 2020, Rol Corte No 2070–2018 cons 6. The relevant article of the Criminal Code is mis-cited in the original (which should read Art 391(1) fifth circumstance). The wording of the relevant part of that provision is: "Anyone who kills another person [...] shall be punished: 1. – With [between 15 years and one day, and 20 years in] prison, or life imprisonment, if they perpetrate the killing with any of the following circumstances: [...] Fifth. – With premeditation".
15 Instructing magistrate Judge Álvaro Mesa Latorre, Judgment of 26 September 2019, Rol No 10.819 cons 1 I, and Judgment of 10 February 2021, Rol No 10.819 cons 1 K.
16 CNVR (1991) (n 7) 103. For details of the subsequent annulments, see chapters by the Observatorio de Justicia Transicional in the annual human rights reports of the Universidad Diego Portales, 2016 et seqq. https://derechoshumanos.udp.cl/informe-anual/ (accessed 15 August 2024).

17 Revolutionary Left Movement.
18 Consejo de Guerra de Valparaíso, Judgment of 4 February 1975, Rol No 344-74.
19 Consejo de Guerra de Calama, Judgment of 13 November 1973, no Rol number.
20 Barros, 'Courts Out of Context: Authoritarian Sources of Judicial Failure in Chile (1973–1990) and Argentina (1976–1983)' in Ginsburg et al (eds) 167 et seq.
21 On the relationships between extrajudicial repression and justice in the paradigmatic case of Germany's Third Reich, see Werle, *Justiz-Strafrecht und polizeiliche Verbrechensbekämpfung im Dritten Reich* (1989) 48 et seqq.
22 See CNVR (1991) (n 10).
23 Investigative magistrate Judge Álvaro Mesa Latorre, Judgment of 26 September 2019, Rol No 10.819 cons 1 I–K.
24 The Caravan of Death was an October 1973 operation whereby a secretive military commission travelled the country by helicopter, meting out summary justice in the form of extrajudicial executions or enforced disappearance, particularly targeting members of the recently deposed government.
25 Stark, an army general, commanded the Caravan of Death. (Author's note).
26 Court of Appeals Santiago, Judgment of 6 August 2020, Rol Corte No 2070–2018 cons 7.
27 Fiscalía Militar de Valdivia, Judgment of 13 September 1976, Rol No 85-73.
28 Fiscalía Militar de Concepción, Judgment of 2 October 1978, Rol No 1.177-72.
29 The victims were 12 men and 1 woman. The woman was pregnant at the time of her disappearance.
30 These agencies were the National Intelligence Directorate (Dirección de Inteligencia Nacional (DINA), 1973–1978) and its replacement, the Central Nacional de Informaciones (CNI), 1978–1990.
31 Chilean Surpreme Court, Judgment of 29 August 2023, Rol No 7885-2022 cons 30–33.
32 Details of the case, giving an account of the blatant dilatory behavior of the court, can be found in Couso/Perret (2023) (n 1) 926–928.
33 A dictatorship-era human rights defense organization set up by the Chilean Catholic Church.
34 See the account at Alejandra Matus, 'Carlos Cerda, el juez indómito' (*Archivo Vicaría*, no date). https://casosvicaria.udp.cl/carlos-cerda-el-juez-indomito/ (accessed 15 August 2024). The judge in question was not judge Cerda.
35 Alejandra Matus, 'Carlos Cerda, el juez indómito' (*Archivo Vicaría*, no date). https://casosvicaria.udp.cl/carlos-cerda-el-juez-indomito/ (accessed 15 August 2024).
36 For which the possibility of hampering, rather than preventing, the crime would suffice.

Bibliography

Barros R, 'Courts Out of Context: Authoritarian Sources of Judicial Failure in Chile (1973–1990) and Argentina (1976–1983)' in Ginsburg T/Moustafa T (eds), *Rule of Law. The Politics of Courts in Authoritarian Regimes* (Cambridge University Press 2008).

Couso J, 'From Nuremberg to Mendoza: Judicial Murder and Its *Aufarbeitung*' in Florian Jeßberger/others (eds), *Strafrecht und Systemunrecht* (Mohr Siebeck 2022).

Couso J/Perret S, 'Responsabilidad penal por intervención en crímenes de dictaduras en el ejercicio de funciones judiciales. Estudio exploratorio del caso chileno y perspectiva comparada' (2023) 18 (36) *Politica Criminal* 904.

Graver H P, *Judges Against Justice. On Judges When the Rule of Law Is Under Attack* (Springer-Verlag 2015).

Reicher H, 'Evading Responsibility for Crimes against Humanity: Murderous Lawyers at Nuremberg' in Steinweis A/Rachlin R D, *The Law in Nazi Germany: Ideology, Opportunism, and the Perversion of Justice* (Berghahn 2013) 137.

Spendel G, '§ 339' in Jähnke B et al (eds), *Leipziger Kommentar zum Strafgesetzbuch, vol. 9* (11th edn, De Gruyter 2006).

Werle G, *Justiz-Strafrecht und polizeiliche Verbrechensbekämpfung im Dritten Reich* (De Gruyter 1989).

6 Self-Representations of the Chilean Judiciary Regarding Their Responsibility in Relation to the Crimes of the Dictatorship

Daniela Accatino

6.1 Introduction: Different Judicial Portraits and Voices

Chile has conducted two official truth commissions since its return to democracy in 1990. The first, which was reported in 1991, focused on human rights violations committed between 1973 and 1990 resulting in deaths or disappearance. The second, reported in 2004, focused on torture and politically motivated imprisonment of survivors in the same period. Both commissions considered it necessary, as part of their reconstruction of the backdrop against which dictatorship-era atrocities took place, to conduct a critical review of the behavior of the judicial branch. The first commission, the National Commission on Truth and Reconciliation (Comisión Nacional de Verdad y Reconciliación) illustrated its analysis by quoting the then-President of the Supreme Court, delivering the 1975 iteration of the official address, which traditionally marks the opening of each year's judicial cycle. The speech contains striking language, made even more memorable by its juxtaposition in the truth commission report with accounts of horrific crimes:

> Contrary to what unworthy Chileans or foreigners operating with a particular political aim have said, Chile is not a land of barbarians; it has striven to give strict observance to (…) rights. With regard to torture and other atrocities, I can state that here we have neither firing squads nor iron curtains, and any statement to the contrary is the product of a press that is trying to propagate ideas that could not and will not prosper in our country.[1]

The absolute certainty with which accusations of atrocity were dismissed is of a piece with what the address went on to say about the courts and their workload:

> As a result of appeals presented, the Appeals Court in Santiago and this Supreme Court have been overwhelmed with a large number of habeas corpus actions that have been introduced, alleging arrests made by the executive branch. The administration of justice has thereby been impeded, since the higher courts, particularly in Santiago, have been prevented from attending to urgent matters entrusted to them.[2]

DOI: 10.4324/9781003470069-7

How has the Chilean judicial branch dealt with these words from the past, which return to haunt it? Has it faced up to the need to give an account of its conduct during the Pinochet dictatorship? This chapter considers these questions by analyzing a range of official communications issued by the judicial branch after the end of the military regime, which address aspects of the question of responsibility for its past performance. The chapter offers these 'non-jurisdictional pronouncements' as a counterpoint to the content of judicial rulings and opinions, very few of which have to date addressed the potential criminal liability of those involved in the exercise of jurisdiction under Pinochet's rule.

The chapter pays particular attention to '*acuerdos del Pleno de la Corte Suprema*', official statements issued by full sittings of the country's Supreme Court. In particular, it deals with statements issued in response to public criticism of the judiciary's role during the military regime and/or to demands for institutional acknowledgments of, or apologies for, the courts' behavior during that period. This focus will be complemented by reference to the communications occasionally emanating from presidents of the Court, for example, at the opening of each judicial year, when the president gives an official address summing up the courts' performance over the past twelve months. Neither the Supreme Court nor its president is authorized to speak on behalf of judges as a whole: the Chilean judiciary does not have an institutional channel for speaking as a single collective subject. For this reason, I also attend to other institutional voices, such as declarations by the Board of the National Magistrates' Association (Asociación Nacional de Magistradas y Magistrados del Poder Judicial), a professional association founded in 1968 to which most of the country's judges belong. As we will see, the Association's expressed views are often in conflict with those of the Supreme Court.

As other chapters in the present volume have shown, insofar as the potential criminal liability of Chile's judicial actors during dictatorship has been considered at all, that discussion has to date been limited to potential liability for active intervention in irregular courts-martial leading to execution or enforced disappearance or for judicial misconduct in the military justice system.[3] By contrast, the official Supreme Court statements and other public declarations analyzed here focus on judicial branch responsibility for omitting to carry out its duties of protection and investigation when faced with arbitrary detention and allegations of dictatorship-era torture and kidnap. This is an area in which no criminal charges have been brought to date.

Considering how these institutional discourses have evolved over time reveals significant changes in the attitude of the courts toward evaluating dictatorship-era judicial behavior. From a starting position where all fault or failing was denied, the Supreme Court's communications, like those of other judicial-institutional actors, gravitate toward greater openness to acknowledging some form of responsibility. I place this responsibility in relationship with the notion of collective or political responsibility as developed by Hannah Arendt and by Iris Marion Young. In giving an account of this evolution, I divide the post-dictatorship period into three periods. These periods, characterized, respectively, by denial, openness, and acknowledgment, correspond roughly to the first, second, and third decades since electoral democracy was recovered. The chapter closes by considering whether changing judicial attitudes, and the type of acknowledgment that they represent, might have any impact on the readiness of the courts to take on future potential criminal investigations of judicial actors for judicial murder, torture, or unlawful detention.

6.2 The Supreme Court Denies Any Judicial Responsibility (1990–1998)

The initial representations offered in public discourse by the judiciary about the actions of judges during the dictatorship constitute a resounding defense of the legality and integrity of what was done. These representations were first articulated during the regime, in response to demands and criticisms emanating from civil society organizations that undertook humanitarian and legal defense of victims during the years of state terror. The work of those organizations generated an extraordinarily complete record, both of crimes and of the fruitlessness of efforts to denounce them before the justice system.[4] After the democratic transition began, these criticisms were brought together and formulated in the truth commission report chapter cited above. The chapter concluded that the judicial branch was "largely, if unintentionally, responsible for aggravating the process of systematic human rights violations, both directly insofar as persons who were arrested and whose cases reached the courts were left unprotected, and indirectly insofar as that stance offered the agents of repression a growing assurance they would enjoy impunity for their criminal actions, no matter what outrages they might commit".[5]

The list of failings the report attributes to the judiciary is long and unedifying. Those of most interest for present purposes can be summarized as follows:

1 The rejection of almost all habeas corpus writs presented on behalf of people who had been illegally detained, many of whom went on to be lost without a trace. This rejection transgressed all applicable rules about the immediate resolution of such writs, judicial oversight of places of detention, and the existence of a duly issued prior warrant.
2 Judges' tendency to place blind faith in information provided by the government in response to questions triggered by habeas corpus writs, contrasted with the lack of attention paid to all other information supplied to them.
3 A lack of due zeal in investigating denunciations of possible criminality and the renunciation of faculties of supervision over the military justice system, compounded by the assumption, once the 1978 amnesty decree was imposed, that its terms required application before investigation or attributing of responsibilities.
4 The Supreme Court's deployment of its disciplinary powers and control over lower court judges' career progression, to the detriment of those who took a stance in favor of investigation of human rights violations.[6]

Upon publication of the first truth commission report, in 1991, a full sitting of the Supreme Court adopted a declaration addressed to the President of the Republic. This reacted vigorously against what they interpreted as "a judgement passed on the courts by an entity that has not even the slightest faculty to do so". This judgement, made – according to the Court – without even listening to the judges and in clear overreach of [the commission's] actual powers, attributed to the judiciary a form of "malicious complicity aimed at shielding the commission of excesses against the liberty and physical integrity of persons", and "culminates by attributing to judges almost the same quota of responsibility as is assigned to the actual authors of abuses of human rights".[7]

It should be noted that the Supreme Court that issued this response was still made up of judges appointed during the dictatorship, as Chile, unlike other countries in similar circumstances, did not reform or renew Supreme Court membership on transition. The conduct that was being criticized was therefore at least in some measure the conduct of its own current members. Its defensive posture can therefore be interpreted as an attempt at self-protection in case the public truths that the truth commission report sought to establish were to lead later to legal consequences. This explains why the Court felt the need to justify itself *as though* allegations of criminality had been leveled. The Court argued, first, that various dictatorship-era obstacles to justice had not been within the control of the courts. Thus, it was claimed, special legislative decrees, a lack of means to act in the absence of cooperation from the authorities, and the clandestine nature of many detention centers had all prevented the judicial branch from acting more effectively. Along the same lines, the Court's declaration added that despite those adverse conditions, the Supreme Court had made the representations and voiced the challenges that it considered proper to its functions and had taken action toward the opportune resolution of habeas corpus writs. According to the Court, this meant that delays had been outside the control of the judicial branch. In fact, the sparse list of actions the declaration spells out is much more likely to leave the reader convinced that the Court's interventions were both too little and too late.

The Court's next step in arguing its freedom from any responsibility concerns the report's mention of the supposed failure of the judicial branch to carry out its legal duties in criminal prosecution of crimes. According to the Supreme Court, this criticism proceeds from a mere discrepancy over the interpretation of the law and the assessment of evidence, upon which the Court insists judges' decisions were based. To turn such discrepancies into an affirmation of unlawfulness would mean affording the executive branch – or the truth commission, which was, according to the Court, "evidently its vehicle"[8] – the power to review the foundation of judicial decisions, something which would contravene constitutional principles.

In support of its argument, the Court seized on two affirmations made in the truth commission report. The first questioned the "excessive rigor with which the courts adhered strictly to formal legality in assessing the proof brought against the perpetrators", while the second criticized "an excessively formal approach to interpreting the law".[9] Although these affirmations were quite secondary to the tenor of the original report, the Court foregrounded them in an effort to suggest that, far from acting unlawfully, judges had in fact adhered strictly to the law. Judges, said the Court,

> have absolutely no authority to depart from the law by giving it a different interpretation to that offered by its literal formulation, when the text [of the law] is clear [and] clearly transmits the intention of the legislator. Were they to do so, they would betray the essence of their mission as instruments of the law.[10]

This attitude of denial persisted through the early years of democratic transition, and using it as a shield, the Supreme Court continued to treat the military Junta's 1978 amnesty decree law as a perfectly valid norm. It was interpreted as allowing judicial investigations to be closed as soon as it was determined that the alleged crime at issue had occurred during the time period covered by the amnesty.[11] 'Correct' interpretation of the amnesty decree law was a contested issue in a period also marked by the continuation of Pinochet in the post of Army commander-in-chief, the gradual dismantling of those human rights organizations that had taken the lead in dictatorship-era litigation, and the government's abandonment of the admittedly challenging policy of directly promoting the derogation or annulment of the amnesty law. Demands for justice seemed destined to dissolve into a debate about legal interpretation, a debate moreover fueled by President Aylwin himself. Aylwin insisted on putting forward an alternative interpretation of amnesty whereby full investigation, and the identification of those criminally responsible, was a necessary prerequisite, going so far as to recommend this interpretation in a communication sent to the Supreme Court president.[12] Against this backdrop, the judicial branch contented itself with continuing to take refuge in a self-image as a mere applier of laws: beyond reproach, susceptible to differences of opinion but never to actual blame.

Judicial branch behavior over dictatorship-era crimes returned to public notice in December 1992, with an attempt to impeach three Supreme Court judges for severe dereliction of duty (*notable abandono de deberes*). The action was over their decision to refer the case of the enforced disappearance of Alfonso Chanfreau back to the military courts. The investigation had been at an advanced state, with various uniformed and other dictatorship agents called to appear. Instead, the military court invoked amnesty and rapidly closed the case. Although the impeachment attempt was rejected by the Senate, the controversy persisted as new investigative measures were ordered in a growing number of cases over dictatorship-era crimes.[13] This newly proactive approach appeared to acquire tacit support in the inaugural speech delivered by the Supreme Court president to mark the opening of the 1993 judicial year. In reply to what he termed the "campaign of calumny launched against the judicial branch, culminating in an attempted impeachment", the Court president insisted that it was not true that the courts were unmoved by the fate of the still-disappeared. On the contrary, he insisted, "investigations have continued until there was no more possibility of achieving satisfactory results" – implying that the amnesty decree did not, after all, prevent the carrying out of investigations. Simultaneously, however, his address reiterated the defense with which the reader is already familiar:

> the judicial branch can in no way be held responsible in this matter: there are absolutely no grounds on which to attribute responsibility [to the courts] for the excesses which may have been committed. As has already been stated, the Court did nothing more than apply the prevailing law of the day, as was its obligation. To have done otherwise would have meant committing the serious offence of dereliction of duty (*prevaricación*).[14]

In the end, the incipient proactive behavior of some judges was usually aborted when the respective case reached the Supreme Court, to the satisfaction of the Armed Forces, who had reacted with a certain amount of sabre-rattling to what they saw as a "parading" (*desfile*) of their members through the courts.

6.3 Changing Judicial Receptivity to Demands for Justice and Criticism of its Dictatorship-Era Actions (1998–2013)

Over the course of the 1990s, a series of reforms carried out under the banner of judicial branch modernization had direct effects on the composition of the Supreme Court. Judicial behavior over human rights case underwent much more notable changes than previously.[15] From 1997 onward, the Supreme Court began to disapply amnesty on a case-by-case basis and on a range of grounds, a position which was strengthened after the arrest of Pinochet in London in October 1998. Meanwhile, there was an increase in case litigation, brought about by the lodging of numerous new criminal complaints.[16]

The Pinochet case led Chile's center-left administrations to adopt a defensive stance that opposed the extradition of the former dictator from the UK to Spain, on the understanding that accountability for his crimes could be achieved at home. This position had institutional effects, as well as effects on judicial culture, over the course of the ensuing decade. Amongst the former featured the creation of a dialogue roundtable – the 'Mesa de Diálogo' – to search for victims of enforced disappearance. Government representatives took part, alongside the Armed Forces and some human rights lawyers and organizations. The results were in the end quite meager, but the exercise did lead the Supreme Court to implement, from 2001, a system for centralized management of the dictatorship-era crime caseload. Specialized judges, known as *ministros/as en visita*, were assigned to investigate such cases on either a preferential or exclusive basis. This added proactive Supreme Court administration of the human rights caseload to the improved jurisdictional receptivity that was beginning to be visible in final Supreme Court verdicts. Analysis of the state of advance of dictatorship-era cases began to feature regularly in each year's Supreme Court presidential address.

A closer look at how this new judicial receptivity was foregrounded and referred to in these addresses reveals signs of allusions to past judicial conduct that amount to a shift in the public image projected by the judiciary regarding its own responsibilities. In 2004, for example, the inaugural address of the judicial year featured the following statements from the Court president:

> The efforts made by the judicial branch to resolve those cases and bring them to completion must be taken into account; [they were cases which], at the time, proved impossible to get to the bottom of as soon as what were later revealed to be security agencies, their commanders, or members became involved. The effective investigation [of these cases] was only possible after the return to democracy in our country. The fact cannot be ignored that justice, like liberty, is only viable in democracy.[17]

Up until this point, the speech reiterates, with different arguments, the previous image of external obstacles preventing the judiciary from pursuing responsibilities at the time violations took place. At this point in his speech, the Court president nonetheless introduced a different note, affirming that:

> In any case, we consider that based on that experience, our judicial branch will never again underperform or allow itself to be inhibited in carrying out its two major roles, which are to protect and oversee the rights of persons, and to control the actions of the authorities.[18]

Although the comment is directed toward the future, it now by implication recognizes deficiencies and inhibitions in dictatorship-era judicial behavior that could have been avoided.

The tension between these two attitudes, to some extent contradictory, is also present in another significant institutional communiqué from the same year. This time, the Supreme Court was responding to Chile's second official truth commission, this one focused on cases of political imprisonment and torture. The commission's report, published in November 2004, reiterated the criticism of judicial conduct formulated by the first commission.[19] The reply that came from a full sitting of the Court was quite different in tone, opening by expressing consternation and solidarity with victims, a sentiment that had been absent in 1991. The resistance to criticism was, however, still present, albeit less vociferous, and the Court's defense against what it called the "grave charge" of "a type of connivance with those who committed excesses and violations" is similar. In other words, this reply also argued that the courts had been prevented from fully carrying out their protective functions because their sphere of action had been circumscribed by the invocation of constitutional states of exception and because they could not count on the effective co-operation of state organisms and authorities, who instead generally hid information. In the very next paragraph, the denial of responsibility was, however, softened by the affirmation that "from a different historical perspective, it could be said that the courts might have tried to carry out more effective actions in protection of individual rights", although it had to be borne in mind that given the aforementioned limitations, this "would not have had significant results".[20] This incipient change in attitude was reinforced with a final reference in the declaration to the jurisdictional work that had been carried out after the restoration of democratic institutionality and a promise that the Court would continue to fulfill to the best of its ability, its jurisdictional mandate and its role in preserving individuals' rights.

Openness to public acknowledgment of responsibility is clearer to see in a declaration issued some days later by the Board of the National Magistrates' Association. This declaration highlighted the fact that "a certain number" of judges had acted in defense of people's rights, at the cost of risks to their own careers and even to their personal safety, often without obtaining useful results. A contrast was drawn between this behavior and that of those judges who "ought to have intervened – and would have been able to do so – in cases in which human rights violations were being alleged". The conduct of such judges in "operating within the bounds of official information of the time" was judged "insufficient" and unequal to the seriousness of the crimes that were being denounced. Two further aspects of this declaration are of interest and help to frame and explain the change that it represented. The first is the observation, made in the statement, that the Association members in whose name it was emitted were not members of the judicial branch, and certainly not of its higher echelons, at the time of the events referred to in the truth commission report. This represents a change – one which judges themselves considered relevant – from the circumstances that prevailed at the time of the Supreme Court's declaration in response to the first truth commission. The second point is that it may have been precisely this distance that allowed, for the first time, a recognition that a public acknowledgment (a "generic and values-based" declaration, in the language of the statement) operates on a different plane from any question of possible individual legal responsibilities "which may come to be established in any particular case and by way of the applicable jurisdictional procedures".[21]

The conflict between different understandings of the judiciary's responsibility for its past conduct became explicit inside the Supreme Court the following year, in the course of a widely reported case that once more called into question the disciplinary control that higher courts exercised over junior judges. The case would go on to cost Chile an adverse verdict from the Inter-American Court of Human Rights. At issue was a disciplinary proceeding to which a serving judge was submitted over his opinion of dictatorship-era judicial conduct. The judge had undertaken further studies in the form of a diploma in human rights. The dissertation he submitted in fulfillment of course requirements argued that "in order for the judicial branch to reposition itself morally and ethically as a guarantor of citizens' rights, its highest governing body has the moral duty to recognise, clearly and without self-justifications, its responsibility for human rights violations".[22] Upon receiving a copy of the judge's dissertation, the Supreme Court ordered a disciplinary investigation against him that later led to a career sanction for having 'censured or attacked the conduct in office of other judges'. Although this decision could be viewed as a sign of the intensity of senior judicial resistance to any form of acknowledgment of responsibility, on the other hand, six of the Court's 21 judges voted against it. The minority opinion issued by the dissenters publicly argued that evaluating the behavior of the courts during the dictatorship was an open question, in respect of which no one could abrogate to themselves the right to determine absolute truths.

This was a time during which national and international public attention was being paid to the outworkings of the Pinochet case, first in London and then back home in Chile, where numerous domestic cases were in train against him and other agents of the dictatorship. It was therefore not surprising either that judges felt interrogated both about their present-day role and the legacy of past judicial behavior or that internal differences of opinion on these issues rose to the surface, becoming visible to the public and eroding the previously monolithic denial that had emanated from the Supreme Court.[23] The disciplinary proceedings analyzed in the previous paragraph are illustrative both of this movement within judicial culture and of the difficult reception faced by any critical understanding of the courts' role during the dictatorship. The judiciary was, after all, still highly constrained by a strongly hierarchical structure, plus the historical weight of an understanding of its own role as purely technical and apolitical.[24] Any movement toward institutional recognition of judicial responsibility of the kind that the censured dissertation had proposed would need to overcome institutional reluctance. This reluctance, while latent, was still intense, as was evidenced by the decision to apply sanctions to the author of the offending text.

6.4 Institutional Recognition of Responsibility for Judicial Behavior during the Dictatorship (Since 2013)

Not until 2013 did the conflicts within the judicial branch resolve themselves in favor of a public taking on of responsibility for the judiciary's dictatorship-era omissions. The year marked the 40th anniversary of the military coup, and everywhere public space was filled with acts of symbolic memory and commemoration.[25] On judicial terrain, the decisive impulse came from the National Magistrates' Association, whose Board declared that

> it is not possible to elude the historical responsibility of our judiciary over the violation of basic rights of the human person that took place during the dictatorial regime. It must be said and acknowledged with clarity and courage: the judicial branch, and in particular the Supreme Court of the day, renounced its essential work of overseeing fundamental rights and protection those who were victims of state abuse.[26]

The same declaration went on to ask forgiveness from victims, their families, and society, as an "expression of the unequivocal, unbreakable commitment of our judiciary in the present and into the future, to guaranteeing, promoting and protecting the fundamental rights of the human person". The declaration closed by inviting the Supreme Court to "also carry out the required critical reflection over its own past actions and omissions", expressing the hope that the Court would not "turn a deaf ear to the heartfelt plea of judges who want to distance themselves from the dark past that they have inherited through no fault of their own".

This time the Supreme Court did make the required declaration, read by its president before the television cameras on 6 September 2013. The statement opened by explaining that it had been prompted by

> a series of pronouncements directed at criticizing, amongst other actors, the judicial branch and in particular the Supreme Court of the time [of the dictatorship], as having allowed a repressive system that gravely affected the fundamental rights of citizens and culminated in deaths, enforced disappearances and torture, amongst other crimes (…) many of which have been proven beyond doubt by the courts, as is public knowledge.[27]

The declaration, issued by a full sitting of the Court, acknowledged that those crimes had taken place

> in part due to the omissions of judges of the time, who did not do enough to determine the truth of the violations (…) but principally due to the Supreme Court of the day, which did not exercise leadership in making representations about this type of illegal activity, considering that [the Court] could not have been ignorant of the fact that [these crimes were] definitely happening, given that numerous denunciations were made via a host of jurisdictional requirements that were made within its sphere of competence.... in this way [the Court] denied the effective judicial guarantees that those affected should have been able to rely on.

In direct contrast to its previous resistance to any form of acknowledgment of responsibility on the part of the judiciary, in this declaration the Supreme Court now affirmed with some vehemence the need for a public gesture of this sort, to make it clear "to all current and future members of the judiciary and to generations of citizens" that the actions and omissions referred to constituted a "dereliction of duty", and to ensure that this did not happen again. The statement concluded by saying that consequently, "this Supreme Court has committed its best efforts to resolving these crimes, and calls on all judges of the Republic and staff of the judicial branch to continue to work toward this end".

The declaration was made public at a time when institutional *mea culpa* were the order of the day, and public opinion appeared inclined to turn a critical eye on dictatorship-era terror. This could lead an observer to judge this to be a relatively empty gesture, were it not for the fact that, as we have already seen, even to get this far had been a struggle. In this author's opinion, what finally made it possible to publish this declaration, and commit to what it promised for the future, was the distance that the final phrase quoted here established between past negligence and current diligence in dealing with the dictatorship's crimes. In 2013 there were, without a doubt, still lacunae and critical obstacles in the judicial response: the annual report of the Observatorio de Justicia Transicional of the Universidad Diego Portales for that year listed, for example, the slow pace of cases; the concession of mitigating circumstances to lower sentence tariffs; a lack of transparency around the granting of post-sentencing benefits, including early release and the invocation of statutory limitation to deny civil claims for damages.[28] Some of these weaknesses still persist. The 2013 Supreme Court declaration, however, expressed, consolidated, and projected for the future an institutional appreciation of its jurisprudential evolution and of institutional improvements that made further case progress possible. These improvements included the designation of special magistrates, already mentioned, and the introduction of a Supreme Court co-ordinator, and then a co-ordination office, dedicated to these human rights-related cases. The contrast with the passivity of former times was evident.[29]

Returning, however, to the central themes of the present volume, what effect if any does this public acknowledgement of dereliction of duty have on broader questions about judicial liability? In particular, could this institutional representation favor eventual pursuit of criminal liability over the ways in which jurisdiction was exercised during Pinochet's rule?

6.5 The Distinction between Collective Responsibility and Individual Guilt of Judges Over Their Past Performance

In answering these questions, it is useful to delineate more precisely in what sense(s) the judiciary takes on responsibility when it acknowledges the existence of judicial passivity in the face of the repressive policies of the dictatorship. Here, the concepts of collective responsibility or political responsibility, as formulated by Hannah Arendt and later developed by Iris Marion Young, can be brought into play. They are well matched to the ways in which responsibility was delineated in the declarations of the Supreme Court and of the National Magistrates' Association.[30] Arendt articulates these notions when she observes that moral or juridical concepts such as blame and guilt lose their meaning if applied to a whole group whose association with wrongdoing is the passive allowing of it – thus, for example, the German people, with regard to Nazi crimes. This is, she says, because the whole purpose of blame and guilt is to "single out". They therefore lose all meaning if used to denote a situation whereby "where all are guilty, nobody is".[31] A collectivity – that is, all those who belong to it – may be responsible for something that one of its members has done, or for that which was done in its name, in a different sense. The foundation of that second type of responsibility is "membership in a group (a collective) which no voluntary act of mine can dissolve".[32] In this sense, says Arendt, every nation assumes responsibility for the deeds and misdeeds of the past: "we are always held responsible for the sins of our fathers as we reap the rewards of their merits".[33] This image of a kind of burden associated with belonging fits surprisingly well with the reference that the Magistrates' Association declaration makes to the "dark past that [judges] have inherited through no fault of their own", and which it asks the Supreme Court to acknowledge.

Discussing Arendt's idea, and precisely in order to be more specific as to what it means to "take on" this collective or political responsibility, Iris Marion Young proposes that while blame or guilt are backward-looking, political responsibility is forward-looking and implies taking on the task of improving matters:

> [t]he meaning of political responsibility is forward-looking. One has the responsibility always now, in relation to current events and in relation to their future consequences. We are in a condition of having such political responsibility, and the fact of having it implies an imperative to take political responsibility. If we see injustices or crimes being committed by the institutions of which we are a part, or believe that such crimes are being committed, then we have the responsibility to try to speak out against them with the intention of mobilizing others to oppose them, and to act together to transform the institutions to promote better ends.[34]

This prospective point of view also fits with the sense of the acknowledgements made by Chile's Supreme Court and Magistrates' Association. These express the sentiment that what we might therefore call the political responsibility of present-day judges with regard to the dictatorship's crimes consists of doing in the present the justice that was not done in the past and avoiding future states of defenselessness.[35]

Thus, recognizing and taking on 'political' responsibility for the legacy of past judicial inaction does not entail retrospective self-reproach or blame. Nor, therefore, is it a first step toward an eventual apportioning of criminal guilt to this or that individual judge for their past omissions. The collective responsibility of the judiciary and the potential individual guilt of particular judges would, in this view, remain on conceptually distinct planes. This is in contrast to what the Supreme Court appeared to fear when, in the early years of transition, it defended itself vigorously against the criticisms of the first truth commission. None of this, of course, excludes the possibility that the general forward-looking commitment made – that the demands of justice will in future be met with diligence – might also come to be applied in future to cases in which the criminal liability of some judicial actor is at issue.[36]

In my view, this prospective notion of political responsibility is well suited to the public acknowledgments that have been discussed here. Nonetheless, an important proviso must be made: the Supreme Court's institutional acknowledgement also implies certain backward-looking commitments that do not have to do with individual attributions of guilt. The proviso takes on board a point made by Martha Nussbaum in her prologue to Young's book. Discussing the degree of precision with which it is possible to draw the boundary between forward-looking and backward-looking projections of political responsibility, Nussbaum says, "it is a little hard to see how we ever get to the future without a critique of the past".[37] In the case that is the focus of our attention here, the Supreme Court's acknowledgement of responsibility aims to emphasize the distance between former judicial passivity and current judicial proactivity and project that distance into the future. Nonetheless, the identification of that former passivity cannot completely escape a retrospective dimension that it is also important to underline.

The Court's declaration affirms the existence of past omissive practices by the courts regarding dictatorship-era crimes and the causal incidence of omissions on the persistence of that systematic state violence. That public affirmation about the past commits the Court, in the sense that it establishes that general fact as incontrovertible, thereby *prima facie* relieving parties in future cases of the burden of proving the same, under the doctrine of judicial notice. This type of general fact could become relevant in a hypothetical future criminal prosecution for judicial murder, torture, or unlawful detention, for example, for the purposes of examining the trustworthiness of a particular piece of evidence. It could, however, also become relevant in other types of cases, such as where a possible example of fraudulent *res judicata* might be at issue,[38] or as part of the discussion as to whether a particular crime can be classed as a crime against humanity.[39]

Therefore, and in conclusion, public self-representations of the responsibility of the Chilean judiciary for the crimes of the dictatorship, as expressed in institutional statements, have evolved from denial to acknowledgment. This movement has been accompanied by the taking on of a notion of responsibility that is conceptually distinct from the notion of criminal liability. This evolution toward the taking on of political responsibility nevertheless entails the assumption of commitments to future action, and to general factual affirmations, that could be relevant in any future jurisdictional addressing of cases over the potential criminal liability of judicial actors.

Notes

1 CNVR, *Report of the Chilean National Commission on Truth and Reconciliation*, English edition (Notre Dame University Press 1993) 141.

2 CNVR (1993) (n 1) 141.

3 See chapter by Jaime Couso in the present volume.

4 This defensive position can be seen in the annual addresses of Supreme Court presidents at the opening of each judicial year, published in the country's paper of record (Diario Oficial), and in the key law report journal *Revista de Derecho y Jurisprudencia y Gaceta de los Tribunales*. It was also in evidence in various declarations issued by full sittings of the Supreme Court, such as the one reported in broadsheet *El Mercurio* on 8 July 1987 under the headline "Supreme Court Rejects Criticisms of the Judicial Branch" (*Corte Suprema rechazó críticas al Poder Judicial)*. On the role of civil society organizations in documenting and denouncing regime atrocities, see Accatino, 'Permanence et reprise des actes écrits qui ont dénoncé par la voie judiciaire les atrocités de la dictature chilienne' (2024) 181 *L&S* 13. The latter analyzes how omissive judicial behavior was recorded in the dossiers that such organizations created, during the dictatorship, of attempted legal actions such as the lodging of writs of habeas corpus and criminal complaints.

5 CNVR (1993) (n 1), 141.

6 Beyond its strictly jurisdictional duties, the Supreme Court also played a significant part in legitimating the dictatorship. The most evocative expression of this came in a 1974 public ceremony in which the then- Supreme Court president presented Chile's ceremonial presidential sash to Pinochet, in effect consecrating the political power of the military Junta. On this legitimizing role, see Hilbink, *Judges beyond Politics in Democracy and Dictatorship: Lessons from Chile* (2007) 157 et seqq.

7 Corte Suprema de Chile, 'Respuesta de la Corte Suprema al Informe de la Comisión Nacional de Verdad y Reconciliación' (1991) 42 *Estudios Públicos* 237, 238.

8 Corte Suprema de Chile (1991) (n 7), 244.

9 CNVR (1993) (n 1), 148 and 150.

10 Corte Suprema de Chile (n 7), 242 and 243. The increased importance afforded to these criticisms of interpretative literalism or formalism may have been influenced by the considerable weight attached to the terms in which first transitional president Patricio Aylwin remonstrated with judges over their dictatorship-era conduct. First, in March 1990, Aylwin delivered a speech to the National Magistrates' Association in which he alleged that instead of effectively protecting people's rights, judges had "restricted themselves to being mere appliers of law". In a press conference a year later, he criticized judges' "lack of moral courage" (*falta de coraje moral*). See Aylwin, *La transición chilena: Discursos escogidos marzo 1990-1992* (1992) 159–165 and Correa, 'Cenicienta se queda en la fiesta. El poder judicial chileno en la década de los 90' in Drake/Jaksic (eds), 299.

11 Resolving a writ of unconstitutionality in August 1990 – i.e., after the transition had begun – the Supreme Court expressly found the amnesty decree law to be constitutional, dismissing the argument that it should be invalidated on the grounds that it contravened various norms contained in the Geneva Conventions. See Hilbink (2007) (n 6) and Collins, 'Human Rights Trials in Chile during and after the Pinochet Years' (2009) 4 *IJTJ* 1.

12 On Alywin's message to the Supreme Court, and also for a critical view of the controversy about Chilean judges and dictatorship-era formalism, see Atria, *'La hora del derecho: los "derechos humanos" entre la política y el derecho'* (2003) 91 *Estudios Públicos* 45.

13 In just one example, investigations were reopened into the 1976 homicides of former Chilean foreign minister Orlando Letelier and his US colleague Ronni Moffitt, a crime that had taken place on US soil (in Washington, DC) and had been expressly excluded from Decree Law 2.191 (the amnesty decree law). New efforts were also made in the case of the death of Carmelo Soria, a UN diplomat and Spanish national killed in Santiago in the same year (see Hilbink (2007) (n 6) 189 et seqq.). The year 1993 even saw a conviction handed down in a case of two young people forcibly disappeared during the period covered by the amnesty law: the verdict declared that the amnesty did not apply because the crime was an ongoing offense (*delito de ejecución permanente*). See Observatorio de Justicia Transicional, 'Jurisprudential milestones in human rights cases: Chile 1990-2024' (Universidad Diego Portales 2024). https://derechoshumanos.udp.cl/publicacion/major-jurisprudential-milestones-in-dictatorship-era-human-rights-cases-chile-1990-2024/ (accessed 26 August 2024).

14 Aburto, 'Discurso de inauguración del año judicial 1993' (1993) XC/1 Revista JCS XI.

15 Reforms included the introduction of a retirement age for senior judges, alongside an increase in the number of Supreme Court members (from 17 to 21). The combined effect of the changes was to allow the appointment of 11 new Court members. See Correa (1999) (n 10).

16 See Hilbink (2007) (n 6); Collins (2009) (n 11) and Collins, *Post-transitional Justice. Human Rights Trial in Chile and El Salvador* (2010) 81 et seqq.

17 Libedinsky, 'Discurso de inauguración del año judicial 2004'. www.pjud.cl/docs/download/894 (accessed 26 August 2024).

18 Libedinsky (2024) (n 17).

19 The report, and the Court's reply, can be seen in (2006) 97 *Estudios Públicos* 527. The Supreme Court's response, issued after a full sitting, was emitted after various branches of the Armed Forces and security services had also provided institutional responses. These responses were very different in tone from those that had been produced in 1991, with various of the new replies including acknowledgments of responsibility. On this

general change of attitude, see Sierra, 'Reabrir y cicatrizar: Notas sobre el informe Valech y sus reacciones' (2005) 1 *DOAJ* 157.

20 Corte Suprema de Chile, 'Declaración de la Corte Suprema al Informe de la Comisión Nacional sobre Prisión Política y Tortura' (2006) 97 *Estudios Públicos* 527, 528.

21 Asociación Nacional de Magistrados del Poder Judicial de Chile, 'Declaración de la Asociación Nacional de Magistrados del Poder Judicial de Chile' (2006) 97 *Estudios Públicos* 530, 531.

22 Author's translation. The facts of the case are summarized in IACtHR, 27 August 2020, Series C No 409, *Urrutia Laubreaux v. Chile*, 14 et seqq.

23 Other expressions of these emerging critical views from within the judiciary about the institution's past behavior began to surface in media sources, publications, and off-the-record interviews: see Huneeus, 'Judging from a Guilty Conscience: The Chilean Judiciary's Human Rights Turn' (2010) 35 *LSI* 1, 114 et seqq.

24 On these as two distinctive features of the Chilean judiciary, see Hilbink (2007) (n 6) 269 et seqq.

25 See Waldman, 'A cuarenta años del golpe militar en Chile. Reflexiones en torno a conmemoraciones y memorias' (2014) 221 *Rev. mex. cienc. polít. soc.* 243.

26 Asociación Nacional de Magistrados del Poder Judicial de Chile, 'Declaración pública' (2013).

27 Corte Suprema de Chile, 'Declaración Pública'. https://media.elmostrador.cl/2013/09/Declaraci%C3%B3n-Corte-Suprema.pdf (accessed 26 August 2024).

28 Collins, 'Truth, Justice and Memory for Dictatorship-Era Human Rights Violations, 40 Years after Chile's Military Coup' in Collins et al (eds), 29.

29 On the evolution of jurisprudence surrounding statutory limitation, gradual recognition of the category of crimes against humanity, and interpretation of the amnesty decree law – which has not to date been derogated or annulled – see Observatorio de Justicia Transicional, 'Jurisprudential milestones…' (n 13). Other judicial branch initiatives dating from around the same time provide further evidence of an institutional approval of the shift in judicial receptivity: these include, for example, the 2013 release of a judicial branch documentary film recounting progress made by judge Héctor Solís in a case known as the Paine massacre: Poder Judicial Chile (2013) 'Ministros en visita en causas de derechos humanos: el caso Paine'. www.youtube.com/watch?v=GJ3kIT2G9F4 (accessed 1 August 2024). The Supreme Court also launched a project entitled Digital Historical Memory of the Judicial Branch (Memoria Histórica Digital del Poder Judicial), aimed at creating a historical archive of all case files in completed dictatorship-era investigations. The same project included the publication, less than two years later, of a 'Historical Report on Human Rights Violations and the Work of the Judicial Branch' ("Informe histórico de las violaciones a los Derechos Humanos y la labor del Poder Judicial"). See 'Observatorio de Justicia Transicional de la Universidad Diego Portales' (2016) 33 *Boletín informativo* 10.

30 See Arendt, *Eichmann in Jerusalem: A Report on the Banality of Evil* (1963) and Arendt, 'Collective Responsibility' in Bernauer (ed); Young, *Responsibility for Justice* (2011).

31 Arendt (1987) (n 30) 43.

32 Arendt (1987) (n 30), 45.

33 Arendt (1987) (n 30).

34 Young (1987) (n 30) 92.

35 It is particularly interesting to note that this interpretation has a point of contact with the thesis developed by Alexandra Huneeus that a key factor in explaining the Chilean judiciary's prosecutorial turn from 1998 was a gradual taking on by judges of

a "counterhegemonic understanding of the judicial role", whereby "(j)udges came to understand the judiciary as stained by its past, and to view the prosecutions as a means toward redemption". See Huneeus (2010) (n 23).

36 In June 2013, i.e., a few months prior to the formulation of its historic declaration, the Supreme Court had had to pronounce in a case of this sort. On that occasion the Court agreed to allow an extradition petition to proceed against former Argentine prosecutor Otilio Romano Ruiz. Romano, an Argentine national, was wanted in Argentina for his part in various counts of false imprisonment, torture, illegal searches, and a crime against the administration of justice consisting of failing in his official duty by neglecting to promote the pursuit and sanctioning of criminals (crimes committed during the Argentine dictatorship of 1976–1983). See Corte Suprema de Chile, 18 June 2013, Roll No 290–2012, *Extradición de Otilio Romano Ruiz* and chapter by Omar Palermo in the present volume.

37 Nussbaum, 'Foreword' in Young (ed) (2011) (n 30).

38 See the chapter by Juan Pablo Mañalich in the present volume.

39 See, for example, Corte Suprema de Chile, 16 May 2019, Roll No 4.568–18, *Homicidio de Gabriel Salinas*. The case involved discussion of whether the elements of a crime against humanity were present for purposes of ruling on the applicability of amnesty and statutory limitation. The victim's death had come about due to a shot fired by a uniformed policeman when arresting him on suspicion of having taken part in the theft of some tools the previous night. The Court ruled that a crime against humanity had been configured, "because the authorities, the prevailing legal-political context, and the military jurisdiction of the time favoured impunity and defencelessness, promoting the elimination of invisible or undesirable persons".

Bibliography

Aburto M, 'Discurso de inauguración del año judicial 1993' (1993) XC/1 *Revista de Derecho y Jurisprudencia y Gaceta de los Tribunales*.

Accatino D et al, 'Permanence et reprise des actes écrits qui ont dénoncé par la voie judiciaire les atrocités de la dictature chilienne' (2024) 181 *Langage & Société* 13.

Arendt H, *Eichmann in Jerusalem: A report on the Banality of Evil* (Penguin Classic 1963).

Arendt H, 'Collective responsibility' in Bernauer S. J. J. W. (ed), *Amor Mundi: Explorations in the Faith and Thought of Hannah Arendt* (26th edn, Martinues Nijhoff Publishers 1987).

Asociación Nacional de Magistrados del Poder Judicial de Chile, 'Declaración de la Asociación Nacional de Magistrados del Poder Judicial de Chile' (2006) 97 *Estudios Públicos* 530.

Asociación Nacional de Magistrados del Poder Judicial de Chile, 'Declaración pública' (2013). https://media.elmostrador.cl/2013/09/Declaraci%C3%B3n-de-la-Asociaci%C3%B3n-de-Magistrados.pdf.

Atria F, 'La hora del derecho: los 'derechos humanos' entre la política y el derecho' (2003) 91 *Estudios Públicos* 45.

Aylwin P, *La transición chilena: Discursos escogidos marzo 1990-1992* (Editorial Andrés Bello 1992).

Bernasconi O, *Resistance to political violence in Latin America. Documenting atrocity* (Palgrave Macmillan 2019).

Collins C, 'Human Rights Trials in Chile during and after the "Pinochet Years"' (2009) 1 *The International Journal of Transitional Justice*.

Collins C, *Post-transitional justice. Human Rights trial in Chile and El Salvador* (Pennsylvania University Press 2010).

Collins C et al, 'Truth, Justice and Memory for Dictatorship-Era Human Rights Violations, 40 Years after Chile's Military Coup' in Vial T (ed), *Informe Anual Derechos Humanos* 2013 (Universidad Diego Portales 2013). Translation of chapter originally published in Centro de Derechos Humanos, Informe anual sobre derechos humanos en Chile 2013 (Universidad Diego Portales). https://papers.ssrn.com/sol3/papers.cfm?abstract_id=2628430# (accessed 17 July 2024).

Comisión Nacional de Verdad y Reconciliación, *Report of the Chilean National Commission on Truth and Reconciliation*, English edition (Notre Dame University Press 1993). www.usip.org/sites/default/files/resources/collections/truth_commissions/Chile90-Report/Chile90-Report.pdf.

Comisión Nacional sobre Prisión Política y Tortura, 'Informe de la Comisión Nacional sobre Prisión Política y Tortura' (2006) 97 *Estudios Públicos*.

Correa J, 'Cenicienta se queda en la fiesta. El poder judicial chileno en la década de los 90' in Drake P/Jaksic I (eds) *El modelo chileno: democracia y desarrollo en los noventa* (LOM 1999) 299.

Corte Suprema de Justicia de Chile, 'Respuesta de la Corte Suprema al Informe de la Comisión Nacional de Verdad y Reconciliación' (1991), 42 *Estudios Públicos* 237, 238. www.estudiospublicos.cl/index.php/cep/article/view/1447/2452.

Corte Suprema de Justicia de Chile, 'Declaración de la Corte Suprema al Informe de la Comisión Nacional sobre Prisión Política y Tortura' (2006) 97 *Estudios Públicos*.

Corte Suprema de Justicia de Chile, 'Declaración Pública' (2013). https://media.elmostrador.cl/2013/09/Declaraci%C3%B3n-Corte-Suprema.pdf.

Hilbink L, *Judges beyond Politics in Democracy and Dictatorship: Lessons from Chile* (Cambridge University Press 2007).

Huneeus A, 'Judging from a guilty conscience: The Chilean judiciary's human rights turn' (2010) 35 *Law & Social Inquiry* 1.

Libedinsky M, 'Discurso de inauguración del año judicial 2004'. www.pjud.cl/docs/download/894 (accessed 17 July 2024).

Nussbaum M, 'Foreword' in Young I M, *Responsibility for Justice* (Oxford University Press 2011).

Observatorio de Justicia Transicional, *Jurisprudential Milestones in Human Rights Cases: Chile 1990–2024* (Universidad Diego Portales 2024). https://derechoshumanos.udp.cl/cms/wp-content/uploads/2023/09/Chile-Justice-Milestones-Human-Rights-Cases-1990-2024-ENG.pdf.

Observatorio de Justicia Transicional de la Universidad Diego Portales, *Boletín informativo Nº 33* (2016). https://derechoshumanos.udp.cl/cms/wp-content/uploads/2020/12/Boletin_33_Observatorio_JT_juicios_ddhh_Chile_dic_2015_ene_feb_2016_1.pdf.

Sierra L, 'Reabrir y cicatrizar: Notas sobre el informe Valech y sus reacciones' (2005) 1 *Anuario de Derechos Humanos* 157.

Waldman G, 'A cuarenta años del golpe militar en Chile. Reflexiones en torno a conmemoraciones y memorias' (2014) *Revista mexicana de ciencias políticas y sociales* 221.

Young I M, *Responsibility for Justice* (Oxford University Press 2011).

Other Resources

Poder Judicial de Chile, 'Ministros en visita en causas de derechos humanos: el caso Paine' (2013). www.youtube.com/watch?v=GJ3kIT2G9F4.

Part II

Judicial Immunity and the Invalidation of Judicial Decisions

7 Judicial Immunity and Its Limits

The Anglo-American Approach[1]

Nancy Amoury Combs

7.1 Introduction

The doctrine of judicial immunity shields judges from lawsuits that challenge the acts they performed in the course of their judicial duties. Judges are not the only government officials who benefit from some measure of immunity. In many jurisdictions, state governors,[2] police officers,[3] prison officials,[4] and even schoolteachers[5] can assert what is known as 'qualified' immunity, which protects these officials from civil liability for their improper behavior unless they knew or should have known that their conduct was wrongful.[6] By contrast, Anglo-American countries typically bestow 'absolute' immunity on judges and legislators.[7] Absolute judicial immunity prevents judges from being held liable for their wrongful conduct even when they act purely in pursuit of malicious or corrupt ends.[8]

Section 7.2 of this chapter will describe the contours of judicial immunity in common-law countries, with a particular focus on the United States and England.[9] As a comparison with other chapters in this volume reveals, the Anglo-American legal tradition is considerably more protective of judicial acts than is the civil-law tradition. Moreover, as summarized, the doctrine of absolute judicial immunity seems counterintuitive, if not utterly wrong-headed, even outside of the mass atrocity context that is the subject of this book. Why would we want to provide judges with a 'free pass', as it were, against all manner of liability for all manner of misconduct? Anglo-American courts have ready answers to that question, which we will discuss in Section 7.3. But as Section 7.4 explores, those answers have faced more scrutiny and a more skeptical reception in recent years. Scholarly commentators, in particular, have come to view absolute judicial immunity as unwarranted and as undermining some legitimate policy goals. Finally, Section 7.5 of the chapter suggests that the divergence between common law and civil law approaches to judicial immunity, though significant in most realms, is dramatically reduced in the context of mass atrocity. That is, although we cannot be sure because we do not have a plethora of Anglo-American examples in which efforts were made to hold judges responsible for international crimes, our understanding of the judicial immunity doctrine suggests that it might be flexible enough to accommodate efforts to promote international criminal accountability.

DOI: 10.4324/9781003470069-9

7.2 The Doctrine of Judicial Immunity in Anglo-American States: Contours and Limits

In general, the doctrine of judicial immunity protects judges from civil or criminal suits that challenge their judicial acts. This recitation of the rule, though accurate, glosses over a number of constituent elements and limitations. These must be explored in order to fully understand the contours of the doctrine, not least because they vary to some degree from jurisdiction to jurisdiction. To that end, this section will address, in turn: (1) the individuals who can claim judicial immunity; (2) the nature of the acts that are shielded by judicial immunity; (3) jurisdictional exceptions that limit judicial immunity; and (4) judicial immunity as applied to criminal prosecutions and allegations of human rights violations. Although the first three subsections concern elements of judicial immunity that have developed in the context of civil, not criminal, litigation, they are relevant to this volume for two reasons. First, precedent concerning criminal liability is scarce. Second, some Anglo-American jurisdictions bestow on judges the same immunity for criminal and civil acts.

7.2.1 Who Can Claim Judicial Immunity?

Historically, the contours of the judicial immunity doctrine varied depending on the court and the status of the judge. Specifically, judges on inferior courts and judges on courts of limited jurisdiction were provided a more restricted form of judicial immunity than superior court judges.[10] Judicial immunity in England still varies to some degree according to the status of the judge,[11] but judicial immunity "protects all judges, from the lowest to the highest court" in the United States.[12] The same expansive protection applies in other Anglo-American jurisdictions such as Australia,[13] New Zealand,[14] and some Canadian provinces.[15] Moreover, the doctrine of judicial immunity extends to those who perform duties of a judicial nature but who are not judges.[16] Early English cases, for example, extended immunity to (non-judge) members of the General Council[17] and the Board of Guardians.[18] Later cases sought to generalize the principle by providing judicial immunity to all tribunals established under the authority of Parliament or the Crown "which exercise equivalent functions by equivalent procedures and are manned by equivalent personnel as those of the recognized courts of the land".[19] In a similar vein, American and Canadian law provides judicial immunity to administrative law judges and hearings examiners in administrative agencies,[20] as well as to law clerks[21] and those appointed by judges to perform services for the court.[22]

7.2.2 Which Acts Benefit from Judicial Immunity?

Judicial immunity, even as far back as Lord Coke's 17th-century formulation of the doctrine, protected only *judicial* acts.[23] Historically, in England, many functions of the British government were carried out by justices of the peace, whose work was traditionally categorized as either judicial or ministerial.[24] Whereas the ministerial acts of justices of the peace were not protected by immunity, their judicial acts were.[25] This distinction proved unsatisfactory,[26] and for the next several centuries, English courts struggled to define a 'judicial act' in a way that transcended the particularity of context.[27] The courts eventually ended their attempts to formulate a universal rule, instead adopting a flexible approach that emphasized the different characteristics of judicial, administrative, and legislative functions. As relevant to immunity, judicial functions were typically characterized by "the power to hear and determine a controversy, the application of objective standards for the determination of an issue, the declaration of alteration of the rights and obligations of individuals and certain procedural attributes".[28]

US courts seeking to distinguish judicial acts (which are immune) from non-judicial acts (which are not) have considered such factors as whether the act is a typical judicial function; whether the events occurred in a courtroom or somewhere adjacent thereto; whether the act pertained to a case pending before the judge; and whether the events arose from an interaction with the judge in his or her official capacity.[29] These factors are to be construed in favor of finding immunity.[30] Administrative acts are the primary class of acts considered non-judicial.[31] Employment actions taken by judges (such as demotions and dismissals) are typically considered administrative,[32] as is the selection of jurors for county courts.[33] Australian law, by contrast, provides judges with immunity even when they are performing administrative duties.[34]

7.2.3 Jurisdictional Exceptions That Limit Judicial Immunity

Judges may not have immunity when they act outside of their jurisdiction. This jurisdictional limitation on judicial immunity appears to be formulated slightly differently amongst the Anglo-American jurisdictions, but despite the different phrasing, the interpretation of this limitation has largely converged. The English formulation provides immunity even for judicial acts that extend beyond the judges' jurisdiction, so long as the judge holds a good faith belief that she or he had jurisdiction.[35] Similar tests are employed in New Zealand[36] and Australia.[37] The US formulation, by contrast, appears to place little or no emphasis on the judge's perception of his or her jurisdiction, instead providing that judges retain immunity for all judicial acts except those that are undertaken in the "clear absence of jurisdiction".[38] US case law reveals, however, that a judge acts in the clear absence of jurisdiction when she or he acts without jurisdiction, *knowing* that he or she lacks jurisdiction.[39] Because a judge who acts while knowing that she or he *lacks* jurisdiction is the opposite of a judge who holds a good-faith belief that he or she *has* jurisdiction, the US and English positions converge to the rule that immunity is lost when judges deliberately exceed their jurisdiction.[40]

7.2.4 Judicial Immunity as Applied to Criminal Prosecutions

Although Anglo-American jurisdictions uniformly shield judges from civil liability, they vary in their willingness to protect judges from the consequences of their criminal actions. To be sure, everyone agrees that judges "are potentially subject to the criminal law, like all other members of the community".[41] That is, judges have no immunity for criminal behavior that stems from non-judicial acts.[42] So, judges who abuse their spouses, cheat on their taxes, or sexually assault their neighbors will be criminally responsible for those acts, just like anyone else.

But what about criminal acts that judges commit in the course of their judicial duties? Cases and commentary on judicial immunity for criminal suits are somewhat scarce,[43] so our answers must be somewhat tentative in some jurisdictions. Perhaps the least protective jurisdiction is the United States, where authorities appear to agree that judicial immunity does not protect judges from criminal liability.[44] To be sure, US cases have held that the misfeasance of a judge, when acting in his or her official capacity, does not constitute a criminal offense.[45] But judicial immunity also does not protect US judges from criminal liability for acts that would be deemed judicial if a litigant sought money damages from the judge.[46] For that reason, judges charged with criminal corruption, fraud, or soliciting bribes have not been able to assert immunity against those charges.[47] Most commonly, US courts will deny immunity claims against criminal charges on the straightforward ground that "[j]udicial title does not render its holder immune to crime even when committed behind the shield of judicial office".[48] But other cases hold that in committing a crime, a judge acts outside the realm of judicial action.[49] That statement is not wholly accurate, however: judges who rule in favor of a particular litigant for corrupt or pecuniary purposes are engaged in a judicial action. For instance, two judges in the United States who profited from corruptly assigning juveniles to a for-profit detention center were unable to assert immunity to prevent their criminal convictions,[50] but were considered immune from the victims' civil actions for monetary damages.[51] Canadian commentators likewise suggest that common-law judicial immunity does not extend to criminal charges.[52]

Other Anglo-American jurisdictions, by contrast, provide judicial immunity for criminal acts in the same way that they do for civil acts.[53] In *Yeldham v. Rajski*, for instance, Australia's New South Wales Court of Appeals held that the policy supporting judicial immunity for civil actions "is equally applicable to criminal proceedings"[54]; consequently, the court found the criminal action barred. In *Fingelton v. The Queen*,[55] the High Court of Australia highlighted this common-law holding in its interpretation of Queensland legislation that extended judicial immunity to criminal acts. Article 30 of the Queensland Criminal Code provided that, unless contradicted by another provision in the code, "a judicial officer is not criminally responsible" for any acts or omissions "in the exercise of the officer's judicial functions", even if the acts or omissions exceed the officer's judicial authority. Other provisions of the code, including those that criminalized judicial corruption, did contradict article 30's grant of immunity, so the High Court deemed judges to have no immunity from such charges. But absent such a clear contradiction, the Court concluded that "the public policy which supports immunity from civil liability even in respect of conduct alleged to be malicious … extends to immunity from criminal responsibility".[56] Some New Zealand authorities likewise indicate that criminal acts are shielded through judicial immunity,[57] but others suggest that there can be no immunity against criminal prosecutions "in respect of the corrupt exercise of judicial functions".[58]

7.3 The Purposes of Broad Judicial Immunity

Modern Western legal systems generally adhere to the ancient maxim *ubi jus ibi remedium* (where there is a wrong, there is a remedy). Any immunity is thus exceptional and must be justified by important policy considerations,[59] considerations that must be all the more compelling when they need to justify the broad absolute immunity bestowed on Anglo-American judges.

Although commentators have always highlighted the societal benefits that judicial immunity provides, the early US cases that expansively constructed the doctrine did so after harkening to the doctrine's long historical pedigree.[60] Notably, Justice Field proclaimed in 1872 that judicial immunity "has been the settled doctrine of the English courts for many centuries and has never been denied, that we are aware of, in the courts of" the United States.[61] Although the US Supreme Court appealed to this same historical precedent nearly a century later when deciding its most important modern case on judicial immunity,[62] contemporary historians maintain that the US courts misunderstood the English precedent. Feinman and Cohen show that English law does not provide support for a broad rule of judicial immunity and that the precedents were "misread and misapplied by successive generations of American judges".[63] As for 19th-century US precedents on judicial immunity, commentators disagree, with some maintaining that 19th century US courts held "many, if not most judicial officers liable for their wrongful acts much, if not most, of the time"[64] whereas others conclude that the doctrine of judicial immunity was "universally accepted in the state courts of the United States".[65]

Judicial immunity's lengthy historical pedigree, even if it were able to be well established, is not itself a policy justification for that doctrine.[66] So in addition to history, absolute judicial immunity has been said to be supported by a number of important policies. One is the need for finality.[67] Specifically, if litigants were permitted to challenge judges for their behavior on the bench, then, in theory, the litigation may never end: disappointed parties could challenge the actions, first, of the initial judge who ruled against them on the merits of the case and, subsequently, of the judges who ruled against their challenge to the initial judge's actions.[68] Next, it has been claimed that judicial immunity is necessary to maintain the authority of, and respect for, judges. Specifically, the concern is that subjecting judges to lawsuits and scrutinizing their potential mistakes 'would certainly cause a loss of stature'.[69] Third, it is desirable for competent, capable individuals to seek judicial office, and judicial immunity is alleged to be necessary to encourage their willingness to undertake the position.[70] This argument assumes that qualified persons would be unwilling to accept judicial office if doing so meant subjecting themselves to litigation every time a litigant was dissatisfied with one of their rulings.[71]

Although these policy arguments frequently appear in the literature, they are typically dismissed as not particularly weighty, largely because they hypothesize scenarios that are highly unlikely to occur. Litigation is costly, commentators point out, so litigants are not likely to launch *ad infinitum* legal challenges against every judge who ever ruled against them. Moreover, any challenges that they do launch can be summarily dismissed when obviously lacking in merit.[72] Further, capable individuals might be deterred from seeking judicial office if they were provided no immunity whatsoever from litigant suits, but absolute immunity is probably not a *sine qua non* for attracting and retaining qualified judicial candidates. Competent candidates certainly seek other governmental positions, although they are not provided with absolute immunity.[73]

If judicial immunity were supported only by the foregoing arguments, it would stand on a very questionable base. However, another far more persuasive rationale is most commonly invoked in support of absolute immunity: its value in maintaining an independent judiciary.[74] This argument presumes that judges who are not protected from lawsuits will take into account the threat of subsequent litigation when making their decisions.[75] Fear of these lawsuits might cause judges to consciously or unconsciously favor a litigant who seems particularly able and willing to sue if disappointed in the case's outcome.[76] It has thus been said that the primary purpose of judicial immunity "is the preservation of a fearless and independent judiciary whose members will be able to resolve difficult and controversial matters based on their own convictions, uninfluenced by apprehension of civil suits against them by disappointed litigants".[77]

This appeal to judicial independence appears not only in cases[78] and scholarship[79] addressing judicial immunity but also in literature and reports addressing judicial independence.[80] Indeed, the United Nations General Assembly's Basic Principles on the Independence of the Judiciary include a provision recommending that judges have personal immunity for civil suits seeking damages for improper acts in the performance of their judicial duties.[81] In sum, the provision of immunity is considered a core component of an independent judiciary.

7.4 Judicial Immunity: The Backlash

Perhaps judicial immunity always generated considerable controversy. Withholding a remedy to which a victim would otherwise be entitled is predictably fraught and likely to prove unpopular. In recent years in particular, however, judicial immunity has garnered an exceptional number of critics.[82] In the United States, much of this criticism followed the United States Supreme Court case of *Sparkman v. Stump*, where the Court provided especially broad immunity to a judge whose behavior was especially reprehensible.[83] But even cases affording judicial immunity for more matter-of-fact harms have generated widespread discussion and dissatisfaction.[84]

Although most critics of judicial immunity recognize the benefits the doctrine provides, they consider the doctrine's costs to exceed those benefits.[85] These costs pertain primarily to victims who are left without a remedy for the harms they have suffered but also negatively affect a judiciary that faces no accountability or deterrence for wrongful acts.[86] Despite these criticisms, commentators typically do not call for the elimination of judicial immunity but rather seek its qualification.[87] In particular, they propose narrowing some of the elements earlier described.

Thus, although current law broadly considers any judicial act to garner immunity, some reformers would except acts committed with malice.[88] 'Malice' is understood differently by different commentators, with some excepting only acts that are committed in the knowledge that they are illegal or with conscious disregard for their illegality.[89] Others define malice more broadly, to except from immunity any acts motivated by "malice, bad faith, gross negligence, or recklessness".[90] Regardless of the precise contours of the definition, the basic argument is that the justifications for immunity break down when it comes to malicious acts, both because victims of malicious acts are in greater need of a remedy[91] and because when it comes to judges who commit malicious acts, we need to worry less about threatening their independence and more about deterring their malice. Other commentators take aim at the ever-increasing cast of characters who perform tasks deemed sufficiently judicial to generate immunity, maintaining that this expansion is unwarranted.[92] Finally, some reformers adopt a process-based perspective and recommend excluding immunity when the judge's acts prevented the complainant from seeking appellate correction of error[93] or limiting immunity to instances where the judge's actions are consistent with the procedural standards typically expected of judges.[94] One commentator more specifically advises that judicial acts should be immune only when the judge in question has afforded the victim notice, a chance to be heard, and a method of appeal.[95]

Although absolute judicial immunity has been the subject of a great deal of critical commentary both in scholarly literature and in the pages of dissents,[96] these critical views have not prompted courts or legislatures to restrict the doctrine. Indeed, if anything, the doctrine has expanded as more quasi-judicial acts and actors have been provided with immunity[97] and the broad protections once reserved for judges of superior courts have been extended to lower-court judges.[98] Given this recitation of the law and history, one might conclude that Anglo-American judges would surely have immunity for judicial acts that assist in the commission of mass atrocities. Section 7.5, however, suggests that that conclusion may be unwarranted.

7.5 Anglo-American Immunities and Mass Atrocities

Because Anglo-American countries typically bestow absolute immunity on those who perform judicial functions, it might seem difficult, if not impossible, to hold Anglo-American judges criminally responsible for judicial actions that assist or result in mass atrocities. This volume has highlighted two sets of factual scenarios in which efforts have been made to hold judges criminally responsible for such acts. These include judges who sentence defendants to death after trials that are patently unfair, thereby failing to protect the defendants' procedural and due process rights, and judges who fail to provide appropriate legal protection, after which victims are forcibly disappeared, murdered, tortured, or otherwise subjected to illegal violence. As the chapters in this volume have described, efforts to hold judges criminally responsible for acts such as these can easily be foiled by the stringent application of other legal doctrines. These include, in particular, those pertaining to the elements of accomplice liability and *mens rea*. However, my tentative prediction is that

Anglo-American judicial immunities would not pose insurmountable impediments to such prosecutions.

First, as noted in Section 7.4 (above), some Anglo-American jurisdictions draw a sharp distinction between civil suits and criminal prosecutions, providing judges with immunity only for the former. In those jurisdictions, therefore, judicial immunity presents no impediment to a criminal prosecution. To be sure, other jurisdictions bestow the same broad immunity on judicial acts regardless of whether those acts subsequently become the subject of a civil suit seeking damages or a criminal prosecution. Even in these jurisdictions, however, there may be a path to criminal liability, at least when the crimes are mass atrocities.

For one thing, even jurisdictions with expansive judicial immunity doctrines limit their protections to judicial acts that fall within the judge's jurisdiction. To be sure, judges can commit crimes through acts that are self-evidently in the course of their judicial duties. Receiving bribes in exchange for a favorable ruling is just one obvious example of a self-evidently judicial act that constitutes a crime. But, as noted in Section 7.3, courts are often inclined to characterize a judge's criminal acts as non-judicial or as outside of the court's jurisdiction. Thus, if we routinely see courts characterizing run-of-the-mill criminal acts such as bribery and corruption as non-judicial or as in excess of the judges' jurisdiction, then we might expect that that characterization would be all the more prevalent when the crime in question is complicity in a mass atrocity consisting of torture, rape, or murder. That is, we might reasonably predict that courts will find a way to interpret the existing elements of immunity in a way that locates mass atrocities outside of them.

Second, the jurisdictions that bestow the same absolute immunity on both civil and criminal acts do so because the policy reasons justifying immunity in the civil setting apply equally to the criminal setting. Consider, for instance, a judge who inappropriately holds a defendant in pre-trial detention when the law clearly permits that defendant to remain free before trial. Absent immunity, the judge would be vulnerable both to a civil suit seeking damages for false imprisonment and criminal prosecution for the crime of false imprisonment. To the extent that we believe judicial immunity is necessary to permit judges to make independent decisions without threat or fear, then we need to immunize them from both civil suits and criminal prosecutions. Indeed, because deprivation of liberty is a more onerous sanction than money damages, we might conclude that immunity from criminal prosecution is even more important to maintaining judicial independence.

It is, however, difficult to discern any legitimate policy basis for immunizing harms that are as severe as mass atrocities. As noted above, immunity is exceptional and generally considered justified only to advance societal goals that exceed the harms wrought to victims who are denied an otherwise-deserved remedy. Anglo-American jurisdictions generally – perhaps more than they should – weigh this balance in favor of the societal benefits provided by immunity. However, when the victims are as numerous and deserving as those who have suffered mass atrocities, that balance almost certainly shifts. Because we have little or no precedent to appeal to in Anglo-American countries, we can make only educated guesses. The widespread criticism and pushback that greeted absolute judicial immunity when employed to shield ordinary judicial misbehavior nonetheless suggest that shielding the extraordinary judicial misbehavior that results in mass atrocities will generate a tsunami of (justified) opposition.

Notes

1 Ernest W. Goodrich Professor of Law, Robert E. and Elizabeth S. Scott Research Professor, and Director of the Human Security Law Center, William & Mary Law School, United States.
2 See, e.g., SCOTUS, Decision of 29 June 1978, No 76–709, *Butz v Economou,* 438 US 478 (1978) (hereinafter SCOTUS, *Butz*).
3 See, e.g., SCOTUS, Decision of 25 February 1975, No 73–1285, *Wood v Strickland*, 420 US 308 (1975).
4 SCOTUS, Decision of 26 June 1975, No 74–8, *O'Connor v Donaldson*, 422 US 563 (1975).
5 SCOTUS, Decision of 17 April 1974, Nos 72–914, 72–1318, *Scheuer v Rhodes*, 416 US 232 (1974).
6 SCOTUS, *Butz* (n 2).
7 Barth, 'Immunity of Federal and State Judges from Civil Suit – Time for a Qualified Immunity?' (1977) 27 *Case W Rsrv L Rev* 727, 727, 737 n 49.
8 Shaman, 'Judicial Immunity from Civil and Criminal Liability' (1990) 27 *San Diego L Rev* 1, 2.
9 The United Kingdom has three separate legal systems. The one described here applies to England and Wales.
10 Feinman/Cohen, 'Suing Judges: History and Theory' (1980) 31 *S Carolina L Rev* 201, 224–230; Feinman/Cohen 240, explaining the basis for the distinctions.
11 UK Court of Appeals, Decision of 30 July 1974, 1972 S. No 1660 (1975) 1 QB 118, *Sirros v. Moore* held that the distinction between inferior and superior judges was not sustainable, but the *Sirros* judges differed regarding the precise level of immunity to which judges were entitled. Ananian-Welsh/Williams, *Judicial Independence from the Executive* (2014). See also Shetreet/Turenne, *Judges on Trial: The Independence and Accountability of the English Judiciary* (2013) 274 et seq, noting that "superior" judges must act beyond their jurisdiction and in bad faith to lose immunity, whereas inferior judges need only act beyond their jurisdiction.
12 Shaman (1990) (n 8) 5; see also Feinman/Cohen (1980) (n 10) 246, reporting that Justice Field's analysis in *Bradley v Fisher* "began the merger of the doctrinal treatment of superior and inferior judges".
13 In Australia, it is unclear whether the common law provides differing levels of immunity to superior as opposed to inferior judges, though a uniform approach has been cited positively in a number of cases, viz. High Court of Australia, Decision of 28 June 1990, S. 90/001, *Gallo v Dawson* (1988) 82 *ALR* 401, 404; High Court of Australia, Order of 31 March 2011, S97/1998, *Herijanto v Refugee Review Tribunal* (2000) 170 *ALR* 379. The point is largely moot, however, because Australian federal, state, and territory legislation provides inferior court judges with the same immunity as that enjoyed by superior court judges. Ananian-Welsh/Williams (2014) (n 11) 51.
14 New Zealand District Court Act 1947 Section 119 (as substituted on May 20, 2004, by Section 7 of New Zealand District Courts Amendment Act 2004); see also New Zealand Court of Appeal Wellington, Decision of 4 August 1977, Case No Unknown,

Nakhla v McCarthy [1978] 1 *NZLR* 291; Supreme Court New South Wales, Decision of 9 Dec. 1985, CLD No 14007/85, *Moll v Butler* [1985] 4 *NSWLR* 231. See also Harris, 'Remedies and Accountability for Unlawful Judicial Action in New Zealand: Could the Law be Tidier' (2008) *New Zealand L Rev* 483, 494, noting that in 2004, the New Zealand Parliament removed the distinction between superior and inferior judges.

15 See Kligman, 'Judicial Immunity' (2011) 38 *Advoc Q* 251, 256 et seq.

16 Olowofoyeku, *Suing Judges: A Study of Judicial Immunity* (1993) 79.

17 UK Court of Appeal, Decision of 5 May 1890, Case No Unknown, *Partridge v General Council* (1890) 25 QBD 90.

18 UK House of Lords, Decision of 7 March 1921, Case No Unknown, *Everett v Griffiths* (1921) 1 AC 631.

19 Court of Appeal (Civil Division), Decision of 11 April 1979, EWCA Civ J0411-1, *AG v BBC* (1979) 3 All ER 45, 53.

20 SCOTUS, *Butz* (n 2); Kligman (2011) (n 15) 256 et seq.

21 US District Court, S. D. New York, Decision of 18 August 1987, 86 Civ. 8082 (MJL), *Oliva v Heller*, 670 F Supp 523 (SDNY 1987).

22 Scott, *Dismantling American Common Law: Liberty and Justice in our Transformed Courts* (2008) 95. For a discussion of the extension of judicial immunity to those who perform judicial functions, see Chemerinsky, 'Absolute Immunity: General Principles and Recent Developments' (2008) 24 *Touro L Rev* 473, 488–490, and for critical commentary on that extension see generally Johns, 'A Black Robe is not a Big Tent: The Improper Expansion of Absolute Judicial Immunity to Non-Judges in Civil-Rights Cases' (2006) 59 *SMU L Rev* 265.

23 UK Court of King's Bench, Decision of 1 January 1607, Case No Unknown, *Floyd v Barker* (1607) 77 ER 1305, 1307, restricting immunity to anything done by a judge 'as Judge'.

24 Block, '*Stump v. Sparkman* and the History of Judicial Immunity' (1980) *Duke L J* 879, 887.

25 Hawkins, *Pleas of the Crown* (1795) ch 8, § 74.

26 Block notes, for instance, that the judicial-ministerial distinction served to classify many of a justice of peace's administrative duties as judicial, thereby protecting them with immunity. Block (1980) (n 24) 889.

27 Block (1980) (n 24) 891.

28 Block (1980) (n 24) 892.

29 Shaman (1990) (n 8) 9. For a fuller discussion of the qualities of a judicial act, see Olowofoyeku (1993) (n 16) 38–52.

30 US Court of Appeals, Ninth Circuit, Decision of 8 July 1986, No 84-1580, *Ashelman v Pope*, 793 F2d 1072, 1075–1076 (9th Cir 1986).

31 Shaman (1990) (n 8) 10. In Australia, judges have immunity from suits challenging their administrative acts. Magistrates Act 1991 s 21A (Qld). However, it is possible that some acts classified as administrative in Australia would be classified as judicial in the United States. Moreover, US judges who perform administrative acts, though not entitled to absolute immunity, may benefit from the qualified immunity that would be bestowed on other government officials. SCOTUS, Decision of 12 January 1988, No 86–761, *Forrester v White*, 484 US 219, 228–230 (1988) (hereinafter SCOTUS, *Forrester v White*); SCOTUS, Decision of 2 June 1980, No 79–198, *Supreme Court of Virginia v. Consumers Union*, 446 US 719, 731–734 (1980); Crowell, 'North Carolina Superior Judges' Benchbook' (2015) 3.

32 SCOTUS, *Forrester v White* (n 31).

33 SCOTUS, Decision of 1 October 1879, Case No Unknown, *Ex Parte Virginia* 100 US 339 (1879).
34 Judicial Officers Act 1986 (New South Wales) s 44A; Magistrates Act 1991 (Queensland) s 21A; Ananian-Welsh/Williams (2014) (n 11) 49.
35 Olowofoyeku (1993) (n 16) 54.
36 Harris (2008) (n 14) 494.
37 High Court of Australia, Order of 23 June 2005, B58/2004, *Fingleton v The Queen* [2005] HCA 34.
38 SCOTUS, Decision of 28 March 1978, No 76-1750, *Stump v Sparkman*, 435 US 349, 357 (1978) (hereinafter SCOTUS, *Stump*).
39 Olowofoyeku (1993) (n 16) 57.
40 Olowofoyeku (1993) (n 16) 57.
41 Harris (2008) (n 14) 490.
42 Shaman (1990) (n 8) 18. As Olowofoyeku puts it "a judge who commits theft, assault, or murder ... would not be able to claim judicial immunity, since these would have nothing to do with his office as a judge". Olowofoyeku (1993) (n 16) 77.
43 Olowofoyeku notes that the conviction of judges for crimes "is virtually unheard of in England". Olowofoyeku (1993) (n 16) 77; Rosenberg, 'The Doctrine of Judicial Immunity' (1978) 64 *Va L Rev* 833, 856.
44 Shaman (1990) (n 8) 18; Stafford, 'An Overview of Judicial Immunity' (Summer 1977) *State Ct J* 3, 4 ("It is axiomatic that common law judicial immunity has never been extended to shield judges from criminal liability"). See also SCOTUS, Decision of 15 January 1974, No 72-953, *O'Shea v Littleton*, 414 US 488, 503 (1974); SCOTUS, Decision of 2 March 1976, No 74-5435, *Imbler v Pachtman*, 424 US 409, 429 (1976); SCOTUS, Decision of 17 November 1980, No 79-1186, *Dennis v Sparks*, 449 US 29, 31 (1980).
45 See generally Court of Appeals of Kentucky, Decision of 4 May 1951, Case No Unknown, *Commonwealth v Tartar*, 239 SW2d 265 (Ky 1951). In some jurisdictions, the immunities apply only for malfeasance in the performance of judicial tasks undertaken in good faith. See Supreme Court of Alabama, Decision of 1 January 1855, Case No Unknown, *Hamilton v Williams* 26 Ala 527 (1855).
46 Shaman (1990) (n 8) 20.
47 US Court of Appeals, Eighth Circuit, Decision of 8 March 1945, No 12841, *Braatelien v United States* 147 F2d 888 (8th Cir 1945) (hereinafter USCA, *Braatelien*); Supreme Court of Nebraska, Decision of 26 May 1961, No 34916, *McFarland v State*, 172 Neb 251 (1961) (hereinafter S. C. Nebraska, *McFarland*).
48 USCA, *Braatelien* (n 47) 895.
49 S. C. Nebraska, *McFarland* (n 47) 260; US Court of Appeals, Ninth Circuit, Decision of 5 March 1984, No 84-1009, *United States v Claiborne* 727 F2d 842, 848 (9th Cir 1984).
50 Stengel, 'Absolute Judicial Immunity Makes Absolutely No Sense: An Argument for an Exception to Judicial Immunity' (2012) 84 *Temp L Rev* 1071, 1072–1073.
51 Stengel 1074. See also US District Court for the Middle District of Pennsylvania, Memorandum of 9 November 2009, No 3:09-cv-286, *Wallace v Powell* (MD Pa Nov 20, 2009), at 19 et seq finding that the doctrine of judicial immunity necessitated the dismissal of certain claims.
52 Justice Ian Binnie, on behalf of the Supreme Court of Canada, "Judicial Independence in Canada" (Paper delivered at the 2nd Congress of the World Conference on Constitutional Justice, Rio de Janeiro, 16–17 January 2011) at 2.

53 Australia is one of these jurisdictions. See Tsavdaridis/Luo, 'Immunity of Administrative Decisions by Judicial Officers' (2023) 35 *JOB* 14, 14: "Judicial officers enjoy an 'indefeasible' immunity from civil and criminal sanctions for certain acts connected to their office".

54 Court of Appeal, New South Wales, Decision of 4 October 1989, Case No Unknown, *Yeldham v. Rajski*, 18 *NSWLR* 48, 69 (1989).

55 *Fingleton* (n 37).

56 *Fingleton* (n 37) 40.

57 Harris (2008) (n 14) 490 ("If the alleged criminal action taken by the judge is within his or her jurisdiction, that jurisdiction may prevent what would otherwise be regarded as criminal action being held to be such by the courts").

58 Law Commission, *Crown Liability and Judicial Immunity: A Response to Baigent's case and Harvey v Derrick* (Law Com No 37, 1997) para 140.

59 See, e.g., US District Court for the Western District of Wisconsin, Decision of 14 October 1981, No 78-C-155, *Mason v Melendez* 525 F Supp 270, 275 (WD Wis 1981): "Immunity from damages ... represents a sharp departure from the principle that persons are responsible for the harm they inflict upon one another, and that the victims may seek compensation from the perpetrators".

60 Feinman and Cohen (1980) (n 10) 254: "The most important reason usually offered for a rule of judicial immunity is the weight of the past".

61 SCOTUS, Decision of 01 December 1871, Case No Unknown, *Bradley v Fisher* 80 US 335, 347 (1871) (hereinafter *Bradley*).

62 See SCOTUS, *Stump* (n 38) 355.

63 Feinman and Cohen (1980) (n 10) 254; see also Note, 'Judicial Immunity at the (Second) Founding: A New Perspective on § 1983' (2023) 136 *Harv L Rev* 1456, 1464.

64 Feinman and Cohen (1980) (n 10) 237; see also Note, 'Judicial Immunity at the (Second) Founding: A New Perspective on § 1983' (2023) 136 *Harv L Rev* 1456, 1474; Barth (1977) (n 7) 731.

65 Block (1980) (n 24) 900.

66 See Feinman and Cohen (1980) (n 10) 264.

67 Barth (1977) (n 7) 741; Olowofoyeku (1993) (n 16) 187–188; see also *Floyd* (n 23) 1307: "For if the judicial matters ... should be drawn into question, ... there will never be an end of causes, but controversies will be infinite".

68 Barth (1977) (n 7) 741; Feinman and Cohen (1980) (n 10) 266–267.

69 Feinman and Cohen 267; Feldthusen, 'Judicial Immunity: In Search of an Appropriate Limiting Formula' (1980) 29 *UNB L J* 73, 79; Barth (1977) (n 7) 742; Harris (2008) (n 14) 487; SCOTUS, Decision of 1 December 1868, Case No Unknown, *Randall v Brigham* 74 US 523, 536 (1868).

70 Feinman and Cohen (1980) (n 10) 267.

71 Olowofoyeku (1993) (n 16) 189.

72 Barth (1977) (n 7) 741–743.

73 Olowofoyeku (1993) (n 16) 190.

74 Olowofoyeku 193; see also Harris (2008) (n 14) 484; Kligman (2011) (n 15) 251; Law, 'A Tale of Two Immunities: Judicial and Prosecutorial Immunities in Canada' (1990) 28 *Alberta L Rev* 468, 480, 484. SCOTUS, *Stump* (n 38) 354–356 and *Bradley* (n 61) 347.

75 Feinman and Cohen (1980) (n 10) 267; Barth (1977) (n 7) 743; Craig Burgess, 'Judicial Immunity—Right or Wrong' (2006) 31 *Alternative L J* 39, 39.

76 Harris (2008) (n 14) 487.

77 Rosenberg (1978) (n 43) 855.

78 SCOTUS, *Stump* (n 38) 354–356; *Bradley* (n 61) 347.
79 See authorities cited in note 75.
80 Binnie (2011) (n 52) 27: "A further bulwark of judicial independence is that judges enjoy immunity from civil liability for actions taken in the performance of their judicial duties"; Ananian-Welsh/Williams (2014) (n 11) 48: "Judicial immunity from suit is a crucial facet of personal independence"; UNODC, 'Expert Group Meeting on the Role of Judicial Immunities in Safeguarding Judicial Integrity', Vienna, Austria, 26–27 August 2019, Summary Report.
81 UNGA Res 40/32 (29 November 1985) and 40/146 (13 December 1985), para 16 (1988).
82 Sinclair, 'Casenotes Torts – Judicial Immunity: A Sword for the Malicious or a Shield for the Conscientious? Stump v. Sparkman, 98 S.Ct. 1099 (1978)' (1978) 8 *U Balt L Rev* 141, 155; Law (1990) (n 74) 483, maintaining that absolute judicial immunity primarily serves one interest: "the personal interests of the judge who, in acting maliciously, has abused his office".
83 Judge Stump approved the *ex parte* petition of Ora McFarlin to have her 15-year-old daughter surgically sterilized, without conducting a hearing or providing notice to the daughter. SCOTUS, *Stump* (n 38) 349. Critical commentary includes Rosenberg (1978) (n 43) 855 et seq.
84 Burgess (2006) (n 75) 39 (noting that the Australian High Court's provision of immunity in Fingleton v. Queen "has excited much public debate"); Chris Merritt, 'Judicial Immunity Needs an Overhaul' *The Australian*, 4 July 2005.
85 Nagel, 'Judicial Immunity and Sovereignty' (1978) 6 *Hastings Const L Q* 237, 238, 244, arguing that the "weighty policies asserted by the Court in support of absolute judicial immunity do not justify the result".
86 Note, 'Judicial Immunity at the (Second) Founding: A New Perspective on § 1983' (2023) 136 *Harv L Rev* 1456, 1475.
87 See, e.g., Johns (2006) (n 22); Nagel (1978) (n 85) 239, 253.
88 Harris (2008) (n 14) 514–515; Kates, 'Immunity of State Judges under the Federal Civil Rights Acts: *Pierson v. Ray* Reconsidered' (1970) 65 *NWU L Rev* 615, 624; Law (1990) (n 74) 482. As Olowofoyeku puts it, "[a] malice based liability is many commentators' favourite means of setting the limits". Olowofoyeku (1993) (n 16) 205.
89 Block (1980) (n 24) 922.
90 Harris (2008) (n 14) 514.
91 Harris (2008) (n 14) 514.
92 Johns (2006) (n 22) 299.
93 Block (1980) (n 24) 924.
94 Feinman and Cohen (1980) (n 10) 263–264.
95 Waters, 'Judicial Immunity vs. Due Process: When Should a Judge be Subject to Suit?' (1978) 7 *Cato J* 461, 471.
96 See, e.g., Barth (1977) (n 7) 728. See generally, Block (1980) (n 24); see also SCOTUS, Decision of 11 April 1967, Nos 79, 94, *Pierson v Ray*, 386 US 555, 564 (Justice Douglas, dissenting): "To deny recovery to a person injured by the ruling of a judge acting for personal gain or out of personal motives would be 'monstrous.'".
97 See Johns (2006) (n 22).
98 See Harris (2008) (n 14) 484.

Bibliography

Ananian-Welsh R/Williams G, *Judicial Independence from the Executive* (Judicial Conference of Australia 2014).

Barth D K, 'Immunity of Federal and State Judges from Civil Suit – Time for a Qualified Immunity?' (1977) 27 *Case Western Reserve Law Review* 727.

Block J R, 'Stump v. Sparkman and the History of Judicial Immunity' (1980) *Duke Law Journal* 879.

Burgess C, 'Judicial Immunity — Right or Wrong' (2006) 31 *Alternative Law Journal* 39.

Chemerinsky E, 'Absolute Immunity: General Principles and Recent Developments' (2008) 24 *Touro Law Review* 473.

Crowell M, 'North Carolina Superior Judges' Benchbook' (2015) 3.

Feinman J/Cohen R S, 'Suing Judges: History and Theory' (1980) 31 *South Carolina Law Review* 201.

Feldthusen B, 'Judicial Immunity: In Search of an Appropriate Limiting Formula' (1980) 29 *University of New Brunswick Law Journal* 73.

Harris B V, 'Remedies and Accountability for Unlawful Judicial Action in New Zealand: Could the Law Be Tidier' (2008) *New Zealand Law Review* 483.

Hawkins W, *Pleas of the Crown* (7th edn, 1795).

Johns M Z, 'A Black Robe Is Not a Big Tent: The Improper Expansion of Absolute Judicial Immunity to Non-Judges in Civil-Rights Cases' (2006) 59 *Southern Methodist University Law Review* 265.

Kates D B, 'Immunity of State Judges under the Federal Civil Rights Acts: Pierson v. Ray Reconsidered' (1970) 65 *North Western University Law Review* 615.

Kligman R D, 'Judicial Immunity' (2011) 38 *The Advocates Quarterly* 251.

Law J M, 'A Tale of Two Immunities: Judicial and Prosecutorial Immunities in Canada' (1990) 28 *Alberta Law Review* 468.

Nagel R F, 'Judicial Immunity and Sovereignty' (1978) 6 *Hastings Constitutional Law Quarterly* 237.

Olowofoyeku A A, *Suing Judges: A Study of Judicial Immunity* (Oxford University Press 1993).

Rosenberg I M, 'The Doctrine of Judicial Immunity' (1978) 64 *Virginia Law Review* 833.

Scott K, *Dismantling American Common Law: Liberty and Justice in our Transformed Courts* (Lexington Books 2008).

Shaman J M, 'Judicial Immunity from Civil and Criminal Liability' (1990) 27 *San Diego L Rev* 1.

Shetreet S/Turenne S, *Judges on Trial: The Independence and Accountability of the English Judiciary* (2nd edn, Cambridge University Press 2013).

Sinclair J B, 'Casenotes: Torts – Judicial Immunity: A Sword for the Malicious or a Shield for the Conscientious? Stump v. Sparkman, 98 S.Ct. 1099 (1978)' (1978) 8 *University of Baltimore Law Review* 141.

Stafford S P, 'An Overview of Judicial Immunity' (Summer 1977) *State Court Journal* 3.

Stengel T M, 'Absolute Judicial Immunity Makes Absolutely No Sense: An Argument for an Exception to Judicial Immunity' (2012) 84 *Temple Law Review* 1071.

Tsavdaridis T/Luo D, 'Immunity of Administrative Decisions by Judicial Officers' (2023) 35 *Judicial Officers Bulletin* 14.

Waters R C, 'Judicial Immunity vs. Due Process: When Should a Judge be Subject to Suit?' (1978) 7 *Cato Journal* 461.

8 Judicial Immunity

A South American Approach

Javier Wilenmann

This chapter reports on special protections against prosecution or punishment afforded to judges in seven South American countries (Argentina, Bolivia, Chile, Colombia, Ecuador, Peru, and Uruguay). More specifically, it seeks to answer the question of whether immunity protections play a role in defining the conditions under which judges may be held criminally liable for murder and other crimes committed in contexts of dictatorship and state abuse and, generally, for criminal offenses committed while in office.

The chapter makes three claims in this regard. First, faced with the common problem of balancing judicial independence and judicial responsibility, South American legislators have generally used procedural safeguards (rather than substantive rules such as the common law doctrine of absolute immunity). The chapter provides an overview of the content and purposes of these safeguards.

Second, in contrast to common law countries and some civil law jurisdictions, there is no doctrine of immunity or substantive protection of judges in South American law. No South American legal system within the scope of this study has specific provisions on the general conditions under which a judge is held liable for crimes committed while exercising his or her role. Explicit doctrines of this type have played no role in cases such as the Mendoza 'megacase' (*megacausa).*[1] In principle, positive law addresses the problem of balancing judicial independence and judicial responsibility only through procedural safeguards.

Third, and to close, I claim that despite the absence of a doctrine on special substantive conditions for judges' criminal liability, South American countries are still faced with the same institutional challenge that common law addresses through the doctrine of absolute immunity,[2] or German law, through the doctrine of the *Sperrwirkung* of *Rechtsbeugung.*[3] Judges do make decisions that have significant impact on individual rights and can certainly raise a justification defense based on acting within the scope of their jurisdiction. The configuration of a system in which judges are commonly held criminally liable for their actions might impact their independence and willingness to apply certain laws. At the same time, if the defense is too broad, judicial responsibility would be jeopardized. Tracing the contours of what I refer to as the 'exercise of jurisdiction defense' is thus a significant task, one that has not yet been undertaken by Chilean doctrinal work and

DOI: 10.4324/9781003470069-10

caselaw. I apply the insights obtained from the exchanges contained in this volume to tackle the contours of the exercise of jurisdiction defense in relation to three different types of cases identified throughout this volume.

8.1 The Question of Judicial Criminal Liability and the South American Model of Judicial Protection

Legal orders face several challenges regarding the question of whether judges should be made criminally liable for offenses committed in their office, such as when, under dictatorial regimes, they apply the regime's rules to impose harms on others or willfully tolerate state crime and fail to defend its victims. On the one hand, judges commonly impose forms of coercive harsh treatment on others that would count as criminal offenses when applied outside of the scope of their office. Imposing the death penalty implies killing someone and would in most contexts be judged to constitute murder, just as sentencing someone to imprisonment would ordinarily amount to kidnapping. It is, however, the duty of judges to impose punishments as set down in law. Moreover, it is commonly accepted that judicial independence is an important pillar of the rule of law: judges should be protected from harassment by the parties on which they impose the law or by political or other powerful actors.

In theory we can differentiate two broad types of provision that may limit the criminal conviction of judges or may make it more difficult. We can use the term 'substantive limitations' to denote those rules or doctrines that establish specific, more stringent conditions for criminal liability of judges. For example, a certain legal order may require that judges should have acted with intent or malice if they are to be held criminally liable, whereas common citizens can be held criminally liable for acts executed with knowledge or recklessness.[4] Procedural safeguards, on the other hand, do not alter the rules of criminal liability but rather alter the rules applicable to ordinary criminal trials.

In most South American countries, judges are protected against prosecution by the existence of special criminal procedural safeguards. Table 8.1 provides an overview of these protections.

The special provisions that benefit judges may appear in three different forms: admissibility procedures, special procedures for charging a judge and placing them on trial, and (apparent) substantive limitations on the scope of criminal liability.

The admissibility model can be found in countries including Argentina and Chile. Here, procedural safeguards take the form of pre-trial procedures that control the admissibility of indicting a judge. These procedures are meant to limit the tactical use of criminal charges against judges. A criminal investigation will not take effect unless a tribunal with special standing admits it in a special procedure. If admitted, the judge will be suspended from office, and ordinary procedural measures – including pre-trial detention – will be applicable. The case can then move to a normal criminal trial.

Table 8.1 Legal safeguards against prosecution of judges in South American countries

Country	*Procedural safeguards against prosecution*	*Type of procedure*	*Constitutional origin of safeguards*	*Substantive immunity provisions*
Argentina	Yes	Pre-indictment jury	Yes	No
Bolivia	No	N/A	No	No
Chile	Yes	Pre-indictment admissibility procedure	Yes	Apparent
Colombia	Yes	Special procedure to indict judges	Yes	No
Ecuador	Yes	Special procedure to indict judges	Yes	Apparent
Peru	Yes	Special procedure to indict judges	Yes	No
Uruguay	No	N/A	No	No

In Argentina, a committee composed of legislators, judges, and lawyers decides on the admissibility of an indictment against a judge.[5] In Chile, that same process takes place before a Court of Appeals via a special procedure known as a '*querella de capítulos*'.[6]

Other countries go beyond the establishment of a pre-indictment admissibility procedure of this sort. Colombia, Ecuador, and Peru, for example, establish special procedures for the entirety of any criminal process involving a judge. In Colombia, Art. 235 of the Constitution makes the standing to investigate and charge a judge the sole prerogative of the country's chief prosecutor,[7] and requires that all related procedures be heard before the Supreme Court. The rationale for such stipulations varies from offering protection against intimidation to ensuring that the parties responsible for charging and adjudicating will have enough power or prestige to hold the judge accountable.[8]

Finally, it is not uncommon in the South American constitutional tradition to establish some provisions that seem to limit the substantive scope of judicial criminal liability. These could be used as provisions granting some sort of immunity for offenses committed in office. Article 79 of the Chilean Constitution – like Art. 172 of the Ecuadorian constitution – provides a fitting example. Art. 79 declares that "judges are personally liable for the offences of bribery, malfeasance and denial of justice, and in general for all forms of prevarication that they incur in the exercise of their office (…)".[9] Article 324 of Chile's Organic Code of Courts rules out application of the offence(s) of malfeasance and denial of justice to members of the Supreme Court.[10]

In theory, such provisions could be construed as rules that limit the scope of criminal liability of judges for acts in office solely to corruption and malfeasance offenses or that require such an offense to have occurred in order to allow judges to be charged and sentenced for other crimes (such as judicial murder). Nonetheless, this does not seem at all to be the case when we consider how the law actually operates in action, as will be seen in the next section, below. Accordingly, then, the 'South American model' for dealing with the question of the criminal liability of judges is mostly procedural. What are the ideas and objectives that have given rise to these procedures?

8.2 Judicial Independence, Responsibility, and Separation of Powers in the Protection of Judges against Criminal Prosecution

The provisions that limit the criminal liability of judges in the South American countries examined here are generally connected to questions of judicial independence, judicial responsibility,[11] and, in some cases, separation of powers.[12]

By far the most prevalent approach is to connect the question of judicial criminal liability to tensions between judicial independence and judicial responsibility[13] – an approach that is also commonly adopted in the common law in regard to absolute immunity.[14] Judicial independence is generally seen as a predictor of high-quality justice, the absence of corruption, and therefore the legitimacy of justice.[15] Judicial independence would potentially be threatened if there were to be a permanent risk of prosecution of judges for their decisions: the instrumental use of such powers of public prosecution would amount to a political danger.[16] Despite the inaction displayed by judges in contexts of dictatorship,[17] South American commentators still assume that law and the courts act as a check on political authoritarianism and provide protections to citizens. The principle of separation of powers is sometimes invoked to justify limits or conditions on liability: the concern being that the executive branch could instrumentalize prosecutorial services to harass judges and thereby limit their independence. Although this argument has lost some of its relevance as criminal prosecution services have acquired an ad-hoc form of constitutional autonomy, it is still invoked by some scholars.

The argument moreover gains some plausibility if we consider the incentives that private parties may have to harass judges (and prosecutors). In South America, private prosecution initiated through the presentation of criminal complaints (*querellas*) is not uncommon.[18] Private parties could therefore put pressure on judges by threatening them with private prosecution or by attempting to force prosecutors to make certain decisions regarding the bringing of charges. Private actors could (and do) file criminal complaints for malfeasance of justice and/or abuse of office over judges' or prosecutors' decisions. This would further jeopardize judicial independence unless safeguards are set.

Questions of independence are typically balanced against questions of judicial responsibility. It has become commonplace to resist special protections for higher authorities, including judges. Constitutional provisions with long-ago origins, such as article 79 of the Chilean Constitution (which is rooted in constitutional texts from the 1820s and 1830s), already championed explicit declarations of judicial responsibility. More recent constitutions tend to go even further, not including any special safeguards, and simply declaring that judges are to be held responsible for their acts in the same way as any other citizen. This is the case of the new (2009) constitution of Bolivia. Perhaps its most striking manifestation is, however, to be found in article 23 of the current Constitution of Uruguay: "All judges are liable before the law, for even the smallest aggression against the rights of private persons, and for any deviation from the procedures established by law".[19] Most legal systems, however, tend to assume that they have reached a balance between independence and responsibility by establishing procedural safeguards.

8.3 Lack of Acceptance of Explicit Doctrines of Substantive Limitation of Judicial Liability

On the basis of the above, then, I would argue that immunity arguments have played little or no role in South America as far as the judgment of cases of judicial murder is concerned.

No South American country included in the study has established, in practice, limitations to the general responsibility of judges. Such an argument is nowhere to be found in Argentina's 2017 Mendoza *megacausa* sentence,[20] for example, nor do any such considerations feature in the Chilean Supreme Court's grant of extradition of Argentine judge Otiliano Romano in connection with that same *megacausa*.[21]

This assertion is not based solely on factors connected to the *law on the books*. On the contrary, the law on the books – at least in Chile – offers some grounds on which an immunity defense could be built. The provision enshrined in Art. 79 of the Chilean Constitution could, in theory, be mobilized as an argument to limit the criminal responsibility of judges for actions in office, solely to crimes connected to malfeasance of justice. Such a reading would moreover exclude altogether criminal responsibility of any sort for members of the Supreme Court. To construe the article in this way would entail reading the textual phrases "judges are personally responsible for bribery (...) and in general all forms of malfeasance of justice in office" as "judges are *only* responsible for bribery (...) and all forms of malfeasance of justice in office" or "judges are *only* personally responsible in office if they have perpetrated bribery (...) or any form of malfeasance of justice in office".

An argument of this sort would proceed as follows: the article 79 provision would – it is contended – have no effect if construed simply as a declaration that judges are responsible for malfeasance of justice in office. This is given that there is no provision in the Chilean Constitution limiting the power of the legislature to criminalize corrupt judicial actions, and considering that by the time of the enactment of Chile's Constitutions of 1832 (and especially, of 1925 and 1980), malfeasance of justice had been long part of criminal law. For the provision to have any meaningful content, it must therefore, runs the argument, be construed as a limitation of liability whereby judges are only to be held responsible for these specific crimes in respect of their actions in office. Or, in an alternative reading, they could not be held criminally liable unless they had incurred responsibility for malfeasance of justice.

Such an argument has several shortcomings as a matter of constitutional interpretation. For one, it transforms the meaning of the constitutional provision from a declaration that judges must be considered liable in such cases to a declaration that they are only liable in those cases. Secondly, it is simply wrong to assume that the provision would have no effect unless construed as a limitation to criminalization: it is first and foremost a political declaration that the reach of responsibility (also) stretches to judges.[22]

Notwithstanding the argument's formal merits or demerits, the central point for our purposes is its current (lack of) acceptance. In South America, the construction of special standards for prosecuting a judge over criminal offenses committed in office – as in the notorious case of US criminal law -[23] is to this author's knowledge neither accepted in practice nor defended in the literature. As an argument with no acceptance, then, a technicality such as an immunity defense is particularly unlikely to convince when applied to questions of judicial murder and other heinous crimes committed in dictatorial contexts.

8.4 On Liability of Judges for Offences Perpetrated in Office: The 'Exercise of Jurisdiction' Defense

I have argued so far that neither statutory provisions nor doctrines provide substantive immunity to judges for crimes committed in office, including crimes committed when they exercise jurisdiction. Such a notion is alien to South American legal culture, as far as the countries examined here are concerned.

This contention does not, of course, imply that the prosecution of criminal offenses committed by judges in office is free of particular challenges and specific defenses; it only claims that what is in play is not special doctrine.

Judges can make use of an ordinary defense when faced with prosecution for crimes committed in office. The argument functions as follows: when acting according to law and within the confines of their office, judges are allowed to impose certain hardships on defendants and parties that would otherwise amount to felonies. Criminal judges can deprive a person of their liberty in various ways: by issuing a warrant for their arrest, by placing them on remand (i.e., pretrial detention), or by imposing a custodial sentence. Several other judicial actions that would otherwise amount to criminal offenses are similarly mandated by law. Their lawfulness is a consequence of the fact that the judge is using legal powers and acting within the scope of his or her office. Thus, acting within one's jurisdictional powers is very obviously a justification that can be mobilized as a defense against a criminal accusation. I will refer to this, as above, as the 'exercise of jurisdiction' defense.

Although no South American country in this study has a specific provision relating to the exercise of jurisdiction justification, most criminal codes contain general provisions that allow an officeholder to raise a defense of having acted within the scope of their duty or powers. This is the case, inter alia, of article 10, no. 10 of the Chilean Criminal Code; article 34, no. 4 of the Argentine Criminal

Code; article 32, no. 2 of the Colombian Criminal Code; and article 20, no. 8 of the Peruvian Criminal Code. Criminal courts will normally connect the exercise of jurisdiction defense to such provisions.[24]

Unfortunately, there is no strong track record of doctrinal work or caselaw that would allow the tracing of the precise contours of this defense. From a functional point of view, the challenges of adequately demarcating the content of the exercise of jurisdiction defense are expressions of the same problem faced by German law in regard to the '*Sperrwirkung*' doctrine or Anglo-American law over absolute immunity. Namely, if the justification is too narrowly constructed, judges could be made criminally liable for any error in applying law. If the justification is too broadly constructed, there would be no criminal accountability of judges whatsoever.

By identifying at least three types of cases connected to the issue of judicial criminal responsibility, the insights provided by this volume may prove an invaluable starting point for tracing the contours of this defense.

A first group of cases relates to judicial decisions in anomalous state contexts, leading to the death of persons or other significant forms of harm against individuals. There are two significant issues surrounding the application of the exercise of jurisdiction defense in such cases. First, the 'legal' provisions applied by the judge may in fact have a weak legal pedigree, as in anomalous state contexts, the production of law ceases to follow its normal conditions or procedures. The exercise of jurisdiction defense is not applicable if based on legal provisions with an ostensibly weak pedigree. While it is true that judges may be pressured to comply with an anomalous regime, the relevant defense in that case is duress. Second, even when judges apply laws that do not have a weak legal pedigree, their decisions may be based on dubious legal grounds and oriented only at complying with the regime. Judges who make ostensibly wrong decisions that lead to the death or harm of a regime's victims should face responsibility for their actions.

A second group of cases relates to failure to protect individuals in contexts of state violence. This has been the most prevalent ground of contestation in the aftermath of South American dictatorships. Making judges individually liable for the consequences of state violence in such contexts would be exaggerated. This objection is not, however, based primarily on the exercise of jurisdiction defense, but rather on the more stringent conditions under which individuals are liable for failing to prevent harm. The exercise of jurisdiction defense plays only a limited role in this regard. If, under the applicable law, judges did not have the legal duty and power to prevent harm, then they cannot be made liable.

Finally, a third group of cases relates to harm brought about through the application of law in normal state contexts. The exercise of jurisdiction defense should play a major role in these cases. First, judges cannot face any negative legal consequence for correctly applying the law. Second, even if their decisions end up being erroneous, they should not be held liable if they acted under a plausible construction of law or of the facts of a case. They can only be made liable when knowingly making decisions that cannot be construed as a proper application of law.

Notes

1 A large-scale criminal case pursued in Argentina, in which a total of four judges and prosecutors were convicted, in 2017, over dictatorship-era crimes against humanity, including aggravated homicide and illegal deprivation of liberty. See, in particular, Palermo's chapter in this volume and other contributions.

2 For which, see Nancy Combs' chapter in this volume.

3 In essence, the preclusive effect of the absence of malfeasance, i.e., a block on prosecution of judges for criminal offenses unless there has (also) been judicial perversion of justice (*Rechtsbeugung*) See the opening chapter of this volume and discussion of these doctrines in various other contributions, including the chapter by Rojas.

4 See Nancy Combs' chapter in this volume for a reconstruction of the doctrine of absolute immunity – a very stringent form of substantive limitation.

5 These procedures are regulated in Articles 53 and 115 of the Argentine Constitution and in Act 25320 – also known as the "*Ley de Fueros*" (Act of Special Protections).

6 See Chilean Code of Criminal Procedure, art. 424.

7 Fiscal General de la Nación.

8 See Gómez Pajaveau/Farfán Molina, 'El fuero de investigación y juzgamiento penal de altos funcionarios del Estado. Problemas procesales' (2015) 36 *Rev. derecho penal criminol.* 87, 89 et seq.

9 "Los jueces son personalmente responsables por los delitos de cohecho, falta de observancia en materia sustancial de las leyes que reglan el procedimiento, denegación y torcida administración de justicia y, en general, de toda prevaricación en que incurran en el desempeño de sus funciones. Tratándose de los miembros de la Corte Suprema, la ley determinará los casos y el modo de hacer efectiva esta responsabilidad".

10 "Esta disposición no es aplicable a los miembros de la Corte Suprema en lo relativo a la falta de observancia de las leyes que reglan el procedimiento ni en cuanto a la denegación ni a la torcida administración de la justicia".

11 In this sense, they are seen as functional equivalents of absolute judicial immunity in Anglo-American law. See Shaman, 'Judicial Immunity from Civil and Criminal Liability' (1990) 27 *San Diego L Rev* 1, 2 et seq.

12 There is little academic literature on the subject. The most prevalent type of publication on the subject consists of theses published by law students at the end of their studies. In Colombia, publications of this type generally treat the question of protection against prosecution as a matter of separation of powers. See, for example, López, *Segunda instancia para los aforados constitucionales* (2021). Aguirre/Cárdenas, *Integralidad del fuero constitucional colombiano* (2015).

13 This is the frame adopted by Bordalí, 'Independencia y Responsabilidad de los Jueces' (2003) 14 *Rev derecho (Valdivia)* 164; Bordalí, 'El Régimen de Responsabilidad Disciplinaria de los Jueces Chilenos y su Inadecuación a las Exigencias Constitucionales' (2018) 24 *Ius et Praxis* 516; Atria, 'Jurisdicción e independencia judicial: El Poder Judicial como poder nulo' 4 *REJ* (2004) 119, 133.

14 See Shaman (1990) (n 11) 4. In contrast, because of the specific configuration of the Nazi (national-socialist) regime, the driving force behind the German discussion of judicial liability was not the balance between independence and responsibility but rather the delineation of the outer boundaries of strict formal adherence to the law. See the contribution by Jeßberger and Kuhli in this volume.

15 This assumption has been challenged recently, specifically in the case of Chile, where indicators of independence have substantially risen and yet trust in the judicial branch has

plummeted. Hilbink, 'Jueces, ciudadanía, y estado democrático de derecho: Construir la confiabilidad para recuperar la confianza' (2019) 5 *LALS* 4–6.

16 There is an emerging literature on the use of prosecution to harass political rivals in Latin America. Vegh Weis, 'What Does *Lawfare* Mean in Latin America? A New Framework for Understanding the Criminalization of Progressive Political Leaders' (2023) 25 *Punishm Soc* 909, 917–920. So far, the literature has not addressed its link to questions of judicial independence.

17 See, for instance, Garretón/Garretón, 'La Democracia Incompleta En Chile: La Realidad Tras Los Rankings Internacionales' (2010) 30 *RCP* 114, 122 et seq; Hilbink, *Judges beyond Politics in Democracy and Dictatorship: Lessons from Chile* (2007).

18 On the subject of private prosecution in Latin America, see the (generally optimistic) approach taken by Michel/Sikkink, 'Human Rights Prosecutions and the Participation Rights of Victims in Latin America' (2013) 47 *Law Soc Rev* 873, or Michel, *Prosecutorial Accountability and Victims' Rights in Latin America* (2018).

19 "Todos los jueces son responsables ante la ley, de la más pequeña agresión contra los derechos de las personas, así como por separarse del orden de proceder que en ella se establezca", author's translation.

20 Tribunal Oral Federal de Mendoza 1, Decision of 22 November 2018, Sentencia No. 1836. The reasoning can be found at: https://juiciosmendoza6.files.wordpress.com/2018/12/fundamentos-14000125-2006.pdf.

21 (Chilean) Corte Suprema, Judgment of 18 June 2013, Roll No. 290-2012.

22 In this sense, see also Bordalí (2018) (n 13) 516.

23 See Nancy Combs' contribution to this volume.

24 A similar point is made by Viganó, in this volume, regarding Italian criminal law.

Bibliography

Aguirre I/Cárdenas V, *Integralidad del fuero constitucional colombiano* (2015). https://repository.eafit.edu.co/server/api/core/bitstreams/ff43f91a-c299-4001-9b32-4178dd2fb7b6/content.

Atria F, 'Jurisdicción e independencia judicial: El Poder Judicial como poder nulo' (2004) 5 *Revista de Estudios de la Justicia* 119.

Bordalí A, 'El Régimen de Responsabilidad Disciplinaria de los Jueces Chilenos y su Inadecuación a las Exigencias Constitucionales' (2018) 24 *Ius et Praxis* 513.

Bordalí A, 'Independencia y Responsabilidad de los Jueces' (2003) 14 *Revista de Derecho (Valdivia)* 159.

Garretón M A/Garretón R, 'La Democracia Incompleta en Chile: la Realidad tras los Rankings Internacionales' (2010) 30 *Revista de Ciencia Política (Santiago)* 115.

Gómez Pajaveau C A/Farfán Molina F J, 'El fuero de investigación y juzgamiento penal de altos funcionarios del Estado. Problemas procesales' (2015) 36 *Revista Derecho Penal y Criminología* 87.

Hilbink L, *Judges beyond Politics in Democracy and Dictatorship: Lessons from Chile* (Cambridge University Press 2007).

Hilbink L, 'Jueces, ciudadanía, y estado democrático de derecho: Construir la confiabilidad para recuperar la confianza' (2019) 5 *Latin American Legal Studies* 1.

López G, *Segunda instancia para los aforados constitucionales* (2021). https://repository.unilibre.edu.co/bitstream/handle/10901/22615/Art.%20Trabajo%20de%20grado.pdf?sequence=1&isAllowed=y.

Michel V, *Prosecutorial Accountability and Victims' Rights in Latin America* (Cambridge University Press 2018).
Michel V/Sikkink K, 'Human Rights Prosecutions and the Participation Rights of Victims in Latin America' (2013) 47 *Law & Society Review* 873.
Shaman J, 'Judicial Immunity from Civil and Criminal Liability' (1990) 27 *San Diego Law Review* 1.
Vegh Weis V, 'What Does *Lawfare* Mean in Latin America? A New Framework for Understanding the Criminalization of Progressive Political Leaders' (2023) 25 *Punishment & Society* 909.

9 Invalidation of Judicial Decisions in Cases of Farcical Prosecutions

A German Perspective

Markus Abraham

9.1 Overview

There are judicial decisions that are based on farcical prosecutions. Such decisions should be invalidated. This is the premise that I was invited to address in this chapter. I will proceed by exploring, in turn, four questions that arise from the premise. First, what is a farcical prosecution? The chapter approaches the phenomenon of farce through looking at literature, namely, Friedrich Dürrenmatt's novel 'Die Panne'.[1] Second, the text goes on to ask whether it is possible and appropriate to address farcical prosecution by drawing parallels with existing categories of German criminal law doctrine: specifically, the tripartite categorization of deficient judgments as inequitable, unjust, or ineffective per se. The third question, arising from experiences of invalidation in the recent German past, asks how judicial decisions handed down during periods of systemic injustice were dealt with in practice by successor regimes. Here, the chapter provides a broad-brush outline of the post-hoc overturning of gravely flawed Nazi-era and East German socialist-era sentences. A fourth and final question tackled is whether the concept of 'farcical prosecution' makes sense. The chapter argues in the affirmative, positing that a trial should be considered a farce when judges pursue a goal other than a just application of the law. However, since the condition of malice on the part of the judge would seem to narrow the concept of farce unduly, the chapter also proposes making use of what in international criminal law is referred to as the 'policy element', namely, the context element in crimes against humanity.

9.2 What Is a Farce? When Can a Prosecution Be Considered a Farce?

The notion of 'farce' or 'farcical' as applied to prosecutions may at first sight appear stimulating and far-fetched in equal measure. The derivation of the term, from the Latin '*farcire*', has to do with the act of cramming one thing into another, and its possible deployment as a legal term was certainly unfamiliar to this author at the outset of the chapter. However, since the word is in common usage in the field of literature, I decided to see whether literature could be useful for approaching the phenomenon. In particular, I settled on the work of Friedrich Dürrenmatt, a Swiss author renowned for his mastery of satire, paradox, and farce. In his novel 'Die

DOI: 10.4324/9781003470069-11

Panne', Dürrenmatt has three trained lawyers – a prosecutor, a judge, and a defense lawyer – hold a criminal trial. The reader may initially think there is nothing particularly special about this. At least two aspects of the narrative, however, take us into the arena of farce. First, all three of the legal professionals are retired and no longer hold office. Second, the 'prosecution' and resulting decision come about in very peculiar circumstances. The 'defendant', a traveler whose car has broken down, is invited to dinner by chance. What begins as a lavish dinner, however, turns into a trial directed against him on charges that are only established during the course of the meal. At one point, the dialogue famously goes as follows: the traveler asks, "What crime am I charged with?", to which the prosecutor replies, "That's an unimportant point (…) a crime is always to be found".[2] The prosecutor then uncovers, through sharp-witted interrogation, what becomes the basis for an accusation: we learn the traveler is in some sense responsible for the death of his boss. At the end of the trial, as the meal reaches its dessert phase, a guilty verdict is delivered and the death sentence passed.

We have already noted how the status of the protagonists and the entirely accidental circumstances contribute to making the trial a farce. It is worth considering which elements of the trial, as Dürrenmatt describes it do not contribute to the overall identity of the trial contained therein as a farce. It is not the criminal provision – the prohibition on killing – that is farcical here. Nor is the specific interpretation of that prohibition really farcical: the charge of murder is based on two assumptions that, while rather far-fetched, are not entirely implausible. First, it transpires that the accused had known that his boss had previously suffered a severe heart attack, with a high risk of recurrence if subjected to great excitement. Second, while in full knowledge of this situation, the accused had entered into an affair with his boss's wife, later ensuring that his boss found out. The revelation caused another heart attack, this one fatal. While at the dinner table, the accused explicitly confirmed that his conduct had moreover been intentionally harmful. Seen in this light, neither the legal provision nor its particular application is what makes the prosecution appear farcical.[3] It is only the courtroom scenario that turns this trial into a paradigm of farce. While this is due in part to the lack of actual legitimacy as a court, it mainly has to do with the disregard for procedural rules. Particularly, there is no sign of respect for the rules that ought to protect any accused party from becoming the object of a punitive prosecution that, like the one depicted here, displays great creativity in finding and constructing accusations.

This circumstance, i.e., the fact that it is non-compliance with procedural rules that makes the prosecution a farce, is what distinguishes this fictional scenario from many actual instances of injustice occurring within an unconstitutional, unjust, or unlawful state ('*Unrechtsstaat*'). In settings of systemic injustice, it is not uncommon for the criminal provision or its interpretation to also be farcical in and of itself. For an example of farcical law, we might look to *Wehrkraftzersetzung*,[4] an anti-sedition provision under Nazi law that criminalized activities deemed to adversely affect the Armed Forces. Under this norm, which was primarily aimed to stifle any sign of pacifism,[5] statements considered defeatist could be punished with the death penalty. The already capacious notion of defeatism was further expanded by courts' interpretation of the norm.[6] An alternative example is the 1939 "Decree against Public Enemies" (*Verordnung gegen Volksschädlinge*),[7] with its stipulation of 'taking advantage of the state of war' as a particular aggravating circumstance, one which of course could be – and was – deemed to apply in almost any conceivable case. Even the nervous tension felt by most of the population at the outbreak of war was deemed to fall under this definition.[8] Seeking, instead, for examples of farcical interpretation, one could cite the ways in which already vague criminal law provisions were actually applied.[9] The path toward farcical interpretation was smoothed, for example, by invoking the 'common sense of the people' (*gesundes Volksempfinden*) or 'the will of the Führer' (*Führerwille*) as central interpretive criteria and sources of law.[10]

Both substantive law and its interpretation can, then, give rise to farcical decision-making. Where the law itself is at fault, the focus must be on the legislator. If interpretation is the culprit, however, the spotlight falls more directly on judicial actors, and it may be considered more appropriate to attempt to formulate a reproach against them for past misdeeds. A provisional conclusion may be drawn here: some prosecutions are farcical simply and solely because they proceed on the basis of farcical laws. Here, the farce has been created by the legislature. There are also, however, prosecutions that are made farcical by their questionable interpretation of substantive law. A farce that takes place solely in the procedural sphere may meanwhile be invisible from a substantive legal point of view, as Dürrenmatt shows us.

9.3 Categories of Wrongful Judgments in German Criminal Law

Before returning to the idea of substantive and procedural aspects that may make a prosecution a farce, I would like to draw attention to a potentially helpful distinction that has been drawn in German criminal law theory on wrongful judgments. The doctrinal jurisprudence on this topic might be helpful in further developing the concept of farcical prosecution. Three categories are worth exploring for present purposes. First, judgments that have been allowed to stand – for example, by courts of appeal – despite suffering from acknowledged defects. While their shortcomings potentially render these judgments objectionable and excessively harsh, they have been deemed acceptable. They can be labeled inequitable judgments (category one). A second category comprises judgments which, in retrospect, are found to have fundamental flaws that require the annulment of their legal force. The injustice that they entail appears so intolerable that the principle of legal peace that the decision was supposed to establish must take a back seat to ideas of justice or truth. These are unjust verdicts (category 2): judgments that are effective but might be annulled by an act of invalidation.[11] A third category can be detected in jurists' discussion of German criminal law: judgments that are already without effect *per se* (category 3).[12] Within this category a further distinction can be drawn between void judgments, category 3(a),[13] and non-judgments, category 3(b). Void judgments, while succeeding in bringing a trial to conclusion, have extremely serious defects. The examples we will discuss here constitute show trials, in which the outcome was predetermined. This category, category 3(a), also covers judgments which, taken as a whole, are so flawed that the authority of the law and the administration of justice would be more seriously undermined by upholding them than by designating them invalid.[14] Category 3(b), non-judgments, is reserved for pronouncements that merely have the form of a judgment but whose underlying prosecution and/or trial is a farce. This happens when a 'court' is not a court at all, such as in the case of revolutionary tribunals or Dürrenmatt's imagined scenario. In such cases, we can talk about what Spendel has termed 'naked murder by pretending to judge'[15]. The difference between categories 3(a) and 3(b) is not merely formal; it has implications for judicial liability, as we will see below.

An example of category 3 can be seen if we consider the court martial that took place in the German town of Lohr in the spring of 1945, in the final weeks of the Second World War.[16] At a time when US tanks were rolling through the town unchallenged, a local doctor was sentenced to death on the charge of '*Wehrkraftzersetzung*', i.e., subversion of the Armed Forces and giving succor to the enemy. The accusation came about because the man was supposedly poised to go out to meet US soldiers with a white flag, aiming to save the town through surrender. His trial was patently absurd: the role of public prosecutor was taken by someone with no legal knowledge; the application for the death sentence was made by the presiding judge; the accused – known to be suffering from depression and drug addiction – had no defense representation and spoke only one single coherent sentence over the course of the proceedings. The 'facts' were established in just thirty minutes, based on the testimony of a sole prosecution witness.[17] As can be seen, the trial's deficiencies are manifold. Wessel concludes that, in view of the shortcomings, this episode clearly belongs in category three, judgments without effect. In retrospect, however, it is not possible to say with certainty whether the episode's protagonists always intended to carry out the killing, with the trial as solely a pretext – murder in the guise of justice – or whether the summary trial, despite all its legal flaws, was a more or less serious enterprise. As this inevitably remains a matter of speculation, Wessel chooses to classify the proceeding outcome as a void judgment: category 3(a), in the taxonomy suggested here.[18]

In the light of this categorization, three points are particularly noteworthy. The first is how closely the tripartite categorization of inequitable, unjust, and ineffective judgments tracks Gustav Radbruch's formula about unjust law (Radbruch discusses, in turn, harsh laws; laws that constitute intolerable injustice; and laws that do not strive for justice and are therefore no longer law at all).[19] The second point to underline concerns the consequences of this categorization for the criminal liability of judges. Prevailing interpretation of the German provision on judicial misconduct (section 339 of the German Criminal Code) holds that judges' liability for deprivation of liberty or homicide is barred in all types of judgment – with the sole exception of non-judgments, our category 3b[20] – unless deliberate malfeasance in office (i.e., section 339) can be proven. In practice, German courts have historically set such high standards for a finding of such malfeasance[21] that criminal liability has almost always been denied in cases of attempted prosecution of Nazi-era judges.[22] So, for instance, in the Lohr case mentioned above, assessed by

Wessel as falling into category 3(a), an intentional violation of the law would have to be confirmed before the judge could be prosecuted for other charges such as deprivation of liberty or manslaughter.[23]

As a third point, I would like to argue that it does not make sense to reserve the label of farcical prosecution solely for category 3 cases. This is mainly because German judicial practice has made such very limited use of category 3 that any such restriction would risk interpreting the concept of farcical prosecution too narrowly. Outcomes would also depend exclusively on how category 3 is interpreted in legal practice. In other words, while the abovementioned threefold classification of judgments makes sense, it should not be determinant in respect of the possible need for annulment. Dividing unsatisfactory judgments into inequitable, unjust, and ineffective is analytically rigorous and also makes sense given the different consequences of each category for the legal validity of the judgments and the criminal liability of the respective judicial actors. As regards the possible need for a (constitutive or declaratory) act of annulment, however, and from the point of view of the victim – i.e. the person unjustly convicted – this classification is not relevant. To call a trial a farce may be appropriate in situations other than only those that fall into the extreme category 3(b).

9.4 German Practice Surrounding Invalidation

I have argued, then, that category 2 and category 3 sentences can both be candidates to be deemed instances of farcical prosecution. Let us now turn to the question of how such sentences have been dealt with in German legal practice concerning the overturning of gravely unjust sentences in the aftermath of systemic injustice.[24] Since it is obviously impossible to provide a full account here of the injustices visited by the Nazi regime and by the East German socialist regime, a broad-brush outline of subsequent accountability will have to suffice.

One immediately notable point is that category 3 (declaring previous verdicts to be void judgments or non-judgments) has hardly been used at all. One important exception, the so-called Waldheim trials held in East Germany in 1950, dealt with accusations of Nazi crimes;[25] these trials were heavily influenced by East Germany's political leadership of the time. Use of category 3 was moreover even explicitly rejected by post-reunification German courts in a case concerning the attempted assassination of Hitler. The accused, Hans von Dohnanyi, had been sentenced to death, as a conspirator, after a farcical trial.[26] Revisiting this conviction in 1998, the Berlin Regional Court's reasoning was as follows: if the judgment were considered null and void (category 3), it would not be possible to invalidate the original decision. The consequence, in the court's view, would be to deny the possibility of judicially removing the stigma of the decision, an outcome which the court deemed untenable.[27] This argument is not convincing.[28] If the original judgment were to have been deemed void, the Berlin court could still have confirmed this assessment, in a declaratory manner, as a means of removing the associated stigma.

Since the courts, then, have chosen to apply category 3 only in very exceptional cases, in most examples of past injustice the original judgments remain legally binding for the time being. That is, they continue to be decisions with legal force, a situation that can only be altered if they are subsequently actively invalidated. So, if problematic past sentences were, at most, deemed unjust (category 2), how were they then dealt with? Each of the four Allied occupation zones into which Germany was divided immediately after the Second World War applied different mechanisms to invalidate such sentences.[29] In some, unjust past sentences were overturned by law. In others, an application from the convicted person or their relatives was needed. Such applications also often had additional requirements, such as that the act for which the victim had been unjustly convicted had been an act of resistance. In short, rules for invalidation varied widely according to occupation zone.[30] Many past judgments were, nonetheless, overturned immediately after the war, but once German jurisdiction was reestablished in 1949, practice regarding past Nazi sentences was very restrained. West German courts, for the most part, declared such sentences to be legally valid, a situation that persisted until the 1980s.[31]

Only after German reunification in 1990 did uniform regulation come about in the form of invalidation laws passed by the German Parliament. These covered both Nazi injustice and injustice under the former East German socialist regime, albeit with different levels of emphasis and success.[32] While constraints of space make full detail prohibitive, at least the major substantive legal requirements for invalidation will be outlined here. For the East German socialist regime, the relevant legislation is the Act on the Rehabilitation and Compensation of Victims of Criminal Prosecution Measures Contrary to the Rule of Law in the Acceding Territory, of 29 October 1992.[33] The criterion for invalidation here is the "incompatibility of the decision with essential principles of a free democratic order" (Section 1, author's translation). The first section further specifies that the required incompatibility is to be considered as given when the original decision served the ends of political prosecution (a list of offenses is mentioned here) or when the sentence was grossly disproportionate to the underlying offense.

For Nazi injustice, the relevant regulation is the Nazi Repeal Act of 25 August 1998.[34] According to the Act, the criterion for invalidation is that the sentences were passed "in violation of elementary ideas of justice to enforce or maintain the National Socialist regime of injustice for political, military, racial, religious or ideological reasons".[35] To add further specificity to this requirement, a list of Nazi-era laws is included, with the corresponding violation stipulated for any decision that was based on these laws.[36]

Despite the differences in the manner of invalidation – with Nazi sentences collectively invalidated by law, while East German injustices required case-by-case application – both solutions have in common a strong emphasis on the farcical nature of the laws applied. The farcical quality that can result, instead, from the conduct of the proceedings – as seen above – is thus not really taken into account.[37] This latter observation must be somewhat qualified, however: the Nazi Repeal Act did completely invalidate the outcomes of two Nazi-era entities, namely the People's Court (*Volksgerichtshof*),[38] considered particularly unjust and harsh, and courts martial (*Standgerichte*).[39] In these two instances, decisions whose primary flaws were procedural and that had not been invalidated for substantive reasons in the post-war period – were covered by declaring the entire institution to be inadequate.[40]

9.5 Does the Concept of Farcical Prosecutions Make Sense?

Having traced the principal lineaments of practice in Germany regarding the invalidation of past judicial decisions, I conclude by addressing the question of whether the notion of farcical prosecution makes sense as a legal concept. I have argued above that it does not seem sensible to limit the reach of the term farcical prosecution to category 3 (non-judgments or void judgments), inter alia, given that merely unjust decisions – category 2 – can also come about through farcical prosecution. If we are to proceed further, then an attempt must be made to identify definitional criteria that specifically delineate farcical prosecution in this expanded meaning. The following may be considered a preliminary attempt: a trial should be considered a farce when judges, instead of seeking a just application of the law, pursue another goal. (For example, in Dürrenmatt's fictional case, the 'trial' is conducted for fun, that is, as an amusing pastime.) In these cases, at any rate, one should speak of farcical prosecution. Insistence on a state of intentional requirement on the part of the judge, however, seems to unduly limit the reach of the concept of farce. To remedy this, I propose to make use of what is commonly referred to as the 'policy element'[41] in international criminal law, which forms part of the context element in crimes against humanity.[42]

The policy element requires that the act in question, which may constitute a crime against humanity, was committed in furtherance of a policy of a state or organization that has as its objective a widespread or systematic attack against the civilian population.[43] The policy element could now serve as a model for the extended meaning of farcical prosecution: a prosecution would also be deemed farcical if it was carried out in support of, or in execution of the policy of, a state or organization whose aim is a systematic attack against a political opponent or against other groups to be specified and characterized. The crucial point to grasp here is that, as with the policy element in international criminal law, for a trial to be deemed farcical, it would not be necessary for the judge herself to have endorsed the goals of the policy. Rather, the definition turns on the fact that the judgment can be interpreted as subscribing to such a policy.[44] In other words, what renders a prosecution farcical is not the motive (or mens rea) of the judge herself but the motive(s) of the organization whose policy the judge – *nolens volens* – subordinates herself to. This definition makes it clear that a decision can be considered farcical (and must therefore be invalidated, whether by constitutive or declaratory means) regardless of whether the individual judge can be convicted of judicial misconduct. It becomes equally irrelevant whether the judge is subject to other types of criminal liability, such as for deprivation of liberty or homicide.

This describes a possible scenario whereby a prosecution might be deemed farcical, yet the judge responsible cannot be punished for judicial misconduct. This is not meant to support a thesis that a Nazi elite was the decisive factor for Nazi injustice, thereby effectively exonerating Nazi-era legal professionals. Rather, the scenario is intended to make clear that a prosecution can be farcical even in the absence of any evidence of malice by the parties involved in the trial. The possibility of farce even in the absence of malice of the judicial agents is not, either, implausible: according to Bonhoeffer's theory of stupidity, injustice arising from thoughtlessness or stupidity can be more dangerous than the injustice that proceeds from malice.[45] The same applies to the activity of courts.[46]

To summarize, then, the main thesis of this concluding section is that the policy element that I proposed for inclusion in the criterion defining farcical prosecutions has the merit of (also) allowing trials to be classified as farcical in the absence of grounds for attributing ill will to the judge. One final remark: this chapter has focused on farcical prosecution that is detrimental to the accused person. It does not explicitly address the potentially protective uses of farcical prosecution, such as those set out in Rome Statute Art. 20(3), which are dealt with by Cárdenas and by Mañalich in their contributions to the present volume. In such cases, the farcical nature of the proceedings works in favor of the accused person, turning the 'prosecution' into a protective farce and an attempted erasure of the harm suffered by the original victim(s).[47] When this occurs, the concept of the policy element as proposed here can still be applied. If such a shielding judgment is seen as a protective farce, this moreover also opens up the possibility that the judge responsible may incur criminal liability for aiding and abetting a criminal organization or a state of injustice by not conducting a proper prosecution. In this mode of criminal liability, as in the case of the proposed policy element, it is not necessary that the perpetrator be shown to have evil intentions him or herself; it is sufficient that they have willingly been part of an organization that pursues evil goals. It then becomes necessary to consider whether the conduct of merely being part of such an organization should also incur criminal liability.[48] This question would apply not only to omissions – such as the failure of a judge to act in a context where people were disappearing – but also to instances of positive action, such as the passing of unlawful death sentences. The connecting factor for criminal liability is, then, not the act of sentencing per se, nor the omission of inaction conducted with malicious intent on the part of the judge. Rather, it would be the sole fact of her membership in an organization that pursues malicious aims.

Notes

1 Dürrenmatt, *Die Panne*, first published 1956. An English translation was published in 1960 under the title 'A Dangerous Game', although the original German title literally translates as 'The Breakdown'. Written as a radio play, the work was almost immediately novelized.

2 Dürrenmatt, *Die Panne* (1985) 18; author's translation.

3 Although one might argue that the accusation of homicide would be bound to fail, as from a criminal law perspective, informing someone about an affair could be considered socially appropriate behavior.

4 § 5 I Nr. 1 Kriegssonderstrafrechtsverordnung (RGBl. I 1939, 1455).

5 Werle, *Justiz-Strafrecht und polizeiliche Verbrechensbekämpfung im Dritten Reich* (1989) 212.
6 Werle (1989) (n 5) 211.
7 Cf. Werle, 'Das Strafrecht als Waffe: Die Verordnung gegen Volksschädlinge vom 5. September 1939' (1989) 29 *JuS* 952, 952 et seqq.
8 Werle (1989) (n 7) 956, where more examples can be found.
9 Kuhli, 'Grundzüge der Strafrechtsgeschichte. Vom 18. Jahrhundert bis zur Gegenwart – Teil 1' (2021) 13 *ZJS* 25.
10 On the *Führerwille*, see Werle (1989) (n 5) 581 et seqq.
11 Kühne, 'Einleitung Abschnitt K' in Becker et al, *Löwe-Rosenberg, Kommentar zur Strafprozessordnung,* para 110. The label 'void' is also sometimes applied to past judgments after system changes. According to Kühne (para 109 et seq) some state action is, however, required in order to render these judgments void – i.e., they are not void from the outset. I suggest that it is better to refer to such verdicts as 'unjust' (category 2), without excluding the possibility that some such judgments are already deemed void without further state action.
12 On the distinction Lischka, *Umgang mit Unrecht – Die Aufhebung von während der NS- und DDR-Zeit ergangenen strafrechtlichen Unrechtsurteilen* (2021) 10 et seq.
13 To the debate with comprehensive references (and rejecting) Kühne (2016) (n 11), paras 105 et seqq.
14 Peters, *Strafprozess* (1981) § 55 I.
15 Spendel, 'Mord durch ein "Standgericht" – SchwurGer Würzburg und BGH, in: Justiz und NS-Verbrechen, X (1973), S. 205, 233' (1988) 28 *JuS* 857; author's translation.
16 Court martial held on 2 April 1945, reported in LG Aschaffenburg, Judgement of 6 December 1948, which can be found in Rüter/de Mildt, *Justiz und NS-Verbrechen. Die ost- und westdeutschen Gerichtsentscheidungen wegen nationalsozialistischer Tötungsverbrechen seit 1945, Band III*, 1968 et seqq. For a detailed analysis of the case, see Wessel, *NS-Justizverbrechen und Nachkriegsrechtsprechung* (1998).
17 Summary of the case in Wessel (1998) (n 16) 14 et seqq.
18 Wessel (1998) (n 16) 47 et seqq.
19 Radbruch, 'Gesetzliches Unrecht und übergesetzliches Recht' (1946) 1 *SJZ* 105, 107. The parallels are nonetheless not exact, as laws falling into Radbruch's category of 'intolerable injustice' do not require an act of invalidation. See above Peters (1981) (n 14).
20 Spendel (1973) (n 15) 857 argues that the barring effect of section 339 of the German Criminal Code is overturned only in cases falling under category 3b.
21 On the debate, and the restrictive interpretation by the German courts, see Hilgendorf, '§ 339: Rechtsbeugung' in Dombrowski et al, *Leipziger Kommentar zum Strafgesetzbuch,* paras 90 et seqq. The Federal Court of Justice however recently stated – in contrast to previous interpretation – *dolus eventualis* does suffice, something which also makes the barring effect "largely obsolete" (BGH, Judgement of 13 May 2015, 3 StR 498/14, [2015] 11 *NStZ* 651, 653 para 17). Nevertheless, in order for Section 339 requirements to be deemed to have been fulfilled, it is according to the BGH (para. 12) required that the judge "deliberately and seriously departed from the law and justice"; author's translation.
22 See overall, on the de facto non-prosecution of Nazi judges, Schoch, 'Die Zusammensetzung der Justiz in der Bonner Republik' in Koch A et al (eds), 95 et seqq. On the restraint against judicial actors see Wessel (1998) (n 16) 100 et seqq.
23 Wessel affirms that there was malfeasance in office (a finding that runs contrary to the post-war adjudication of the case). He reports that the judge was convicted of negligent

manslaughter, but not of judicial malfeasance, which is irritating as the malfeasance conviction would have been the prerequisite for the former (1998) (n 16), 28 et seqq.

24 Cf. the noteworthy collection of judgments on Nazi crimes by Rüter and de Mildt (2024) (n 16).

25 See Kai Cornelius's chapter in the present volume.

26 Generally on the killings of co-conspirators Canaris, von Dohnanyi, Oster, Sack, Gehre, and Bonhoeffer, see Spendel, *Rechtsbeugung durch Rechtsprechung* (1984) 89 et seqq. Spendel argues (at 98) that the proceedings that led to the death sentence constitute, at the very least, a void judgment.

27 LG Berlin, Judgement of 2. June 1997, 517AR1/97, 2P Aufh.5/96, (1998) 14 *NJW* 1002, 1004.

28 On non-judgment, also see Gribbohm, 'Comment on BGH, Urt. v. 19.6.156 – 1 StR 50/56' (1996) 16 *NStZ* 489. This remains an open question according to Mohr, 'Die Aufhebung des SS-"Standgerichtsurteils" gegen Hans von Dohnanyi' (1998) 51 *NJW* 958, 959 et seq.

29 For an overview of regulations in the federal states, see Schuster, 'Vor § 339' in Becker et al, *Löwe-Rosenberg, Kommentar zur Strafprozessordnung,* para 182. For more details, see Lischka (2021) (n 12) 55 et seqq.

30 In the British occupation zone, the invalidation was only amnesty-like, i.e., it retained the convictions, only revoking the sentences. See Nettersheim, 'Die Aufhebung von Unrechtsurteilen der NS-Strafjustiz. Ein langes Kapitel der Vergangenheitsbewältigung' in Hanack E W et al (eds) 936. In the US-administered zone, the requirement that the offense must have been an act of resistance meant according to Nettersheim (at 935) that perpetrators without a political motive were discriminated against.

31 Lischka (2021) (n 12) 111 et seqq. For a noteworthy exception see Lischka at 113. On the differences in interpretation see Lischka at 120 et seqq.

32 Lischka (2021) (n 12) 164 et seq. The differences are particularly evident in the prosecution of judges, where the impression emerged that East German offenders were being punished much more severely. The Federal Court did eventually acknowledge failings in the prosecution of Nazi perpetrators: BGH, Judgement of 16 November 1995, 5 StR 747/94 (1996) 13 *NJW* 857, 863. On convictions of East German judges for malfeasance in office, see Marxen/Werle/Vormbaum, *Die strafrechtliche Aufarbeitung von DDR-Unrecht* (2020) 54 et seqq (especially at 59, 66, and 68), or the chapter by Werle and Vormbaum in the present volume.

33 "Gesetz über die Rehabilitierung und Entschädigung von Opfern rechtsstaatswidriger Strafverfolgungsmaßnahmen im Beitrittsgebiet" as part of the „Erstes Gesetz zur Bereinigung von SED-Unrecht", BGBl I 1992, 1814; Lischka (2021) (n 12) 148 et seqq.

34 "Gesetz zur Aufhebung nationalsozialistischer Unrechtsurteile in der Strafrechtspflege und der Sterilisationsentscheidungen der ehemaligen Erbgesundheitsgerichte", BGBl I 1998, 2501.

35 Author's translation; see, on this point, Lischka (2021) (n 12) 97 et seqq.

36 Nazi Repeal Act Section 2 No. 3, plus the relevant appendix.

37 Lischka (2021) (n 12) 170.

38 On the Volksgerichtshof, see Marxen, *Das Volk und sein Gerichtshof* (1994), although Marxen (at 90) also points out that even in its late phase, the People's Court had "remnants of judicial action".

39 Section 2, No. 1 and 2 of the Nazi Repeal Act.

40 Regarding the People's Court, the law was based on a (legally non-binding) resolution of the Bundestag, issued on 25 January 1985: The People's Court served as an instrument of terror for the implementation of National Socialist despotism.
41 Werle/Jeßberger, *Völkerstrafrecht* (2020) paras 989 et seqq.
42 Art. 7 of the Rome Statute of the International Criminal Court, ICC, and see Werle/Jeßberger (2020) (n 41) para 972.
43 Art. 7 (para 2a), Rome Statute.
44 On the mens rea requirement of the policy element in respect of crimes against humanity, see Werle/Jeßberger (2020) (n 41) paras 1004 et seq.
45 Bonhoeffer, *Widerstand und Ergebung* (1943) 17.
46 On the point that the fanatical supporters of an unjust regime may have no sense of injustice, see Rudolf Wassermann, 'Rechtsblindheit? – Müssten Roland Freisler und Hilde Benjamin strafrei bleiben?' (1995) 48 *NJW* 2965, 2966 et seq.
47 Cf. also, for East Germany, instances of non-prosecution by East German judges, leading to their subsequent conviction for malfeasance in office. Marxen/Werle/Vormbaum (2020) (n 32) 70 et seqq and see chapter by Werle/Vormbaum in this volume.
48 On the liability for being a member of a criminal organization, see the chapter by Geneuss in this volume.

Bibliography

Bonhoeffer D, *Widerstand und Ergebung* (written in 1943, published by Christian Kaiser 1951).

Dürrenmatt F, *Die Panne* (first published 1956, Diogenes 1985).

Gribbohm G, 'Comment on BGH, Urt. v. 19.6.156 – 1 StR 50/56' (1996) 16 *Neue Zeitschrift für Strafrecht* 489.

Hilgendorf E, '§ 339: Rechtsbeugung' in Brodowski et al (eds), *Leipziger Kommentar zum Strafgesetzbuch, vol 13* (13th edn, De Gruyter 2023).

Kuhli M, 'Grundzüge der Strafrechtsgeschichte. Vom 18. Jahrhundert bis zur Gegenwart – Teil 1' (2021) 13 *Zeitschrift für das juristische Studium* 25.

Kühne H H, 'Einleitung Abschnitt K', in Becker J P et al (eds), *Löwe-Rosenberg, Kommentar zur Strafprozessordnung, vol 1* (27th edn, De Gruyter 2016).

Lischka J, *Umgang mit Unrecht – Die Aufhebung von während der NS- und DDR-Zeit ergangenen straf-rechtlichen Unrechtsurteilen* (Dr. Kovač 2021).

Marxen K, *Das Volk und sein Gerichtshof* (Vittorio Klostermann 1994).

Marxen K/Werle G/Vormbaum M, *Die strafrechtliche Aufarbeitung von DDR-Unrecht* (2nd edn, De Gruyter 2020).

Mohr P, 'Die Aufhebung des SS-"Standgerichtsurteils" gegen Hans von Dohnanyi' (1998) 51 *Neue Juristische Wochenschrift* 958.

Nettersheim G, 'Die Aufhebung von Unrechtsurteilen der NS-Strafjustiz. Ein langes Kapitel der Vergangenheitsbewältigung' in Hanack E W et al (eds), *Festschrift für Peter Rieß* (De Gruyter 2002) 933.

Peters K, *Strafprozess* (3rd edn, C. F. Müller 1981).

Radbruch G, 'Gesetzliches Unrecht und übergesetzliches Recht' (1946) 1 *Süddeutsche Juristen-Zeitung* 105.

Rüter C F/de Mildt D W (eds), *Justiz und NS-Verbrechen. Die ost- und westdeutschen Gerichtsentscheidungen wegen nationalsozialistischer Tötungsverbrechen seit 1945.* https://junsv.nl/home (accessed 15 January 2024).

Schoch M L, 'Die Zusammensetzung der Justiz in der Bonner Republik' in A Koch et al (eds), *Strafrecht in der alten Bundesrepublik 1949-1990* (Nomos 2020) 95.

Schuster F, 'Vor § 339' in Becker J P et al (eds), *Löwe-Rosenberg, Kommentar zur Strafprozessordnung, vol 9/1* (27th edn, De Gruyter 2022).

Spendel G, *Rechtsbeugung durch Rechtsprechung* (De Gruyter 1984).

Spendel G, 'Mord durch ein "Standgericht" – SchwurGer Würzburg und BGH, in: Justiz und NS-Verbrechen, X (1973), S. 205, 233' (1988) 28 *Juristische Schulung* 857.

Wassermann R, 'Rechtsblindheit? – Müssten Roland Freisler und Hilde Benjamin straffrei bleiben?' (1995) 48 *Neue Juristische Wochenschrift* 2965.

Werle G, *Justiz-Strafrecht und polizeiliche Verbrechensbekämpfung im Dritten Reich* (De Gruyter 1989).

Werle, 'Das Strafrecht als Waffe: Die Verordnung gegen Volksschädlinge vom 5. September 1939' (1989) 29 *Juristische Schulung* 952.

Werle G/Jeßberger F, *Völkerstrafrecht* (5th edn, Mohr Siebeck 2020).

Wessel M, *NS-Justizverbrechen und Nachkriegsrechtsprechung* (Cuvillier 1998).

10 Invalidation of 'Judicial' Decisions in Cases of Sham or Show Trials

An International Criminal Law Perspective

Claudia Cárdenas

10.1 Introduction

The issue of *ne bis in idem* is normally approached when examining the possibility of submitting a person that has already been tried to a new criminal proceeding. The approach in this chapter is quite different. Here, provisions on *ne bis in idem* in the statutes of international criminal tribunals will be examined as standards set under international criminal law as to what kind(s) of proceeding should count as mere show trials, unsatisfactory proceedings, or sham trials.[1] Particular attention will be paid to the Statute of the International Criminal Court, ICC (specifically, Article 20(3) of the Rome Statute). The idea is to draw attention to international consensus surrounding groups of decisions that do not produce the effect of *res judicata*, despite having the formal appearance of binding judicial decisions that produce this effect. We are concerned, in other words, with decisions that are not considered worthy of being treated as legitimate judicial decisions.

Attending to this international consensus is useful for the purposes of the present volume. This is because deeming a final judicial decision non-legitimate to the point where it does not prevent the person involved from being tried anew seems tantamount to saying that the decision was the outcome of a show trial or sham trial. This in turn is linked to the possibility of examining judges' responsibility – even their potential criminal liability – for such a decision and its consequences. If this much can be agreed upon, one could say that this international consensus of the 124 States Parties to the Rome Statute on what counts as a show or sham trial could be of use. It supports removal of the status of 'proper judicial decision' from decisions of the sort that are under discussion here. It could also feature as a relevant element in holding accountable judges who have signed such decisions. This might include pursuit of their potential criminal responsibility where killing, unlawful imprisonment, or torture has been committed in the execution of those decisions. Similar considerations would apply where perpetrators of such crimes have been granted impunity because of the inaction of judges whose action would have been required in order to prevent or halt the commission of crimes.

In different parts of the world, and at different times, the power of the state has been used to persecute parts of the population. This has occurred in the most diverse forms, ranging from sheer brute force to state armed forces torturing

DOI: 10.4324/9781003470069-12

people or shooting openly at citizens in the streets to more elaborate forms. A special challenge arises when one later seeks to assess this behavior legally and finds that these actions are covered by legal formalities. In perhaps the most formalized sphere of state action, that of criminal justice, such conduct may have been covered by judicial decisions ordering imprisonment or executions (in regimes that allow the death penalty) or allowing for victims to be disciplined, including by means of measures that domestic law allows for but that constitute torture according to international law. The cloak of legality that covers these acts may prevent states from investigating and judging them. This chapter is dedicated to the parameters that have been developed in international law to deny *res judicata* status to certain acts whose formal appearance allows them to be externally recognizable as judicial decisions (what the Inter-American Court of Human Rights has called 'fraudulent res judicata'). This analysis is undertaken on the assumption that these parameters, once identified, can be useful in addressing a question that is key if prosecuting judges is to be possible: namely, what counts as a (valid) judicial act? Alternatively, when is a judge acting as a judge?

10.2 The Sham Exception in the Statutes of the Ad Hoc Tribunals and the Permanent International Criminal Court

10.2.1 The Road to Rome Statute Article 20 Paragraph 3

The statutes of the ad hoc tribunals[2] each provided for exceptions to their general rule on *res judicata*. Both Article 10(2) of the ICTY Statute (1993) and Article 9(2) of the ICTR Statute (1994) have the same wording:

> *Non-bis-in-idem.* A person who has been tried by a national court for acts constituting serious violations of international humanitarian law may be subsequently tried by the International Tribunal [...] only if: (a) The act for which he or she was tried was characterised as an ordinary crime; or (b) The national court proceedings were not impartial or independent, were designed to shield the accused from international criminal responsibility, or the case was not diligently prosecuted.

The ordinary crime exception set out in 2(a), above, was left out of the Rome Statute. The exception did have value: by procuring the correct labeling of conduct amounting to crimes against international law, it promoted the application of proportionate legal consequences.[3] Nonetheless, its omission from the Rome Statute is comprehensible because the ICC is designed to act only in very few exceptional cases. This is coherent with the fact that the Rome Statute does not oblige its states parties to implement core crimes against international law in their domestic legal orders, even though many of them have found good reasons to do so.[4] By contrast, the Rome Statute retained two of the three processual shortcomings that the ad hoc statutes' shared paragraph 2(b), above, identifies as making new proceedings permissible. These are, first, a lack of impartiality or independence, and second, having aimed to shield the accused from criminal responsibility. The final condition, lack of prosecutorial diligence, was considered unsuitable for an instrument with such a universal vocation as the Rome Statute, creating a court designed to act only in very exceptional circumstances.

The International Law Commission, ILC, included a *ne bis in idem* rule in its 1994 Draft Statute for an International Criminal Court. The rule as proposed would have allowed for a new trial in the same circumstances spelt out in the ad hoc tribunal statutes reviewed above.[5] The various proposals made on this issue by the Preparatory Committee in 1996 did not differ significantly from the ILC's draft.[6] The Preparatory Committee's draft was placed before the Plenipotentiary Conference in 1998.[7] It provided for the following exceptions to the *ne bis in idem* principle when a conviction had been issued by another court for a crime within the ICC's jurisdiction: (a) protective purpose of [those prior] proceedings and (b) conduct of the proceedings "in a manner which, in the circumstances, was inconsistent with an intent to bring the person concerned to justice".[8] The associated footnotes (n. 62–64, inclusive) state that in the Committee's view the question of whether further exceptions to the *ne bis in idem* principle would be necessary should be considered. Nevertheless, the same draft article included an alternative proposal according to which the *ne bis in idem* principle would apply without exception.[9] In the final wording of the Rome Statute, as adopted on 17 July 1998, proposed exception (a), above, was retained as per the Preparatory Committee's draft, while proposed exception (b) was included in a modified form.

10.2.2 The Sham Exception in the Statute of the International Criminal Court (1998)

Article 20, paragraph 3 of the Rome Statute identifies two cases in which decisions that formally appear to be final judgments will not be recognized as having *res judicata* effect:[10]

> (a) When the proceedings were for the purpose of shielding the person concerned from criminal responsibility for crimes within the jurisdiction of the Court; or
>
> (b) When the proceedings were otherwise not conducted independently or impartially in accordance with the norms of due process recognized by international law and [fr. *mais* (but)/ sp. *o* (or)] were conducted in a manner which, in the circumstances, was inconsistent with an intent to bring the person concerned to justice.

Both of the specified instances of fraudulent *res judicata* are often referred to as expressions of the so-called sham exception, according to which sham proceedings should not prevent a retrial. What follows is an examination of the detail of each instance.

10.2.2.1 Article 20(3)(a) of the Rome Statute

According to Article 20(3)(a), then, the accused is not protected by the *ne bis in idem* guarantee if the state-level proceedings served the purpose of protecting the person from criminal liability for crimes under the jurisdiction of the ICC. The intention to protect is also provided for as a ground for inadmissibility in Article 17(2)(a), as a form of lack of will to prosecute. The idea behind the wording is that State exercise of jurisdiction in good faith must be respected.[11] In order to determine whether this variant of lack of will is present, an examination must take place of whether the power of state organs has been purposefully abused with the intention of protection.[12] For determining intention to protect, the will to prosecute as exhibited by the state in its entirety must be taken into account. In other words, it is not sufficient to limit the investigation to the behavior of the competent investigative or prosecutorial organ. The role of (other) state organs with actual control over the proceedings, or of the legislature, in addition to that of organs formally executing or enforcing the law, may be decisive.[13] For example, if a judge applies laws that protect the accused from criminal liability, his or her personal protective intent is no less relevant than that of the legislative powers. The intention to protect the accused must be purposeful ('for the purpose') and must relate to criminal liability, i.e., to the avoidance of punishment. If the provision is interpreted with regard to the meaning and purpose of the Statute, it is sufficient for affirmation of the intention to protect if the protection of the accused can be foreseen as a certain and objective consequence of the state's action. This also applies if other accompanying remote goals are argued as justification for the state's action, because the purpose of the Rome Statute is to combat impunity. According to the Statute, the intention to protect against criminal liability should be with reference to the crimes designated in Article 5 (i.e., crimes within the Court's jurisdiction). This does not mean that precisely these *nomina iuris* must have been applied in the domestic proceedings: what is at issue here is criminal liability arising from those acts or omissions that the Statute designates as crimes.

If there is an authoritarian government in power in a country, which leads to massive and systematic breaches of the law, and if that government at the same time controls the state's courts, it could be possible for a domestic process to be carried out solely in order to give the appearance of legitimacy to certain decisions, such as the granting of impunity to perpetrators. This is precisely what should be avoided, and so in such circumstances, the ICC is called upon to take action.[14] One important indicator of the intent to grant impunity is the lenient nature of penalties.[15] It is worth keeping in mind that the ICC was created to 'put an end to impunity', and to ensure that "the most serious crimes of concern to the international community as a whole [do] not go unpunished".[16] An unequivocal intent to protect the accused will be present, in particular, when the state departs from its usual practice in comparable cases.[17] Of course, the presumption of innocence applies to suspected criminals under international law, just as it does in general. The decisive factor in determining an intention to protect is therefore whether the decision was made on the basis of the actual procedure as carried out or whether political criteria were involved.[18] Determination of the appropriate sentence is closely related to the legal assessment of the act, for which the prosecuting state is in principle not accountable to the ICC. Nevertheless, acts that are punishable as crimes under international law are not domestic matters. Even where a state has the authority to determine the status of the offense, if this power is misused as a means of protecting a person from criminal responsibility, the procedure has the aim of protecting the accused.

The use of pardons or amnesties for perpetrators of crimes under international law is also an expression of the intention to protect against criminal responsibility.[19] In subsuming pardons under Article 20(3) of the Rome Statute, it is decisive whether or not the enforcement proceedings are to be regarded as a part of the proceedings within the meaning of this provision. 'Proceedings', referring to state activity in a particular case, seems to be an overarching term. Accordingly, enforcement proceedings would also be considered part of the proceedings. Thus, Article 20(3) of the Rome Statute is to be interpreted in such a way that when a pardon is granted for conduct that materially constitutes crimes against international law, the proceedings have the purpose of protecting the accused from criminal liability for the acts punishable as core crimes. This interpretation also does justice to the purpose of the norm, which is to prevent 'shielding'.

Bearing in mind that some plans or policies that underlie the commission of international crimes include the granting of impunity,[20] the conduct of producing decisions that shield perpetrators from criminal responsibility could be seen as itself constituting a form of criminal responsibility. This inasmuch as this conduct contributes to the commission of crimes (by a group of persons acting with a common purpose), which may cover conduct engaged in after the crimes, with the aim of furthering the criminal activity or criminal purpose of the group.[21] One would think that judges involved in a plan to grant impunity after the commission of crimes could be prosecuted for that, given that their decisions are not recognized as valid judgments.[22]

10.2.2.2 Article 20(3)(b) of the Rome Statute

This provision (see above for wording) reads as if two cumulative conditions for a finding of fraudulent r*es judicata* were set. On the one hand, the prior procedure must have departed from the principles of impartiality and independence. On the other, it must have been conducted in a way that cannot, under the circumstances, be reconciled with an intention to bring the person concerned to justice.[23] The procedure lacks impartiality if the acting body does not make its decisions objectively, according to the merits of the actual process, but instead with consideration of the interests of the parties.[24] The procedure lacks independence if the acting body's decisions are determined not only by the law but also by directives from higher authorities or other persons.[25] As principles of due process, both impartiality and independence are regulated in state legal systems as well as in various international human rights instruments.[26]

Lack of impartiality or independence, combined with incompatibility with the intention to bring someone to justice, are also cited as grounds for admissibility in Article 17(2)(c) of the Rome Statute. Nevertheless, there are differences. In the situation described by Article 20, we are dealing with completed proceedings (as distinct from investigations). Therefore, and unlike under Article 17, independence and impartiality are here always to be interpreted according to the relevant international standards provided in human rights treaties. The addition, in the English language version of the statute, of the requirement of incompatibility with an intention to bring the person in question to justice is therefore redundant, since this incompatibility will naturally exist where there has been a lack of independence and/or impartiality. This redundancy is not found in the French version, where the conjunction '*mais*' ('but') joins the sentence clause referring to independence and impartiality to the subsequent one specifying the lack of the intention to bring the accused to justice.[27] In the binding Spanish wording, the aforementioned two conditions are linked using the conjunction '*o*' ('or'), implying that impartiality and independence could be interpreted as examples of a lack of intention to bring the person concerned before the court. Independence or impartiality seem, then, to be immanent requirements of the legal efficacy of final judicial decisions.

10.3 Setting Criteria for the Status of Documents That Have the Form of Judgments

The aim of Rome Statute Article 20(3) is to determine whether the ICC can hold a new trial. One might think that there is little room before the ICC for cases in which only lit. (b), above, would apply, without lit. (a). However, the proposal here consists of looking at these provisions as standards for declaring certain decisions to be sham decisions, therefore susceptible to being deemed as non-(valid) judicial acts, in turn possibly forming a basis for the responsibility of the issuing judges. From this perspective, one might very well take the view that the required standard could be met where the purpose of judicial action was incompatible with the aim of bringing the accused to justice. That could be the case where a judge ordered the death penalty, or deprivation of liberty, for someone completely undeserving of criminal punishment, or where a judge handed down a punishment that was disproportionately harsh when compared to the deed of which the accused was convicted. These are examples of decisions that would meet the standard set down in lit. (b), but not lit. (a), or vice versa. Were this to be the case, according to the Rome Statute standard, the decision would not be recognized as a binding one. Consequently, the judge that signed off on that decision should be called to account for the consequences of the execution of his or her decision.

The approach presented here is not completely unheard of. Schabas agrees with the declaration issued by the state of Malta, when ratifying the Rome Statute, to the effect that: '[i]t is presumed that under general principles of law a trial as described in paragraphs 3(a) and (b) of article 20 of the Statute would be considered a nullity and would not be taken into account'.[28] The Inter-American Court of Human Rights, IACtHR, has done something similar in referring to Article 20 of the Rome Statute,

Article 10 of the ICTY Statute, and Article 9 of the ICTR Statute, as foundations for the criteria it uses to determine where fraudulent *res judicata* has occurred. There are two main IACtHR cases where this can be seen clearly. The first is the case of Carpio-Nicolle et. al. v. Guatemala, in which the IACtHR's Judgment of 22 November 2004 stated: "[t]he development of international legislation and case law has led to the examination of the so-called 'fraudulent *res judicata*' resulting from a trial in which the rules of due process have not been respected, or when judges have not acted with independence and impartiality".[29] In a footnote, the Court refers to Article 20 of the Rome Statute, Article 9 of the ICTR Statute, and Article 10 of the ICTY Statute as sources.[30]

Almost two years later, in the case of Almonacid-Arellano et al. v. Chile, the IACtHR Judgment of 26 September 2006 stated:

> With regard to the *ne bis in idem* principle, although it is acknowledged as a human right in Article 8(4) of the American Convention, it is not an absolute right, and therefore, is not applicable where: i) the intervention of the court that heard the case and decided to dismiss it or to acquit a person responsible for violating human rights or international law, was intended to shield the accused party from criminal responsibility; ii) the proceedings were not conducted independently or impartially in accordance with due procedural guarantees, or iii) there was no real intent to bring those responsible to justice. A judgment rendered in the foregoing circumstances produces an "apparent" or "fraudulent" *res judicata* case.[31]

Here, as in Carpio-Nicolle, a footnote refers to the abovementioned sources.[32] This regional court jurisprudence was in turn referred to by the hybrid tribunal, the ECCC (Extraordinary Chambers in the Courts of Cambodia). In a 3 November 2011 decision in the case of Ieng Sary,[33] the ECCC cited IACtHR practice in Carpio-Nicolle and Almonacid when deciding on *ne bis in idem*, amnesty and pardon.[34] These examples show how the standards set for international criminal jurisdiction have been used in other international, or internationalised, jurisdictions as standards for deciding whether an act does or does not count as a valid judicial decision.

10.4 Conclusion

The overarching purpose of this chapter was to argue that the cases of fraudulent *res judicata* recognized in Article 20(3) of the Rome Statute constitute – even if written down for the specific purpose of ICC exercise of jurisdiction – an expression of general standards for extending or refusing recognition to documents that seem to be judicial decisions. The chapter has shown that this interpretation of general applicability is both theoretically plausible and de facto utilized in practice: both the Inter-American Court of Human Rights and Cambodia's internationalised special jurisdiction have treated Rome Statute Article 20(3) as a source for declaring fraudulent *res judicata* as a basis for disregarding apparent prior judgments. This usage opens the door to pursuing responsibility of judges for these non-judicial acts. This finding could add a third perspective to existing treatments of *ne bis in idem* regulations in international treaties: together with its role as an individual right and as a tool for the distribution of competences,[35] *ne bis in idem* may have a part to play in setting criteria for the refusal to recognize some decisions as valid judicial decisions.

Notes

1 Schabas, *The International Criminal Court: A Commentary on the Rome Statute* (2016) 508 et seqq; Coracini/Tallgren, 'Article 20 Ne bis in idem' in Ambos (ed), *Rome Statute of the International Criminal Court. Article-by-Article Commentary* (2022) 1091, 1121 et seqq; Berg, 'The 1994 ILC Draft Statute for an International Criminal Court: A Principled Appraisal of Jurisdictional Structure' (1996) *Case W. Res. J. Int'L.* 221, 247. See also Specht, *Die zwischenstaatliche Geltung des Grundsatzes ne bis in idem* (1999), 203 et seqq.

2 The International Criminal Tribunal for the former Yugoslavia (ICTY) and the International Criminal Tribunal for Rwanda (ICTR).

3 Cárdenas, 'Labelling Crimes Against Humanity in Domestic Jurisdictions: Does nomen iuris matter? The Case of the Crimes in Colonia Dignidad' in Jeßberger/Vormbaum et al (eds) 25–35.

4 Werle/Jeßberger, *Principles of International Criminal Law* (2020) 179 et seqq.

5 Article 42(2) ILC Draft 1994. This proposal was not uncontested during the negotiations. Further details appear in Cárdenas, *Die Zulässigkeitsprüfung vor dem Internationalen Strafgerichtshof. Zur Auslegung des Art. 17 IStGH-Statut unter besonderer Berücksichtigung von Anmestien und Wahrheitskommissionen* (2005) 138 et seqq.

6 Summary of the proceedings of the Preparatory Committee during the period 25 March-12 April 1996, UN Doc. A/AC.249/1 (1996), 101.

7 UN Conference of Plenipotentiary on the Establishment of an International Criminal Court (ICC).

8 Report of the Preparatory Committee on the Establishment of an International Criminal Court, A/Conf.183/2 (1998) 29 (Draft Article 18).

9 Report of the Preparatory Committee on the Establishment of an International Criminal Court (n 8) 29.

10 The exceptions were carried over from Article 17(2) (a) and (c) of the ICC Statute. See Sadat, *The International Criminal Court and the Transformation of International Law* (2002) 190.

11 That the intention to protect is simply to be regarded as a lack of *bona fides* is clarified in an alternative draft to the article 'Questions of Admissibility', prepared by the Preparatory Committee ('PrepCom') in 1996. Summary of the proceedings of the Preparatory Committee (n 6), 99 et seqq.

12 For Blakesley, the intention to protect implies the international responsibility of the state for acts contrary to international law. See Blakesley, 'Commentary on Article 6: Obligation to Try or Extradite' (1993) 11 *Nouvelles Études Pénales* 133, 153.

13 Cf. Meißner, *Die Zusammenarbeit mit dem Internationalen Strafgerichtshof nach dem Römischen Statut* (2003) 83 et seqq. The same idea emerges from the OTP, Informal expert paper 'The principle of complementarity in practice' (2003) 14 para 45. www.icc-cpi.int/sites/default/files/NR/rdonlyres/20BB4494-70F9-4698-8E30-907F631453ED/281984/complementarity.pdf (accessed 26 August 2024).

14 Further examples are given by Holmes, 'Complementarity: National Courts versus the ICC' in Cassese/Paola et al (eds) 667, 675: "[o]bvious departures from the formal legal procedures of a State would be another factor that could give rise to serious doubts about the legitimacy of an exercise. [...] The transfer of the case(s) to secret tribunals would also be relevant".

15 Reisinger/Coracini Tallgren, 'Article 20 Ne bis in idem' in Kai Ambos (ed) 1091, 1121 et seqq.

16 Preamble of the Rome Statute, paras 4 and 5, quoted by the Appeals Chamber of the ICC in The Prosecutor v. Germain Katanga and Mathieu Ngudjolo Chui, Judgment on the Appeal of Mr. Germain Katanga against the Oral Decision of Trial Chamber II of 12 June 2009 on the Admissibility of the Case, 2009, and in The Prosecutor v. Saif Al-Islam Gadaffi, Judgment on the appeal of Mr Saif Al-Islam Gadaffi against the decision of the Pre-Trial Chamber I, entitled 'Decision on the "Admissibility Challenge by Dr. Saif Al-Islam Gadaffi pursuant to Articles 17(1)(c), 19, and 20(3) of the Rome Statute"', 2019.

17 Zimmermann, 'Die Schaffung eines ständigen Internationalen Strafgerichtshofes Perspektiven und Probleme vor der Staatenkonferenz in Rom' (1998) 58 *ZaöRV* 47, 98.

18 Agreeing with OTP (2003) (n 13) 14 para 46, whereby the expert group puts forward these considerations under the term 'unwillingness'.

19 The same view is taken by the Draft Additional Protocol for the Penal Enforcement of the International Convention for the Suppression and Punishment of the Crime of Apartheid: Article 25 (exoneration) para 8 (Double Jeopardy) d). UN Doc. E/CN.4/1426 (1981); Van den Wyngaert/Ongena, 'Ne bis in idem Principle, Including the Issue of Amnesty' in Cassese et al (eds), 705, 727. The Group of Experts on Complementarity considers the use of post-trial amnesties to be a significant indication of shielding, but this is not in itself sufficient to establish the existence of this criterion. See OTP (2003) (n 13) 30 et seqq Annex 4 (List of Indicia of Unwillingness or Inability to Genuinely Carry Out Proceedings).

20 This has been demonstrated, for example, in the Chilean situation by many judicial decisions using wording such as '[…] the crime was perpetrated in a context of serious, massive, and systematic human rights violations, committed by State agents […]; where impunity was granted to the executors of said programme by not interfering in their methods […]'. Chilean Supreme Court, Judgment of 24 May 2012, Roll No. 288-12, kidnapping of Rudy Cárcamo, author's translation). Further details in Antonia Marisol Martínez Vargas, 'La descripción del ataque generalizado y sistemático contra una población civil acaecido entre septiembre de 1973 y marzo de 1990' (2020) 103 et seq.

21 See Article 25(3)(d) ICC-Statute, Werle/Jeßberger, *Principles of International Criminal Law* (2020) 262 et seqq.

22 I am, of course, thinking here about decisions based on Rome Statute Article 20(3)(a) as one piece of relevant information for examining criminal responsibility. I do not suggest that this alone should be sufficient to convict someone.

23 Blakesley, 'Comparing the Ad-Hoc Tribunal for Crimes against Humanitarian Law in the Former Yugoslavia and the Project for an International Criminal Court, Prepared by the International Law Commission' (1996) 67 *AIDP/IAPL* 141, 173: '[i]t may well be important also to include in any statute for a permanent court situations where the International Tribunal will be more protective of the human rights of the accused than would be a national court, which may not be "impartial" or "well-disposed"'.

24 See SCSL, Separate opinion of Justice Geoffrey Robertson, 14 March 2004, SCSL-2004-14-AR72(E), Decision on Preliminary Motion Based on the Lack of Jurisdiction (Judicial Independence), *Prosecutor v. Norman AC*, para 2: '"[i]mpartiality" [...] is

generally regarded as the judicial characteristic of disinterest towards parties and their causes'.

25 See also SCSL, Separate opinion of Justice Geoffrey Robertson (n 24), para 2.

26 Article 14(1) sentence 2 International Covenant on Civil and Political Rights; Article 7(1)(d) African Charter on Human and Peoples' Rights (guarantees only impartiality); Article 8 (1) American Convention on Human Rights; Article 6(1) sentence 1 European Convention on Human Rights.

27 The binding French-language version of Article 17(2)(c) reads as follows: « *La procédure n'a pas menée de manière indépendante ou impartiale mais d'une manière qui, dans les circonstances, est incompatible avec l'intention de traduire en justice la personne concernée* ».

28 Schabas, *The International Criminal Court: A Commentary on the Rome Statute* (2016) 510. https://treaties.un.org/Pages/ViewDetails.aspx?src=TREATY&mtdsg_no=XVIII-10&chapter=18&clang=_en#EndDec (accessed 26 August 2024).

29 IACtHR, Judgment of 22 November 2004, Series C no 117, Carpio-Nicolle et. al. v. Guatemala, para 131 (hereinafter IACtHR, *Carpio-Nicolle et. al. v. Guatemala*).

30 '*Cf., inter alia,* Rome Statute of the International Criminal Court, U.N. Doc. A/CONF.183/9 (1998), Article 20; Statute of the International Tribunal for Rwanda, UN Doc. S/Res/955 (1994), Article 9; and Statute of the International Criminal Tribunal for the Former Yugoslavia, UN Doc. S/Res/827 (1993), Article 10'.

31 IACtHR, *Carpio-Nicolle et. al. v. Guatemala*, para 154.

32 '*Cf.* UN, Rome Statute of the International Criminal Court, adopted by the United Nations Diplomatic Conference of Plenipotentiaries on the Establishment of an International Criminal Court, UN Doc. A/CONF.183/9, July 17, 1998, Article 20; Statute of the International Criminal Tribunal for the former Yugoslavia, S/Res/827, 1993, Article 10, and Statute of the International Criminal Tribunal for Rwanda, S/Res/955, November 8, 1994, Article 9'.

33 ECCC, Decision of 3 November 2011, 002/19-09-2007/ECCC/TC, Decision on Ieng Sary's rule 89 preliminary objections (ne bis in idem and amnesty and pardon), *Prosecutor v Ieng Sary.*

34 ECCC, Decision of 3 November 2011, 002/19-09-2007/ECCC/TC, Decision on Ieng Sary's rule 89 preliminary objections (ne bis in idem and amnesty and pardon), *Prosecutor v Ieng Sary*, paragraphs 34 and 35.

35 Bernard, 'Ne bis in idem – Protector of Defendants' Rights of Jurisdictional Pointsman' (2011) 9 *JICJ* 863, 879.

Bibliography

Berg B E, 'The 1994 ILC Draft Statute for an International Criminal Court: A Principled Appraisal of Jurisdictional Structure' (1996) 28 *Case Western Reserve Journal of International Law* 221.

Bernard D, 'Ne bis in idem – Protector of Defendants' Rights of Jurisdictional Pointsman' (2011) 9 *Journal of International Criminal Justice* 863.

Blakesley C, 'Comparing the Ad-Hoc Tribunal for Crimes against Humanitarian Law in the Former Yugoslavia and the Project for an International Criminal Court, Prepared by the International Law Commission' (1996) 67 *International Review of Penal Law* 141.

Blakesley C, 'Commentary on Article 6: Obligation to Try or Extradite' (1993) 11 *Nouvelles Études Pénales* 133.

Cárdenas C, 'Labelling Crimes Against Humanity in Domestic Jurisdictions: Does nomen iuris matters? The Case of the Crimes in Colonia Dignidad' in Jeßberger F et al (eds), *Strafrecht und Systemunrecht* (Mohr Siebeck 2022).

Cárdenas C, *Die Zulässigkeitsprüfung vor dem Internationalen Strafgerichtshof. Zur Auslegung des Article 17 IStGH-Statut unter besonderer Berücksichtigung von Amnestien und Wahrheitskommissionen* (Berliner Wissenschaftsverlag 2005).

Holmes J, 'Complementarity: National Courts versus the ICC' in Cassese A et al (eds), *The Rome Statute of the International Criminal Court* (OUP 2002).

Martínez Vargas A M, *La descripción del ataque generalizado y sistemático contra una población civil acaecido entre septiembre de 1973 y marzo de 1990* (2020). https://repositorio.uchile.cl/bitstream/handle/2250/179737/La-descripcion-del-ataque-generalizado-y-sistematico-contra-una-poblacion-civil-acaecido-entre-septiembre-de-1973-y-marzo-de-1990.pdf?sequence=4

Meißner J, *Die Zusammenarbeit mit dem Internationalen Strafgerichtshof nach dem Römischen Statut* (Beck 2003).

Reisinger Coracini A/Tallgren I, 'Article 20 Ne bis in idem' in Kai Ambos (ed), *Rome Statute of the International Criminal Court. Article-by-Article Commentary* (4th edn, Beck-Hart-Nomos 2022).

Sadat L, *The International Criminal Court and the Transformation of International Law* (Transnational Publishers 2002).

Schabas W, *The International Criminal Court: A Commentary on the Rome Statute* (2nd edn, OUP 2016).

Specht B, *Die zwischenstaatliche Geltung des Grundsatzes ne bis in idem* (Springer 1999).

Van den Wyngaert C/Ongena T, 'Ne bis in idem Principle, Including the Issue of Amnesty' in Cassese A/Gaeta P et al (eds), *The Rome Statute of the International Criminal Court* (OUP 2002) 705.

Werle G/Jeßberger F, *Principles of International Criminal Law* (4th edn, OUP 2020).

Zimmermann A, 'Die Schaffung eines ständigen Internationalen Strafgerichtshofes Perspektiven und Probleme vor der Staatenkonferenz in Rom' (1998) 58 *Zeitschrift für ausländisches öffentliches Recht und Völkerrecht* 47.

11 Fraudulent *Res Judicata* and Impunity

A Chilean Perspective

Juan Pablo Mañalich R.

11.1 The Context: Fraudulent *Res Judicata* in the '*Quemados*' Case

11.1.1 The 'Quemados' Case Under the Principle of Ne Bis in Idem

On 21 March 2019, Judge Mario Carroza issued his decision in the '*quemados* case'.[1] The originating incident occurred on 2 July 1986, when a dictatorship-era military patrol attacked two young people, doused them in petrol, and set them on fire. One of the victims, Rodrigo Rojas De Negri, died shortly after the attack, while the other, Carmen Gloria Quintana Arancibia, survived with severe burns. In his 2019 ruling on the case, Judge Carroza convicted three of the 13 defendants as perpetrators of the murder of Rodrigo Rojas and the attempted murder of Carmen Gloria Quintana. He also found eight other defendants guilty as accomplices to both crimes while acquitting the remaining two defendants. One of those acquitted, to whom I will refer, in what follows, as 'the defendant', had in fact been the highest-ranking officer among the state agents involved. Judge Carroza nonetheless concluded that although his responsibility as a co-perpetrator of both felonies had been established, the defendant was nevertheless to be acquitted. This was on the basis that he had already faced a previous trial, culminating in a final decision exhibiting the legal force of *res judicata*.[2] In fact, the defendant had indeed been previously convicted – albeit of the lesser charges of negligent homicide and negligent bodily injury – receiving a notably lenient sentence ultimately ratified by the Chilean Supreme Court in 1994.

Judge Carroza's ruling raised the question of whether the previous decision convicting the defendant was to be recognized as an impediment to further prosecution according to the *ne bis in idem* principle. The crux of the matter was whether that previous conviction ought instead to be regarded as an instance of fraudulent *res judicata* (henceforth, 'FRJ'), thus incapable of preventing a new prosecution. This was the line taken by the Court of Appeals of Santiago, which in 2022 overturned Carroza's acquittal of the defendant and instead convicted him as a co-perpetrator of both crimes.[3] The Chilean Supreme Court upheld the latter ruling in January 2024.[4]

The first trial faced by the defendant took place during a transitional period encompassing the last phase of the 1973–1990 Pinochet dictatorship and the first

DOI: 10.4324/9781003470069-13

years of post-dictatorial democratic rule, years characterized by institutional fragility. The case was initially tried and adjudicated by the Second Military Court of Santiago in 1989.[5] On that occasion, the military judge imposed a suspended sentence of 300 days' imprisonment, granting the defendant the benefit of conditional remission. The Court Martial upheld the conviction on the first charge only – negligent homicide – acquitting him on the charge of negligent bodily injury.[6] The Supreme Court, however, reinstated the conviction for the second charge, upon reviewing the case in 1994. The definitive outcome was therefore conviction on both charges with a single sentence of 600 days of imprisonment.[7]

As Judge Carroza remarked in his 2019 ruling, those first proceedings faced by the defendant had been 'anomalous in [both] process and ruling, due to lack of impartiality and objectivity'.[8] Indeed, the cursory initial investigation strove to 'preserve a state of impunity or play down the seriousness of what actually happened'.[9] In virtue of this bias, according to Judge Carroza, the military judge had systematically '[...] ruled out anything that corroborated the version of the victims, as if that version did not exist'.[10] Judge Carroza thus concluded that the outcome of the initial investigation was overdetermined by 'different stratagems, deployed to alter the circumstances of the events'.[11]

Notwithstanding these considerations, which he explicitly linked to transitional justice concerns,[12] Judge Carroza ultimately decided to acquit the defendant based on his contention of *res judicata*. This is somewhat striking, since the recognition of the inhibitory force of the previous judgment should, if anything, have led to the dismissal of the new prosecution, rather than to the defendant's acquittal as a result of this further trial.[13] Despite having depicted the investigation conducted by the military court as 'spurious or illegitimate',[14] in the final analysis Judge Carroza allowed the fact that this first trial had led to a conviction issued by the country's Supreme Court to prevail. In his view, this fact precluded any assertion that the case had been adjudicated with the aim of 'shielding one of those responsible from a probable criminal sanction or favoring his impunity'.[15] Taking into account both that the sentence finally imposed by the Supreme Court was more severe than the one originally handed down by the Second Military Court of Santiago and the absence of 'sufficient reasons to suppose the existence of fraud',[16] Judge Carroza decided to grant the acquittal based on the claim of *res judicata*.

11.1.2 The Admissibility of the Defendant's New Conviction Based on the Fraudulent Nature of His Previous Conviction

However, as we have seen, the Court of Appeals of Santiago reversed Judge Carroza's ruling on the grounds that the *res judicata* effect of the previous conviction was 'merely apparent'.[17] The crucial premise for this proposition was that the 1994 Supreme Court decision, 'regardless of the fact that it was pronounced in a historical era of transition to democracy', had relied on

> a factual substratum emanating from a process in respect of which it is not possible to predicate that it had been conducted [...] in an independent or impartial

> manner, in accordance with the due process of law recognized by international law; being furthermore incompatible with the intention of bringing [the defendant] to justice.[18]

On the basis of this disavowal of the legal force of the sentence previously imposed on the defendant, the Santiago Court of Appeals proceeded, as we have seen, to convict the defendant on the charges of murder and attempted murder. He was sentenced to a twenty-year prison term.[19] In support of its decision, the Court explicitly referred to the doctrine of FRJ developed by the Inter-American Court of Human Rights ('IACtHR'), the canonical formulation of which can be found in *Almonacid Arellano v. Chile*.[20] According to this doctrine, the protection afforded to a putative defendant against a subsequent prosecution regarding the same factual framework does not apply:

> (i) when a court had dismissed the case or acquitted an alleged author in order to shield the accused party from criminal responsibility; (ii) when the proceedings 'were not conducted independently or impartially in accordance with due procedural guarantees'; and (iii) when 'there was no real intent to bring those responsible to justice'.[21]

Until recently, the doctrine of FRJ had been very occasionally invoked by Chilean courts, the Supreme Court amongst them,[22] when adjudicating cases involving crimes perpetrated under the Pinochet regime. Salient among those decisions was the one issued by the Rancagua Court of Appeals some years after the IACtHR ruling against Chile in *Almonacid Arellano*. Both rulings concerned the summary extrajudicial execution of a member of the Chilean Communist Party by police officers during the dictatorship.[23] The IACtHR's 2006 ruling declared that under the American Convention on Human Rights (ACHR), the definitive dismissal of the case that had been pronounced by a domestic military court in virtue of Chile's 1978 Amnesty Decree Law could not be allowed to bar a new prosecution against the alleged perpetrator.[24] In its 2013 ruling, the Rancagua Court accordingly rejected the defense's contention of *res judicata*, falling into line with the IACtHR's decision concerning the fraudulence of the original dismissal of the case.

In the *quemados* case, however, there was no explicit ruling by the IACtHR requiring a new prosecution. The Santiago Court of Appeals nevertheless based its reversal of the defendant's acquittal on the IACtHR's doctrine of FRJ. This doctrine was then explicitly validated by the Supreme Court when upholding the defendant's new conviction. In so doing, the Supreme Court acknowledged that its own previous decision was affected by a kind of fraudulence that rendered the decision without effect as a bar against the new prosecution faced by the defendant. Indeed, the Supreme Court asserted that 'the decision pronounced under those conditions [...] lacks the force of real *res judicata* of a final decision'.[25]

The remainder of this chapter will first present an account of the doctrine of FRJ in light of some prominent decisions issued by the IACtHR, before enquiring as to whether FRJ may be held to apply to cases where what is involved is a form of relative – as distinct from absolute – impunity.

11.2 The Doctrine of Fraudulent *Res Judicata*

11.2.1 Fraudulent Res Judicata: Grounds and Scope

The phrase 'fraudulent *res judicata*' denotes a criterion, or set of criteria, for bypassing the force of a (purportedly) final judicial decision as a *de jure* obstacle to a new prosecution against a person who has faced a previous prosecution in respect of the same factual framework.[26] According to the doctrine of FJR, such bypassing is justified when either the decision itself or the process of which it is the result has been irregular to the point that its legal authoritativeness should be regarded as merely apparent.[27]

When recognized as an institution of criminal procedural law, FRJ works as a mechanism for disregarding the material juridical force of a judicial decision. The characterization of an instance of *res judicata* as fraudulent accordingly purports to deprive the defendant of the immunity that, as per the *ne bis in idem* principle, would otherwise protect her against a new prosecution.[28] Insofar as FRJ functions as a criterion for disavowing a procedural defense that a person facing a new prosecution would otherwise be entitled to raise against it, FRJ cannot be assimilated to what, under Chilean law, is known as the 'revision' of a definitive judicial decision.[29] A revision of this sort takes the form of a procedural action that aims to invalidate a judicial decision already in force. The distinction between these two institutions becomes critical once we consider that, under Chilean law, the revision of a definitive judicial decision can only operate in favor of a person convicted by the decision in question.[30]

This aspect of Chilean procedural law explains why the revision mechanism has indeed been available for invalidating sentences issued during the early phase of dictatorial rule by so-called 'war councils' (*consejos de guerra*). These were military courts, operating under the pretext of a state of war that supposedly existed at the time. They irregularly tried both military officers, and civilians taken to be supporters of the deposed Allende government.[31] Such proceedings amounted to mock trials, with no respect for minimal standards of due process and many supposed 'defendants' facing charges for acts that had been criminalized *ex post facto*. Chile's first official truth commission report documented 50 death sentences carried out as a result of war councils, a figure that represents only a small fraction of the total number of sentences unlawfully imposed in this manner.[32] In the aftermath of a subsequent IACtHR decision, in *Omar Maldonado v Chile*, the Supreme Court has granted revisions resulting in the annulment of a large number of the sentences imposed by these war councils.[33]

By contrast, where a defendant has unjustly benefited from an irregularly produced judicial decision – as occurred in the *quemados* case – the doctrine of FRJ provides the only institutional mechanism for enabling a new prosecution. The fact that this mechanism lacks any explicit recognition at the level of legislatively enacted procedural rules could be taken as a decisive reason for disallowing its operation. Any such determination would, however, overlook the fact that the doctrine of FRJ seeks to make explicit an immanent limit of the procedural closure normally achieved through a final judicial decision. In this sense, to speak of such a limit as 'immanent' suggests that it can be inferred from the self-same basis on which any given legal institution rests.

Consider, for instance, the impediment to prosecution represented by statutory limitation. Its operation may be understood as grounded on the assumption that prosecution of the alleged crime has been possible – at least in legal terms – during the period upon whose expiry prosecution will become barred. Hence, if prosecution of an alleged felony turns out to have been impossible during all or part of said period due to some legally recognized obstacle, one should be able to claim that the lapse during which that obstacle was in effect ought not to count for the purposes of calculating the date at which prosecution ceases to be admissible.[34] In this way, the very rationale for having an arrangement of statutory limitation at all signals an intrinsic constraint regarding the conditions of its application.[35]

Can we recognize such an immanent limit to the efficacy of a final judicial decision as an obstacle to a new prosecution concerning the same factual framework? To answer this question requires us to identify the rationale underlying the (procedural) principle of *ne bis in idem*. One well-known rationale points to a concern for avoidance of the kind of state harassment that would befall someone who comes to be exposed, on more than one occasion, to the procedural risk of being declared guilty of criminal behavior and thus punished in connection with the same world fragment.[36] The relevant procedural risk consists in the chance that the accused be convicted, according to the law, of whatever she could have been accused of under the same factual framework that provides thematic unity to the process. Thus, a person who has faced prosecution via a judicial process resulting in a final judgment becomes protected by acquiring immunity against the possibility of a new prosecution concerning the same factual framework. The justification for this immunity lies in the consideration that the state will already have had an opportunity to hold the defendant accountable for her putatively criminal behavior linked to the relevant world fragment.

However, the operation of this obstacle presupposes that the defendant was indeed exposed to the relevant procedural risk. In reality, this depends on whether the first trial served as the setting for a genuine prosecution.[37] Thus, to the extent that the previous trial was conducted in a way that rendered the procedural risk – or 'jeopardy' – either negligible or non-existent for the defendant, the legal force of the corresponding final decision ought to be treated as merely apparent.[38] In such a case, the defendant will not have faced a minimally serious risk of being convicted for what, given the factual framework that makes up the subject matter of the trial, she could have been accused of. In its decision concerning the *quemados* case, the Santiago Court of Appeals acknowledged this latter rationale as the basis for disregarding the contention that the defendant's first conviction could bar a new prosecution. As the Court observed, the original trial had not been conducted in a way compatible with the intention

> to try [the defendant] and, if appropriate, to sentence him to the penalties that were legally his due given [what] actually occurred, according to the historical truth that the criminal proceedings [...] were meant to uncover.[39]

11.2.2 The Case Law of the IACtHR

A review of the case law of the IACtHR should shed further light on the scope of its doctrine of FRJ.[40] We have already seen how, in *Almonacid Arellano*, the Court stated three alternative criteria for fraudulence in relation to judicial decisions over charges of crimes constitutive of human rights violations. The satisfaction of any one of these three criteria would render inapplicable the *ne bis in idem* principle, which, as recognized by Art 8.4 of the ACHR, protects against a new prosecution 'for the same facts'.[41] According to the Court, this protection against a new prosecution, however, ceases to apply whenever: (1) the trial court's handling of the case was guided by 'the purpose of absolving the accused of criminal responsibility'; (2) the proceedings were not conducted independently and impartially under 'due process of law', or (3) there was no 'real intention to bring the potentially responsible party to justice'.[42]

It has been observed that criterion (1) applies to situations that exemplify the central case of FRJ, since a final judicial decision thus issued would be nothing more than a judgment issued by a 'partial court',[43] resulting in the defendant being immunized against the procedural risk that, *de jure*, she should have faced. The same consideration would seem to apply, *mutatis mutandis*, to situations covered by criterion (3). Here, however, the neutralization of the corresponding procedural risk would be the consequence of the interference of some other state organ in the outcome of the trial.[44] Thus understood, these two criteria apply only to cases in which the (mock) proceedings have not resulted in a conviction. Although this is not made explicit in the formulation of criterion (3), it should be clear that a purportedly final judicial decision reflecting the lack of any real intention of bringing the defendant to justice will take the form of either a dismissal or an acquittal.

The same cannot be said of criterion (2), which applies to cases where there are 'violations of the safeguards of a fair trial that, without them being directly present in the decisions that put an end to the proceedings, enable their invalidation'.[45] According to Article 8.1 of the ACHR, the standard that a judicial process must meet in order for the resultant decision to be recognized as *res judicata*, thus capable of inhibiting a new prosecution against the same person for the same facts, is that the given court act independently *and* impartially. Hence, either a lack of independence or a lack of impartiality exhibited by the court in question would suffice for the fraudulence of the decision produced through a trial conducted by such a court. This holds true regardless of whether the decision takes the form of an acquittal or dismissal, on the one hand, or a conviction, on the other.

Within the case law of the IACtHR, the characterization of a judicial decision as fraudulent on the basis of the lack of impartiality or independence of the court from which it emanated is further linked to the principle of the 'exceptionality of military jurisdiction'.[46] In *Nadege Dorzema v Dominican Republic*, the Court observed that *res judicata* can be deemed 'apparent' when, given the particular circumstances of the case, it is evident that "judicial investigation, the proceeding and the judicial decisions were not truly intended to elucidate the facts, but rather to obtain an acquittal of the accused", and "judicial officials lacked the requisite independence and impartiality".[47] According to the Court, this was so in the case at hand, not least because the case had been placed under military jurisdiction, in contravention of "the parameters of exceptionality and restriction" that ought to characterize that jurisdiction. This in turn had resulted in "the application of a personal jurisdiction that operated without taking into account the nature of the acts involved".[48] The Court concluded that

> [t]he intervention of military jurisdiction in this kind of case does not refer only to the prosecution by a court, but essentially to the investigation itself, because it constitutes the initiation and the necessary presumption for the subsequent intervention of an incompetent court.[49]

11.3 Fraudulent *Res Judicata* and Impunity

The recognition of FRJ as an immanent limit to the inhibitory force of final judgments is intertwined with the IACtHR's attitude toward the issue of impunity. To appreciate what this connection consists of, we need to specify the scope of the concept of impunity.

In a legal sense, to speak of 'impunity' presupposes that someone liable to punishment is not, in the end, so punished.[50] This means, among other things, that the lack of criminalization of a particular form of conduct cannot be seen as giving rise to a situation of impunity, at least if the latter notion is interpreted relative to the (domestic) legal system of the respective state.[51] Nevertheless, it ought to be clear that not every situation in which a person who should, according to the law, have been punished is not punished can be pejoratively or critically characterized as a situation of impunity. For the latter to be the case, it is also necessary that the absence of punishment be due to factors that do not correspond to the normal operation of the given criminal justice system. In other words, impunity arises where the absence of punishment can be seen as the result of a prior injustice or irregularity.[52] We find examples of procedural anomalies of this kind in cases where the trial judge accepts a bribe to decide in favor of the defendant, a witness is coerced to lie in court in the interests of the defendant, or political pressure leads to a prosecution not being pursued.[53] Cases of this sort involve *de facto* impunity. However, one should also acknowledge the possibility of *de jure* impunity.[54] This can occur through, for instance, the granting of amnesties or executive pardons, but also by placing the prosecution of crimes attributed to agents of the state under the jurisdiction of military courts.

The distinction between *de facto* and *de jure* impunity needs to be further combined with a second distinction, namely, between absolute and relative impunity. A situation of absolute impunity is one in which a person liable to punishment for some criminally significant behavior is shielded from any and all punishment. By contrast, a situation of relative impunity is one in which a person is shielded from a punishment minimally adequate to the seriousness of the criminally significant behavior imputable to her. This last possibility is compatible with some measure of punishment being imposed, insofar as that punishment is significantly less severe than the one deserved. In a situation of relative impunity, the punishment actually imposed can be considered ludicrous.[55]

We can now revisit the three criteria of fraudulence put forward by the IACtHR. Criteria (1) and (3) point to ways in which the neutralization of the risk that the defendant be (appropriately) punished for what is imputable to her becomes manifest through a final decision of dismissal or acquittal. The fraudulence they indicate is accordingly linked to expressions of absolute impunity. The same cannot be said of criterion (2), which applies to cases in which the defendant does not come to face the risk of being punished adequately for what is imputable to her. Although she may end up being convicted of some offense, the punishment imposed is so significantly inferior to the magnitude of the punishment deserved that it can only be taken as ludicrous. This means that the fraudulence indicated by criterion (2) is linked to expressions of relative impunity.

There will be cases in which it may be highly uncertain whether the punishment imposed on the defendant should be considered ludicrous. However, this need not prevent us from recognizing clear cases of the phenomenon under consideration. By way of example, suppose that a man who, driven by jealousy, has intentionally killed his wife ends up being convicted of a charge of negligent homicide. Now let us suppose that this outcome was due to steps taken by the prosecuting body – motivated by, say, a bias of 'gender solidarity' toward the defendant – that resulted in the manipulation of evidence that would otherwise have supported a conviction on a charge of femicide (or, at least, murder). In the hypothetical situation described, there should be no doubt that the trial, despite having ended in the conviction of the defendant, would have given rise to a situation of impunity.[56]

We may now conclude by re-examining the decision by the Court of Appeals of Santiago that reversed the acquittal of a defendant as a result of the retrial of the *quemados* case, a decision that the Supreme Court ultimately validated. Does this decision find actual support in the doctrine of FJR? The answer should be affirmative. Although the defendant was indeed convicted as a result of the first process, both the Santiago Court and the Supreme Court established that he did not face a minimally serious risk of being punished in congruence with the seriousness of the two crimes of which he could have been convicted. Hence, one can assert that the first trial resulted in relative impunity, which correlates with the second criterion of fraudulence stated by the IACtHR. Moreover, it seems warranted to say that this impunity outcome was a consequence of the lack of impartiality and independence with which that first process was conducted from the outset.

Notes

1 Judgment by Judge Mario Carroza, Role No 143-2013 (21 March 2019). For a thorough outline of both crimes and the proceedings to which they gave rise, see Mañalich, *Derecho penal y terrorismo de Estado* (2023) 103 et seqq.
2 As suggested by Javier Escobar, the 'finality' of a judicial decision possessing the force of *res judicata* consists in its being irrevocable, such that 'no further ordinary remedies are available' to challenge it, or 'the parties have exhausted such remedies or have permitted the time limit to expire without availing themselves of them'. Javier Escobar, *Ne bis in idem and Multiple Sanctioning Systems* (2023) 183.
3 Santiago Court of Appeals, Judgment of 21 March 2022, Role No 4483-2019. More precisely, the attempted murder in question was (properly) labelled as a 'last-act' (or complete) attempt, which under the Chilean Penal Code (*Código Penal*) leads to a more severe punishment than a 'first-act' (or incomplete) attempt.
4 Supreme Court of Chile, Judgment of 5 January 2024, Role No 22276-2022.
5 Military Court of Santiago, Judgment of 24 August 1989, Role No 1609-1989.
6 Court Martial, Judgment of 2 January 1991, Role No 1132-1986.
7 Supreme Court of Chile, Judgment of 14 December 1994, Role No 4110.
8 Judgment by Judge Mario Carroza, Role No 143-2013 (21 March 2019), cons 4(9). Translations from domestic Chilean court decisions are the author's, here and throughout.
9 Judgment by Judge Mario Carroza, Role No 143-2013 (21 March 2019), cons 33.
10 Judgment by Judge Mario Carroza, Role No 143-2013 (21 March 2019), cons 35.
11 Judgment by Judge Mario Carroza, Role No 143-2013 (21 March 2019), cons 38.
12 Judgment by Judge Mario Carroza, Role No 143-2013 (21 March 2019), cons 89.
13 As stated in Art. 408, No 7 of the Chilean Code of Penal Procedure (*Código de Procedimiento Penal*).
14 Judgment by Judge Mario Carroza, Role No 143-2013 cons 87.
15 Judgment by Judge Mario Carroza, Role No 143-2013 cons 92.
16 Judgment by Judge Mario Carroza, Role No 143-2013 cons 92.
17 Santiago Court of Appeals, Judgment of 21 March 2022, Role No 4483-2019.
18 Santiago Court of Appeals, Judgment of 21 March 2022, Role No 4483-2019 cons 15.
19 The Santiago Court ruled that the 600 days of imprisonment that the defendant had served as a result of the previous sentence were to be discounted from the time to be served as a consequence of this new conviction. This is tantamount to a clear recognition that the inapplicability of the protection provided by procedural *ne bis in idem* against multiple prosecution is perfectly compatible with the applicability of the protection provided by substantive *ne bis in idem* against multiple punishment. On this point see Mañalich, *Estudios sobre la fundamentación y la determinación de la pena* (2018) 67 et seqq, 75 et seqq; Escobar (2023) (n 2) 173.
20 IACtHR, Judgment of 26 September 2006, *Almonacid-Arellano et al v. Chile*.
21 Medina, *The American Convention of Human Rights* (2017) 321; see also Escobar (2023) (n 2) 182.
22 See, for instance, Supreme Court of Chile, Judgment of 4 August 2010, Role No 7089-2009 (4 August 2010), as well as Supreme Court of Chile, Judgment of 25 May 2017, Role No 78951-2016.
23 Rancagua Court of Appeals, Judgment of 14 January 2013, Role No 103-2011.
24 The domestic Amnesty Decree Law, *Decreto Ley* 2191, was imposed by the regime in April 1978.
25 Supreme Court of Chile, Judgment of 5 January 2024, Role No 22276-2022 cons 22.

26 See Mañalich (2023) (n 1) 114 et seqq.
27 On this point, Morgenstern, *Cosa juzgada fraudulenta* (2015) 11 et seqq.
28 See Escobar (2023) (n 2) 181 et seq.
29 See Mañalich, 'Justicia, procedimiento y acción de revisión' (2020) 26 (1) *IP* 28 et seqq, 30 et seqq, 36 et seqq.
30 This contrasts with what under German law takes the form of a *Wiederaufnahme* – a term which can be rendered in English as 'resumption' – enabling a retrial regarding the same factual framework. This can also operate against the person who faced the accusation that produced the purportedly final decision. See Lindemann/Lineau, 'Mechanisms for Correcting Judicial Errors in Germany' (2020) 4 *ELR* 73, 76 et seqq.
31 Salvador Allende (1970–1973) was the elected socialist president deposed by the 1973 coup. For more on war councils, see Hau, 'Consejos de guerra y justicia transicional' (2021) 17 (2) *DOAJ* 357 et seqq.
32 Hau, 'Consejos de guerra y justicia transicional' 363 et seqq.
33 IACtHR, Judgment of 2 September 2015, *Maldonado et al v Chile*, requiring the Chilean state to provide reparations to a group of former Air Force officials convicted by war councils after being tortured. The Supreme Court's first post-Maldonado judgment annulling sentences passed by war councils was Role No 27543-2016 (3 October 2016). For more detail see Hau (n 31) 369 et seqq.
34 See Mañalich, *Terror, pena y amnistía* (2010) 208 et seqq, 211 et seqq.
35 This argument is neutral with regard to whether there are also transcendent limits, imposed by international law, on the operation of procedural institutions that, by inhibiting prosecution, may prevent the imposition of punishment in a manner tantamount to granting impunity to the responsible agents. Such transcendent limits become particularly salient when it comes to the prosecution of crimes against humanity and other international crimes. As we shall see below, in the main text, what underlies the doctrine of FJR as developed by the IACtHR is rather a combined postulate of both immanent and transcendent limits to the *ne bis in idem* principle.
36 See Mañalich (2018) (n 19) 116 et seqq; Escobar (2023) (n 2) 180 et seqq.
37 On this, see Morgenstern (2015) (n 27) 25 et seqq, 33 et seqq.
38 It accordingly suffices that the risk be significantly reduced, as opposed to completely eliminated. On this issue, in direct reference to the scope of the double jeopardy clause of the Fifth Amendment of the US Constitution, see Rudstein, 'Double Jeopardy and the Fraudulently-Obtained Acquittal' (1995) 60 *MLR* 607 et seqq, 638 et seqq, although Rudstein argues against the sufficiency of a mere reduction of the relevant risk.
39 Santiago Court of Appeals, Judgment of 21 March 2022, Role No 4483-2019 cons 15.
40 Mañalich (2023) (n 1) 124 et seqq.
41 See Medina (2017) (n 21) 320 et seqq. The wording of the ACHR provision is rightly criticized for restricting the protection in favor of the accused who has been 'acquitted' by a final decision. The consequence is that only through a rather liberal interpretation of the text can that same protection be extended to someone who has been convicted by a final decision. See, on this matter, Ottaviano, *El principio* ne bis in idem. *La prohibición de doble sanción y de doble enjuiciamiento penal en el Derecho Internacional* (2008) 229 et seqq; 234 et seqq.
42 IACtHR, Judgment of 26 September 2006, *Almonacid Arellano v Chile* para 154. It should be noted that, in this same context, the IACtHR postulated a further restriction on the applicability of the *ne bis in idem principle*, which transcends the realm of FRJ and concerns cases in which 'new facts or evidence come to light that may allow for the identification of those responsible for human rights violations, and even more so, those

responsible for crimes against humanity'. For a critical assessment of this last approach, see Mañalich (2023) (n 1) 135 et seq.

43 Ottaviano (2008) (n 41) 265.

44 See Ottaviano (2008) (n 41) 266.

45 Ottaviano (2008) (n 41) 267.

46 The leading decisions on this issue are the judgments by the IACtHR, both in *Las Palmeras v Colombia* (6 December 2001) and in *Diecinueve comerciantes v Colombia* (5 July 2004). See Dondé Matute, 'El concepto de impunidad: leyes de amnistía y otras formas estudiadas por la Corte Interamericana de Derechos Humanos' in Sistema Interamericano de Protección de los Derechos Humanos y Derecho penal Internacional (ed) 263, 290 et seq; Ottaviano (2008) (n 41) 261 et seq.

47 IACtHR, Judgment of 24 October 2012, *Nadege Dorzema v Dominican Republic* para 196.

48 IACtHR, Judgment of 24 October 2012, *Nadege Dorzema v Dominican Republic* para 197.

49 IACtHR, Judgment of 24 October 2012, *Nadege Dorzema v Dominican Republic* para 198.

50 Duff, 'Crimes Against Humanity and Hostes Generis Humani' (2018) 47 (2) *NJLP* 138 et seqq, 144; also Pensky, 'Impunity: A Philosophical Analysis' in Bergsmo/Buis (eds) 241 et seqq, 251; although Pensky contrasts this strict notion of impunity with a broader notion by which impunity should rather be understood as a lack of accountability.

51 On the considerably broader extension given to the concept of impunity within the case law of the IACtHR, see Dondé (2010) (n 46) 263 et seqq, 265 et seqq, 268.

52 Pensky (2019) (n 50) 251 et seq.

53 Pensky (2019) (n 50) 252.

54 On this distinction, see Ambos, *Impunidad y derecho penal internacional* (1999) 34 et seq.

55 On the relevance of the *quantum* of the sanction eventually imposed as a possible indicator of impunity, Ollé, 'Derecho penal, amnistías, indultos y cosa juzgada fraudulenta en los procesos transicionales' in Turégano (ed) 79 et seqq, 82.

56 This consideration finds support in the restrictions some jurisdictions impose on the *ne bis in idem* principle. For an overview of cases in which, under the double jeopardy clause of the Fifth Amendment of the US Constitution, a previous conviction deemed fraudulently obtained has not been recognized as a barring to subsequent prosecution, see Rudstein (1995) (n 38) 627 et seqq.

Bibliography

Ambos K, *Impunidad y derecho penal internacional* (2nd edn, Ad-Hoc 1999).

Dondé Matute J, 'El concepto de impunidad: leyes de amnistía y otras formas estudiadas por la Corte Interamericana de Derechos Humanos' in Elsner/Ambos et al (eds), *Sistema interamericano de protección de los derechos humanos y derecho penal internacional* (Konrad-Adenauer Stiftung 2010) 263.

Duff A, 'Crimes Against Humanity and Hostes Generis Humani' (2018) 47 (2) *Netherlands Journal of Legal Philosophy* 138.

Escobar J, *Ne bis in idem and Multiple Sanctioning Systems* (Springer 2023).

Hau B, 'Consejos de guerra y justicia transicional' (2021) 17 (2) *Anuario de Derechos Humanos* 355.

Lindemann M/Lineau F, 'Mechanisms for Correcting Judicial Errors in Germany' (2020) 4 *Erasmus Law Review* 73.

Mañalich J P, *Terror, pena y amnistía* (Flandes Indiano 2010).

Mañalich J P, *Estudios sobre la fundamentación y la determinación de la pena* (Thomson Reuters 2018).

Mañalich J P, 'Justicia, procedimiento y acción de revisión' (2020) 2 (1) *Ius et Praxis* 28.

Mañalich J P, *Derecho penal y terrorismo de Estado* (Roneo 2023).

Medina C, *The American Convention of Human Rights* (2nd edn, Intersentia 2017).

Morgenstern F, *Cosa juzgada fraudulenta* (BdeF 2015).

Ollé M, 'Derecho penal, amnistías, indultos y cosa juzgada fraudulenta en los procesos transicionales', in Turégano I (ed), *La justicia de transición: concepto, instrumentos y experiencias* (Editorial Universidad del Rosario 2013).

Ottaviano S, *El principio* ne bis in idem. *La prohibición de doble sanción y de doble enjuiciamiento penal en el Derecho Internacional* (Universidad Austral de Buenos Aires 2008). https://riu.austral.edu.ar/handle/123456789/124

Pensky M, 'Impunity: A Philosophical Analysis' in Bergsmo M/Buis E (eds), *Philosophical Foundations of International Criminal Law* (Torkel Opsahl Academic EPublisher 2019).

Rudstein D, 'Double Jeopardy and the Fraudulently-Obtained Acquittal' (1995) 60 *Missouri Law Review* 607.

Part III

Intent, Mistake of Law, and Other Issues of Imputation

12 Judicial Abuse and Mistake of Law

A Normative Approach Based on a Comparative Law Perspective

Antonio Martins

12.1 Judicial Abuse of Office, Facts, and Law

In many legal systems, judicial abuse of office is treated as a special offence. That is the case, for example, in Spain or in Germany.[1] Furthermore, in German criminal law the offence of judicial perversion of justice (*Rechtsbeugung*)[2] is intended to have a barrier effect (*Sperrwirkung*),[3] precluding other charges such as murder, torture, and unlawful detention unless it is recognized that there has been judicial abuse. Thus, an analysis of judges' criminal responsibility cannot circumvent the question of whether the judge has deliberately broken the law. In Brazilian law there is no specific offense of judicial abuse, but art. 319 of the Brazilian criminal code rules that there has been a general abuse of law if a public official performs or fails to perform an official act against the law.[4] Also in this case we see that the intention to break the law is a requisite for commission of the offense.

The fact that the knowledge of law is an element of the legal prohibition makes the situation in all the aforementioned legal systems more interesting, as the usual distinction between *Tatbestandsirrtum* (a mistake concerning the objective elements of the legal definition of an offense) and *Verbotsirrtum* (a mistake concerning the knowledge of the conduct's prohibition)[5] loses its obviousness.

I will refer to the first kind of mistake, from now on, as a 'mistake of fact', even though this is not quite exact (because the distinction between mistake of fact and mistake of law is now considered obsolete by the prevailing doctrine in Germany).[6] While a mistake of fact excludes intention or conditional intent (*dolus eventualis*), the second kind of mistake (which I will henceforth call 'mistake of law') excludes culpability, if unavoidable, or mitigates it, if avoidable. Whether someone knows a fact, or is aware that a behavior is interdicted, is a matter of fact. Whether a mistake of law was avoidable or not is, however, a normative matter.

This means that, while the difficulties regarding a mistake of fact lie particularly in questions about proof and evidence, the difficulties surrounding a mistake of law also include a normative issue: namely, the reasonableness of a mistake, and thus the normative acceptability of a defense. The dilemma touches on the question of how far we are willing to accept that someone could not know the law. This normative issue involves socialization problems, cultural diversity, religious preferences, etc., and accordingly it challenges the factual validity of a legal

DOI: 10.4324/9781003470069-15

system. An affirmative answer to the question of whether a mistake of law was unavoidable means that law had no coercive force in a given situation. It means, furthermore, that the legal system or the state was itself responsible for a failure of communication with a citizen or a non-citizen.

If the legal definition of the offense requires knowledge about the law – as we have already seen that it does, at least, in German, Spanish, and Brazilian law – then a mistake of law excludes not only culpability but (also) the intention to break the law. Does this imply that we are faced with what is exclusively a question of fact, with no normative content? This chapter will address itself particularly to this problem, prefacing its analysis with the following three sets of opening remarks.

The first relates to the meaning of 'law' or 'legal' as referenced by § 339 of the German criminal code (Strafgesetzbuch, StGB). It is disputed whether this should be read as including positive law as well as natural law, whether it depends on the real interpretation and application of law in a given legal community, or whether we can presuppose that there are universal legal principles that have to be respected by every legal system.[7] This question must be faced if we intend to draw general conclusions regarding two different types of scenario: first, where judicial perversion of justice consists of applying (very) unjust – possibly illegal – law, and second, where judicial perversion of justice consists of not applying positive law.

The second set of opening remarks concerns the fact that the theoretical conclusions that we draw about intention and mistake of law for judicial abuse of office cannot be generalized to other kinds of offense (such as murder, torture, and unlawful detention). They will, however, play a specific role in determining the framework within which we will analyze the possibility of a mistake of law in those abovementioned kinds of offense. An affirmative answer to the question of whether the judge knew that he or she was acting against the law binds us to a conclusion about his or her knowledge or lack of knowledge of the fact that through his or her decision, he or she was actually committing murder, torture, or another crime.

If this is the case – and here is my third opening remark – the two main subjects that we will have to address in our discussion become, on the one hand, the analysis of the concept of law that grounds the responsibility for general or judicial abuse of law, and, on the other, the subjective requisites needed in order to affirm or deny that a judge knew that he or she was breaking the law. This holds true for all the crimes we are interested in.

12.2 Law as a Fact

12.2.1 Law as a Normative Element of an Offense

The classical distinction between mistake of fact and mistake of law is based on the distinction between the knowledge of a fact and knowledge of a rule or rules that say how people should act. This distinction does not apply to our case, in which both levels of knowledge intermingle. If law is a normative element of the offense of judicial abuse, then the expectation that an official knows what he or she is doing as a matter of fact includes the awareness that he or she is violating the law. In other words, knowledge about the law can be compared to the knowledge of any factual element of an offense, such as property, in the case of theft, or the concept of the person, in the case of murder. The practical consequence is that ignorance of law does exclude intention and conditional intent.

12.2.2 Law as an Institutional Fact

As an element of the legal definition of crime, I may suggest that we conceive of the concept of law as an institutional fact after the usage of John Searle.[8] In so doing, we accept that the legal system depends on collective intentionality,[9] which we therefore count on as a system of commands and constitutive rules that gives a specific form and order to social life. From this point of view, we cannot ignore the fact that this system has much to do with the view of a given society at a given time. The way people see and interpret this system is an essential element of its concept. Such views may include interpretations that are wrong or unacceptable when made from within other normative parameters.

This concept refers to law in the sense of the whole legal system, even an unjust one. We live, however, in a complex world of norms established at different levels, including strong moral rules, parochial moral conventions, human rights norms or law, and international law. Only the overlap of all these levels will give us a more precise concept of valid law, meaning that we are bound to accept a marked flexibility in the shape of the concept of law. This flexibility responds to the normative cultural context but also depends on individual standpoints, social position, and evaluations. A judge normally has a more consciously considered notion of the intersection between local and international legal rules than does an ordinary citizen. Otherwise, however, the judge is mostly more influenced by existing legal culture than a normal citizen would be.

One problem that emerges from this kind of conception of law concerns the tension between the facticity and the normativity of law. It cannot be seriously doubted that what judges really do, what judicial practice actually is, is relevant at least to some extent to a broad conception of law. Nonetheless, how can we argue that judges who make the law act deliberately against the law, especially if they can use the argument that other courts apply the law in the same way? This paradox can only be circumvented if we formulate the problem in terms of a system of normative claims, in which the weight of the court's practices is less than the weight of other normative variants.

We should not lose sight of the fact that this conception of a system of claims in which different factors apply is already what allows us to condemn past judicial decisions. In other words, faced with additional normative elements such as international law and human rights, we assume that those previous judicial decisions were wrong, that they were against the law. Thus, the problem does not consist of recognizing that conflictive system of normative claims and its imbalance as a model but of asking to what extent the allegation of a mistake of law is acceptable – if at all – within this system.

12.2.3 Intersections between Normative Systems

The abovementioned normative 'force field' will be generated by a set of claims that can be better understood as competing discourses that each want to contribute to answering the question of whether or not a decision is correct. Naturally, legal arguments neutralize alternative and conflicting reasons coming from other social fields, e.g., morality.[10] This neutralization occurs through discursive control. Reflexive recourse to other discursive languages is, however, constitutive of legal discourse, as well as being part of its functioning.[11] In hermeneutic terms, we can say that the process of interpreting and applying norms only takes place once they are inserted into a social ethos, i.e., an ethical and political community, however pluralistic and contradictory that community may be.[12] In operational terms, we have to recognize, first, that the language of law is insufficient to account for the reality to which its norms refer, and second, that legal decisions (including doctrine) will have to demonstrate a certain social plausibility in relation to other normative systems and maintain some degree of compatibility with these.[13]

A correct understanding of the normative element 'law' therefore presupposes more than simply a reference to the system of abstract norms of the legal system. It must also encompass the field of normative references that contribute to the collective understanding of that system. The understanding of this system depends on the relationship between these abstract norms and what is accepted as law. Elements of this field of normative discourses include morality, ethics, and, to a lesser extent, religion, politics, judicial customs, etc. This field of normative discourses itself, however, gives law an autonomous existence, recognizing the authority of its norms, its exclusionary character, and – above all – the decision-making positions attributed to certain members of the justice system.[14]

Having defined in general terms a concept of law of which social actors may be ignorant, let us turn to the specific problem of the knowledge of the law and its normative consequences.

12.3 Knowing the Law

What does an offender need to know in order to act with awareness of violating the law? What could exclude his or her responsibility by virtue of an ignorance of fact? (here, of the institutional fact, 'law')? Although the content of the required knowledge is an institutional fact, I want to argue that its determination coincides with the normative parameters for determining what is acceptable as a mistake of law. In other words, the concept of law required for the imputation of judicial abuse will be determined by the same normative considerations developed to solve the problem of the reasonableness or unreasonableness of a mistake of law. Why is this so? My suggestion is that the doctrine of the mistake of law has done the work of determining which arguments are acceptable in that system of normative coordinates to which we referred in the previous section. Or, at least, has paved the way for discussion of the limits of the use of arguments from other normative systems. Let us now turn, then, to the doctrine of the mistake of law and its justification.

12.3.1 Normative Reasons for the Recognition of Mistake of Law as a Defense

If ignorance of law is not caused by a naturalistic incapacity of the offender recognized by the legal system (for example, mental incapacity),[15] there are in principle three possible normative solutions:

1 The offender cannot argue, vis-à-vis the legal system, that he or she did not recognize the wrongfulness of the act committed. The effectiveness of norm communication is thus presupposed.
2 It is possible that there has been a lack of effectiveness of norm communication, but this is exclusively the fault of the offender and can only be attributed to him or her.
3 The lack of effectiveness in the communication of norms does not have to be borne by the offender alone. The legislator also recognizes other reasons, beyond objective, normative-psychological ones, why the offender did not recognize the wrongfulness of the act committed.

I must point out that, independent of the formal structure of a functioning democracy, alternative (1) shows a clear tendency towards an authoritarian picture of criminal law. It presupposes a legal and political homogeneity in the population that allows us to assume that individuals always have an awareness of right and wrong, lawful and unlawful conduct. This also implies an ethical homogeneity, without which this legal and political homogeneity is inconceivable. These assumptions are not compatible with pluralistic democracy.[16] Deciding between solutions (2) and (3) is, meanwhile, a political decision which hinges on two questions. First, is the attribution of the lack of effectiveness of norm communication exclusively to the offender compatible with the principle of culpability? Second, what reasons are to be taken into account in solution (3)?

I will argue here, for reasons I cannot go into at length, that there is in fact an incompatibility between the principle of culpability and solution (2). First of all, we have to recognize that if the state has a duty to make criminal law known to its citizens, to the extent that it fails to fulfill this obligation, it should be possible to hold the state responsible for the lack of normative communication.[17]

Regardless of legal or judicial recognition of the relevance of the mistake of law as an exclusion or mitigation of culpability, its acceptance as a defense stems from the plausibility of its social recognition, i.e., the intersection between the social discourse of attribution of moral responsibility and the legal concept of culpability. It does not seem appropriate to consider that someone who has broken the law knowing that their conduct was prohibited should be held responsible in the same way as someone who has acted without this knowledge.[18]

This argument of social plausibility must be complemented in political terms. Knowledge of the unlawfulness of an act gives culpability a concrete democratic content. Because the citizen knows and understands the content of the law, he or she not only knows that the law is binding but can also judge its correctness. The binding nature of the law arises historically from contexts of force, but normatively – at least in democracies – from its malleability. The possibility of using the democratic process to judge, and subsequently object to, a law that is deemed incorrect forces the citizen into a de facto acceptance of its current legal status or, at least, into taking responsibility for the violation of this status.[19] This reveals a normative link between culpability and politics, culpability and democracy, which I will not be able to investigate in depth here.

12.3.2 Reasonable and Unreasonable Mistake of Law

As I have pointed out, the recognition of ignorance of law will always be an indicator of a break in the communicative chain between the state and individuals. It can point to the erosion of fundamental norms that are expected to be shared in order to guarantee the integrity and cohesion of a legal system.

It will be necessary to establish a difference between reasonable and unreasonable ignorance of the law.[20] Continental and Latin American doctrine usually treat these, respectively, as unavoidable and avoidable mistakes, the former excluding culpability while the latter mitigates it.[21] It is necessary to understand the argument about the reasonableness or unreasonableness of the mistake of law in terms of a dialogue about the responsibility of a social actor. The argument in favor of a defendant must be reasonable in terms of social acceptability. This means that there is a mutual (albeit counterfactual) acceptance that one is engaging in the same space of reasons[22] – which, in this case, derives from the very institutional character of law – and that the arguments used can be understood, and claim to be accepted, by all those who engage in the same space of reasons. We can also understand this phenomenon in the sense of a praxis of justification,[23] in which the process of imputation reflects the normative structure of social practices.

12.3.3 A Normative Framework

Hence, when we talk about a mistake of law, we assume that its acceptance as an excuse depends to some extent on normative concerns. Only an inevitable (reasonable) mistake excludes culpability, whereas an avoidable (unreasonable) one can mitigate culpability. This distinction does not apply to mistakes of fact, but it should help us to determine the knowledge of law required to commit judicial abuse.

Can the judge argue that he or she just ignored established human rights or international law because the judge was convinced that those kinds of norms did not apply to the internal legal system? Are we prepared to accept as a defense that someone was aware of international rules, human rights, or strong moral norms that interdicted his or her act but thought that those norms were not binding for his or her judicial activity because they did not belong to the concept of law? The intuitive answer would seem to be a negative one. On the other hand, though, if we introduce a very strong normative notion of reasonableness into the definition of a mistake of fact, we risk coming too close to very problematic conceptions such as willful blindness or *Rechtsblindheit*, conceptions that contribute to an extreme lack of legal certainty in the attribution of criminal responsibility.[24]

So, then, if a normative approach to the problem of ignorance of law as an objective element is as inevitable as it is dangerous to individual liberty, the real task consists of developing criteria for establishing the theoretical framework within which this kind of normative interpretation of facts takes place. A convergence between the doctrine of mistake of law, on the one hand, and a justifiable universal tendency in tracing the outlines of law, on the other, could offer a realistic and fruitful starting point. Such a tendency would have to work with the positive content of human rights, but not with such an open category as that of *mala in se* offenses, since this is not even precise for defining the contents of national criminal law.[25] Nor should it work with vague ideas of natural law, where the praxis – and hence the reality – of a legal system remains out of focus.[26]

Reflection on these normative issues invites us to think about mistakes of law in conjunction with theories and principles of criminalization. These theories, such as the harm and the offense principle in the Anglo-American tradition,[27] or the doctrine of legal good in the Continental and Latin American traditions,[28] seek to offer arguments for rational criminal legislation.

Considering this aspect, an adequate theory of criminalization must understand the criminalizing society as a heterogeneous field, marked by discontinuities, differences, and contingencies, and encapsulating a multiplicity of conflicting interests.[29] Criminal law tries – hegemonically, and following the preferences of classes holding greater political capital – to impose such interests. It would therefore be appropriate to use the idea of competing interests as a starting point for a theory of criminalization.[30]

Interests can have a greater or lesser degree of universality, although no interest is recognized as having absolute universality. Among those interests with a higher degree of universality are those which pertain, for example, to physical integrity. The center of a material concept of crime is thus occupied by interests whose degree of universality is proven by their legislation as universally valid human rights in principle. As we move away from this centre, we find interests that are more widely accepted in a given social order but which are not necessarily common to the various social groups that make up the political field in question.

The further we move away from that center, the less universal and more problematic the protected interests are, and the less legitimate the criminal prohibition of their violation will be. This is the case for avowedly ethical interests that result from a discourse that seeks to identify cultural or religious values or the best way of life for a specific group. Such interests are, by definition, partial interests, which, in accordance with the principles of subsidiarity and *ultima ratio*, should be progressively eliminated from criminal law.

Criminal norms with religious or simply organizational content may be an expression of the preferences of certain social groups or of expectations of economic regulation linked to market interests, but they do not demonstrate the degree of universality enjoyed by the norms of the so-called core of criminal law. On the other hand, it will be much more difficult to accept the argument that perpetrators of crimes against humanity were unaware of the unlawfulness of their acts and that, in the context of an authoritarian state, this ignorance would be excusable. This is especially so if the perpetrators in question are judges.

In this sense, the further we move from the axis of prohibitions that make up the so-called 'core of criminal law', the less likely it is that a perpetrator will be expected to have knowledge of the wrongfulness of the act. On the other hand, if we are very close to that center of serious human rights violations, it will seem unreasonable to argue that the offender did not know he or she was breaking the law. This argument will therefore not be accepted in the space of reasons in which the offender engaged when he or she acceded to being part of the legal community.

12.3.4 The Importance of the Context of Justification of Decisions

This penultimate section offers one final remark: speculation about belief or psychological issues should be of secondary importance when assessing the kinds of cases dealt with here. The most important thing, including in terms of guaranteeing legal certainty, will be the reasoning used to support the decisions in question. Therefore, it is in the declared context of the justification of decisions – and not in the supposed mental process by which individuals make decisions – that the existence of a reasonable or unreasonable mistake of law should be investigated.

This is not solely because we can assess the offender's reasons and knowledge – which could serve as a basis for the imputation process – directly in the sentence. It is rather because, in taking on judicial activity, the offender assumed the justification of decisions as the institutional space where he or she will make use of public reason. Therefore, insofar as the offender engages in a dialogue of responsibility, it makes sense to investigate the legal meaning of the conduct using, as a starting point, that same institutional context where the offender had previously engaged in the same space of reasons.

12.4 Conclusions

This closing section summarizes some of the ideas outlined in this chapter. First, the offense of judicial abuse, present in different legislations, requires violation of the law. The allegation of ignorance of law thus becomes a question of fact, which presupposes the recognition of the intention to violate the penal norm (*dolus eventualis*).

Law must therefore be treated as an institutional fact, the recognition of which depends on the collective acceptance of its contours by the members of the community. Furthermore, this concept will not only be made up of an abstract body of rules but also of interpretations of these rules in the face of a common social ethos and arguments from other normative systems. The prevalence of one concept of law, however, will depend on the prevalence of some discourses over others in a system of normative coordinates.

Although the ignorance of law is in this constellation a mistake of fact, the instrument for articulating the normative coordinates involved will be sought in the doctrine of the mistake of law. In order to understand the logic of this argument, we had to look at the rationale for accepting the mistake of law as a defense. There we could see that the question of a reasonable mistake of law treats the individual as participating in a public dialogue in which his or her arguments must make sense in the context of a space of reasons in which they have engaged.

The normative determination of this reasonableness will require recourse to the theory of criminalization, which will help to show which kinds of ignorance of law seem acceptable in a given legal community, based on a core of prohibitions linked to the recognition of fundamental human rights. It is in the space of justification of judicial decisions that we must try to verify the existence of a mistake of law.

Notes

1 Art. 446 of the Spanish criminal code (Código Penal) reads as follows:
Any judge or magistrate who knowingly renders an unjust sentence or decision shall be punished:

1 With a prison sentence of one to four years, if it is an unjust sentence against the defendant in a criminal case for a serious or less serious offense and the sentence has not been carried out, and with the same penalty, in its more serious range, plus a fine of twelve to twenty-four months, if the sentence has been carried out. In both cases, the penalty of absolute disqualification shall also be imposed for a period of ten to twenty years.
2 With the penalty of a fine of six to twelve months, plus special disqualification from public employment or officeholding for a period of six to ten years in the case of an unjust sentence handed down against the offender in proceedings for a minor offense.
3 With the penalty of a fine of between twelve and twenty-four months, plus special disqualification from public employment or officeholding for a period of between ten and twenty years, if any other unjust sentence or ruling is handed down.

For an analysis, see Muñoz Conde, *Derecho Penal, Parte Especial* (2017) 797 et seq: "The injustice of the decision must be understood as its illegality, which constitutes a specific normative element of the offence. Its determination implies (...) an assessment which must be made on the basis of the specific case and in accordance with postulates of material justice and not purely formalistic ones" (author's translation, here and throughout).

2 § 339 German criminal code: "A judge, other public official or arbitrator who, in conducting or deciding a case, is guilty of bending the law in favor of or to the detriment of a party, shall be punished by imprisonment from one year to five years".

3 See Kuhlen, '§ 339: Rechtsbeugung' in Kindhäuser et al (eds), *Nomos Kommentar zum Strafgesetzbuch* paras 17, 91 et seqq; Rengier, *Strafrecht Besonderer Teil II* (2015) 555.

4 Art. 319 of the Brazilian criminal code refers to "Improperly delaying or failing to perform an official act, or performing it against an express provision of law, to satisfy personal interest or feelings" and imposes a penalty of between 3 and 12 months' imprisonment, plus a fine. See Busato, *Direito Penal, Parte Especial* (2017) 530.

5 See Roxin/Greco, *Strafrecht Allgemeiner Teil* (2020) 591 and 1053; Frisch, *Strafrecht* (2022) 1421 and 385.

6 This applies, e.g., to criminal provisions that refer to different provisions, with recent exceptions. See Roxin/Greco (2020) (n 5) 607, 609. For the history of the legal treatment of mistake of law in Germany, see Köhler, *Strafrecht, Allgemeiner Teil* (1997) 412.

7 Therefore, even if they are not part of a legal culture, this does not mean that they are not valid for this legal community.

8 Searle, *Sprechtakte* (1983) 87, 275; Searle, *Die Konstruktion der gesellschaftlichen Wirklichkeit* (2017) 40; Searle, *Wie wir die soziale Welt machen* (2017) 153.

9 Searle (2017) (n 8) 46; Searle (2017) (n 8) 76.

10 See Raz, *The Authority of Law* (2009) 22, 26.

11 See Martins, *Flüchtige Grenzen. Hermeneutik und Diskurstheorie im Recht* (2013) 286, 336.

12 Gadamer, *Wahrheit und Methode* (1990) 312.

13 See Neumann, *Zurechnung und Vorverschulden* (1985); see also the discussion in Martins, 'Soziale Normen und strafrechtliche Zurechnung' in Saliger et al (eds) 665.

14 Regarding the discussion of Hart's recourse to social rules as founding elements of the validity of law and its conventionalist interpretation, see Marmor, *Social Conventions* (2009) 155. For a critique and interpretation of Hart's understanding of social rules in the sense of a plural subject theory, see Gilbert, *Sociality and Responsibility* (2000) 71.

15 In this case, the person will not have to answer for her action. There will be no dialogue about responsibility in the sense that we develop further here. On the distinction between excuses and exemptions, see Duff, *Answering for Crime* (2007) 284.

16 See Küchenhoff, 'Die staatsrechtliche Bedeutung des Verbotsirrtums' in Spendel (ed) 80.

17 See Horder, *Principles of Criminal Law* (2013) 220.

18 See Husak/von Hirsch, Culpability and Mistake of Law in Shute et al (eds) 161. The arguments against recognition of the mistake of law as an excuse are summarized and discussed in Horder, *Principles of Criminal Law* (2022) 219. For a critique of these arguments, see Husak, *The Philosophy of Criminal Law* (2010) 258.

19 This seems to me to be an adequate response to the problem of the duty to obey the law related to the mistake of law pointed out by Husak/von Hirsch (1993) (n 18) 165.

20 See Horder (2022) (n 18) 221; Husak/von Hirsch (1993) (n 18) 166, 170.

21 See Jescheck/Weigend, *Lehrbuch des Strafrechts. Allgemeiner Teil* (1996) 457; Tavares, *Fundamentos de Teoria do Delito* (2022) 570.

22 See Laden, *Reasoning. A Social Picture* (2012) 229. Because of the institutional character of law, the idea of an 'invitation' to join the same space of reasons must be understood in political terms, decided previously when people engage in social praxis within a legal community. It nonetheless remains true that a normative account of the dialogue of responsibility that constitutes the process of imputation presupposes the use of acceptable arguments by both sides, thereby including the arguments raised by the defendant.

23 See Forst, *Das Recht auf Rechtfertigung* (2007) 23, 29; Forst, *Kritik der Rechtfertigungsverhältnisse* (2011) 53; Forst, *Normativität und Macht* (2015) 37.

24 The German version is also historically problematic. See Mezger, 'Rechtsirrtum und Rechtsblindheit' in Bockelmann et al (eds) 182. The crimes to which this theory should apply are crimes such as racial dishonor or the practice of homosexual acts.

25 See Ashworth, 'Ignorance of Law, and Duties to Avoid it' (2011) 74 (1) *Mod. L. Rev.* 9.

26 Regarding the importance of judicial praxis for the determination of what law is, see Neumann, 'Rechtspositivismus, Rechtsrealismus und Rechtsmoralismus in der Diskussion um die strafrechtliche Bewältigung politischer Systemwechsel', in Prittwitz et al (eds) 109.

27 Simester/von Hirsch, *Crimes, Harms, and Wrongs* (2014).

28 Roxin/Greco, (2020) (n 5) 26; Hassemer/Neumann, 'Vorbemerkung zu § 1' in Kindhäuser et al (eds), *Nomos Kommentar zum Strafgesetzbuch* para 131.

29 Marchart, *Das unmögliche Objekt. Eine postfundamentalistische Theorie der Gesellschaft* (2013) 30, 336, 345.
30 Hassemer/Neumann (2017) (n 28) para 138.

Bibliography

Asworth A, 'Ignorance of the Criminal Law and Duties to Avoid it' (2011) 74 (1) *The Modern Law Review* 1.
Busato P C, *Direito Penal, Parte Especial, vol. 3* (2nd edn, Atlas 2017).
Duff R A, *Answering for Crime* (Bloomsbury Publishing 2009).
Forst R, *Das Recht auf Rechtfertigung* (Suhrkamp 2007).
Forst R, *Kritik der Rechtfertigungsverhältnisse* (Suhrkamp 2011).
Forst R, *Normativität und Macht* (Suhrkamp 2015).
Frisch W, *Strafrecht* (Vahlen 2022).
Gadamer H-G, *Wahrheit und Methode* (Mohr Siebeck 1990).
Gilbert M, *Sociality and Responsibility* (Rowman & Littlefield Publishers, 2000).
Hassemer W/Neumann U, 'Vorbemerkung zu § 1' in Kindhäuser et al (eds), *Nomos Kommentar zum Strafgesetzbuch zum Strafgesetzbuch* (5th edn, Nomos 2017).
Horder J, *Ashworth's Principles of Criminal Law* (10th edn, Oxford University Press 2022) 219.
Horder J, *Principles of Criminal Law* (7th edn, Oxford University Press 2013).
Husak D/von Hirsch A, 'Culpability and Mistake of Law' in Shute et al (eds), *Action and Value in Criminal Law* (Clarendon 1993) 156.
Husak N H, *The Philosophy of Criminal Law* (Oxford University Press 2010).
Jescheck H-H/Weigend T, *Lehrbuch des Strafrechts – Allgemeiner Teil* (5th edn, Duncker & Humblot 1996).
Köhler M, *Lehrbuch des Strafrechts* (Springer 1997).
Küchenhoff G, 'Die staatsrechtliche Bedeutung des Verbotsirrtums' in Stock/Spendel (eds), *Studien zur Strafrechtswissenschaft. Festschrift für Ulrich Stock* (Holzner Verlag 1966) 80.
Kuhlen L, '§ 339: Rechtsbeugung' in Kindhäuser et al (eds), *Nomos Kommentar zum Strafgesetzbuch* (5th edn, Nomos 2017).
Laden A S, *Reasoning. A Social Picture* (Oxford University Press 2012).
Marchart O, *Das unmögliche Objekt. Eine postfundamentalistische Theorie der Gesellschaft* (Suhrkamp 2013).
Marmor A, *Social Conventions* (Princeton University Press 2009).
Martins A, 'Soziale Normen und strafrechtliche Zurechnung' in Saliger F et al (eds), *Rechtsstaatliches Strafrecht. Festschrift für Ulfrid Neumann zum 70. Geburtstag* (C. F. Müller 2017) 665.
Martins A, *Flüchtige Grenzen. Hermeneutik und Diskurstheorie im Recht* (Nomos 2013).
Mezger E, 'Rechtsirrtum und Rechtsblindheit' in Bockelmann P/Kohlrausch E (eds), *Probleme der Strafrechtserneuerung. Festschrift für Eduard Kohlrausch* (De Gruyter 1944) 182.
Muñoz Conde F, *Derecho Penal: Parte Especial* (21st edn, ValTirant lo Blanch 2017).
Neumann U, *Zurechnung und Vorverschulden* (Duncker & Humblot 1985).
Neumann U, 'Rechtspositivismus, Rechtsrealismus und Rechtsmoralismus in der Diskussion um die strafrechtliche Bewältigung politischer Systemwechsel' in Prittwitz C et al (eds), *Festschrift für Klaus Lüderssen zum 70. Geburtstag* (Nomos 2002) 109.

Raz J, *The Authority of Law* (2nd edn, Oxford University Press 2009).
Rengier R, *Strafrecht Besonderer Teil II* (16th edn, C. H. Beck 2015).
Roxin C/Greco L, *Strafrecht Allgemeiner Teil* (5th edn, C. H. Beck 2020).
Searle J R, *Die Konstruktion der gesellschaftlichen Wirklichkeit* (Suhrkamp 2017).
Searle J R, *Sprechakte* (Suhrkamp 1983).
Searle J R, *Wie wir die soziale Welt machen* (Suhrkamp 2017).
Simester A P/von Hirsch A, *Crimes, Harms, and Wrongs* (Hart Publishing 2014).
Tavares J, *Fundamentos de Teoria do Delito* (4th edn, Tirant lo Blanch 2022).

13 Defending the Indefensible

The Mistake of Law Defense Applied to the Case of Judges in Dictatorships and Rogue Regimes – A Comparative Approach

Alejandra Castillo Ara

13.1 Facing the Question of Justice in Times of Dictatorship: An Overview of the German and Chilean cases

Many countries have faced the question of applying justice both during and after periods of dictatorship. This article aims to examine the possibility of offering mistake of law or other culpability defenses in two emblematic settings: post-totalitarian Germany and post-dictatorship Chile. The article also considers whether it makes any difference whether a mistake of law defense is presented in its civil law or common law interpretation.

Germany is a special case because it has twice been confronted, in the recent past, with problems associated with the rule of law in totalitarian regimes. First in 1945, after the defeat of the National Socialist (Nazi) regime, and then in 1989, after the collapse of the German Democratic Republic (East German socialist regime). On both occasions, the question that had to be addressed was whether what had been deemed lawful under the positive law of the defunct legal system should still be considered lawful, even if it violated fundamental principles of justice and the rule of law. The core battle was between strict positivism and a common sense of justice, where belief in the latter implies asserting that the content of justice is somehow self-evident, and so adherence to it can be demanded of any person in any context and at any time. To answer the questions that this battle raised, Radbruch's now-famous formula regarding the invalidity of law in situations of extreme injustice was applied.

Chile, for its part, has had to face the aftermath of atrocities committed by a long-running dictatorship (17 years), as have many other countries, including Argentina, Myanmar, and Cambodia. In this article, I will limit the consideration of possible criminal responsibility to judges who operate in such regimes. The article asks if it is ever possible to raise a plausible defense of judges who have sentenced someone under positive dictatorial law, whether on the grounds of mistake (or ignorance) of law or some other form of reduced liability. This question is similar to the one asked by Monroe Freedman in his paper, 'Must You Be the Devil's Advocate?'[1] A reasonable person may instinctively tend to deny even the possibility of admitting a mistake of law defense or similar. As jurists and practitioners, we are, however, duty-bound to consider such a possibility if we want an administration of

DOI: 10.4324/9781003470069-16

justice where the right to a defense and the presumption of innocence are protected, even in the most obvious cases of apparently vile behavior.

13.2 Time and Locally Framed Understandings of Right and Wrong

Radbruch's formula, whereby extremely unjust laws can be denied validity because extreme injustice is not and cannot be law,[2] has placed positivism in jeopardy. Radbruch, and later challenges by Robert Alexy, return us to a naturalistic conception of law that is quite far removed from the positivism that purports to provide legal certainty and security.[3] Criminal law exists, after all, to protect us not only through the law but also from the law. Accordingly, a situation where we do not or cannot know with any certainty what the law is – because it might be considered unfair or unjust at any time – collides with Feuerbach's almost universally recognized principle of legality (premised on *lex certa stricta, scripta*, and *praevia*). Criticisms of Radbruch's formula from the perspective of concerns about its detrimental impact on legal certainty were certainly not unknown to its author, who undoubtedly appreciated the value of legal certainty.[4] Radbruch's mention of 'serious' and 'tremendous' dangers for legal certainty shows he knew what was at stake.[5] Radbruch's concerns seem reasonable, but it is, in fact, difficult to regulate *ex-ante,* rather than solely as an *ex-post* evaluation, which could in some cases be considered to amount to an unfair, or – as I describe it – 'cheating', reformulation of the law. Legal certainty is also one of the main problems when it comes to determining whether or not there has been a mistake of law, since the requirement of knowledge or understanding of the law does not refer to a written section or paragraph – what the Germans call *formelle Rehtswidrigkeit* (formal wrongfulness) – but applies, rather, to *materielle Rechtswidrigkeit* (material wrongfulness).[6] The relevant concept of knowledge or understanding of the law is not a fully moral conception of right and wrong but a kind of assertion of the obviousness of right or wrong, with a claim to universality. Thus, it approaches what the Anglo-Saxon legal world considers a *mala in se* crime.[7] This understanding of the law as premised on the obviousness of the just and unjust has increasingly been problematized among scholars who debate the potentially Western and/or Eurocentric perspective of the whole human rights system.[8] If we are in agreement with the notion of obviousness, then according to Radbruch's formula, most of the world is barbaric, and its laws are invalid. Such a conclusion, if misused, could lead to the adoption of a paternalistic and imperialistic point of view. Should it be assumed that there is only one concept of justice, one that is moreover so obvious that it ought to be always understood and internalized by everyone, everywhere?[9]

13.3 The Legal Order as Positively and/or Materially Corrupt

Dictatorial or totalitarian regimes cannot be treated as always and everywhere equivalent, or even similar. In some totalitarian or rogue regimes, the rule of law has been corrupted so as to make atrocities such as torture or imprisonment of opponents 'legal'. Examples include Cambodia, or wartime Germany,[10] where deportations and genocide were formally accepted. In these settings, unjust behaviors take place within the framework of the positive written law. A completely different scenario obtains where the rule of law has not been formally corrupted, and illegality occurs outside the law. Thus, torture and disappearance are not legalized, but instead occur *de facto*, as was the case with the Chilean dictatorship of 1973-1990. On paper, such a jurisdiction has the appearance of validity and legality: the appearance of a rule-of-law-respecting state is upheld, and unjust behaviors occur outside the law. So, either the law is not applied, or there is a lack of compliance with valid law.

In the first of these scenarios, where the law is corrupted, unjust laws become valid according to a positivist concept of validity. Radbruch´s formula would therefore require self-reflection on the part of the judiciary to declare enacted law as invalid because it is unjust. In this case, I would argue, one could almost indisputably have recourse to a mistake of law defense, since no indication of unlawfulness would have been available to anyone applying the law. Mistakes of law would be unavoidable – and therefore excusable – since the lawfulness of the law, and the fact subsumed in it, had never been called into question. Even if, after reflection, the judge is able to conclude that a particular rule is invalid, to fail or refuse to apply it would mean running the risk of reprisals, as it would require defying the State.

The second case, where atrocities are committed without being legalized, is completely different, because lawlessness does not take place according to the written law. The legal system is not corrupted – or, at least, is not extremely corrupted. Instead, repression happens outside the scope of the law, under a prevailing framework of legality.[11] Here, there is undeniable wrongdoing, such as in the example of the Chilean case, especially its treatment of habeas corpus writs (known as *recursos de amparo*). Hilbink (2007) reports that: "[a]ccording to a 1985 report by the Inter-American Commission of Human Rights, Chilean courts accepted only ten of the fifty-four hundred *recursos de amparo* filed by human rights lawyers between 1973 and 1983 [... and] in the remaining seven years of the military regime, only twenty more".[12] Courts only challenged the legality of military regime detentions in a few cases.[13] Chilean judges invoked a range of far-fetched excuses, from formalistic obstacles to a blind reliance on police statements, to avoid actually checking on the physical condition of a detainee or visiting one of the many clandestine detention centers whose existence and location were an open secret. Chile's judges *chose* not to investigate further when presented with habeas corpus writs. I would argue that they can accordingly be prosecuted for murder, or for other related crimes, for failing to carry out their duty properly. This is so because judges are bound by a duty to act (*Garantenpflicht*), with failure to act therefore placing them in a position of liability by omission. A possible line of defense, in such a case, would be to explore the limits of that duty to act, but this would become a matter of mistake of fact rather than mistake of law.

The German case of the Berlin Wall shooters, in which Radbruch's formula was applied,[14] is quite far removed from the abovementioned situation of Chilean judges and follows different principles. I would argue that the German case, involving soldiers acting in a totalitarian regime, could be subsumed most clearly to a defense based on non-exigibility or possible mistake of fact.[15] Moreover, I am not referring to the situation of a judge who has cooperated or collaborated, as a co-perpetrator, with the murderer, but rather to one who has simply carried out their job in applying the law, without having directly themselves experienced or inflicted murder or torture. In this respect it is not the same to be a judge of a lower court as it is to be a judge of the Supreme Court: the latter are also politically linked to state power. Non-exigibility is *prima facie* inapplicable unless the judge is acting under a threat (and not just a general fear) of possible reprisals, such as, for example, direct threats to his or her life or physical integrity. Judges – unlike soldiers, who can be punished for desertion – could have simply resigned at any time. If they instead continue to exercise their judicial function, they are exercising a choice. The circumstances for non-exigibility accordingly do not apply.

13.4 Mistake of Law in Civil and in Common Law Systems

The admissibility of a mistake of law-based defense could differ widely according to whether it is evaluated from a common law or a civil law perspective. This can usefully be illustrated by comparing and contrasting approaches to mistakes of law in Germany and in the US. From a comparative criminal law perspective, these are competing systems of regulation that moreover understand the mistake of law excuse at different levels. For Germany this is a problem of guilt, while for the US it is a matter of *dolus*.

Even at face value, the treatment or recognition of mistake of law is fundamentally different in German, and in US, legislation because the latter's common law tradition is based on the historical assumption that mistake of law is no defense. Although *error iuris non excusat* is repeated like a mantra in the literature,[16] the application of it is not consistent. For instance, the Model Penal Code (MPC) – the US's most influential (albeit non-binding) reference rule – recognizes mistake of law as a defense in certain cases. According to MPC Art. 2.04, ignorance or mistake is a defense if "the ignorance or mistake negatives the purpose, knowledge, belief, recklessness or negligence required to establish a material element of the offense; or the law provides that the state of mind established by such ignorance or mistake constitutes a defense". It is clear that, according to the MPC, acceptance of mistake of law as a defense is inextricably linked to the subjective part of the crime – i.e., to mens rea, as intention or purpose (*dolus*), since mistake of law would only be recognized if the offense requires special criminal intent, mostly expressed by use of the terms 'knowingly' or 'willfully'.[17] In any case, it seems evident that the academic mantra that 'mistake of law is no defense' is not entirely accurate. This is also recognized in more than a few court decisions.[18] As previously stated, the acceptance of the mistake of law as a possible defense by the jurisprudence and MPC is structured as a *dolus* approach and not a culpability issue.

The German approach to the mistake of law is more honest on paper about its recognition as an excuse, since almost no one disputes[19] that it is an excuse that excludes or negates culpability (*Entschuldigungsgrund*), but it is not open in practice. The relevant section of the StGB (German Criminal Code), § 17, states: "If, at the time of the commission of the offense, the offender lacks the awareness of acting unlawfully, then the offender is deemed to have acted without guilt if the mistake was unavoidable. If the mistake was avoidable, the penalty may be mitigated under section 49 (1)".[20] Despite the legal recognition in the German system of mistake of law, however, its acceptance as a defense in a particular case is subject to examination of its avoidability (*Vermeidbarkeit*). If it was unavoidable (*unvermeidbar*), culpability is excluded and the perpetrator cannot be convicted and punished. If the mistake was avoidable (*vermeidbar*), there is culpability, but the legal response may not be the same as if there had been no mistake at all. Punishment may be mitigated.[21]

At an international level, the Rome Statute also has a recognition of mistake of law in Art. 32. The result is not significantly different from that of the MPC: "mistake of law as to whether a particular type of conduct constitutes a crime within the jurisdiction of the Court shall not be a ground for excluding criminal responsibility. A mistake of law may, however, be a ground for excluding criminal responsibility if it negates the mental element required for such a crime, or as provided for in Article 33".[22] Therefore, the non-recognition of a mistake of law would indeed be a manifest violation of the principle of culpability and of the defendant's capacity to be found guilty as a reasonable requirement for criminal liability.[23] Nonetheless, I defend the German concept of culpability applied to the mistake of law as the most appropriate. This, as we have seen, treats the question of judicial liability as a culpability issue in terms of the judge's capacity and free will to decide according to the law and not against it. The problem with a mistake of law is not whether the person concerned was able to know, and recognize, a factual description of a legal issue. After all, a mistake of law raises the question of a judge's understanding, not of a factual scenario, but of the unlawfulness of a prohibition or mandate. Were judges able to understand the unlawfulness of their actions when exercising judicial functions in the case at hand? Well, it depends.

13.5 Corrupted and Non-corrupted Rule of Law States

13.5.1 Mistake of Law Based on Internal Law in a Non-corrupted Rule of Law State

The term 'non-corrupted rule of law state' refers to one of the situations described above, namely, the one where a state's legal system has not converted written law into unjust law, and the appearance of a rule of law is therefore preserved. Mistake of law could not apply if judges in such a setting exercised their functions according to the written law,[24] applying interpretations consistent with the purpose of the law and in accordance with the time of its application. There is no possibility of escaping the understanding of the law that could reasonably justify using mistake of law as a defense, since judges have at some point enjoyed freedom of interpretation of the law. The standard of mistake of law (whether avoidable or unavoidable) would not apply to a judge here. In other words, judges would never be able to act "in doubt of the law", because of their status. As a figure who is, in a certain sense and at a certain point, the incarnation of the law, a judge cannot, by definition, act in ignorance of that law. So, either judges are the law, because they create it – which is an interpretation coherent with a case law system – or they are simply not allowed to ignore the law or to misunderstand and fail to apply it. If we accept judges' duty to act, they also become liable for crimes committed because of their omissions.

13.5.2 Mistake of Law Based on the Internal Law of a Corrupted System

In the case of a corrupted system, where unjust laws have been formally recognized as valid laws, it might be admissible to allege a mistake of law. In such a case, the overarching system was formally changed. Under mistake of law, the non-applicability of valid law would therefore exceed the requirement of avoidability and would imply a demand for disregard of the norm by extra-normative criteria of justice. It would exceed the requirement of material wrongdoing (*materielle Rechtswidrigkeit*) and would come close to a requirement of a *mala in se* understanding of wrongfulness. This is in the sense that some behaviors or actions are wrong and unlawful because they are inherently bad, not because they are prohibited (*mala prohibita*). This is a conception of the law, and of internal moral patterns, as self-evident, that would fail Platzgummer's test of *Paralellwertung in der Laiensphäre* (parallel evaluation in the ordinary sphere or layperson's sphere, i.e., the requirement that the offender, as a layperson, would understand what the legislator meant by the specific legal circumstances of the offense, without the need for a correct legal subsumption).[25] It would not even meet the 'reasonable person' parameter, because any judge in that place at that time would have applied the law as it was written. The only room for interpretation would be regarding the range of the avoidability, but the point of reference would have to be either an international comprehension of human rights or a retroactive parameter. That would be openly unfair, even for people who were also part of unfair systems.

One remote possibility for mounting a mistake of law defense could draw on what is sometimes called the 'exotic socialization' argument. This contends that due to a change in the values of society, judges did not or could not internalize the wrongfulness of their actions due to oppression and collective delirium. Persons – including judges – living in such extreme circumstances would tend, it is argued, to confuse good and evil, or right and wrong. There would be a fundamental realignment of their basic values, manifesting itself in a lack of internalization of the pre-corrupted rules, because they are no longer identified as those aligned with the new conception of justice, due to the collective distorted standard of rightness and justice. This would be due, in Jakobs' words, to 'exotic socialisation'[26] into the new prevailing social, political, and cultural reality.

13.6 The Test of Avoidability of a Mistake of Law

If a mistake of law is at all an option for mounting a defense, it would still have to pass the test of avoidability of the mistake. In the civil law systems, the core of this test is the understanding of material wrongdoing (*materielle Rechtswidrigeit*) rather than formal wrongdoing (*formelle Rechtswidrigkeit*). This means that the ignorance or lack of understanding of the law does not involve knowledge of a certain section or wording of a codified rule, but understanding of the natural meaning of the criminal behavior as something that is almost obviously or naturally wrong. Such an assumption must have been easier before globalization and pluralism, but today it seems difficult to make it workable. The conception of something as 'naturally wrong' must at some point serve the existing positive laws; otherwise, such a concept promotes chaos and operates to the detriment of the written norm.[27] Furthermore, the relativism involved in invoking a self-evident understanding of just and unjust laws and values is a double-edged sword: such a statement of right and wrong could be used by the oppressors as easily as by the oppressed. It is, however, difficult to trace a clear dividing line between the two conceptions of wrongfulness: the natural wrongfulness and the positive wrongfulness. It should also be noted that politics, and society in general, tend to divide the world into 'good' and 'evil'. Under dictatorships or situations of collective mass delusion, "many evil acts are 'performed by people who believe they are doing something supremely good'".[28] A functional equivalent, in common law systems, to formal and material wrongdoing in civil law systems is the recognized category of the *mala in se* crime,[29] which assumes that some crimes are humanly and inherently bad. They are not necessarily forbidden acts or omissions in the same sense as *mala prohibita* crimes, which are wrong because they are forbidden but are not obviously (*selbstverständlich*) wrong.[30]

It is supposed, then, that a core set of crimes exists, about whose inherent badness there is no doubt. Examples would include crimes against life or liberty. But is this obviousness really universal? Certainly not. The ways in which an average German, a Chilean, a Saudi Arabian person, and a Congolese person understand freedom would probably differ as regards the content of freedom and its limits. We might consider, for instance, the phenomenon of male circumcision, which is accepted and practiced historically by Muslims and Jews as a religious ritual. In Germany, a very famous case heard in Cologne in 2012 deemed a religiously inspired circumcision, carried out on a boy, to have constituted bodily harm. The correct scope of the prohibition of circumcision on cultural grounds in a pluralistic society has been the subject of much discussion in Germany in the wake of this ruling.[31] The Regional Court of Cologne dealt with the question of how to assess in law the actions of the pious and experienced Muslim doctor, who performed the circumcision for religious reasons at the request of the boy's Muslim parents. The court first determined that the consent of the parents was not justified, inter alia, on the grounds of the legal value that section § 1631, paragraph 2, sentence 2 of the German Civil Code (BGB) affords to the non-violent exercise of care of the person. Next, the court assumed that the doctor, who, according to his subjective conscience, assumed the lawfulness of his act, had committed an unavoidable mistake of law within the meaning of § 17, paragraph 1 of the German Criminal Code (StGB). This particular approach to the consideration of culturally conditioned deviating values of the perpetrator in a case of circumcision was not, however, able to create acceptable legal certainty as a result. Nor did it prove, in ensuing public debate, to represent a satisfactory legal-political approach to the criminal-legal assessment of Jewish or Islamic circumcision rituals. Subsequently, § 1631 of the German Civil Code (BGB) was created, explicitly to regulate and set parameters relating to decisions to be taken about religiously motivated circumcision of male children. The outcome shows that consideration of divergent cultural values may require legal supplementation in order not to risk disturbing legal peace through national criminal law that attaches only limited importance to values prevalent among religious minorities. This example is employed here only to illustrate that what is considered to be obvious, or to constitute a *mala in se* crime, cannot lay claim to universality.

13.7 Conclusion

This chapter revolved around two questions, the first one being, when is a law so unjust that it can lose its validity, even if it was legitimately created and is in force? A related subsidiary question is: who decides on the justice or injustice of that law? According to Radbruch's formula, extremely unjust law is no law, to which Robert Alexy objects that this perspective could jeopardize legal certainty and lead to relativism.[32] Which is consistent with the fact that testimonies in some trials show that many perpetrators believe that what they have done was right, not only for themselves but also for their people, their country, and even democracy.[33]

There is no doubt that international criminal law has developed rapidly over the past 70 years, following the horrors of the First and Second World Wars and of dictatorships and armed conflict in Latin America, Africa, Asia, and the Balkans. This development reflects a relatively sudden and marked departure from the centuries-old practice of tolerating, or even perpetuating, conduct now considered to constitute international crime – such as public executions, torture, and enslavement.[34]. However, just as this was not always the case, nor is it presently the case everywhere. It seems that half the world has still not learned about human rights: at least, not in the classical Western sense of the term.

Although an ex post analysis of justice may sound unrepentantly brutal, I hold to the view that extemporaneous external verification of material wrongdoing (*materielle Rechtswidrigkeit)* is 'cheating', the result of which could be both indefensible and extremely unfair. Radbruch's argument about injustice is, in the last analysis, utilitarian. It is obvious that many acts committed under dictatorship are inhumane and brutal, and that the need for justice is a priority – inter alia for the sake of peace and transitional justice – but the argument that obvious injustice can invalidate positive law could also be a two-faced solution. It is an argument that can be used for both good and evil, depending on which government is in power at the time. The context for which the Radbruch formula was developed may certainly be an example where it was used for good, but that does not guarantee that if the barometer of what is patently unjust varies, the formula will not be used to invalidate positive law and commit atrocities in the name of justice. The wrongfulness or otherwise of behavior, and whether it should or should not be deemed *mala in se*, should be judged within the temporal, local, and cultural context of that behavior. However, the evaluation of whether specific laws are or are not just must be conducted retrospectively, as it is impossible to perform this reflective analysis concurrently with the occurrence of atrocities. Such an analysis is inherently post hoc, necessitating a spatial-temporal distance from the events. This approach is essential in the aftermath of any conflict that disrupts social peace, as it allows for the healing of societal wounds and the reconstruction of democratic institutions.

Notes

1 See Freedman, 'Must You Be the Devil's Advocate?' (1993) *Legal Times* 19.
2 See Radbruch, 'Gesetzliches Unrecht und übergesetzliches Recht' (1946) *SJZ* 105, 107, reprint in: Hassemer (ed), *Gustav Radbruch, Gesamtausgabe,* Band 3 (1990).
3 See Alexy, *The Argument from Injustice. A reply to legal positivism* (2002) 51 et seq.
4 See Radbruch (1946) (n 2) 07; Radbruch, 'Statutory Lawlessness and Supra-Statutory Law (1946)' (2006) *Oxf J Leg Stud* 1, 7.
5 See Radbruch (1946) (n 2). As Alexy states in his work *The Argument from Injustice*, Radbruch's formula is not the result of a natural law intuition or an emotional reaction to National Socialism, but the result of carefully weighing up the three elements of which, for Radbruch, it is composed. These three elements are justice, adequacy, and legal certainty. It could be seen as a third way between positivism and naturalism. Alexy (2002) (n 3) 85 seq.
6 See Baumann/Weber et al, *Strafrecht Allgemeiner Teil* (2003) 48 et seq; Kindhäuser, *Strafrecht Allgemeiner Teil* (2013) 228; Neumann, '§ 17: Verbotsirrtum' in Kindhäuser et al (eds), *Nomos Kommentar zum Strafgesetzbuch* para 22; Rudolphi, *Unrechtsbewusstsein, Verbotsirrtum und Vermeidbarkeit des Verbotsirrtums* (1969) 56 seq.
7 See Travers, 'Mistake of Law in Mala Prohibita Crimes' (1995) 62 (3) *The University of Chicago Law Review*, 1301–1331; Varela, 'Strict-Liability Como Forma de Imputación Jurídico-Penal' 3/12 (2012) *InDret* 1 et seqq.
8 See Mende, 'Are Human Rights Western – And Why Does It Matter? A Perspective from International Political Theory' (2021) 17 (1) *JIPIT* 38 et seqq.
9 About the concept of internalization of the law, as a deeper concept than the mere knowledge or understanding of it, see: Bustos, 'Was ist Schuld?' in Sieber et al (eds) 351 et seq names this "fehlende Verinnerlichung". Laubenthal and Baier understand it as the standard for people alien to the dominant culture: Laubenthal/Baier, 'Durch die Ausländereigenschaft bedingte Verbotsirrtümer und die Perspektiven europäischer Rechtsvereinheitlichung' (2000) *GA* 209. See also Köhler, *Strafrecht Allgemeiner Teil* (1997) 437; Mayer, *Rechtsnormen und Kulturnormen* (1965) 17 and Valerius, *Kultur und Strafrecht, die Berücksichtigung kultureller Wertvorstellungen in der deutschen Strafrechtsdogmatik* (2011) 179. This concept is close to Jakobs' "exotische Sozialisation": see Jakobs, *Strafrecht Allgemeiner Teil* (1993) § 19 para 7. In the Argentine literature a similar idea has been raised by Eugenio Zaffaroni. See Zaffaroni/Alagia et al, *Derecho Penal* (2003) 736.
10 Accepting the Nuremberg Race Laws passed by the Reichstag on 15 September 1935, including the Law for the Protection of German Blood and German Honour, as those that allowed the deportation and deprivation of civil rights of Jews, Roma, and other groups, and began official Nazi Socialist propaganda. See Roller/Höschel, *Judenverfolgung und jüdisches Leben unter den Bedingungen der nationalsozialistischen Gewaltherrschaft: 1930-1946* (1996) 259.

11 See Hilbink, *Judges beyond Politics in Democracy and Dictatorship. Lessons from Chile* (2007) 115.
12 Hilbink (2007) (n 11).
13 See Hilbink (2007) (n 11) 116.
14 BGH, Judgment of 3 November 1992 – 5 StR 370/92, (1993) 2 *NJW* 141, 144.
15 Due to a lack of evaluation of the circumstances grounding a justification clause.
16 See Keedy, Ignorance and Mistake of Law (1908) 22 *Harv L Rev* 76.
17 See Hall/Seligman, 'Mistake of Law and mens rea' (1941) 64 *Univ. Chic. Law Rev.* 259.
18 SCOTUS, Decision of 16 December 1957, No 47, *Lambert v California* (1957) 355 U.S. 229-230; SCOTUS, Decision of 8 January 1991, No 89-658, *Cheek v. United States*, 498 U.S. 192 (1991).
19 Other than some isolated scholars, such as Schmidhäuser, *Strafrecht Allgemeiner Teil* (1982) § 7 para 87 et seq.
20 Author's translation.
21 Some scholars still advocate for obligatory mitigation. See Perron, '§ 21: Verminderte Schuldfähigkeit' in Eser et al (eds), *Kommentar zum Strafgesetzbuch* paras 6 et seq.
22 This recognition has been used by defenders of the mistake of law defense as its ultimate validation, considering that even at an international level, the non-recognition of mistake of law could lead to extremely unjust results, since it entails a lack of culpability.
23 "[N]o man shall be held criminally responsible for conduct he could not reasonably understand to be proscribed", SCOTUS, Decision of 7 June 1954, No 32, *United States v. Hariss* [1954] 347, U.S. 612, 618.
24 Either in sections or as a case law section or paragraph.
25 Platzgummer, *Die Bewußtseinsform des Vorsatzes* (1964) 81 seq.
26 Jakobs (1993) (n 9).
27 In this sense also see Keedy (1908) (n 16).
28 See Smeulers, 'Why Serious International Crimes Might Not Seem 'Manifestly Unlawful' to Low-level Perpetrators, A Social Psychological Approach to Superior Orders' (2019) 17 *JICJ* 109.
29 See Travers (1995) (n 7) 1327; Varela (2012) (n 7).
30 See Travers (1995) (n 7); Varela (2012) (n 7).
31 LG Köln, Judgment of 7 May 2021; see Hörnle/Huster, 'Wie weit reicht das Erziehungsrecht der Eltern? Am Beispiel der Beschneidung von Jungen' (2013) 68 (7) *JZ* 328–339.
32 See Alexy (2002) (n 3) 53.
33 See Smeulers (2019) (n 18) 110.
34 See Smeulers (2019) (n 18) 110.

Bibliography

Alexy R, *The Argument from Injustice. A Reply to Legal Positivism* (Oxford University Press 2002).

Baumann J/Weber U et al, *Strafrecht Allgemeiner Teil* (Verlag Ernst und Werner Gieseking 2003).

Bustos J, 'Was ist Schuld?' in Sieber U et al (eds), *Strafrecht und Wirtschafsstrafrecht-Dogmatik, Rechtsvergleich, Rechtstatsachen. Festschrift für Klaus Tiedemann zum 70. Geburtstag* (Heymann 2008) 351.

Freedman M, 'Must You Be the Devil's Advocate?' (1993) *Legal Times* 19.

Hall L/Seligman S, 'Mistake of Law and mens rea' (1941) *University of Chicago Law Review* 641.

Hilbink L, *Judges beyond Politics in Democracy and Dictatorship. Lessons from Chile* (Cambridge University Press 2007).

Hörnle T/Huster S, 'Wie weit reicht das Erziehungsrecht der Eltern? Am Beispiel der Beschneidung von Jungen' (2013) 68 Heft 7 *JuristenZeitung* 328.

Jakobs G, *Strafrecht Allgemeiner Teil* (De Gruyter 1993).

Keedy E, 'Ignorance and Mistake of Law' (1908) 22 *Harvard Law Review* 75–96.

Kindhäuser U, *Strafrecht Allgemeiner Teil* (Nomos 2013).

Köhler M, *Strafrecht Allgemeiner Teil* (Springer 1997).

Laubenthal K/Baier H, 'Durch die Ausländereigenschaft bedingte Verbotsirrtümer und die Perspektiven europäischer Rechtsvereinheitlichung' (2000) *Goltdammer's Archiv für Strafrecht* 140.

Mayer M, *Rechtsnormen und Kulturnormen* (Wissenschaftliche Buchgesellschaft 1965).

Mende J, 'Are Human Rights Western – And Why Does It Matter? A Perspective from International Political Theory' (2021) 17 *Journal of International Political Theory* 38. https://journals.sagepub.com/doi/10.1177/1755088219832992 (accessed 8 December 2023).

Neumann U, '§ 17' in Kindhäuser U/Neumann U et al (eds), *Nomos Kommentar zum Strafgesetzbuch* (3rd edn, Nomos 2010).

Perron, W, '§ 21: Verminderte Schuldfähigkeit' in Eser A et al (eds), *Kommentar zum Strafgesetzbuch* (28 edn, Beck 2010).

Platzgummer W, *Die Bewußtseinsform des Vorsatzes* (Springer 1964).

Radbruch G, 'Gesetzliches Unrecht und übergesetzliches Recht' (1946) 1 *Süddeutsche Juristen-Zeitung* 105, reprint in: Hassemer W (ed), *Gustav Radbruch, Gesamtausgabe*, Band 3 (1990).

Radbruch G, 'Statutory Lawlessness and Supra-Statutory Law (1946)' (2006) 26 *The Oxford Journal of Legal Studies* 1.

Roller W/Höschel S, *Judenverfolgung und jüdisches Leben unter den Bedingungen der nationalsozialistischen Gewaltherrschaft: 1930-1946* (Verlag für Berlin-Brandenburg 1996).

Rudolphi H J, *Unrechtsbewusstsein, Verbotsirrtum und Vermeidbarkeit des Verbotsirrtums* (Schwartz 1969).

Smeulers A, 'Why Serious International Crimes Might Not Seem "Manifestly Unlawful" to Low-level Perpetrators, A Social Psychological Approach to Superior Orders' (2019) 17 (1) *Journal of International Criminal Justice* 17.

Travers M, 'Mistake of Law in Mala Prohibita Crimes' (1995) 62 (3) *The University of Chicago Law Review* 1301.

Valerius B, *Kultur und Strafrecht, die Berücksichtigung kulturelle Wertvorstellungen in der deutschen Strafrechtsdogmatik* (Duncker & Humblot 2011).

Varela L, 'Strict-Liability Como Forma de Imputación Jurídico-Penal' (2012) 3 *Indret: Revista para el Análisis del Derecho* 1.

Zaffaroni E/Alagia A et al, *Derecho Penal* (Ediar, Sociedad Anómia Editora, Commercial, Industrial y Financiera 2003).

14 Judicial Murder, Torture, and Unlawful Detention

An Overview from the Italian Legal System

Francesco Viganò

14.1 Introduction

Can judges be held criminally liable for murder, torture, and unlawful detention committed through acts or omissions linked to the exercise of their judicial functions? If so, under what conditions can such a liability be established? This chapter attempts to answer these basic questions from the perspective of the Italian legal system. It is important to underline at the outset that the answers provided here will be necessarily tentative, given the dearth of relevant case law or scholarly investigation on this topic. In Italy, judges and prosecutors have sometimes been convicted of corruption, or of complicity with the Mafia, in connection with acts performed in their official capacity.[1] As far as this author has been able to establish, however, no judge or prosecutor has ever been convicted or investigated in Italy on charges of murder, torture, or unlawful detention committed in the performance of their duties. Prosecutions of this sort did not even take place after the 1943 fall of Italy's fascist government, when a series of laws aimed at punishing crimes of the fascist regime were enacted and implemented.[2]

In principle, judicial actors in Italy are subject to criminal liability in the same way as any other individual. While special limitations apply to judges' civil liability,[3] there is no equivalent, in the domain of criminal law, of the judicial immunity that is generally recognized across the Anglo-American world.[4] Nor are there any particular procedural hurdles that protect judges from ordinary prosecution.[5] At the same time, there is no offense of specifically judicial perpetration, i.e., there is nothing akin to the German criminal code figure of '*Rechtsbeugung*', or judicial perversion of justice, which could produce a '*Sperrwirkung*', i.e., the effect of excluding the establishment of any other criminal offense.[6] At most, Italian judges and prosecutors are subject to certain forms of possible liability for corruption offenses, a condition that they share with all other civil servants. Such offenses include the general offense of 'neglecting official duties (Article 328), which carries a sentence tariff of between six months and two years. There is, however, nothing that would in theory shield judicial actors from much more serious charges should they be involved, through action or omission linked to their official capacity, in crimes such as murder, torture, or unlawful detention.

DOI: 10.4324/9781003470069-17

Establishing such liability in concrete cases would nonetheless be problematic for a number of reasons. The following sections of the chapter will address some of these reasons, working on the familiar ground of the distinction between liability for acts, on the one hand, and for omissions, on the other.

14.2 Liability Through Acts

To commence with the matter of possible criminal liability for acts committed in office, no serious question would arise as to the existence of liability where a course of conduct undertaken by a judicial actor falls manifestly outside the scope of his or her judicial duties or is in blatant contradiction with them – such as involvement in 'show trials' or 'farcical prosecutions'.[7] For example, there would be no doubt but that a judge or prosecutor would incur criminal responsibility were she to preside over questioning of a prisoner using some kind of tough interrogation technique amounting to torture. Since torture is not allowed in the Italian legal system under any circumstance, not even under the law of necessity,[8] a judge or prosecutor who acts as described would surely be held responsible as perpetrator or co-perpetrator of the offense of torture as established by the criminal code. Should the same official informally order that a prisoner be tortured by someone else – for example, by police officers on police premises – she would incur liability as an instigator of the offense committed by the other. The practical consequences would potentially be the same for her in both situations: since Italian law does not differentiate between the various forms of participation in a crime, the applicable sentencing framework is, in principle, the same for perpetrators and mere participants.[9]

A more complex situation would arise where a judge issues a formal decision entailing deprivation of liberty that, despite having the appearance of legality, later turns out to be unlawful. Such a decision might, for example, take the form of an order to remand in custody or even of a capital sentence, were the death penalty ever to be restored to the Italian statute books. Would or should such a judge be subsequently liable to charges such as false imprisonment (*sequestro di persona*) or voluntary homicide, respectively?

Under Italian law, any action that is causally linked to the commission of an offense by someone else is considered to be an act of participation (*concorso*) in the offense when committed with the intent to contribute to the carrying out of the offense.[10] It is not, however, necessary that the (immediate) perpetrator himself should be punishable: it is sufficient that he carries out the *actus reus* of such an offense.[11]

Now, a judge who issues an order of detention or passes a death sentence is in effect bringing about a (necessary) precondition of the victim being deprived of liberty or meeting their death. The law enforcement official executing the order would, then, fulfill the elements of the *actus reus* of false imprisonment or homicide, and the judge could be deemed as a participant in the relevant offense. A similar situation would arise in the event that a deportation or extradition order is issued, sending a person to a country where they face the prospect of torture or the death penalty. Here, the judicial decision likewise operates as a necessary precondition for the subsequent inflicting of harm by public officials in the destination country.

In all these hypothetical scenarios, however, causation is only a first step toward the assessment of the judge's criminal responsibility. In other words, the tracing of causality only establishes a *prima facie* case against her. In order to hold her criminally responsible, under the general principles of Italian criminal law, it would also be necessary to establish that her judicial decision was unlawful (Section 2.1) and that she acted with the necessary *mens rea* (Section 2.2).

14.2.1 Unlawfulness of the Judicial Decision

A common principle in criminal law is that criminal liability cannot arise from a particular course of conduct that causes a particular result or causes others to bring about this result unless that course of conduct is itself unlawful. This condition is generally not present when, for example, a judge imposes the death penalty on a person convicted of a criminal offense for which capital punishment is provided by law. Indeed, if the crime in question is mandatorily punishable by death, there is obviously a duty upon the judge to apply that particular sentence. In situations where the death penalty is discretionary, the judge is surely allowed to apply it if the relevant statutory requirements are met. *Mutatis mutandis*, the same could be said for a custodial sentence falling within the boundaries allowed by law.

Scholars in Italy and in other legal systems influenced by German legal doctrine might argue whether the reasons for not punishing the judge in the example given are to be found in the lack of grounds for objective imputation (*imputazione oggettiva, objektive Zurechnung*) of the result of her action or in the lack of unlawfulness (*antigiuridicità, Rechtswidrigkeit*) of her action, on the grounds of the fulfillment of a duty inherent to her office. Ultimately, however, all would agree that if the judge has acted in conformity with her legal duty – including by exercising discretion when choosing an appropriate penalty among those the law allows – her action cannot be considered criminal. And this for objective, rather than merely subjective, reasons (such as lack of mens rea).

The pivotal question for our purposes is, therefore, whether it is possible – and if so, under what conditions – to brand a particular judicial decision condemning someone to death, or to imprisonment, as an unlawful decision capable of generating possible criminal responsibility on the part of the judge.

Before embarking on this discussion, it is important to recall that every non-final decision can be quashed on appeal and that most final decisions can be reviewed, following extraordinary appeals, if specific new circumstances arise. The success of any such appeal necessarily implies that the previous decision was in some way flawed: at a minimum, in the sense that the original judge misinterpreted or misapplied the law or did not correctly assess the facts. Nevertheless, it would clearly be excessive to consider every decision later quashed on appeal to be *ipso facto* 'unlawful', for the purposes of postulating potential criminal liability on the part of the judge who made it.[12] Since judicial decisions very often presuppose complex assessments of fact and of law, all that can reasonably be expected from a judge is that she complies with a basic duty to carefully examine the relevant issues before rendering her decision, irrespective of whether or not this decision is later annulled because of an error of fact or law.

On the other hand, one can hardly see any compelling reason to rule out in absolute terms possible criminal responsibility of a judge for decisions that disregard the aforementioned basic duty and, in so doing, cause serious harm to others, such as the loss of life or personal liberty. The legal question becomes, then, where the bar for possible criminal liability should be set. In this respect, two diametrically opposed dangers should be avoided: on the one hand, that judges are deterred, by fear of possible criminal prosecution, from passing rightful and fully deserved sentences; on the other, that judges enjoy absolute impunity, even where there has been blatant abuse of power or inexcusable negligence. The risks entailed by the latter situation should not be underestimated: judges and prosecutors are often crucial instruments in the hands of authoritarian regimes. To grant them total impunity for every possible circumstance is, therefore, simply not an option.

In the search for a balanced solution to assessing the unlawfulness of a judicial decision, it therefore seems necessary to draw a crucial distinction between two categories of situation:

1. situations where the unlawfulness of the decision proceeds from a *misinterpretation*, or a *flawed application*, of a *valid law* (see Section 14.2.1.1), and
2. situations where the unlawfulness of the decision proceeds, rather, from the application of an *invalid law* (see Section 14.2.1.2).

14.2.1.1 Unlawful Decision-Making through Misinterpretation or Flawed Application of a Valid Law, or Violation of Procedural Rules While Applying Such a Law

The first category we have identified above describes the scenario in which a judge issues a flawed decision while applying a law that is fully valid (for example, a law specifying an entirely reasonable term of imprisonment for a particular crime).

The flaw in such a decision may turn on a misinterpretation of the law (such as where the judge wrongly considers that the defendant's actions fall within the scope of application of an offense, whereas a correct interpretation of the relevant legal provisions would have led her to the opposite conclusion). Alternatively, it may consist of a flawed application of that law in the proceeding, based, for example, on a wrongful appreciation of the evidence (a correct reading of which would have led to the conclusion that the defendant was not responsible). The flaw may also come about due to a disregard of procedural rules, operating to the detriment of the defendant, during the application of the law. In each of these three situations, the key issue in establishing criminal responsibility on the part of the judge is the identification of a viable standard for *ex post* evaluation of the 'unlawfulness' of her decision.

A case could be made for the reasonableness of the following approach: as a general rule, a judicial decision rendered within a legal proceeding subsequently annulled due to errors of fact or law remains, nonetheless, a 'lawful' decision.

Its legal force is simply set aside by a subsequent decision based on a more thorough appreciation of the relevant law or facts. As a 'lawful' decision, it must, then, be respected by everyone – including the person affected – unless and until it is annulled by a higher court. Even after any such annulment has taken place, the judge who issued the original decision should not ordinarily be held criminally responsible for it (just as she would ordinarily not be liable, under Italian civil law, for damages arising).

However, some exceptions to this general rule should be recognized, at least in cases of manifest error. In such an eventuality, the Italian legal system already envisages the judge's potential personal civil liability for damages,[13] thereby signaling that the manifestly erroneous decision is being classified as unlawful. The same criterion should arguably apply when it comes to the possible criminal liability of the judge, insofar as the manifest nature of her error shows that she has not complied with her basic duty to carefully examine the relevant matters of law and fact. For example, one might suggest that such an error occurs when a given interpretation of the law or a given appreciation of the facts, would appear *wholly implausible to any reasonable lawyer experienced in criminal law.*

Where this is the case, it might be argued that an 'unlawful' act of participation in false imprisonment, or homicide resulting from a capital sentence, has thereby been established. The test moreover operates from a purely objective perspective, irrespective of the judge's state of mind.[14] In particular, it applies regardless of whether she *intended* to break the law – something that, under German law, would be required for the purposes of attributing criminal liability for '*Rechtsbeugung*' – or did so out of inexcusable ignorance of the law, or gross negligence in the assessment of evidence. Only once the decision has been deemed objectively unlawful, the judge's actual intention and knowledge will become relevant, in connection with establishing *mens rea* regarding the specific criminal offense with which she will be charged (see Section 14.2.2).

14.2.1.2 Unlawful Decision-Making through Application of an Invalid Law

Let us now turn to our second category of unlawful decision-making, probably of greater significance for the purposes of the chapter. Here, we are interested in whether a judge's due application, to a particular defendant, of an invalid law can result in an 'unlawful' judicial decision.

Let us assume that an authoritarian regime enacts a law imposing imprisonment on anyone who engages in political activity in opposition to the government, even without using violence or any other intrinsically illicit means.[15] In all likelihood, should liberal-democratic governance be restored in the aftermath, such a law will be (retrospectively) considered invalid: persons previously convicted under it will see their convictions quashed and will regain their freedom if they had been imprisoned. What, though, will happen to the prosecutors and judges who brought charges, handed down convictions, and imposed sentences of imprisonment and even of death, according to the law then in force? Should or could those people be brought to justice as participants in the criminal offenses of homicide and/or false imprisonment?

One well-known way to address this question was first proposed by Gustav Radbruch at the end of the Second World War.[16] At its core, Radbruch's thesis is that a law once enacted by means deemed 'legal' in a given legal system may still, exceptionally, be considered invalid because of its 'injustice'. This injustice consists of its manifest departure from the imperatives of justice, or the foundational principles of natural law. A law of this sort should, argued Radbruch, be considered incapable of sustaining a conviction (or any other decision limiting a person's rights). This would clear the path to recognizing that the judge who handed down such a conviction or decision acted in a way that was not only unjust but also unlawful.

It seems to me, however, that this question needs to be thoroughly reconsidered today in the light of new frameworks of national constitutional and international law, whose existence and contents Radbruch could hardly have anticipated or imagined. Two basic situations should be discussed here: (1) a legal system where a liberal and democratic constitution is still in force and (2) a system that has undergone an authoritarian turn that has impaired – *de iure* or *de facto* – the functioning of such a constitution.

Taking situation (1) first, let us imagine for the sake of argument that an elected Italian government has legislated to reintroduce the death penalty. Now let us assume that a case involving a capital offense comes before a judge who has satisfied herself to the required standard – i.e., beyond reasonable doubt – that the defendant has indeed committed the crime. Is the judge bound to apply the new law? Before discussing whether the provision could be held contrary to natural law, as Radbruch would have suggested, a contemporary Italian judge ought first to carefully assess its validity according to Italian positive constitutional law. At least three alternative scenarios could, then, be imagined:

(1.1) Absent a prior constitutional amendment repealing the ban on the death penalty contained in Article 27(4) of the Italian Constitution, the new provision would be manifestly unconstitutional. The presiding judge ought therefore to refer the matter to the Constitutional Court, who should go on to declare the provision null and void.

(1.2) Even if Article 27 (4) had, in point of fact, been repealed before the enactment of the new law, the provision would still run counter to Protocols 6 and 13 of the European Convention on Human Rights (ECHR). In this scenario it ought also, therefore, to be considered unconstitutional under Article 117(1) of the Constitution, which explicitly states that domestic laws must be compatible with international legal obligations that are binding on Italy.

(1.3) In a hypothetical situation where, prior to the passing of the law in question, Article 117(1) of the Constitution has been repealed and Italy has also withdrawn from ECHR Protocols (likely finding itself suspended from the Council of

> Europe for that very reason), an Italian judge could – and indeed, should – argue that a general ban on the death penalty is still in place. This would derive from fundamental principles enshrined in the Constitution, including respect for the equal dignity of every individual and their inviolable rights. (Those principles are in all likelihood included among the principles subject to an unwritten 'eternity clause', the existence of which has been recognised by the Constitutional Court). In consequence, even in this third scenario the reintroduced death penalty could be held unconstitutional, and its enacting law therefore invalid, according to positive constitutional law (i.e., without any recourse to natural law).[17]

In sum, in a constitutional system it no longer appears necessary to invoke natural law in order to have a legislative provision deemed invalid. Constitutional law is largely sufficient to this end, particularly when it works in synergy with international human rights law. Crucially for the present discussion, it follows that a judge who applies a law that is clearly unconstitutional – and, therefore, invalid – is indeed issuing an 'unlawful' decision. Indeed, her duty to carefully examine the questions of law arising from the case cannot but include the preconditions of validity of the law she is called upon to apply. Hence, should she impose a death sentence or custodial sentence on someone in application of a clearly unconstitutional law, her decision would represent an 'unlawful' act of participation in false imprisonment or homicide, potentially engaging her own criminal responsibility.

One might object that even in modern constitutional states, and certainly in Italy, a law is presumed to be valid until it is declared null and void by the Constitutional Court. This being so, a judge could not be said to have applied an 'unlawful' law until such a declaration is actually issued. However, it would be easy to reply that every judge has a duty to ascertain whether the law to be applied in the case at hand is compatible with the Constitution. Certainly, in those cases where a defendant raises doubts about the constitutionality of the law, or its unconstitutionality is manifest, the judge is under an obligation to refer the question to the Constitutional Court before applying the provision. A failure to do so would in itself amount to a 'unlawful' application of the law.

Let us now turn to situation (2), where there has been an authoritarian turn. We might assume that a military coup has transformed a previously democratic state into an authoritarian one, as occurred in various Latin American countries in the 1970s and 1980s or envision democratic backsliding or decay such as can be observed today in various European countries following regular elections.[18] After a coup, fundamental rights and constitutional principles are generally suspended or even formally repealed, with constitutional courts dismissed. In the event of democratic backsliding, it is more common to see ordinary and constitutional courts continue to function, but 'packed' with personnel loyal to the government, therefore unable to perform their functions as guardians of the constitution.[19]

In contexts such as these, ordinary constitutional remedies are no longer viable. Indeed, the dividing line between 'valid' and 'invalid' laws itself becomes blurred wherever higher courts are unable to discharge their duty to ensure respect for the constitution. Nevertheless, once again it seems to me that today's conditions are significantly different from those prevailing when Radbruch formulated his theory, i.e., during the first half of the twentieth century. If we consider Europe, for example, European Union law has remained in force within the national legal order of those states that have experienced democratic backsliding. EU law still enjoys primacy over domestic law where the two come into conflict, despite any attempts by national (including judicial) authorities to claim the contrary.[20] Now, one essential part of EU law is the Charter of Fundamental Rights. Its provisions actually work in the same way as constitutional and human rights guarantees, and they have, for the most part, direct effect in member states. Consequently, every judge within the EU is still under a legal duty to disapply a national law that disregards one of the rights enshrined in the Charter. Sending someone to jail, or sentencing them to death, based on a national provision incompatible with the Charter[21] would, then, arguably constitute an *actus reus* of false imprisonment or of homicide, committed 'unlawfully' by the judge. Consequently she could well be brought to justice, at any subsequent point in time, to answer for those crimes.[22]

But even outside the EU, after the Second World War, international human rights law has also become a well-established normative reality well beyond the confines of the EU. Its basic principles are widely considered today to be binding on all states (and, crucially, on every state actor), independent of the status of formal recognition in specific treaties. Thus human rights law has become part and parcel of general (customary) international law,[23] or even, in respect of a growing number of issues, part of international *ius cogens*.[24]

As a consequence, national laws clearly contravening the basic tenets of international human rights law[25] – at least, as enshrined in universally recognized instruments such as the Universal Declaration of Human Rights or the International Covenant on Civil and Political Rights – cannot be held to be valid even within legal orders that have officially turned their back on the principles of constitutionalism. This holds true regardless of whether such national laws meet the prevailing domestic conditions necessary to be considered as formally legally enacted.

This being so, in every single case where the application of such a law actually led to a capital penalty or a deprivation of liberty, the judicial decision itself could well be considered constitutive of 'unlawful' participation in an *actus reus* of homicide or false imprisonment.

Finally, should the application of domestic law by a judge amount to an international crime, due – for example – to forming part of a systematic or widespread attack against a particular sector of the civilian population (e.g., political opponents) that judge's criminal liability would be indisputable.[26] International criminal law, after all, has clear precedence over domestic law, and thus not even a judge or prosecutor could claim to be exempt from its scope of application based on domestic provisions.

14.2.2 Mens Rea

A final necessary step, if a judge is to be convicted of homicide or false imprisonment committed through an act of office such as a judicial order, would be to show not only that her decision was 'unlawful' but also that she acted with the necessary mens rea.

As a general rule, neither the offense of voluntary homicide nor that of false imprisonment requires any special form of intention or knowledge.[27] In Italy, as in many other European continental and Latin American countries, every form of *dolus* would suffice, including *dolus eventualis*. Now, intention and knowledge, which are both essential to the modern notion of *dolus*, usually refer to the material consequence of the action, i.e., the death or loss of liberty that affects the victim. The judge is certainly aware that her decision will cause such consequences.

The question remains, though, whether assessment of the judge's *mens rea* – or, more broadly speaking, her culpability – also requires some kind of awareness of the unlawful nature of her decision.

In the specific sub-case where law has been applied in a flawed manner to a particular set of facts, e.g. due to an incorrect reading of the evidence, the rules on *mens rea* should be combined with those on the establishment of the objective 'unlawfulness' of the act. The question about 'mistake as to justification' is one of the most heavily discussed among scholars influenced by German doctrine[28] and cannot be adequately addressed here. Suffice it to say that prevailing opinion on the matter in Italy is that no criminal liability for a criminal offense requiring *dolus* – such as false imprisonment – could ever be established if the defendant has acted in the honest, albeit mistaken, belief of the occurrence of facts that, if present, would have allowed her to act.[29] Therefore, if a judge sentences someone to prison in the honest belief that the defendant has committed a crime, under Italian law her criminal responsibility for false imprisonment is always ruled out due to lack of the necessary *mens rea*. This is so even if her judgment was 'unlawful' due to being so manifestly erroneous as to appear wholly implausible to any reasonable lawyer experienced in criminal law. In the event of such a blatant error, criminal responsibility for false imprisonment on the part of the judge could only arise if she was positively aware that the defendant did not commit the offense with which he was charged and nonetheless decided to convict him.[30]

The situation could be different, however, if what is at issue is a judge's possible responsibility for homicide, arising from a judicial death sentence decision based on a manifestly flawed assessment of the evidence. In the Italian legal system, homicide is also punishable when committed by mere negligence.[31] Malicious intent on the part of the judge would therefore not be required in order for her to be punished as a participant in a merely 'negligent' homicide. The question about her criminal responsibility would instead hinge, in practice, on whether her judgment could be considered unlawful according to the standard set out above. In fact, negligence would necessarily be established once the conclusion is reached that no reasonable lawyer experienced in criminal law would have fallen into the same error. In such a situation, therefore, the path would be open to asserting the judge's liability for negligent homicide arising from her sentence. Alternatively, should there be grounds for suspecting her to have acted with actual malicious intent against a particular defendant, she would have no protection against liability for voluntary homicide.

Greater complexity arises when the flaw in the judicial decision lies either in a gross misinterpretation of a valid provision or with a failure to refuse to comply with an invalid law. Both of these situations may lead to the issuing of an unlawful decision, and both raise questions as to whether a judge may invoke a (proper) 'mistake of law' defense. Under normal circumstances, criminal law systems tend to allow only very limited space for any such defense.[32] In Italy, following a decision of the Constitutional Court,[33] a defendant may only be granted the excuse of mistake of law if said mistake was unavoidable. This would be taken to mean that the law in question was objectively obscure or so inconsistently interpreted by the Supreme Court that even a legal expert would not be able to provide reliable information as to its content.[34] In practice, for a defendant to successfully escape conviction by adducing mistake of law would be rare, happening only in exceptional cases. When a legal system has, however, been perverted to a point where basic rule of law tenets are no longer in force, the possibility that a judge may be acting *bona fide* while applying a law formally enacted following the ordinary rules within that system should be carefully considered.

I have argued above that the fundamental principles of international human rights law – and certainly of international criminal law – should be considered as binding on courts, even within legal systems that have departed from the rule of law. This self-same point is, however, always denied by authoritarian governments, which usually claim instead that domestic principles of law have precedence over international law. In such situations, judges and prosecutors are often also trained according to prevailing official legal doctrine, appointed by government officials, and subject to disciplinary proceedings in the hands of the regime. These professionals will, to put it mildly, enjoy fewer opportunities to recognize the 'invalid' character of laws enacted by the regime than would their counterparts who serve in free and democratic states. On the other hand, an overgenerous margin of toleration in allowing such considerations to justify the defense of mistake of law would produce generalized impunity for judicial actors who are often key participants in the criminal policies of authoritarian governments. Therefore there is a need, particularly in transitional justice contexts, to develop some more precise setting-specific criteria for evaluating such mistakes. This would help strike a proper balance between the need to re-establish justice after transition and assessment of the degree to which defendants are personally at fault. Such an assessment would involve taking into consideration how fully judges and prosecutors would have been able to appreciate the unlawfulness of their acts at the time of commission.

14.3 Liability Through Omission

Our final last question concerns whether a judge could be held criminally liable for failing to intervene to impede acts of murder, torture, and unlawful detention carried out by other individuals.[35]

In Italy, criminal liability for the offense of neglecting official duties could be easily established in such circumstances. This is a charge that, however, attracts very light punishment. A more relevant question, then, is whether the same judge could be held accountable for homicide, false imprisonment, or torture under the law of liability by omission.

In my view, at least, the starting point here ought to be the recognition of a general duty, applicable to all state agents, to protect the human rights of individuals within their jurisdictions. Judges and prosecutors would, of course, feature among the agents so obligated, within the limits of their institutional competence.

Such a duty can be derived, first and foremost, from states' international commitments to protect the rights that are recognized in the relevant regional spaces, instruments, and mechanisms. That is, for instance, in the European legal space, the European Convention on Human Rights, and in Latin America, the American Convention on Human Rights, each as interpreted by the respective regional human rights system. As both of the respective Courts[36] have repeatedly stated in well-established case law, every state party is under an obligation to take active steps to protect the individuals in its jurisdiction against any assault on their basic human rights, whether emanating from state agents or third parties. These active steps include a duty to investigate when any such assault or violation is taking place or has taken place, as well as the duty to identify, prosecute, convict, and sentence those responsible for it.[37]

However, in order for charges to be leveled against a judge or prosecutor alleging criminal liability for omission, a key element of proof would be needed. It would have to be shown that the result – the death, torture, or unlawful detention – would not have taken place, or could at least have been brought to an end, had the judge or the prosecutor acted according to her duties. In other words, a causal link between omission and result[38] would have to be established, according to some predefined interpretation or definition of what could be held to constitute such a link.[39] Unfortunately, the cases we are considering here are extremely resistant to the establishment of such a link. One might be able to imagine some hypothetical situations in which such a link would be clearly present: if, for example, a public prosecutor has full knowledge of the whereabouts of a person unlawfully detained by paramilitary forces but does not order the police to intervene and free the victim. Even here, however, a proviso applies: there would need to be good reason to believe that, given prevailing conditions, such an order would have been complied with. In many other possible situations, however, it would be virtually impossible to demonstrate a causal pathway even of this contingent kind. The criminal liability of a judge or a prosecutor for failure to intervene would therefore be impossible to establish without disregarding basic principles of criminal law regarding liability for omission.[40] In such situations, the only form of criminal responsibility that could potentially come into play would therefore be possible responsibility as accessories-after-the-fact (i.e., as perpetrators of the offense of *favoreggiamento*,[41] '*encubrimiento*', and '*Begünstigung*').[42]

Notes

1 For a corruption case, see (Italian) Court of Cassation, Decision of 8 August 2017, n. 47602. For a thorough discussion on case law related to Mafia complicity, see Fernando Londoño's contribution to the present volume.

2 For a thorough analysis of these laws, Caroli, *Transitional Justice in Italy and the Crimes of Fascism and Nazism* (2022) 18 and 102.
3 According to Italian Law N. 117 of 13 April 1988.
4 See an extensive exploration of this topic in Nancy Combs's contribution to this volume.
5 Such as those in place in various South American countries, as illustrated in chapters by Luis Emilio Rojas and Javier Wilenmann in this volume.
6 In this respect, therefore, the Italian situation significantly differs from that prevailing in Germany, which is analyzed in chapters by Milan Kuhli, Florian Jeßberger, Kai Cornelius, and Luis Emilio Rojas in this volume.
7 See, on 'show crimes' and 'farcical prosecutions, respectively, chapters by Jaime Couso and Markus Abraham in this volume.
8 See Scaroina, *Il delitto di tortura* (2018) 326, with further references.
9 Article 110 of the Italian Criminal Code.
10 On all these principles, see Marinucci et al, *Manuale di diritto penale. Parte generale* (2022) 579.
11 Marinucci et al, *Manuale di diritto penale. Parte generale* (2022) 576.
12 According to Héctor Hernández's contribution to this volume, indeed, 'every legal system accepts miscarriages of justice as normal and not criminal, at least in principle'.
13 See article 7 (1) of Italian Law N. 117 of 13 April 1988.
14 For a different approach, see, however, Héctor Hernández's contribution to this volume.
15 For another example (the Nazi law criminalizing intermarriages between 'Arians' and Jews), see Florian Jeßberger and Milan Kuhli's contribution to this volume.
16 In Italian legal doctrine, on Radbruch's thesis and its impact in contexts of transitional justice, see Giuliano Vassalli's book, *Formula di Radbruch e diritto penale* (2001). In this volume, see also chapters by Florian Jeßberger and Milan Kuhli and Luis Emilio Rojas.
17 Such a recourse is rightly considered by Hernández, in his contribution to this volume, as 'highly problematic'.
18 See, for example, Levitsky/Ziblatt, *How Democracies Die* (2018) 72. About the Hungarian case, see Levitsky/Ziblatt, *Tyranny of the Minority* (2023) 60.
19 See, among many possible sources, Sadurski, *Poland's Constitutional Breakdown* (2019); Śledzińska-Simon 'The Rise and Fall of Judicial Self-Government in Poland: On Judicial Reform Reversing Democratic Transition' (2018) 19 *GLJ* 1839.
20 See, in this regard, the jurisprudential saga that has produced multiple decisions by the CJEU (5 June 2023, Case C-204/21, *Commission v Poland IV*; 16 February 2022, Case C-157/21, *Poland v European Parliament and Council of the European Union*; 16 November 2021, Joined Cases C-748/19 to C-754/19 *W.B. et al.*; 5 November 2021, Case C-487/19 *W.Z.*; 15 July 2021, Case C-791/19 *Commission v Poland III*; 19 November 2019, Joined Cases C-585/18, C-624/18 and C-625/18 *A. K. v Krajowa Rada Sądownictwa et al.*) opposed by the Polish Constitutional Court (Judgement of 20 April 2020, Ref. No. U 2/20; Decision of 21 April 2020, Ref. No. Kpt. 1/20; Judgement of 14 July 2021, Ref. No. P 7/20; Judgement of 7 October 2021, Ref. No. K 3/21 and Judgment of 24 November 2021, Ref. No. K 6/21). See also, with respect to the same issue, the case law of the ECHR: Judgment of 24 October 2023, App no 25226/18, *Pajak et al. v. Poland et al.*; Judgment of 3 February 2022, App no 1469/20, *Advance Pharma sp. z o.o. v. Poland*; Judgment of 8 November 2021, App no 49868/19 and 57551/19, *Dolinska-Ficek and Ozimek v. Poland*; Judgment of 22 July 2021, App no 43447/19, *Reczkowicz v. Poland*; Judgment of 7 May 2021, App no 4907/18, *Xero Flor w Polsce sp. z o.o. v. Poland.*
21 Such as, let us say, provisions criminalizing political dissent or consensual homosexual relationships.

22 For discussion of the deployment of criminal law against judges who have issued decisions running counter to EU law, with particular regard to the Polish situation (albeit with exclusive reference to the offence of 'perversion of justice'), see von Bogdandy/Spieker, '*Restoring the Rule of Law Through Criminal Responsibility*', *VerfassungsBlog*, 10 December 2021. https://verfassungsblog.de/restoring-the-rule-of-law-through-criminal-responsibility/ (accessed 2 January 2024).

23 De Schutter, *International Human Rights Law* (2019) 59.

24 De Schutter, *International Human Rights Law* (2019) 85.

25 Such as the ban on torture or execution of children – principles that, by the way, can surely hardly be viewed as expressions of a 'paternalistic or imperialistic point of view'. On this critique regarding the universality of human rights, see Alejandra Castillo's impressive contribution to this volume.

26 On the possible responsibility of judicial actors according to international criminal law, see the chapters by Elies van Sliedregt and Claudia Cárdenas in this volume.

27 In particular, unlike in the German offense of *Rechtsbeugung*, no *specific intent* is required. This marks probably the essential difference between the Italian and German contexts as far as our topic is concerned.

28 For an extended discussion, see, for example, Roxin/Greco, *Strafrecht. Allgemeiner Teil I* 735.

29 This conclusion is based on Article 59 (4) of the Italian Criminal Code.

30 The practical outcome would not, here, significantly differ from the one that would result in Germany from the application of the offence of *Rechtsbeugung* (judicial perversion of justice).

31 Article 589 of the Italian Criminal Code.

32 See, on this topic, chapters by Antonio Martin and Alejandra Castillo in this volume.

33 Italian Constitutional Court, Judgment of 24 March 1988, No 364/1988.

34 More on this standard in Marinucci et al (2022) (n 11) 470.

35 For some illustrative examples, see Jaime Couso's contribution to this volume. It is interesting to note that a failure to act may also take the form of an apparent action, such as a decision to reject a *habeas corpus* (see, on this point, the example offered by Luis Emilio Rojas in his contribution to this volume).

36 The European Court of Human Rights and the Inter-American Court of Human Rights.

37 On this case law, see Viganò, 'La arbitrariedad del no punir. Sobre las obligaciones de tutela penal de los derechos fundamentales' (2014) 9 *Política criminal* 428.

38 As rightly pointed out by Héctor Hernández in his contribution in this volume. According to the standard understanding of causality, furthermore, a link should be established between a *single* individual's failure to act and a particular event (here: the commission of a specific crime by someone else), in the sense that, had that individual (here: the judge) acted in conformity with her duties, the crime in question would not have been committed (for example, by police or military officers). For a wholly different perspective, linking the inaction by *the whole judiciary* of a country – seen as a 'collective person' – with the commission of *all* crimes carried out during the Argentinean dictatorship, see Omar Palermo's contribution in this volume.

39 More on this question in Viganò, 'Riflessioni sulla c.d. "causalità omissiva" in materia di responsabilità medica' (2009) 52 *RIDPP* 1679.

40 A different way to approach the problem, which cannot be further examined here due to space constraints, would be to argue that the inaction of a particular judge – faced with say, a *habeas corpus* petition – amounts to an instigation to (further) unlawfully detain a prisoner. The inaction would mean, here, implicit encouragement – under the specific

circumstances of the case, and with regard to some existing relationship between the judge and the actual perpetrators – of the unlawful action committed by third persons. Even in this case, though, a specific causal link between the judge's conduct and the commission of the offense should be carefully established.

41 Article 378 of the Italian Criminal Code.

42 For this solution, see also Luis Emilio Rojas' contribution to this volume.

Bibliography

von Bogdandy A/Spieker L D, '*Restoring the Rule of Law Through Criminal Responsibility*', *VerfassungsBlog*, 10 December 2021. https://verfassungsblog.de/restoring-the-rule-of-law-through-criminal-responsibility/ (accessed 2 January 2024).

Caroli P, *Transitional Justice in Italy and the Crimes of Fascism and Nazism* (Routledge 2022).

De Schutter O, *International Human Rights Law* (3rd edn, Cambridge University Press 2019).

Levitsky S/Ziblatt D, *How Democracies Die* (Penguin Random House LLC 2018).

Levitsky S/Ziblatt D, *Tyranny of the Minority* (Penguin Random House LLC 2023).

Marinucci G/Dolcini E/Gatta G L, *Manuale di diritto penale. Parte generale* (11th edn, Giuffrè 2022).

Roxin C/Greco L, *Strafrecht. Allgemeiner Teil*, I (5th edn, Beck 2020).

Sadurski W, *Poland's Constitutional Breakdown* (Oxford University Press 2019).

Scaroina E, *Il delitto di tortura* (Cacucci Editore 2018).

Śledzińska-Simon A, 'The Rise and Fall of Judicial Self-Government in Poland: On Judicial Reform Reversing Democratic Transition' (2018) 19 *German Law Journal* 19.

Vassalli G, *Formula di Radbruch e diritto penale* (Giuffrè 2001).

Viganò F, 'La arbitrariedad del no punir. Sobre las obligaciones de tutela penal de los derechos fundamentales' (2014) 9 *Política criminal* 428.

Viganò F, 'Riflessioni sulla c.d. "causalità omissiva" in materia di responsabilità medica' (2009) 52 *Rivista italiana di diritto e procedura penale* 1679.

15 On the Relationship between Judicial Perversion of Justice and Judges' Participation in Crimes against Humanity

Luis E. Rojas A.

15.1 Introduction

In 1925, Adolf Merkl argued that the category of miscarriage of justice ('*Justizirrtum*') was a *contradictio in adiecto*. Indeed, at the beginning and at the end of his 1925 work *Justizirrtum und Rechtswahrheit*, he adduced the example of 'judicial murder' (*Justizmord*) as a species of such an alleged error: "Judicial homicide is not only no homicide, it is not even a wrongdoing".[1] The historical context of Merkl's writing was the mid-point of the Weimar Republic. It would be an interesting hypothetical exercise to speculate whether Merkl would have stood by his thesis when faced with some of the examples that presented themselves two decades later. What, for instance, would he have made of the case of the German judicial official who reported a merchant for scrawling a piece of toilet stall graffiti that read "Hitler is a serial killer and is guilty of the war"? The decision to report the man led to his being sentenced to death.[2] Or what of the case of the German general who, shortly before the end of the war, organized a court martial to pass the death sentence on two men – one an alleged deserter from the Armed Forces, and the other a peasant farmer – for having disarmed a group of Hitler Youth?[3] Merkl would more likely than not have stood by his previous statement, especially if one bears in mind that Kelsen himself, in the later, second, edition of his *Pure Theory of Law*, maintained the same with regard to the legal system then in force.[4]

Almost half a century after Merkl published *Justizirrtum und Rechtswahrheit*, and geographically almost half a world away, Chile suffered its 1973 military coup d'état. There followed a brutal persecution of supporters of the overthrown government, unleashed by agents of the Armed Forces and security services. This persecution took the form of murders, sometimes preceded by perfunctory courts martial, and the kidnapping or illegal detention of opponents of the military regime. There was frequent use of torture, including in the form of sexual violence. Courageous victims' relatives filed thousands of writs of habeas corpus and/or criminal complaints before the courts. Many of them were represented by lawyers from social organizations linked to the Catholic Church. Practically all the habeas corpus writs were, however, rejected, first by the respective district Court of Appeals and then by the Supreme Court itself. At first, the reasons given included

DOI: 10.4324/9781003470069-18

the claim that the ordinary court system lacked jurisdiction because the new military regime had decided to declare a state of siege. Later, when a handful of writs were admitted and information was duly requested from the *de facto* authorities, the courts simply accepted at face value official falsehoods stating that the named person's whereabouts were not known. As for the investigative proceedings that were, or ought to have been, initiated by the complaints, these were routinely suspended by the investigative magistrates overseeing them, particularly after 1978, when an amnesty was decreed.[5]

This chapter addresses the relationship between judicial perversion of justice and the participation of judges in crimes against humanity. It does so by comparing the categories developed in the German legal tradition with the rules in force in Chilean law at the time of the military dictatorship. Turning first to Germany, the chapter proceeds via a brief historical exploration of the origins of the rules of judicial liability in the German tradition and the 'blocking effect' of the absence of judicial perversion of justice in that tradition. Next, Chile is discussed. Stark contrasts emerge between the German experience and the principles and rules of judicial liability in the Chilean tradition.

15.2 Judicial Perversion of Justice and the Participation of the Judge in Other Crimes in the German Legal Tradition

Within Germany's civil law tradition, the revolutionary ideology that sought to prevent the creative work of judges, reducing their role to the mere application of the law, did not penetrate deeply into the German kingdoms.[6] Throughout the 19th century, the work of jurists in the conceptual elaboration of the common law was still indispensable. This was reflected in the study of Roman law and the conducting of ongoing discussion with legal commentators by civil and criminal jurists alike. By the time the process of codification of criminal and civil law began, in the latter part of that century, German judges seemed to enjoy great confidence and authority in the interpretation and application of the law. This was true to such an extent that it was not deemed necessary to even attempt to regulate their work by establishing rules of interpretation, as had been done elsewhere. This is the only possible explanation for the fact that the framework of the codification process incorporated only two rules of ministerial responsibility, common to all public officials. The first appeared in a section on 'unlawful actions', under the heading of 'specific obligational relationships': § 839 part 2 of the German Civil Code (Bürgerliches Gesetzbuch, BGB) stipulated that an official who violates his or her duty of office in judging a legal matter is only liable for the damage thereby inflicted:

> [W]hen the breach of duty is punishable by a state penalty to be imposed by means of a judicial criminal proceeding. This rule is not applicable to refusal or delay, contrary to duty, in the exercise of office.

The second rule was initially set down as § 336 of the *Reichsstrafgesetzbuch* (RStGB), German Criminal Code of the day. Although now modified, the wording survives, virtually unchanged, in the current § 339. This article introduced a criminal penalty rule for *Rechtsbeugung*, judicial perversion of justice, in the following terms:

> any judicial officer or arbitrator who, in the conduct or decision of a legal matter, intentionally distorts the law in favor or to the detriment of one of the parties, shall be punished with imprisonment of up to five years.

It is of considerable interest to note that the first rule, i.e., § 839.2 of the Civil Code, made the liability of the official for the damage caused to one of the parties dependent on the fact that the breach of duty of office was subject to a criminal penalty to be imposed via judicial proceedings.[7] It is even more interesting to note that in the case of possible liability of a judge for damage caused by a decision adopted in breach of his or her duty of office, the rule on punishment of judicial perversion of justice expressly required *dolus*. Accordingly, if such damage instead occurred as a result of the judge's negligence or inexcusable ignorance, she or he would be exempt from judicial responsibility.

In any case, what is clear is that underlying these rules of liability is a vision of the judge that goes far beyond that of a mere interpreter and applicator of the law. Rather, the judge is being conceived of as a sort of mediator between the law and the parties, in such terms that the rights and obligations of the latter are subordinated to the recognition and declaration of the court in the specific case.[8] This conception of the role of the judge is clearly reflected in a brief work by Josef Kohler in 1904 on the concept of judicial perversion of justice.[9] Given the wording of § 336 of the Criminal Code (*Strafgesetzbuch*, StGB), Kohler understood that the judge commits perversion of justice in civil law when he or she arbitrarily does not recognize a subjective right of whose existence he or she is convinced or, conversely, when she or he arbitrarily declares the existence of a right that she or he knows does not exist. On what grounds the judge arrives at that conclusion is, said Kohler, the judge's own affair: "in the *sacrosanct* sphere of the founding conviction upon which judicial activity is based, no one has the right to enter" (emphasis added). In particular, Kohler maintained that the meaning that a judge attributes to the sources of law is entirely a matter of individual conviction:

> In any case, the judge who sacrifices his conviction seriously disregards his high position. It follows that nothing would be more wrong than to aspire to submit the reliable treatment of the law to the prosecutor's examination and the investigation of the criminal judge.

Kohler's prediction came true almost in its entirety: as both Sarstedt and Spendel report, from the time the *Reichsstrafgesetzbuch* came into force (1871) until before the Second World War, only four high court (*Reichsgericht)* judgments on perversion of justice can be found. Two of these moreover relate to other public officials (i.e., not judges).[10] When post-war legislators and jurists took on the task of clarifying the responsibilities of judges for past war crimes and crimes against humanity, the faultlines that opened up in the bedrock of tradition must have caused much perplexity and even consternation. How could it be conceivable that the very authority called upon to rule on the law in specific cases – charged with declaring the existence or non-existence of the rights of the parties – could, by its judicial decisions, be party not only to the commission of crimes but crimes of such magnitude?

It was against this historical backdrop that Radbruch coined his well-known formula.[11] The main case he had in mind was the one mentioned at the outset of this chapter, concerning the official who reported the merchant who had written a "pristine truth" (*blanke Wahrheit)*: "Hitler is a serial murderer and is guilty of the war".[12] Radbruch argues that if the complainant filed his report with 'principal's *dolus*', then he is liable as the principal-by-means of the homicide that was thereby enacted through the ensuing trial and death sentence. This is a kind of liability that supposes the judge was instrumentalized by the complainant. However, says Radbruch, if the complainant did not act with such *animus* but intended only to place the facts in the hands of the authorities, leaving the subsequent course of events to the decision of the court, then he can at most be treated as an accomplice "insofar as the judge, for his part, has been guilty of a homicide through the sentence and its execution". This thesis would have been followed by the court called to resolve the case in the post-war period:

> The punishability of the judge for the homicide presupposes the *simultaneous* concurrence of a perversion of justice [*'Rechtsbeugung'*] committed by him (§§ 336, 344). For, the *judgment of* the independent judge can only be punished when he has precisely violated the principle of subjection to the legislation, that is, to the *law*, a principle which was precisely the purpose of that independence.[13]

Applying his formula, Radbruch argues that if in the specific case it can be verified that the judge has applied a rule that was not law – for example, because the measure of punishment implied a disregard of any will to justice – then *objectively* there is prevarication. Radbruch goes on to speculate:

> [B]ut could judges who had been so trained under the reigning positivism that they knew no other law than the legislated law, be *guilty of judicial perversion of justice ['Rechtsbeugung']* in the application of positive laws?.[14]

As can be seen, Radbruch here discusses the responsibility of the judge as principal 'through an innocent agent', a form of intervention that is relevant because the judge does not carry out the homicide 'by his or her own hand', as it were, but by means of a death sentence that is then carried out by other judicial officials.[15] The external or objective aspect of homicide is present, insofar as there is a causal link between the conviction and the carrying out of the death sentence. But, as Radbruch himself had previously clarified with respect to the complainant, perpetration-by-means implies intention on the part of the perpetrator, differentiated only by this subjective nuance from complicity. Here the action of the intervener – this time, the judge – consists of a judicial decision, issued to the detriment of one of the parties, i.e., the unjustly accused defendant. The 'principal's *dolus*' accordingly translates into the corresponding '*dolus* of judicial perversion of justice' by declaring the right of the State to execute the condemned person knowing that the sentence is improper – either because the person is in fact innocent or because the death penalty is manifestly disproportionate to the crime. This is why Radbruch goes on to ask whether the recalcitrant, strictly 'positivist' judges – those who mistakenly believed that '*Gesetz ist Gesetz*'[16] – really had '*dolus* of judicial perversion of justice', even though they objectively committed judicial perversion of justice by applying unlawful legislation.

Strangely enough, later jurisprudence and majority doctrine deduce, from these passages of Radbruch's work, the existence of something akin to an additional presupposition that must be met if a judge is to be punishable for murder, torture, or kidnapping. This extra element would lie in the prior configuration of the crime of judicial perversion of justice (with the practical consequence that, if this were not the case, judges would remain unpunished). In other words, jurisprudence and doctrine derive an implicit rule that would privilege judges in comparison with other mortals.[17] Radbruch was writing just one year after the end of the war. Could it have been his intention to conceptually elaborate a filter creating privilege for judges? Surely the contrary is more likely. The textual argument of those who advocate for the additional presupposition is based on Radbruch's mention of the principle of judges' independence, which serves the maxim of their subjection to the law. This reading, however, overlooks the fact that in that passage Radbruch uses the verb '*verletzen*' – which can be rendered as to injure or infringe. He alludes, in other words, to a situation where there has been an injury to or infringement of the duty to submit exclusively to the law at the moment of resolving a legal matter. The reading also forgets that, in the entire period between the end of the 19th century and the Second World War, '*Rechtsbeugung*' was conceptualized on the basis of this infringement of duty in a *subjective* sense. That is, the term was taken as denoting the *internal* betrayal of the law, such as when a judge would declare the existence of a right that she or he knew did not exist or would ignore the existence of a right, knowing that it existed.[18]

Current doctrine refers to this filter or condition of punishability under the label of '*Sperrwirkung*', or the preclusive effect of the absence of judicial perversion of justice. The use of this term in this particular sense, i.e. to describe a blocking effect, was coined by Friedrich Christian Schroeder.[19] Commentaries to the German Criminal Code usually deal with the issue of *Sperrwirkung* under the heading of 'concurrence' with the crime of judicial perversion of justice.[20]

15.3 Judicial Perversion of Justice and Responsibility of Judges in the Chilean Legal Tradition

The Chilean legal tradition dates back to the dawn of the Chilean Republic at the beginning of the 19th century. It is marked from its origins by a distrust of judges.

In normative terms, the synallagmatic relationship between the judge's freedom and the judge's responsibility is clearly weighted in favor of the latter. The Chilean tradition has moreover always favored the principle of personal responsibility of judges, a principle that is already reflected in the country's founding 1833 Constitution. Indeed, the scope of the principle of judges' liability was established and regulated by the 1875 Law of Organisation and Powers of the Courts (LOPC), which would later serve as the structural basis for the Organic Code of Courts (OCC) currently in force.[21] In addition to recognizing the principle of independence of the judiciary – at Art. 11 – the LOPC law included the principle of the liability of judges in the same terms as were used in the Constitution, although excluding members of the Supreme Court. As for civil liability, given that the Civil Code did not itself contemplate special rules of liability for damages caused to parties, the LOPC proceeded to regulate this liability in several provisions (Arts. 160–162).

In line with the models offered by the Spanish criminal codes of 1820 and 1848, the exhaustive regulation of the personal responsibility of judges was, however, entrusted to Articles 223, 224, and 225 of Chile's 1874 Criminal Code. Here, no fewer than fifteen different hypotheses of judicial perversion of justice were set down. All described conducts that were punishable by penalties, including deprivation of liberty. In general terms, and in contrast with the rules on '*Rechtsbeugung*' in the German Criminal Code of the same period, the Chilean style of regulation can be said to be based on two pillars. One, the norm contained in Art. 223 of the Criminal Code, punishes conduct that fits the original idea of prevarication. This evokes the Roman tradition as expressed in Digest 47, title XV, 1. *Ulpianus*, commentaries to the Edict, book VI: "The *praevaricator* is like one who stands on two sides, who helps the opposing party by betraying his own cause". In Article 223, this takes forms such as accepting gifts "for doing or failing to do some act of his office" or exercising "the functions of his employment or using the power it gives him", to seduce or solicit sexual favors from a woman who is being prosecuted or who litigates before him (without necessarily requiring that harm be done to the opposing party or to the case). The second pillar of Chilean regulation of judges' liability consists *inter alia* of the rules set down in Articles 224 and 225 of the Criminal Code. These are triggered if a judge dictates a resolution during a process or at its conclusion that is 'manifestly unjust' (*manifiestamente injusta*) (Art. 224), in the sense of being harmful to one of the parties or to the case. Thus, for example, issuing a resolution that denies or delays the administration of justice and the assistance or protection that is legally requested, or keeping prisoner an individual who under the terms of the law is entitled to be released. Another very relevant point to note – evidence that the Chilean judge's freedom tends to be sacrificed in favor of his or her responsibility – is the fact that infractions of most of these rules can be committed either intentionally, or through negligence or inexcusable ignorance.[22]

Nevertheless, as a counterpart to the exhaustive regulation of judicial perversion of justice contained in the Criminal Code and the rules of civil liability, Chile's LOPC established a filter of a *procedural* nature in the following terms:[23]

> No accusation or civil action brought against a judge to enforce his or her criminal or civil liability may be processed without first being ruled admissible by the judge or court called upon to hear it.

In the case of criminal liability, the procedure for the prior declaration of admissibility of the accusation was later regulated by the Code of Criminal Procedure of 1906 (Código de Procedimiento Penal, henceforth, CCP) under the name of the '*querella de capítulos*' (CCP Arts. 623 and ff.). The existence of this procedural filter is what explains the notable mismatch between the apparent desire of the original legislator to comprehensively regulate judicial perversion of justice – imposing penalties for more than fifteen hypothetical infractions – and the very few actual convictions for this crime. Over the entire course of the 20th century, there are no more than a handful of examples.[24]

The same 1906 CCP, which was clearly inquisitorial in nature, however, established a series of duties to which judges were subject. These included the obligation to receive complaints (Art. 24), the obligation to report facts constituting a crime that came to their knowledge (Arts. 83 and 84), and even the duty to proceed *ex officio* upon becoming aware of such facts by other means (Art. 105). The CCP also undertook detailed regulation of procedures for enforcing writs of habeas corpus (Arts. 306 and ff.), imposing judicial duties to protect and denounce in cases of unlawful deprivation of liberty. The Constitution of 1925 maintained the principle of personal responsibility of judges in the same terms. Almost two decades later, in 1943, the OCC reiterated the principle of judicial independence of the judiciary (OCC Art. 12) and kept the framework of rules set down by the preceding LOPC practically intact. These established a series of procedural filters that were required if judicial responsibility was to be activated.

Finally, it is worth mentioning that the Chilean Criminal Code, in its general section, considers as a hypothesis of direct perpetration a situation in which a subject prevents or tries to prevent the avoidance of a crime (Art. 15 n. 1, 2nd part); defines complicity in very broad terms; and considers concealment to be a form of intervention subsequent to the total or partial execution of the crime by the perpetrator and his or her accomplices.

15.4 The Responsibility of Judges in Crimes against Humanity: Solely a Problem of Punishable Participation

Considering the potential responsibility of judges for crimes against humanity committed during the Chilean dictatorship requires distinguishing the exact moment at which a judge intervenes through his or her judicial decisions, as well as, of course, taking into account the framework of legal rules that were in force at the time of the act. In material terms, the acts committed by State agents – which included homicides, kidnappings, and torture, perpetrated to the detriment of a political subgroup of the population – have the *status* of crimes against humanity and, where applicable, war crimes. Nonetheless, it cannot be ignored that formally they were not yet classified as such in domestic law.[25] As far as the material facts are concerned, moreover, there is a pertinent difference relating to judges' intervention in them that should be borne in mind.

At least three groups or types of case should be distinguished.[26] First, cases such as those heard in the period corresponding to Germany's post-Second World War phase, in which it is the judge him or herself who initiated, through a decision, the commission of the homicide. This may be, for example, by means of a manifestly unjust sentence or a court martial based on false accusations and evidence. Second, cases in which state agents initiated a state of unlawful deprivation of liberty, a judge acquired knowledge of this (by means of writs of habeas corpus or other resorts to law), and intervened while the unlawful state persisted; and, third, cases in which the state of unlawful detention had ceased, and the homicide or torture had been carried out, before the judge acquired knowledge of the facts and intervened, or ought to have intervened, by means of judicial resolutions.

In the first group of cases, there is a causal link between the judicial decision and the homicide. Accordingly, the only thing that remains at issue in order for the judge's intervention to be subsumed under Art. 15 n. 1 or n. 2 of the Criminal Code is whether the additional requirements developed by the dogmatics of perpetration are fulfilled. In the second and third groups of cases, by contrast, asserting the judge's liability as an accomplice or concealer after the fact requires further justification.

In the second group of cases, the filing of a writ of habeas corpus to put an end to a state of unlawful deprivation of liberty counts as a 'saving course' (*curso causal salvador*), whose interruption by action makes the subject a direct perpetrator under the terms of Criminal Code Art. 15 n. 1, 2nd part. However, in the context of the dictatorship, the agents of the armed forces had acquired such de facto power that initiating and pursuing a habeas corpus proceeding did not necessarily entail a high probability of cessation of the unlawful state. Members of the competent Court of Appeals and, where relevant, of the Supreme Court might accordingly be held liable as accomplices, rather than as perpetrators, as regards the crimes of kidnapping or illegal detention. However, since judges act through their judicial decisions, liability in this capacity would mean that, presented with credible indications of unlawful deprivation of liberty, judges' rejection of, or failure to properly carry out, habeas corpus would entail a violation of the legal duties of conduct described above. (The violation would consist, for example, in not adopting the measures provided for in Articles 309 or 310 of the CCP when faced with excessive delay on the part of the authorities in providing information about the whereabouts of the protected person.)

In the third group of cases, i.e., where a judge intervened after the execution of a kidnapping or illegal detention, implying that the state of unlawful deprivation of liberty, homicide, or torture by Armed Forces agents had already come to an end, the judge would be responsible for concealment to the extent that he or she had acquired knowledge after the fact regarding the carrying out of acts in whose execution the judge had not previously participated. Once again, however, since judges act through their resolutions, liability under this title would lead to the initiation of criminal proceedings via a criminal complaint or lawsuit. Upon hearing of the commission of any of these crimes by others, a judge of the Republic is *ipso facto* called upon to carry out the law and to ensure the correct *internal* administration of justice. Consequently, if a judge acquired post hoc knowledge of the enforced disappearance of a person, or a consummated homicide, or acts of torture against a person, and did not go on to promote investigation and prosecution or exercise jurisdiction, he or she would be in violation of said duties. In this way, through her or his judicial decisions, the *corpus delictus* would, quite literally in some cases, have been concealed. Or, by not prosecuting the perpetrators of such crimes or exercising jurisdiction over them, in violation of his or her duties, the judge would in effect have concealed those guilty of having committed them (viz., Art. 17.3 of the Criminal Code).

Each group of cases also contains some hypothesis of judicial perversion of justice, as exhaustively regulated by the original legislator. Accordingly, in each group there would be a concurrence of crimes (Art. 75 of the Criminal Code). In the first group of cases, in addition to responsibility as a direct or indirect perpetrator of homicide or similar, one of the hypotheses of judicial perversion of justice in the strict sense is configured (namely, Arts. 223.1, 224.1, 224.2, or 225.2 of the Criminal Code, which either require malice or can be satisfied if there has been negligence or inexcusable ignorance on the part of the judge).[27] In the second group of cases, in addition to liability for complicity in kidnapping or illegal detention, there is the hypothesis of "holding as a prisoner an individual who should be released according to the law", an act that, as above, can be committed by a judge either with malice or simply as a consequence of negligence or inexcusable ignorance (Arts. 224.5 or 225.5 of the Criminal Code). Finally, in the third group of cases, as well as responsibility as an accessory after the fact to kidnapping, homicide, or torture, the judge may be criminally liable for "denying or delaying the administration of justice and the assistance or protection legally requested", which can similarly be committed intentionally or only as a consequence of negligence or inexcusable ignorance (Arts. 224.3 or 225.3 of the Criminal Code).

In conclusion, the relationship between judicial perversion of justice and the participation of judges in crimes against humanity is a concurrent relationship between crimes, not one of reciprocal exclusion between the absence of judicial perversion of justice and criminal liability.

Notes

1 Merkl, 'Justizirrtum und Rechtswahrheit' (1925) 45 *ZStW* 452, 457 et seqq, 462 (author's translation, here and throughout, unless otherwise specified).

2 See Radbruch, 'Gesetzliches Unrecht und übergesetzliches Recht' (1946) 1 *SJZ* 105.

3 BGHSt 10, 294.

4 Kelsen, *Reine Rechtslehre* (1960) 88 et seqq. The first edition was published in German in 1934, the second, in 1960. An English translation of the second edition was published, under the title *Pure Theory of Law* in 1967.

5 Decree Law 2.191 of 1978. See *Report of the CNVR* Notre Dame, University Press (1993), Part Two, chs. 1, 3 and 4; also Lira/Loveman, *Poder judicial y conflictos políticos (Chile: 1973-1990)* vol 3, 26 et seqq, 61 et seqq, 69 et seq, 109 et seqq.

6 See Merryman/Pérez-Perdomo, *La tradición jurídica romano-canónica* 64 et seqq.
7 At present, the rule requires that such a breach of duty must constitute a *punishable act*. As far as the liability of the state is concerned, there is a rule at the constitutional level: Art. 34 Grundgesetz.
8 See Binding, *Lehrbuch BT* 514 et seqq, on the position of the judge in the state.
9 Kohler, 'Ueber den Begriff der Rechtsbeugung' (1904) 13 *DJZ* 613.
10 Judgments issued by the Reichsgericht, Court of the German Empire, which operated pre-1945 as a type of Supreme Court. See Sarstedt, 'Fragen zur Rechtsbeugung' in Lüttger (1972) 427; Spendel, 'Rechtsbeugung und Justiz' (1995) 50 *JZ* 375.
11 See the chapter by Florian Jeßberger and Milan Kuhli in this volume. See also Saliger, 'Rechtsphilosophische Probleme der Rechtsbeugung' (2005) Beiheft 104 *ARSP* 138, 148 et seqq.
12 Radbruch (1946) (n 2) 106.
13 Radbruch (1946) (n 2) 108, emphasis added, author's translation.
14 Radbruch (1946) (n 2) 108, emphasis added, author's translation.
15 With respect to the executing judges, in turn, liability for homicide by means of the execution of a death sentence that should not have been carried out implies the commission of what *Binding* had called "judicial perversion of justice of the sentence": § 345 RStGB.
16 An expression literally meaning 'the [written] Law is the Law', i.e., should be strictly applied.
17 In this sense, Vormbaum, *Der strafrechtliche Schutz des Strafurteils* (1985) 370 et seqq, speaks of a "judicial privilege of liability".
18 In fact, the so-called "objective theory" of judicial perversion of justice, or judicial perversion of justice, only developed under this nomenclature in the second half of the last century, perhaps because of the turning point that these cases represented in the German dogmatic tradition. That is, because of the need to make it clear that although *dolus* might be lacking, the judicial decisions were, at a minimum, "objectively incorrect"; critics of the objective theory Heinitz, *Probleme der Rechtsbeugung* 5 et seqq, 8 et seqq; Sarstedt (1972) (n 10), 428 et seqq.
19 Schroeder, 'Der Rechtfertigungsgrund der Entscheidung von Rechtssachen' (1993) 140 *GA* 389.
20 See Kuhlen, '§ 339: Rechtsbeugung' in Kindhäuser et al, *Nomos Kommentar zum Strafgesetzbuch*, para 89 et seqq; Hilgendorf, '§ 339: Rechtsbeugung' in Brodowski et al, *Leipziger Kommentar zum Strafgesetzbuch*, para 144 et seqq.
21 Respectively, the Ley de Organización y Atribuciones de los Tribunales de Chile, and the Código Orgánico de Tribunales.
22 Overview in Guzmán, *Introducción a los delitos contra la administración de justicia* (2008) 128 et seqq.
23 The historical antecedent of this procedural filter is found in sections XXVI to XXVIII of the Decree of the Cortes of March 24, 1813, issued under the protection of the Cadiz Constitution of 1812 in the Kingdom of Spain. See Quintana, 'Historia del delito de prevaricación: origen, desarrollo y recepción en el sistema jurídico chileno' (2023) 38 *REJ* 29, 37 et seqq.
24 Gaceta de los Tribunales (1905) SC, vol. I, n. 6988, Judgement n 609; (1912) SC, vol. II, Nr. 7965, Judgement n 1312.
25 See Werle/Jeßberger, *Völkerstrafrecht* (2006) 40 et seqq. For the regulation in force in Chile, see Hernández, 'La persecución penal de los crímenes de la dictadura militar en Chile' in Mañalich et al (eds) 203 et seqq.
26 Couso, in J Couso et al (eds) 493 et seqq, proposes another typology of cases.

27 In general, on the crime of judicial perversion of justice, Rojas, 'Sobre el contenido de injusto de la prevaricación judicial' (2021) 48 *RChD* 53, 70 et seqq.

Bibliography

Binding K, *Lehrbuch des gemeinen deutschen Strafrechts Besonderer Teil, vol 2* (Engelmann 1905).

Couso J, 'Responsabilidad penal por la intervención en crímenes de la dictadura en el ejercicio de roles judiciales. Perspectivas comparadas para una exploración en Chile' in Couso J et al (eds), *Libro Homenaje a Jorge Mera* (Thomson Reuters, 2021).

Guzmán J L, *Introducción a los delitos contra la administración de justicia* (INEJ 2008).

Heinitz E, *Probleme der Rechtsbeugung* (Colloquium Verlag Berlin 1961).

Hernández H, 'La persecución penal de los crímenes de la dictadura militar en Chile' in Mañalich J P et al (eds), *La ciencia penal en la Universidad de Chile* (2013).

Hilgendorf E, '§ 339: Rechtsbeugung', in Cirener G, Radtke H, Rissing-van Saan R, Rönnau T and Schluckebier W (eds), *Leipziger Kommentar zum Strafgesetzbuch, vol 13* (12th edn, De Gruyter 2009).

Kelsen H, *Reine Rechtslehre* (2nd edn, Mohr Siebeck 1960).

Kohler J, 'Ueber den Begriff der Rechtsbeugung' (1904) 13 *Deutsche Juristen-Zeitung* 613.

Kuhlen L, '§ 339: Rechtsbeugung", in Kindhäuser U et al (eds), *Nomos Kommentar zum Strafgesetzbuch* (5th edn, Beck 2017).

Lira E/Loveman B, *Poder judicial y conflictos políticos (Chile: 1973–1990), vol 3* (LOM ediciones 2020).

Merkl A, 'Justizirrtum und Rechtswahrheit' (1925) 45 *Zeitschrift für die gesamte Strafrechtswissenschaft* 452.

Merryman JH/Pérez-Perdomo R, *La tradición jurídica romano-canónica* (Fondo de Cultura Económica 2014).

Quintana C, 'Historia del delito de prevaricación: origen, desarrollo y recepción en el sistema jurídico chileno' (2023) 38 *Revista de Estudios de la Justicia* 29.

Radbruch G, 'Gesetzliches Unrecht und übergesetzliches Recht' (1946) 1 *Süddeutsche Juristen-Zeitung* 105.

Rojas L E, 'Sobre el contenido de injusto de la prevaricación judicial' (2021) 48 *Revista Chilena de Derecho* 53.

Saliger F, 'Rechtsphilosophische Probleme der Rechtsbeugung' (2005) Beiheft 104 *Archiv für Rechts- und Sozialphilosophie* 138.

Sarstedt W, 'Fragen zur Rechtsbeugung' in Lüttger H (ed), *Festschrift für Ernst Heinitz* (De Gruyter 1972).

Schroeder F C, 'Der Rechtfertigungsgrund der Entscheidung von Rechtssachen' (1993) 140 *Goltdammer's Archiv für Strafrecht* 389.

Spendel G, 'Rechtsbeugung und Justiz' (1995) 50 *JuristenZeitung* 375.

Vormbaum T, *Der strafrechtliche Schutz des Strafurteils* (Duncker & Humblot 1987).

Werle G/Jeßberger F, *Völkerstrafrecht* (4th edn, Mohr Siebeck 2006).

Part IV

Modes of Responsibility and Criminal Association

16 Superior Responsibility and Judicial Murder

When Judges Are Not 'Superior'

Héctor Hernández Basualto

16.1 Introduction

A characteristic feature of the Chilean military dictatorship between 1973 and 1990 was the submissive attitude of many judges toward the crimes of the regime. During those years, Chilean courts generally failed to protect the victims or prosecute the perpetrators, even though the atrocities were an open secret. Beyond the moral censure that this deserves, the question has arisen of the possible criminal responsibility of these judges, not only for the criminal violation of their judicial duties (prevarication, concealment) but also for the crimes committed by the agents of repression that judges did not prevent or prosecute.

However, if the judges did not directly commit the crimes, nor did they order them, nor did they actively assist in their commission, then the only traditional way to hold them responsible would be through *improper omission*. In other words, the crime would be imputed to them as if they themselves had committed it, because they did not prevent it when they were in a position to do so and had a duty (as 'guarantors') to do so.[1] There are cases for Chile in which this does not appear to present a problem, such as the example known as the '*degollados*', or 'throat-slitting', case. Faced with the kidnapping of three Communist activists in March 1985, a lawyer took all the necessary steps to have a judge go to the place where they were being detained, or otherwise exercise his authority to protect the lives of the prisoners. The judge failed to do so, and the three men were ultimately murdered. In such a case it is quite possible to hold the judge criminally responsible not only for the breach of his duties but also directly for the deaths.[2] However, in many – perhaps most – other cases, this is far from straightforward. Hence the question arises as to whether it is possible to apply other forms of imputation of criminal responsibility that are legitimate but more effective. One possible candidate is the form known as 'superior responsibility'.

16.2 Superior Responsibility as a Possible Alternative

The concept of superior responsibility has become a well-established concept in international criminal law, including in legal texts, since its jurisprudential emergence from the post-World War II Yamashita case.[3] As is well known, this does not

DOI: 10.4324/9781003470069-20

mean that there is clarity or consensus on the nature and scope of the concept. What is indisputable, however, is that at least in its international formulations, superior responsibility represents a significant extension of liability for the act of another. The extension is both subjective (making negligence sufficient) and objective (equating the simple failure to prosecute or report a crime, once committed, with failure to prevent it).

It is true that several national laws implementing the 1998 Rome Statute of the International Criminal Court, ICC, limit the scope of superior responsibility, including by treating the failure to prosecute or denounce as a separate and less serious crime[4] or by considering only intentional cases.[5] The question that arises, however, is whether in the absence of such limitations, superior liability could provide an alternative allowing judges to be prosecuted as though they had committed the crimes they failed to prevent or prosecute. The remainder of this chapter attempts to answer this question.

16.3 Were the Judges 'Superiors' of the Repressors?

Doubts in this respect do not arise from the fact that judges were civilian, rather than military, authorities. The formulation of superior responsibility in Additional Protocol I to the Geneva Conventions, GC, clearly deals with omissions by military commanders, while the formulation that appears in the statutes of the ad hoc tribunals[6] does not explicitly refer to civilian authorities. Nonetheless, the jurisprudence of the ICTY and ICTR recognized the responsibility of non-military authorities – and even of private agents, as will be seen later – as forms of superior responsibility. The Rome Statute later explicitly adopted this recognition. Even earlier, namely, in the post-World War II Tokyo Trials, convictions had been handed down using similar – albeit poorly argued – logic. In 1948, Japanese foreign ministers Koki Hirota and Mamoru Shigemitsu[7] were convicted specifically for having failed to take the necessary measures to prevent the outrages committed by Japanese troops, in various territories, before and during World War II.[8]

Thus, obstacles to the application of superior responsibility to Chilean judges who did not fulfill their duties with regard to the repressive organs of the dictatorship lie not in their non-military identity but rather in the fact that the requirements of the concept would not be met. Let us consider, first, the requirement of the existence of a superior-subordinate relationship between the perpetrator of the crime and the subject of the responsibility in question. In the example at hand, such a relationship would need to exist between the agent of the security services and the judge, to the extent that the latter could be considered superior to the former, who in turn could be considered to be subordinate to the judge.

While the scope of the concept of the superior-subordinate relationship is not entirely clear – and emphasis is often placed, in practice, on the (distinct and additional) requirement of an effective ability to control the behavior of others – there seems to be at least tacit agreement that the qualities of being a superior, and being a subordinate, result from the hierarchical structure of a given organization. It has been said that "the capability to exercise control must be embedded within a hierarchical structure with a certain degree of stability and organization that is independent of the concrete situation".[9] The requirement of authority, in the sense of organizational hierarchy, must be established independently of, and prior to, the exercise of effective control.[10] Also, "The concept of the superior is broader and should be seen in terms of a hierarchy encompassing the concept of control".[11] It has been rightly said that both concepts – superior, and subordinate – implicitly presuppose that the relationship between the two subjects takes place under the auspices of an organization. In other words, there must be a structural framework that serves as a basis for the relationship and gives it meaning. Specifically, this structural framework would be one with a hierarchical order, that is, containing different levels of rank, allowing those who occupy higher levels of the scale to be treated as superiors with respect to others, who occupy lower levels and are therefore considered subordinate to them.[12] While in the military sphere it is the army and its units to which the subjects belong, in the civilian sphere it may be the state apparatus, i.e., the public administration and its departments, but also companies or other private institutions. What is decisive is that, by virtue of this hierarchical order, one subject – the superior – structurally has the power to give commands or instructions to another, who is in turn structurally obliged to obey or follow these.[13]

This requirement of an organizational hierarchy is completely independent of the discussion of whether the relationship of subordination must be *de jure* or can simply be *de facto*. This is so because even if *de facto* relationships are accepted – as seems to be the prevailing opinion – the existence of an organic or organizational hierarchy is a *sine qua non* for any such relationship to arise. It should be recalled that recognition of a merely *de facto* hierarchy was only intended as a way of including in the figure of superior responsibility the kinds of relationships of subordination that often occur within irregular armed forces or other organizations without legal recognition. This was done in recognition of the fact that such forces or organizations are increasingly common given the changing reality of armed conflicts; it does not imply any questioning of the necessity of the existence of membership in a hierarchical organization (as is clear from the ICTY judgment in the Delalić case).[14]

Nor can the hierarchy requirement be avoided by making reference to the fact that it has also been recognized that *indirect* subordination is sufficient for superior responsibility. Thus, for example, GC Additional Protocol I establishes the duties of a commander not only with respect to the members of the armed forces under his or her command but also, significantly, with respect to other persons under his or her control (art. 87.1 and 87.3). These subjects do not have to be integrated into the same organization, notwithstanding that the commander is considered to be their superior. However, as is well known, the scope of this extension is quite limited and depends on extremely specific circumstances. According to the International Committee of the Red Cross (ICRC) Commentary on Art. 87 of Additional Protocol I, the main case where it would be applicable concerns the responsibility of a commander for what happens in occupied territories.[15] Here, precisely by virtue of the occupation, the commander of the occupying troops effectively displaces the rest of the authorities. Although the Commentary itself states that this is not the only possible hypothesis of indirect subordination, the additional examples proposed follow the same general line, in being connected to military control over what happens in a given territory. So, for example, a commander has the duty to prevent the civilian population of her or his own side from attacking prisoners of war in her or his custody, to prevent prisoners from attacking one another, and so on. The same applies when civilian elements are engaged in a military commander's operational sector, without being officially subordinated to that commander.[16]

International jurisprudence also contains references to the decision of the Court of the French Occupation Zone in Germany, in the case against the industrialist Hermann Roechling and others.[17] Here, despite the fact that superior responsibility was not expressly invoked, convictions were handed down against those who did nothing to prevent serious abuses against forced laborers. Although the abuses were perpetrated mainly by members of the Gestapo, over whom the convicted had no formal command, they (i.e., the abuses), however, took place specifically in factories under the direction of the accused. The abuses, however, took place specifically in factories under the direction of the accused, a very relevant position in the context of the war, which was accordingly considered by the court to confer authority and power that would have been sufficient to stop the abuses occurring there. As can be seen, however, even in this case there is a reference to an organization – specifically, a company – and to the power of direction that the accused had over it, or in matters that affected its functioning. Something similar can be seen in the jurisprudence of the ad hoc tribunals with regard to civilians in charge of detention centers,[18] a setting in which the existence of internal organization, from which a hierarchy emerges, is also evident.

The significance of belonging to a hierarchical organization as a prerequisite for superior responsibility is underscored by the fact that it has been strictly applied even in the (limited) number of instances where the concept has been applied in civilian contexts, including in the private (i.e., non-state) ambit. The ICTR offers good examples in its rulings in the Musema[19] and Nahimana cases.[20] Alfred Musema was director of the Gisovu Tea Factory in Kibuye Prefecture during the 1994 genocide in Rwanda. The ICTR Prosecutor alleged that on various occasions Musema transported armed attackers, including factory employees, to a range of locations in the Gisovu and Gishyita districts, ordering them to attack Tutsis seeking refuge there. He had also personally participated in such attacks and killings. It is important to note that Musema was convicted not only for acts in which he actively participated in one of the ways provided for in Art. 6.1 of the Statute ('committing, planning, instigating or ordering the commission of, or in any other way assisting in the planning, preparation or execution of'), but also under Art. 6.3, which refers to the responsibility of the superior for failing to prevent crimes committed by their subordinates. In this regard, the quality of subordinates is attributed exclusively to the employees of the factory when acting in their capacity as such, while Musema's status as a superior is claimed exclusively due to the authority he held over them in his capacity as the factory's director and acting in that capacity. In effect:

> The Chamber finds that it has been established beyond reasonable doubt that Musema exercised *de jure* authority over employees of the Gisovu Tea Factory while they were on Tea Factory premises and while they were engaged in their professional duties as employees of the Tea Factory, even if those duties were performed outside factory premises. The Chamber notes that Musema exercised legal and financial control over these employees, particularly through his power to appoint and remove these employees from their positions at the Tea Factory. The Chamber notes that Musema was in a position, by virtue of these powers, to take reasonable measures, such as removing, or threatening to remove, an individual from his or her position at the Tea Factory if he or she was identified as a perpetrator of crimes punishable under the Statute. The Chamber also finds that, by virtue of these powers, Musema was in a position to take reasonable measures to attempt to prevent or to punish the use of Tea Factory vehicles, uniforms or other Tea Factory property in the commission of such crimes. The Chamber finds that Musema exercised *de jure* power and *de facto* control over Tea Factory employees and the resources of the Tea Factory (§ 880).

It is interesting to note that once it had been established that Musema was the superior of, and had command over, the factory personnel, the question was raised as to whether he could also be considered the hierarchical superior of other persons. Specifically, it was asked whether he "had power of control over persons who a priori were not under his authority..., namely, the soldiers, the Gisovu *Commune* police, and the *Interahamwe*". Despite having established that Musema had great ascendancy over people living where the factory was located (describing him as "a socially and politically prominent person in Gisovu *Commune*", perceived "as a figure of authority and as someone who wielded considerable power in the region", §§ 132, 881), the court did not conclude that Musema actually exercised *de jure* power and *de facto* control over these individuals (§ 881).

Ferdinand Nahimana and Jean-Bosco Barayagwiza, for their part, founded Rwanda's *Radio-Television Libre des Mille Collines* (RTLM). The media outlet RTLM was used during the 1994 genocide as a vehicle to promote extremist Hutu ideology, incite hatred, and incite listeners to murder Tutsis. Again, it is important to note that before the ICTR, both were convicted not only for openly inciting the acts through the radio station (under Art. 6.1 of the ICTR Statute) but also, under Art. 6.3, for failing to prevent crimes committed by their subordinates. This category was considered to be made up exclusively of journalists, broadcasters, etc. who actually worked in the RTLM radio station, rather than external third parties. Indeed:

> The Chamber has considered the individual criminal responsibility of Ferdinand Nahimana and Jean-Bosco Barayagwiza for RTLM broadcasts, by virtue of their respective roles in the creation and control of RTLM. As found..., Nahimana and Barayagwiza were, respectively, "number one" and "number two" in the top management of the radio. They represented the radio at the highest level in meetings with the Ministry of Information; they controlled the finances of

> the company; and they were both members of the Steering Committee, which functioned in effect as a board of directors for RTLM. Nahimana chaired the Program Committee of this board, and Barayagwiza chaired its Legal Committee. While the Chamber recognizes that Nahimana and Barayagwiza did not make decisions in the first instance with regard to each particular broadcast of RTLM, these decisions reflected an editorial policy for which they were responsible. Phocas Habimana, Gaspard Gahigi and all the RTLM broadcasters down the chain of command were ultimately accountable to the Steering Committee, which functioned as a board of directors for RTLM. Nahimana's contention that the board did not intervene directly at the level of journalists has no legal relevance to his and Barayagwiza's exercise of authority at the highest decision-making level. They intervened at a higher managerial level (§ 970).

In summary, then, except for extremely specific extensions, the relationship of subordination presupposes that both the superior and the subordinate are in some way part of the same organization. The question now is whether this can be said of the relationship between judges and agents of repression under the Chilean dictatorship.

To analyze this point, it should be borne in mind that dictatorships differ in type and also in the manner and degree to which each seeks to integrate the courts into its repressive apparatus. Some dictatorships with totalizing pretensions integrate the judiciary completely into the political action of the regime, with the consequence that repression is often formally and openly channeled through laws and judges. In fact, in such dictatorships, it is the courts that, to a significant extent, cause expropriation, exile, imprisonment, and even death (capital punishment) through their rulings. This was the case of, for example, the Nazi dictatorship in Germany between 1933 and 1945, where one part of repression was legally formalized and exercised through the courts. This reality explains why one of the subsequent Nuremberg Trials – the one known as the Judges' Trial – was dedicated specifically to addressing responsibility for atrocities committed directly by members of the judiciary in the course of exercising their positions in it.[21]

In other dictatorships, however, the judiciary is not integrated into the repressive apparatus. Instead, it is simply tolerated by the regime, dealing with the day-to-day matters for which courts are needed in all societies, including dictatorships. Indeed, even in dictatorships, contractual or family disputes arise, and common crimes are committed, which need to be dealt with by courts. This does not mean that the courts in such regimes function independently, without political interference of various kinds, nor that judges critical of the dictatorship can remain in office. It simply means that repression is basically conducted through other channels, without the courts being used for this purpose. In such a context, courts function relatively normally to the extent that they do not interfere with the regime, which in turn sets *de facto* limits on their jurisdiction. In this type of dictatorship, repression takes place outside the courts, yet without their interference.

This second category in our typology is the one that fits the relationship that existed between organs of repression and the judges under the Chilean military dictatorship that extended between 1973 and 1990. In contrast to the fate of Chile's legislature – dissolved almost simultaneously with the 1973 military takeover – the courts were not formally touched by the regime,[22] and there is no evidence that the dictatorship openly used the courts for its repressive purposes. Although there was, in fact, judicially channeled repression immediately after the coup, this was carried out by 'Consejos de Guerra', special courts composed of military personnel whose decisions were beyond the control or supervision of the regular court system. This state of affairs was certainly congruent with the open sympathy the Chilean Supreme Court expressed for the dictatorial regime from its outset, a gesture that in a way guaranteed that the courts would not interfere in matters that the dictatorship chose to reserve for itself. On the other hand, much of Chile's repression was carried out in a clandestine fashion, with the dictatorship denying the existence of the crimes and, in some way, concealing them. This context explains why, over the course of the dictatorship, and especially in its early years, a large proportion of the Chilean judiciary at the time systematically failed to take the necessary actions. Requests for protection and denunciations of crimes went unheeded when to do otherwise would have meant upsetting the military authorities.

In this second type of dictatorship, then, it does not seem possible to conclude either that judges were the superiors of repressive agents or that the latter were subordinate to the former. It is true that police officers are subordinate to the judiciary in those areas where the police force's role involves, specifically, carrying out orders from the judicial system. In Chile, however, the involvement of police officers in repressive activities was, like that of the military or other state agents involved, carried out on a separate track, not subject to judicial control or supervision.

This does not mean, of course, that judges had no duty to prevent crimes of which they were aware and for which their intervention was requested. For these duties are owed not only to subordinates. Police officers are also guarantors, and the same could be said of judges,[23] who can also give orders to anyone, including other agents of the State, regardless of their hierarchy, even if they do not belong to the same organization. But the question of the powers and duties of one subject is not the same as the question of the hierarchical superiority of one subject over another. The fact that police and judges have the duty to prevent crimes in general, and that they must respond criminally when they fail to do so, does not, of course, imply that they are hierarchical superiors of the criminals who commit them. The importance of this clarification lies in the fact that the liability of a guarantor under the general rules of punishable omission has stricter requirements and a narrower scope than those governing the liability of the superior, mainly in terms of subjective requirements. Therefore, it is important to determine whether the basic requirement of this special form of liability is met.

In the case of the Chilean dictatorship, for the reasons mentioned above, it was not the judges who were the superiors of the repressive agents, but other subjects, namely the commanders of the respective security agencies, as well as the senior officers of the military or police institutions to which these agencies belonged, and in principle also the civilian or military government authorities, in the area of defense and internal security, though ultimately in some other area as well. There is no doubt that the judges should and could have tried to do something in favor of the victims or against impunity. However, aside from debating whether they were truly capable of doing so, their conduct cannot be assessed through the lens of superior responsibility simply because they did not hold the status of superiors.

16.4 Did Judges Have Effective Control over the Repressors?

The power of the judges in a constitutional state is strong because the orders of the judges have an unquestionable force, so that their disobedience has certain, direct, or indirect negative consequences for the disobedient. But it is precisely this that can be called into question in the context of dictatorships that do not use the courts for their criminal activities but only tolerate their existence for the dispatch of everyday legal matters that are of no particular interest to the regime. This brings us to the second major obstacle to the application of superior responsibility to judges under the Chilean dictatorship, which is that judges did not have effective control over the agents of the repressive apparatus, a control that is essential for this type of responsibility.

Effective control presupposes that the subordinate, when given an order by the superior, is not free to obey or disobey it, provided that he or she can expect that there will be effective harmful consequences in case of disobedience. This is the criterion that makes it possible to distinguish between mere influence and the power of command that is the basis of the superior's responsibility.

As mentioned above, the criminal activities of the Chilean military dictatorship were not carried out through the criminal justice system but rather outside it, literally *manu militari*, in a more or less clandestine manner. In this context, it is clear that the judges exercised no direct control over the repressors, while indirect control through the exercise of their prosecutorial powers was practically illusory.[24] In fact, in the few dictatorship-era cases where criminal judges attempted to interrogate intelligence agents, the government protested that this would compromise intelligence work, and the Supreme Court, while affirming judicial power,[25] ordered the scope of the criminal investigation to be curtailed.[26] Formally, this was reinforced by an Amnesty Law (Decree Law No. 2,191 of 19 April 1978). The decree covered a series of crimes committed between 11 September 1973 (i.e., the date of the coup) and 10 March 1978, including those related to human rights violations. The few judges who attempted to disregard this regulation were disciplined by the Supreme Court, even after the dictatorship had ended.[27] This censure still occurred even as the conditions for the prosecution of human rights violations that had taken place post-March 1978, i.e., outside of the temporal scope of amnesty, began to improve.[28] It is clear, then, that the judges had no control over the agents of repression during the dictatorship.

The importance of effective control, even with regard to those who are undoubtedly superior, is illustrated by the ICTY's judgment in the Boškoski case,[29] which dealt with crimes committed by the Macedonian police and military against ethnic Albanians in the village of Ljuboten in August 2001. Ljube Boškoski was the Macedonian Minister of the Interior at the time, and in that capacity, in addition to his effective leadership, he was the hierarchical superior of the police and other operational employees of his ministry (§§ 513–516), but he was not punished for failing to repress the crimes (he only reported them, § 519 ff.), simply because he had neither the power to punish (§ 518) nor the authority over those who had the power to punish (§§ 517, 536). Among the latter were the judges, but, significantly, in a context of institutional normality (§ 514),[30] which was what was lacking in the Chile of the dictatorship.

Perhaps the Chilean judges could have been more courageous, or, unable to change the conditions, they could have resigned. But it does not seem plausible that they would have been able to effectively prevent or punish the crimes of the repressors, as required by the superior responsibility. Consequently, this form of responsibility does not offer a viable alternative for their prosecution.

Notes

1 On the other hand, the lack of prosecution of a crime is not a cause of liability for that crime.

2 There have been significant convictions for the facts (6th Criminal Court Santiago, Judgment of 31 March 1994, Case No 118.284; Santiago Appeals Court, Judgment of 30 September 1994, Case No 16.196–94; Supreme Court, Judgment of 27 October 1995, Case No 31.030), but the possible criminal liability of the judge has never been raised.

3 Art. 86.2 Additional Protocol I to the Geneva Conventions; Art. 7.3 ICTY Statute; Art. 6.3 ICTR Statute; Art. 28 Rome Statute of the ICC.

4 In Chile, Art. 35 Law No 20.357. In Germany, § 15 VStGB, where a distinction is also made between non-avoidance per se (§ 4 VStGB), and violation of the duty to supervise (§ 14 VStGB, carrying a lesser penalty). In Spain, art. 615 bis 3 and 5 of the criminal code, Código Penal.

5 Such is the case of Article 35 of the Chilean Law No 20.357.

6 The International Criminal Tribunal for the former Yugoslavia (ICTY) and the International Criminal Tribunal for Rwanda (ICTR).

7 Also mentioned is Prime Minister Hideki Tojo, who, however, was not only Minister of Defence [Defense] for much of the war, but also a general and the undisputed leader of the army.

8 IMTFE, Judgment of 12 November 1948, count 55, as cited in Pritchard J/Zaide S M (eds), *The Tokyo War Crimes Trial* (Garland Pub. 1981), Vol. 22, 48.424.

9 Werle/Jeßberger, *Principles of International Criminal Law* (4th edn, Oxford University Press 2020) para 690; see Ambos, *Internationales Strafrecht* (4th edn, C.H. Beck 2014) § 7 para 56. Reference has also been made to a "chain of command" associated to the same hierarchical structure: Mettraux, *The Law of Command Responsibility* (Oxford University Press 2009) 146 et seqq.

10 Ronen, 'Superior responsibility of civilians for international crimes committed in civilian settings' (2010) 43 *Vanderbilt j. transnatl. Law* 340.

11 ICRC, Commentary on the Additional Protocols of 8 June 1977 to the Geneva Conventions of 12 August 1949 (Martinus Nijhoff Publishers 1987) 1013.

12 Burghardt, *Die Vorgesetztenverantwortlichkeit im völkerrechtlichen Straftatsystem* (Berliner Wissenschafts-Verlag 2008) 171.

13 Burghardt (n 12) 174.

14 ICTY, Judgment of 16 November 1998, IT-96-21-T, *Prosecutor v. Zejnil Delalić et al* § 354. See Mettraux (n 9) 143 et seq; Karsten, *Die strafrechtliche Verantwortlichkeit des nicht-militärischen Vorgesetzten* (Duncker & Humblot 2010) 41 et seq; Garrocho, *La responsabilidad del superior por omisión en Derecho penal internacional* (Aranzadi 2017) 93 et seq.

15 ICRC, Commentary on the Additional Protocols of 8 June 1977 to the Geneva Conventions of 12 August 1949 (Martinus Nijhoff Publishers 1987) 1020.

16 ICRC, Commentary on the Additional Protocols of 8 June 1977 to the Geneva Conventions of 12 August 1949 (Martinus Nijhoff Publishers 1987) 1020, footnote 9.

17 General Tribunal of the Military Government of the French Zone of Occupation in Germany, Judgment rendered on 30 June 1948 in the case against Hermann Roechling et al.

18 See Karsten (n 14) 49ff.

19 ICTR, Judgment of 27 January 2000, ICTR-96-13-T, *The Prosecutor v. Alfred Musema.*

20 ICTR, Judgment of 3 December 2003, ICTR-99-52-T, *The Prosecutor v. Ferdinand Nahimana, Jean-Bosco Barayagwiza and Hassan Ngeze.* The portion of the case of interest here involves Nahima and Barayagwiza.

21 NMT, Judgment of 4 December 1947, 6 LRTWC 1 (1948), *United States of America v. Altstötter et al.*

22 Article 3 of Decree Law No 1 of 11 September 1973 states that the Government Junta "shall guarantee the full effectiveness of the powers of the Judiciary". In turn, Article 1 of Decree Law No 128 of 16 November 1973 – after recalling that the Government Junta had assumed the exercise of the constitutional, legislative, and executive powers – states that "The Judiciary shall exercise its functions in the manner and with the independence and powers established by the Political Constitution of the State". Author's translation.

23 Not to mention that there is a big difference between police and judges in that the former, despite having less authority, are the only ones who have the power to act directly (whereas judges must act through others).

24 At the time of the events, judges in Chile had the functions not only of adjudicating, but also of investigating and prosecuting.

25 With no further consequences, the Supreme Court presented it directly to the President of the Republic, Augusto Pinochet, in a letter dated 10 March 1976.

26 See, for example, Supreme Court Official Letter No 3688, 17 September 1976, regarding the decisions of Judge Tomás Dahm.

27 A famous case is that of the Santiago Appeals Court Judge Carlos Cerda, who, in the context of the so-called "case of the 13", was sanctioned in October 1986 and January 1991 for refusing to close the proceedings.

28 A change that became incipient even before transition. One paradigmatic case was the prosecution of 13 police officers – including commanders – of the uniformed police service (Carabineros de Chile). The case, investigated by Santiago Appeals Court judge José Cánovas, was over the 'throat-slitting' murders of August 1985. The conduct of the case led to the resignation of then-Police Commander César Mendoza, Director General of the Carabineros and a member of the governing junta. (Although no convictions were secured until after the advent of democracy.)

29 ICTY, Judgment of 10 July 2008, IT-04-82-T, *Prosecutor v. Ljube Boškoski and Johan Tarčulovski.*

30 "Ljube Boškoski was the minister of a structured, disciplined and heavily regulated ministry in a government that was functioning effectively and which had available the full and normal supportive structures of government, including judiciary, police and military agencies".

Bibliography

Ambos K, *Internationales Strafrecht* (4th edn, C.H. Beck 2014).

Burghardt B, *Die Vorgesetztenverantwortlichkeit im völkerrechtlichen Straftatsystem* (Berliner Wissenschafts-Verlag 2008).

International Committee of the Red Cross, *Commentary on the Additional Protocols of 8 June 1977 to the Geneva Conventions of 12 August 1949* (Martinus Nijhoff Publishers 1987).

Garrocho A, *La responsabilidad del superior por omisión en Derecho penal internacional* (Aranzadi 2017).

Karsten N, *Die strafrechtliche Verantwortlichkeit des nicht-militärischen Vorgesetzten* (Duncker & Humblot 2010).

Mettraux, G, *The Law of Command Responsibility* (Oxford University Press 2009).

Ronen Y, 'Superior responsibility of civilians for international crimes committed in civilian settings' (2010) 43 *Vanderbilt Journal of Transnational Law* 313.

Werle G/Jeßberger F, *Principles of International Criminal Law* (4th edn, Oxford University Press 2020).

17 Jurists' Responsibility for Crimes of Dictatorships

An International Criminal Law Perspective

Elies van Sliedregt

As a preliminary observation, I would posit that prosecuting and adjudicating jurists and judges before a *domestic* court for their participation in human rights violations encompassing murder, torture, and unlawful detention means that domestic law applies.[1] When it comes to prosecuting international crimes, domestic law applies to general principles, i.e., the law on mens rea, causation, and modes of perpetration and participation. As I have argued elsewhere,[2] then, the 'general part' of criminal law applies to international crimes just as it does to 'ordinary' garden-variety crimes. There are arguably two exceptions: command/superior responsibility and superior orders, which are both concepts with an international law pedigree. They hence require incorporation in domestic law, and the application of relevant international case law, when applied in domestic cases. Moreover, and despite these stipulations, international criminal law may be a source of inspiration, and it is from that perspective that I have prepared this chapter.

17.1 Introduction

The Nuremberg *Justice* case is a good place to start when discussing attribution of criminal liability to jurists or judges. The court held that:

> The charge, in brief, is that of conscious participation in a nationwide government-organized system of cruelty and injustice, in violation of the laws of war and of humanity, and perpetrated in the name of law by the authority of the Ministry of Justice, and through the instrumentality of the courts. The dagger of the assassin was concealed beneath the robe of the jurist. The record is replete with evidence of specific criminal acts, but they are not the crimes charged in the indictment.[4]

I distill three elements from this quote. First, criminal responsibility of jurists or judges is premised on *conscious* participation in a system of cruelty and injustice. Second, the commission of crimes is done in the name of the law. Third, evidence does not amount to the crimes charged in the indictment. I translate this into three specific legal problems that this chapter explores: (1) conceptualizing liability as

DOI: 10.4324/9781003470069-21

part of a system; (2) attributing crimes for generic contributions (i.e., acts that are not criminal on the face of it, or have an everyday nature), and (3) dealing with deviation between the crime on the ground and the conduct that triggered it at decision-making level (e.g., in the courtroom or in policymaking circles). This exploration requires discussion of the following modes of responsibility: common purpose or joint criminal enterprise (JCE) liability; aiding and abetting; and leadership liability (interlinked JCE and indirect co-perpetration).

Before embarking on further consideration of these legal problems and modes of responsibility, the chapter offers brief comments on other cases of judicial participation in international crimes. This is done in order to delineate the concept of judicial murder by seeking potential similarities in factual patterns and analogous concepts in international criminal law (ICL). The chapter by Rojas in this volume discusses how Radbruch describes the criminal responsibility of the judge who imposes a death sentence as that of a principal 'through an innocent agent', insofar as the judge would not carry out the murder with his or her own hands, but by means of a death sentence, which is carried out by other judicial officials (who are not innocent *stricto sensu*). The actus reus is present insofar as there is a causal link between the conviction imposed by the judge and the execution of the death sentence. This perpetration-by-means/innocent agency form of criminal responsibility implies that the judge had the intent to kill. This is different from complicity liability, Radbruch points out, since the latter does not require proof that the accomplice or accessory shares the mens rea of the direct perpetrator. The complication when dealing with judges is that there might not be a mens rea to kill: a judge may objectively but erroneously *believe* that he or she is abiding by the law in imposing this sentence. The judge would commit the crime of prevarication or malfeasance, rather than murder. We will return to this issue when discussing forms of what I call 'leadership liability'.

Regarding liability by omission, the Mendoza case, as discussed by Omar Palermo in this volume, is interesting. The case concerned the prosecution of former magistrates who served as prosecutors and judges during the Argentine dictatorship of 1976–1983. The magistrates were accused of not having investigated the kidnappings of dozens of people who had been charged with violating the infamous Law 20.840 while knowing that the armed and security forces were acting illegally and committing crimes.[3] Regarding Chile, Alejandra Castillo and Jaime Couso argue, in their contributions to this volume, that dictatorship-era judges who chose not to investigate disappearances could be prosecuted for murder (or other related crimes) for failing to carry out their duty properly, because judges have a duty to act. Ergo, in both the Argentine and Chilean cases, the question of liability by omission is central to the charges. We will therefore proceed by exploring what lessons, if any, ICL can provide for imputing crimes based on omission liability.

ICL is the place to look for complex questions on attribution of liability. ICL deals primarily with the 'bureaucratic murderer' (*Schreibtischtäter*), the prototypical case being that of Adolf Eichmann. Judicial murder may be regarded as a subspecies or offshoot of that idea. Both bureaucratic murderers and judicial murderers are remote, non-physical perpetrators. This raises tricky questions around causation and non-criminal, 'generic' activity, i.e., conduct that is not unlawful *per se* or that does not fulfill the material element of a crime. The sections that follow discuss, in turn, participation in systemic criminality with a focus on common purpose/joint criminal enterprise (JCE) liability (Section 17.2), aiding and abetting and generic contributions (Section 17.3), and leadership liability and deviation of crimes on the ground (Section 17.4).

17.2 Common Purpose and JCE

The Tribunal in the Nuremberg *Justice* case held that:

> As we have said, the defendants are not charged with specific overt acts against named victims. They are charged with *criminal participation in government-organized atrocities* and persecutions unmatched in the annals of history. Our judgments are based upon a consideration of all of the evidence which tends to throw light upon *the part which these defendants played* in the entire tragic drama. We shall, in pronouncing sentence, give due consideration to circumstances of mitigation and to the proven character and motives of the respective defendants.[4] (emphasis added)

To make clear that there was no normative difference between direct (physical) involvement and indirect (functional) involvement in a crime, prosecutors and judges in post-Second World War proceedings largely refrained from using the principal-accomplice terminology. Instead, they used terms such as 'participating in a criminal organization' or 'pursuing a common criminal design'. The US military tribunal attributed liability on the basis of the division of tasks in an organization. Strictly speaking, defendants were accomplices to the crimes, yet the court held that:

> (...) the person who persuades another to commit murder, the person who furnishes the lethal weapon for the purpose of the commission, and the person who pulls the trigger are all principals or accessories to the crime.[5]

In the trial of *Franz Holstein & Twenty-Three Others*, the Permanent Military Tribunal in Dijon divided the accused, all charged with crimes against the French resistance, into three categories: 'those found guilty as instigators, mainly by issuing orders; those found guilty as perpetrators; and those found guilty as their accomplices'.[6] The accused, who had been in command of the men who committed the crimes, were held responsible as instigators. Those who could not be labeled instigators were found guilty as accomplices for having facilitated and prepared the crimes before the fact. Others were found guilty as accomplices for supplying means during the crime.[7] The court made clear, however, that no fundamental distinction existed between these types of accomplices:

> It is a universally recognised principle of modern penal law that accomplices during or after the fact are responsible *in the same manner* as actual perpetrators

> or as instigators, who belong to the category of accomplices before the fact.[8] (emphasis added)

It is important to remind ourselves here that accomplices are also convicted for the crime proper. The practical value of distinguishing between principals and accessories is limited: it does not come with a sentence reduction. Most of the judges in the *Justice* case were convicted of war crimes and crimes against humanity, but each accused person's contributions were recognized and weighed differently.

The following factors played a role in findings of guilt for war crimes and crimes against humanity:

- Membership of the SS (it was assumed that SS members had knowledge of crimes);
- High position (this concerned defendant Klemm: it was found that he had knowledge and had acted '*con amore*');
- Widespread nature of crimes (this points to knowledge of crimes);
- Connection to the execution and carrying out of the Nacht und Nebel decree (this concerned defendant Mettgenberg, who was held liable as a principal);
- Taking a consenting part (this concerned defendant Rothenberger, who was regarded as having aided and abetted crimes. He participated in a morally corrupt system, and as a result was found guilty of war crimes and crimes against humanity. He received a lenient sentence).

The Nuremberg cases are still relevant today. They constitute international precedents that were relied upon in case law at the International Criminal Tribunal for the former Yugoslavia, ICTY, mainly to carve out the contours of JCE liability.[9] JCE requires proof of the existence of a plurality of people who pursue a common criminal purpose and can be held liable for the crimes that result from this common criminal plan. This even when – as in the ICTY Tadić cases – the crimes were not intended but merely foreseen and accepted as natural and foreseeable consequences (*dolus eventualis*). The latter form of JCE liability is referred to as Third Category JCE or extended JCE.

In principle, all members of a JCE are equally liable for the crimes. JCE liability enables reference to political and military superiors as 'participants' in a JCE rather than accessories, which they would be under a theory of complicity (derivative liability). The JCE complicity model has been the dominant approach at the ad hoc Tribunals. Some critics have argued that it does not meet the demands of 'fair labeling', which requires that liability is expressed in a way that fairly represents the nature and magnitude of the law-breaking.[10] In the context of masterminded violence, using the term 'accessory' sounds inappropriate. Schabas observes that:

> [t]he 'accomplice' is often the real villain, and the 'principal offender' a small cog in the machine. Hitler did not physically murder or brutalize anybody; technically, he was 'only' an accomplice to the crime of genocide.[11]

Judges at the ICTY have insisted on the non-normative meaning of terms such as 'principal', 'perpetrator', and 'co-perpetrator' when referring to a participant in a JCE.[12] They are merely terms of 'convenience'.[13] This is to make it clear that variance in role and blameworthiness has no place when attributing criminal responsibility: it is, rather, at the sentencing stage that each contribution to a crime is weighed. This position also implies that reference to accomplice or aiding/abetting liability does not imply 'lesser' liability. This non-normative complicity model has been difficult to sustain, and it is undeniable that aiding and abetting liability at the Tribunals has developed into a form of 'lesser liability' vis-à-vis JCE liability.[14] This non-differentiation in normative terms has evoked criticism. The extended form of JCE,[15] which requires a *dolus eventualis* test, differs from the basic form of JCE liability (closely akin to co-perpetration), which requires participants to *share* the intent. Critics feel that extended JCE, with its lower degree of mens rea and more attenuated link to the crime, should translate to lesser rather than equal liability.[16] This is why extended JCE is controversial.

Article 25(3)(d) of the Rome Statute captures criminal liability for contributing to a group acting with a common purpose. It is referred to as 'JCE light' since it does not provide for extended JCE: *dolus eventualis* is not accepted as a mental element. There has to be at least proof of an awareness that crimes 'will occur' (versus 'might occur').[17] On the face of it, 'JCE light' has a very low contribution/causal requirement: the provision confers responsibility upon persons who '[i]n any other way contribute to the commission or attempted commission of (…) a crime by a group of persons acting with a common purpose'. In *Mbarushimana*, the ICC Pre-Trial Chamber, however, considered that it would be inappropriate to interpret the term 'in any other way' as including *every* possible contribution to a group crime:

> Without some threshold level of assistance, every landlord, every grocer, every utility provider, every secretary, every janitor or even every taxpayer who does anything which contributes to a group committing international crimes could satisfy the elements of 25(3)(d) liability for their infinitesimal contribution to the crimes committed.[18]

In this way, the Pre-Trial Chamber sought to exclude normal economic and social activities from the scope of Article 25(3)(d), considering that such activities do not constitute a culpable and blameworthy contribution to a crime that justifies criminal punishment. Accordingly, the *Mbarushimana* Pre-Trial Chamber held that for there to be liability, the accused's contribution to the group crime should be at least 'significant' – a finding that was later confirmed by the Trial Chamber in *Katanga*. The significant contribution standard entails that the accused influences or has a bearing on whether and how the crime is committed.[19] Conduct that is immaterial or inconsequential to the commission of crimes cannot generate common purpose liability.[20] Having said that, it is not required that the commission of the crime *depends* on the accused's contribution, i.e., that contribution need not be a *conditio sine qua non*. Translating this to a dictatorial regime, where judges are asked to apply law that violates fundamental rights, this behavior should quite easily meet the significant contribution threshold. The trickier question is around omission liability and hypothetical causality, i.e., whether the crimes could have been avoided had it not been for the omission of judicial intervention.

Let us now turn to so-called 'dual-use' contributions, i.e., everyday contributions that are not unlawful *per se*. Examples might include delivering weapons or providing logistical support to armed groups. There has been debate about whether there is a need for specific criteria (such as the "specific direction" requirement) to establish a criminal (causal) linkage for this type of remote and/or dual-use contributions.

17.3 Aiding and Abetting Liability and Generic Contributions

Aiding and abetting constitutes accessorial liability that applies to persons who have assisted others in committing crimes. Liability for aiding and abetting is included in the statutes of all international criminal courts, including the ICC, the International Criminal Tribunals for Yugoslavia and Rwanda (ICTY and ICTR), and the Special Court for Sierra Leone (SCSL). As regards causality, international case law generally requires that the aider and abettor made a substantial contribution to the crime (which of course begs the question of differentiation between a 'significant' and a 'substantial contribution'). According to the ICTY, 'significant contribution' entails that 'the criminal act most probably would not have occurred in the same way had not someone acted in the role that the accused in fact assumed'.[21]

In 2013, the ICTY Appeals Chamber delivered a controversial judgment in the case of Momčilo Perišić. As Chief of the General Staff of the Yugoslav Army, Perišić had provided military and logistical aid to the Bosnian-Serb army (VRS) during the Balkan war by sending weapons and seconding officers. In the first instance, the Trial Chamber convicted Perišić of aiding and abetting international crimes perpetrated by the VRS, finding that the accused had made a substantial contribution to these crimes.[22] The Appeals Chamber nonetheless reached a different conclusion, acquitting Perišić of all charges.[23] The change in outcome came about because the Appeals Chamber took a different view regarding the causal connection between the accused's contribution and the crimes with which he was charged. In addition to a 'substantial' contribution, the Appeals Chamber required that Perišić's assistance had been 'specifically directed' toward the crimes charged. According to the Appeals Chamber, the 'specific direction' element requires an essential link between the accessory's assistance and the crimes committed by the principal. This in particular considering, in the case at hand, that Perišić had been geographically and operationally remote from the crimes, having made a neutral/generic contribution that could have been used for lawful purposes.[24] Specific direction would exist, said the Chamber, if (i) 'the VRS was an organization whose sole and exclusive purpose was the commission of crimes' and (ii) Perišić had 'endorsed a policy of assisting VRS crimes'.[25] As neither of these scenarios was proven beyond reasonable doubt,[26] the outcome was a full acquittal.

The *Perišić* appeal judgment was heavily criticized from the start,[27] and its reasoning was rejected within the year by a differently composed bench of the same court of appeals. In *Šainovic et al*, and in *Stanišic & Simatovic*, the Chamber found a violation of prevailing jurisprudence on the actus reus of aiding and abetting and rejected the *Perišić* judgment on this point.[28] While specific direction was conclusively rejected as a requirement for aiding and abetting, it has not completely disappeared from the field of international criminal law. Pursuant to Article 25(3)(c) of the Rome Statute, aiding and abetting entails that the accused assists the (attempted) commission of a crime, with the purpose of facilitating the commission of such crime. As commentators have observed,[29] the requirement of acting 'with the purpose of facilitating' resembles the 'specific direction' requirement and serves a similar purpose, namely, to limit criminal liability for the neutral conduct of remote actors.

If we apply these considerations to our thinking about judges, in situations where judicial figures are not part of a dictatorial regime whose sole and exclusive purpose is to commit crimes, there must then be proof of intent on the part of judges if criminal responsibility is to be generated. With regard specifically to omission liability in Argentina and Chile, if a case can be made that there has been willful blindness – where 'looking away' can be equated to intent – combined with a high position, we draw quite close to the 'purpose' element of aiding/abetting under the ICC Statute.

Let us next turn briefly to the subject of complicity by omission. One specific category of aiding and abetting by omission can be found in so-called approving spectator cases. Presence without an overt action can generate liability when such presence amounts to having a 'substantial effect' on the commission of a crime. The ICTR Trial Chamber held, in *Kayishema et al*, that in such an instance, "[i]ndividual responsibility is based, not on a duty to act, but on the encouragement and support that might be afforded to the principals of the crime from [the] omission [of action]".[30] An approving spectator who is held in such esteem by the perpetrators that his or her presence encourages them to commit, or continue to commit, a crime, may be guilty of aiding and abetting by omission.[31] Mere presence as part of a crowd does not suffice—it needs to be coupled with a certain status before such presence can qualify as aiding and abetting the commission of a crime.[32] In *Akayesu*, the ICTR Trial Chamber held that the defendant, a local mayor (*bourgomestre)*, aided and abetted by being present at the scene of the crime, because his inaction coupled with his status had had an encouraging effect on the actual perpetrators.[33] A variant of 'mere presence' is having a role in a system that comes with particular duties attached. Here again, the analogy with judges in a dictatorial regime is easily drawn.

Despite the affirmation of aiding and abetting by omission in ICTY and ICTR case law, close analysis reveals that this type of liability is underdeveloped.[34] Existing jurisprudence provides only a thin legal basis: it is not clear under what exact circumstances aiding and abetting by omission generates liability. This is problematic, especially when alternative, better-established theories of liability – such as superior responsibility – are available for use.

17.4 Leadership Liability and Deviation

This final section discusses the ICC's theory of indirect co-perpetration, which was first developed at the ICTY as what I have termed 'interlinked JCE'. The discussion requires us to consider the ICTY's *Brđanin* case. Radoslav Brđanin was a fairly high-level political figure who formulated, together with other Bosnian Serb military and political leaders, a 'strategic plan' to link Serb-populated areas in Bosnia and Herzegovina. The objective was to gain control over these areas in order to create a separate Bosnian state, from which non-Serbs would be removed. The implementation of the strategic plan involved the commission of crimes against humanity and war crimes, including the setting up of detention camps where such crimes were committed. The ICTY Appeals Chamber relied on JCE as a basis for liability, although the defendant had no direct link with the physical perpetrators. In its ruling the Appeals Chamber accepted an 'interlinked JCE', whereby the principal perpetrator does not have to be a member of the JCE. Instead, the appellate judges found that,

> [w]hat matters is...not whether the person who carried out the actus reus of a particular crime is a member of the JCE but whether the crime in question forms part of the common purpose.[35]

To hold a member of the JCE responsible for crimes perpetrated by a non-member, it is sufficient to show that at least one member of the JCE can be linked to a non-member. When the latter is used by the former as a tool to carry out the common criminal purpose, the other co-perpetrators of the JCE can be held equally liable for the crimes.[36] The Appeals Chamber further held that the extended form of JCE may also trigger liability where crimes committed by non-members are concerned. This applies as long as it can be shown that the member who uses non-members as tools to carry out the *actus reus* had the requisite intent, i.e., that in the circumstances of the case: (i) it was foreseeable that such a crime might be perpetrated by one or more of the principal/physical perpetrators (non-members), and (ii) the member willingly took that risk.[37]

The appellate ruling in *Brđanin* was a breakthrough in the law on JCE. This judgment enabled the prosecutor at the ICTY (and, later, at the ICTR) to apply JCE entirely at the leadership level if it could be shown that one of the participants was linked to the physical perpetrator who was used as a tool to carry out the crime(s). The *Brđanin* ruling effectively loosens the link between participants in a JCE and the physical perpetrator(s). Such 'delinking' is expressed through the courts' acceptance of non-membership on the part of the physical perpetrator. It is also reflected in the Appeal Chamber's finding with regard to mens rea in the basic form of JCE. The Appeals Chamber held that determining the link between the member and non-member of the JCE does not require proof of a shared agreement. So, the mens rea requirement for participants and for non-participants may diverge.

A similar concept exists at the ICC, where it is treated as indirect co-perpetration based on the concept of control. Here, remote (joint) perpetrators use others as tools to commit crimes, a notion that is developed from Roxin's theory of *Organisationsherrschaft*. In this theory, dominance over physical perpetrators is channeled through an organization with a tight hierarchical structure and replaceable members (fungibility), which operates outside the legal order. Remoteness from the crime is compensated for by control over the organization.[38] The ICC Pre-Trial Chamber (PTC) in the case of *Katanga & Ngudjolo* considered indirect co-perpetration to be the appropriate liability theory for imputing crimes committed by militia in the Congolese village of Bogoro to the two defendants who commanded these militia. The judges affirmed that control over the direct perpetrator can be exerted by means of an organization, namely, an organized structure of power (OSP).[39] The PTC held that the accused had control over an apparatus based on hierarchical relations between the accused and their subordinates. In the view of the Chamber, this OSP consisted of 'sufficient subordinates', and, as commanders, the accused were 'perpetrators behind the perpetrators' who mobilized authority and power within the organization to secure compliance with their orders.[40] Execution of the crime was secured by automatic compliance, and the crimes could be mutually attributed to both accused. This theory, while somewhat controversial, was accepted by the ICC Appeals Chamber in *Ntaganda*.[41]

If we compare the two models (JCE and indirect co-perpetration), we can conclude that in general terms the ICC model is more objective, because it hinges more on causation than on mens rea. This, however, does not guarantee a close link between senior defendants (political and military masterminds) and physical perpetrators on the ground. The accused need not contribute to the actual crime, as a contribution to the common plan may trigger liability even if not itself criminal. It suffices, for liability, that the relevant common plan contains an element of criminality. For senior defendants, this means that mere contribution to the creation or implementation of a criminal context is sufficient to trigger liability. Just as in the case of interlinked JCE, this means there may be only a tenuous link to the actual crimes on the ground.

With this model of leadership liability, based on remote perpetrator-principals, crime disappears into the background. This means, in my view, it is not a good model for attributing liability to judges who carry out their functions in a dictatorial regime, handing down judgments and imposing sentences that violate fundamental human rights.

17.5 Concluding Thoughts

Having discussed various international modes of liability, aiding and abetting (by omission) seems to come closest to accurately describing and capturing the liability of judges who function within a dictatorship. JCE and indirect co-perpetration, as forms of principal liability, appear more appropriate to describing liability attaching to those at the top, who dominate individuals or an organization. Judges are, however, more likely to function as 'enablers' than as instigators and leaders in a system of criminality, hence the inadequacy of theories such as indirect perpetration and interlinked JCE.

Notes

1 See Greenawalt, 'What is an International Crime?', in Heller et al (eds) 293.
2 van Sliedregt, 'International Criminal Law and Legal Pluralism: Straddling Cosmopolitan Aims and Distributed Enforcement' in Schiff B (ed) 575.
3 A 'national security' law that criminalised what it called "subversive activities of all types" ('*actividades subersivas en todas sus manifestaciones*').
4 NMT, Judgment of 4 December 1947, 3 Trials of War Criminals Before the Nuremberg Military Tribunals Under Control Council Law No. 10, *USA v. Altstötter* (hereinafter Justice Trial) 1177.
5 Justice Trial (n 5) 1063.
6 UNWCC, Vol. VII, 26.
7 Their liability was regulated by Article 60 (2) and (3) of the French Criminal Code: 'Those who have furnished arms, instruments or any other means which have served in the action knowing that they would serve this purpose; Those who knowingly have aided or assisted the perpetrator or perpetrators of the action in the facts which have prepared or facilitated or in those which have consummated the action', in UNWCC, Vol. VII, 33.
8 UNWCC, Vol. VII, 32.
9 van Sliedregt, 'Joint Criminal Enterprise as a Pathway to Convicting Individuals for Genocide' (2007) 5 *JICJ* 184, 185 et seq.
10 Guilfoyle, 'Responsibility for Collective Atrocities: Fair Labeling and Approaches to Commission in International Criminal Law' (2011) 64 *CLP* 255, 261.
11 Guilfoyle, 'Responsibility for Collective Atrocities: Fair Labeling and Approaches to Commission in International Criminal Law' (2011) 64 *CLP* 286. See Chapter 6 Section 6.6.1 on the origin of the complicity terminology and the classification of 'secondary principal' for those who were closely involved in committing the crime as non-principals.
12 Consider Judge Hunt's view: "No such distinction exists in relation to sentencing in this Tribunal, and I believe that it is unwise for this Tribunal to attempt to categorise different types of offenders in this way when it is unnecessary to do so for sentencing purposes. The Appeals Chamber has made it clear elsewhere that a convicted person must be punished for the seriousness of the acts which he has done, whatever their categorisation". ICTY, Separate Opinion of Judge David Hunt, Decision of 21 May 2003, IT-99-37-AR72, AC, Decision on Dragoljub Ojdanic's Motion Challenging Jurisdiction – Joint Criminal Enterprise, *Milutinović et al.* para 31.
13 See ICTY, Judgment of 15 July 1999, IT-94-1-A, AC, *Prosecutor v. Dusko Tadic* (hereinafter ICTY, '*Tadić* appeal judgment) para 192; ICTY, Judgment of 15 March 2002, IT-97-25-T, TC II, *Prosecutor v. Milorad Krnojelac* para 77.
14 van Sliedregt, *Individual Criminal Responsibility in International Law* (2012) 78 et seq.
15 Also known as Third Category JCE. The Appeals Chamber in *Tadić* recognized three categories: (i) related to cases where all co-defendants possessing the same intent pursue a common criminal design, for instance, the killing of a certain person; (ii) concerning the

so-called 'concentration camp' cases, where the requisite actus reus comprises the active participation in the enforcement of a system of repression, as could be inferred from the position of authority and the specific functions performed by each accused. (Here, the mens rea element comprises (a) knowledge of the nature of the system, and (b) the intent to further the common concerted design to ill-treat inmates. Intent may also be inferred from the accused's position within the camp.); (iii) cases where 'one of the perpetrators commits an act which, while outside the common design, was nevertheless a natural and foreseeable consequence of the effecting of that common purpose'. *Tadić* appeal judgment (n 14) para 204.

16 See Ohlin, who argues that "[t]he most basic problem with the doctrine of joint criminal enterprise" is "its imposition of equal culpability for all members of a joint enterprise". Ohlin, 'Three Conceptual Problems with the Doctrine of Joint Criminal Enterprise' (2007) 5 *JICJ* 69, 85. See also Boas et al, *International Criminal Law Practitioner Library: International Criminal Procedure* (2011), 65 et seq. One scholar has proposed abandoning differentiation and modes of liability altogether: James Stewart argues in favor of a unitary approach to criminal participation that collapses all modes of liability into a single standard. Stewart, 'The end of 'modes of liability' for international crimes' (2012) 25 *LJIL* 165.

17 Article 30 of the ICC Statute stipulates, "For the purposes of this article, 'knowledge' means awareness that a circumstance exists or a consequence *will occur in the ordinary course of events*. 'Know' and 'knowingly' shall be construed accordingly. [emphasis added, *EvS*]"

18 ICC, Judgment of 16 December 2011, ICC-01/04-01/10, *Prosecutor v. Callixte Mbarushimana* Decision on the Confirmation of Charges para 277. This argument has been rejected by Judge Fernandez de Gurmendi: Separate opinion of Judge Sylvia Fernandez de Gurmendi, Judgment of 30 May 2012, ICC-01/04–01/10 OA4, *Prosecutor v. Callixte Mbarushimana* Decision on the Confirmation of Charges para 10.

19 ICC, Judgment of 7 March 2014, ICC-01/04-01/07, *Prosecutor v. Germain Katanga* (hereinafter *Katanga* Trial judgment) para 1632 et seq.

20 *Katanga* Trial judgment (n 20) para 1632.

21 ICTY, Judgment of 14 May 1997, IT-94-1-T, *Prosecutor v. Dusko Tadic* para 688.

22 ICTY, Judgment of 6 September 2011, IT-04-81-T, *Prosecutor v. Momcilo Perišić'.*

23 ICTY, Judgment of 28 February 2013, IT-04-81-A, *Prosecutor v. Momcilo Perišić* (hereinafter *Perišić* Appeal judgment).

24 *Perišić* Appeal judgment (n 24) para 40.

25 *Perišić* Appeal judgment (n 24) para 52.

26 *Perišić* Appeal Judgment (n 24) para 54 et seqq, 65 and 69.

27 See e.g. Sadat, 'Can the ICTY's Šainović and Perišić Cases be Reconciled?' (2014) 108 *AJIL* 475.

28 ICTY, Judgement of 23 January 2014, I-05-87, *Prosecutor v. Šainović et al.* para 1650.

29 Greenawalt, 'Foreign Assistance Complicity' (2016) 54 *CJTL* 531, 539 et seq, 579 et seq; van Sliedregt/Popova, 'Interpreting "for the purpose of facilitating" in Article 25(3)(c)?'; Heller, in 'Milestones in International Criminal Justice: Recent Legal Controversies at the UN Yugoslav Tribunal' (2013) 7 et seq.

30 ICTR, Judgment of 21 May 1999, ICTR-95-1-T, *Prosecutor v. Kayishema et al.* para 202, upheld in ICTR, Judgment of 1 June 2001, ICTR-95-1-A, *Prosecutor v. Kayishema et al.*

para 201 et seq, endorsed in ICTY, Judgment of 3 April 2007, IT-99-36-A, *Prosecutor v. Brđanin* (hereinafter *Brđanin* Appeals Judgment) para. 273.
31 ICTY, Judgment of 10 December 1998, IT-95-17/1-T, *Prosecutor v. Anto Furundžija* (hereinafter *Furundžija* Trial judgment) para 207.
32 ICTY, Judgment of 29 July 2004, IT-95-14-A, *Prosecutor v. Blaskić* para 48; *Furundžija* Trial judgment (n 32) para 245, 249; ICTY, Judgment of 20 February 2001, IT-96-21-A, *Prosecutor v. Delalić et al.* para 352.
33 ICTR, Judgment of 2 September 1998, ICTR-96-4-T, *Prosecutor v. Akayesu* para. 705.
34 Boas et al (n 17) 311–315.
35 *Brđanin* Appeals Judgment (n 31) para 410.
36 *Brđanin* Appeals Judgment (n 31) para 413.
37 *Brđanin* Appeals Judgment (n 31*)* para 411.
38 'Loss of proximity to the act is compensated by an increasing degree of organizational control by the leadership positions in the apparatus', *Brđanin* Appeals Judgment (n 31) para 200.
39 ICC, Decision of 30 September 2008, ICC-01/04-01/07, *Prosecutor v. Katanga and Naudiolo* Decision on the Confirmation of Charges (hereinafter *Katanga and Ngudjolo* confirmation decision) para 498.
40 *Katanga and Naudiolo* confirmation decision (n 40) para 513.
41 ICC, Judgment of 30 March 2021, ICC-01/04-02/06 A, *Prosecutor v. Ntaganda.* See, for a discussion of this judgment, the symposium reported in (2022) 20 *JICJ* Issue 3.

Bibliography

Boas G et al, *International Criminal Law Practitioner Library: International Criminal Procedure* (Cambridge University Press 2011).

Greenawalt A, 'Foreign Assistance Complicity' (2016) 54 *Columbia Journal of Transnational Law* 531.

Greenawalt A K A, 'What is an International Crime?' in Heller K J et al (eds), *The Oxford Handbook of International Criminal Law* (Oxford University Press 2020) 293.

Guilfoyle D, 'Responsibility for Collective Atrocities: Fair Labeling and Approaches to Commission in International Criminal Law' (2011) 64 *Current Legal Problems* 255.

Heller K J, 'Milestones in International Criminal Justice: Recent Legal Controversies at the UN Yugoslav Tribunal' in *Chatham House International Law Summary* (2022). www.chathamhouse.org/sites/files/chathamhouse/public/Meetings/Meeting%20Transcripts/161013Yugoslav1.pdf (accessed 16 April 2018).

Ohlin J D, 'Three Conceptual Problems with the Doctrine of Joint Criminal Enterprise' (2007) 5 *Journal of International Criminal Justice* 69.

Sadat L, 'Can the ICTY's Šainović and Perišić Cases be Reconciled?' (2014) 108 *American Journal of International Law* 475.

van Sliedregt E, 'Joint Criminal Enterprise as a Pathway to Convicting Individuals for Genocide' (2007) 5 *Journal of International Criminal Justice* 184.

van Sliedregt E, *Individual Criminal Responsibility in International Law* (Oxford University Press 2012).

van Sliedregt E, 'International Criminal Law and Legal Pluralism: Straddling Cosmopolitan Aims and Distributed Enforcement' in Schiff Berman P (ed), *Handbook on Global legal Pluralism* (Oxford University Press 2020) 575.

van Sliedregt E/Weißer B, 'Foreword' (2022) 20 (3) *Journal of International Criminal Justice* 627–635.
van Sliedregt E/Popova A, 'Interpreting "for the purpose of facilitating" in Article 25(3)(c)?' (blog). https://cicj.org/2014/12/interpreting-for-the-purpose-of-facilitating-in-article-253c/ (accessed 22 January 2024).
Stewart J G, 'The end of "modes of liability" for international crimes' (2012) 25 *Leiden Journal of International Law* 165.

18 Judges' Responsibility for Participation in a Criminal Association

A Comparative and Theoretical Analysis*

Fernando Londoño M.

18.1 Premises: Two Distinctions and a Taxonomy of Criminal Associations

It is useful to begin with a couple of basic distinctions.

18.1.1 Pathology or Physiology as Legal Background: Practical Consequences

First of all, one can draw a distinction based on the legal background against which criminal involvement by judges occurs. The cases addressed by the majority of the chapters in this book relate to involvement in crimes of dictatorships – especially homicide, torture, and kidnap – through the exercise of judicial roles. In other words, they deal with judicial action carried out within what I will refer to as a 'pathological' legal system (one that is formally, or apparently, valid: where there is law, but it is flawed (*geseztliches Unrecht)*). The cases discussed in the present chapter instead occur against what I call a 'physiological' background. That is, cases in which a judge acts within the framework of a democratic rule of law, nonetheless betrays that physiological background in such a way that his or her decisions benefit a criminal association or its members. (By way of example, this association may be some kind of Mafia group, or may be involved in drugs or weapons smuggling, or human trafficking: these are the types of phenomena of comparative interest here.)

Normally, such a departure from physiology will be made not out of conviction or political ideology but for money or other economic benefits (i.e., corruption). On the other hand, one could imagine the hypothetical case of a judge who acts in such a way as to benefit terrorist associations with political goals, for reasons that may have to do with endorsement for 'reasons other than economic profit'. We may think, for example, of a judge committed to the Basque separatist cause in Spain or to the cause of armed groups who claim or are alleged to favor Mapuche indigenous demands in Chile. We could also, however, consider the case of a judge who participates in criminal associations that are made up of public officials. Such is the case, for example, of Chile's secretive dictatorship-era intelligence, agencies the DINA and the CNI,[1] although to this author's knowledge no Chilean

DOI: 10.4324/9781003470069-22

judge has to date been charged in connection with the crimes of these associations. These three scenarios allow us to discern three different associative patterns or profiles[2]: respectively, (1) common organized crime (drug trafficking, Mafia activities, money laundering, etc.); (2) common terrorism; and (3) 'State criminality' or 'State terrorism',[3] i.e., serious crimes against individuals committed by public officials as part of a systematic policy. Each of these profiles has an associated, and distinctive, set of participation dynamics and motives. In case (1), these are, respectively, corruption/profit; in case (2), they are conviction/ideology (political or religious fanaticism); and in case (3), they are conformity or conviction/ideology (political/legal fanaticism).

If we consider just for a moment what is distinctive about our third scenario (the one that most closely matches the majority of the cases dealt with in this book), the issue can be stated in the following way: in contexts of state terror, formalist approaches by judges appear problematic (insofar as they are intended to serve as an excuse, after the fashion of adducing 'unavoidable error'). On the other hand, in cases of common terrorism and common criminal associations – the types of cases with which this chapter predominantly deals – a straightforward departure from law can easily be observed, and there would be no space for an excuse such as 'error'. In scenario (3), then, judicial wrongs are carried out in the light of a law that is unjust or ailing (however formally valid), whereas in scenarios (1) and (2), the wrong is carried out by departing from a legal system that is *a priori* just or healthy.

At least two practical consequences proceed from this comparison. The first has to do with mens rea attribution. In cases of judicial involvement with common criminal associations and common terrorism, the attribution of mens rea should be unproblematic. At the very least, there should be no room for allegations of unavoidable mistake of law, simply because there will have been no mistake of law. Nor should there be any justification for raising judicial immunity where there has been any kind of participation or complicity with such associations. The second concerns affiliation attribution: actions motivated by any kind of economic benefit (corruption) should be considered generally incompatible with affiliation or membership attribution unless we are dealing with recurring or frequent 'judicial services'. We will return to this matter in Section 18.2.

As can be seen, there remains just one scenario that occupies common ground with the central concern of this volume. This is scenario (3): the case of an association of public officials or State agents – among which judges could be counted – who come together to perpetrate crimes under the vile cover of the form or appearance of validity of the state and the law (cf. Nuremberg's famous dictum concerning "[t]he dagger of the assassin ... concealed beneath the robe...")[4]. I am not aware of any case being brought over such a scenario – i.e., alleging the involvement of judges in this third type of criminal organization – at least, not under Chilean law.[5] As is well known, organizations later recognized as being of precisely this kind operated in Chile during the Pinochet dictatorship (viz., regime intelligence agencies the DINA and the CNI).[6] Nonetheless, to this author's knowledge, no accusation has to date been brought alleging involvement of judges in those or other similar state organizations.[7]

Table 18.1 sums up the main contentions of this subsection to date.

Table 18.1 Profiles of association: consequences for mens rea and membership attribution in cases of judicial involvement

Profiles of Association	*Dynamics of, and Motives for, Affiliation, Active Participation, or Cooperation*	*Legal Backdrop*	*Mens Rea Attribution*	*Attribution of Affiliation or Membership*
(1) Common organized crime (drug trafficking, mafia, money laundering, etc.)	Corruption/profit	Physiology (non-corrupted system)	Unproblematic attribution of mens rea (no 'unavoidable mistake of law' should be accepted)	Actions motivated by economic benefit (corruption) are generally incompatible with affiliation or membership attribution (unless there is a recurring disposition to shield, etc.: see Section 18.2)
(2) Common Terrorism	Conviction/ideology (political or religious fanaticism)	Physiology (non-corrupted system)	Unproblematic attribution of mens rea (no 'unavoidable mistake of law' should be accepted)	General criteria
(3) State Criminality or State Terrorism	Conformity or conviction/ideology (political/legal fanaticism)	Pathology (corrupted system)	Less straightforward attribution of mens rea (some 'unavoidable mistake of law' could be accepted)	General criteria

18.1.2 Proper and Improper Actions (Actions within Judicial Competence, versus Abuse of Position)

A second distinction must be made before proceeding any further: we must distinguish between actions within the specific competence of the judge (proper cases) and actions in abuse of position (improper cases). In the first case, we are dealing with actions of a jurisdictional nature (judicial decisions).[8] This is the main focus of the present volume, which concentrates on the framework of judicial perversion of justice (*Rechtsbeugung*). There is, however, a second area of possible practical interest, at least as far as the question of liability for criminal association is concerned. Namely, the various conceivable cases in which a judge abuses his or her public role (with the knowledge and relationships that it entails) to favor a criminal organization or its members in any way. This could be, for example, by disclosing secret information that is of use to the organization[9] for evading liability or engaging in concealment or obstruction of the investigation, or by 'influence peddling' (*tráfico de influencia*) with a view to obtaining a favorable decision from another judge or court, etc. By way of example, the recent 'El Matanga' case in Chile would fall within the area of improper actions. In this case a judge helped a relative to evade an investigation for drug dealing by disclosing to the defendant the fact that their mobile phone had been tapped (in a criminal investigation that was not under the judge's remit).[10]

In my view, liability for improper judicial acts should follow the same fate as liability for other public officials, depending, of course, on the definitions contained within each legal system. That aside, I foresee no special difficulties at the level of mens rea. The distinction between proper and improper acts does not, however, appear particularly relevant for the attribution of affiliation in the criminal association. In other words, in both scenarios, affiliation may be affirmed or denied according to specific attribution criteria related to the criminal legal provision (*Tatbestand*). Thus, in both cases we could at least claim that there has been judicial collaboration with the organization, its members, or the crimes that constitute its objective. Whether such collaboration is sufficient for the attribution of associative affiliation (as a perpetrator (*Täter*) of criminal association *stricto sensu*) will depend not so much on the kind of contribution (proper or improper, i.e., through judicial decisions or other types of actions) as on other factors or criteria. These would include ritual admission, where applicable; the frequency or regularity of the collaboration; the degree of availability; and the existence of gratuity or remuneration, etc. The second part of the chapter discusses these matters.

18.2 Judicial Liability for Participation in, or Cooperation with, Criminal Associations

The focus of the discussion that follows will mainly be on proper actions and, within this category, especially on those that relate to forms of common criminal associations.

18.2.1 Special or Common Attribution Criteria? On Requirements for Claiming Affiliation or Cooperation by Judges

The first question to be asked is whether the judicial capacity makes any difference for the purposes of organized crime liability. That is, does it set judges apart from ordinary citizens and/or other public officials? A satisfactory answer to this question would require more exhaustive analysis than space permits, but for present purposes certain general ideas can be laid out. I see no reason to claim the need for special or ad hoc criteria for attribution of affiliation or cooperation in the case of judges. In other words, there is nothing specific to the judicial capacity or function that attracts or repels this kind of attribution. Just as any citizen, legislator, or other public official could be regularly 'at the service' of a criminal organization, so too could a judge. If their offense perhaps seems more serious – being a betrayal from within the law, by one who is called upon to 'pronounce' it or authoritatively 'lay it down' – this speaks less to reasons for attributing affiliation or collaboration than to the seriousness of the concrete wrongdoing. In other words, the correct distinction to draw would not be about the yes or no of liability but about the quantum of the applicable sanction.

We might also consider what may be termed the 'non-fungible' character of judicial service. Here, of course, there are grounds for identifying something 'special', although hardly to such a degree as to produce or require a departure from general criteria. According to these, the more exceptional, unavailable, or non-fungible the contribution to the organization – as opposed to a neutral contribution – the more likely it is that a typically relevant form of participation will be attributed. (This will depend, of course, on the concrete solution provided by each legal system: *lege lata*). Another special consideration concerns the nature of the motive. In a typical scenario involving common cases of judicial corruption – i.e., services in exchange for economic benefits – the attribution of affiliation will tend to be more difficult.[11] Indeed, since here the judge's actions are motivated by payment or reward, he or she seems to behave like someone who sells services to the association. This is tantamount to a kind of 'outsourcing' arrangement. This is not something that would usually be undertaken by a true member of the association, who would be incurring 'business risks' rather than selling services. Thus in principle the relevant charge(s) in such cases would be mere complicity or external cooperation with the association, punishable according to the corresponding legal provisions surrounding criminal association,[12] or the general rules on commission and participation (respectively, *Täterschaft* and *Teilnahme*).[13] A different solution – resort to the charge of affiliation – may, however, be claimed where a judge has provided habitual, regular, or high-frequency 'judicial services' to the criminal organization.

Our discussion to date is consonant with the most notorious cases of this type that feature in comparative law: those Italian cases that have led to the conviction of judges for complicity (*concorso esterno*) with *Mafia* associations. We are dealing here, for example, with the *Corrado Carnevale* case,[14] in which a judge who the media had nicknamed 'the decision-killer' (*il giudice ammazzasentenze*) was convicted for complicity with Cosa Nostra in connection with the crime of Mafia association as set down in Article 416 bis of the Italian criminal code. This case was followed by the *Maxi-Processo ter* case,[15] also involving the Sicilian Cosa Nostra, in which a judge who was president of an Assizes Court (*Corte di Assise*) was charged with complicity.

In these cases, the Italian Supreme Court (court of cassation, *Cassazione*) struggled to assimilate the particularities of 'judicial services' under etiological parameters, precisely because it sought to apply the general criteria of complicity (*concorso esterno*), which requires some sort of causal contribution to be appreciated ex post, and not ex ante. That said, the activity of a judge in any jurisdictional system, especially in the context of a collegiate court, is not easily tamed by or accommodated within the traditional causal categories that prevail in the field of complicity or cooperation. This is true not only for Italy, but more widely.[16] The 'guaranteed' vote of a colluded judge who is a member of a collegiate court lacks the contributive efficacy of a traditional material contribution or service such as financing, handling weapons or raw materials, laundering assets, etc. Italian jurisprudence has accordingly been hesitant to frame these judicial cases under the causal paradigm. Nonetheless, as we will see below, the court of cassation would end up denying in the resolutive part of its verdicts what it had itself maintained in the declaratory (i.e., justificatory or doctrinal) sections. It did so by treating a single judge's vote as a contribution to the reinforcement or strengthening of the organization, even when that vote was (at most) hypothetically suitable, while concretely unsuccessful. Thus, in practice, the court of cassation deleted the ex post causal criterion for attributing complicity or external cooperation, replacing it with one of ex ante suitability. In this way, failed complicity became punishable. If you will, and although I am aware of the implied partial self-contradiction, one must perhaps concede that there is, after all, something special operating in the matter of judges' liability.

Here, however, we are straying into the terrain of ideas that deserve treatment in a separate section, even if that treatment will be necessarily very synthetic.

18.2.2 Attribution Criteria: Inward (Affiliation and Active Participation) and Outward (Cooperation-with, Complicity, **'Concorso Esterno'***)*

Given the above, what are the general criteria for attribution of affiliation-in, or cooperation-with, an organization? While an in-depth treatment is not possible here, I believe that what follows is broadly valid.

Two attribution categories can be distinguished for our purposes: attribution within the organization and attribution outside the organization (complicity or external cooperation, *concorso esterno*). Within the first category (inward attribution), we can in turn find two common types of attribution in comparative law: passive participation (or 'mere affiliation') and active participation ('taking active part in': see Art. 5.1.a.ii., Palermo Convention).[17] A brief description of each of these categories appears below. A preliminary consideration is, however, needed before proceeding: these questions must obviously be answered differently depending on the structure of the organization, i.e., according to the degree of complexity or stability that the relevant legal provision requires (associations, organizations, groups, gangs, etc.). Also, of course, the attribution criteria for participation become proportionally softer as one moves from more complex, stable, and severely punished forms of aggregation (associations, organizations); through toward more elementary, volatile, and less severely punished forms (groups or gangs), before the category dissolves into mere forms of co-perpetration or co-criminality. With these considerations in mind, what follows will focus on associations and organizations.

18.2.2.1 Attribution within the Organization: Active Participation and Mere Affiliation

Here we must pay attention to the specific modality by which the quality of principal or perpetrator (*Täter*) is recognized in the corresponding legal provision surrounding criminal association (where 'perpetrator' is understood to refer to the subject punishable with the full basic penalty of that legal provision). In this matter, we can identify models that are centered on the idea of affiliation or membership in the strong sense (i.e., a membership that per se justifies full punishment as perpetrator). The most paradigmatic case is that of the legal provision surrounding Mafia association in Italy (art. 416 bis, Italian criminal code).[18] The common Spanish and Chilean legal provisions (arts. 570 bis[19] and 294,[20] respectively, of the relevant criminal codes) also use this notion as an alternative to active participation, as will be explained below. In these cases, the passive member can be charged as perpetrator or principal for the crime of organization, under a presupposition of affiliation. Different criteria prevail as far as proof of affiliation is concerned: some are more, others less, objective or loose (formal-organic criteria, ritual, intersubjectivity, reciprocal recognition, mere adhesion to purposes, etc.).

Other models make use of the notion of active participation, with or without a presupposition of affiliation. At least two variants exist, therefore: more restrictive models that, presupposing membership, require forms of causal or active contribution; and models that impose the penalty of perpetrator on those who make causal contributions, regardless of proof of affiliation. As an example of the first variant, we can point to the special legal provisions in Chilean law surrounding criminal organization for money laundering and drug dealing.[21] For the second, we can consider the common legal provisions of criminal organization or association in Spanish law (criminal code Art. 570 bis) and in Chilean law (criminal code Art. 294.[22] We can also consider Article 5.1.a.ii.b of the Palermo Convention (which deals with 'taking part in activities of an organized criminal group'), although this is not necessarily matched with a causal approach.

As can be readily understood, these models present two crucial decisions: first, whether the passive member is or is not punished as a perpetrator, and second, whether a mere contributor is or is not punished as a perpetrator (i.e., regardless of whether she is, or is not, a member). As has been said, the Chilean and Spanish common legal provisions answer both questions in the affirmative (as does the Palermo Convention), thus broadening their scope.

None of these legislative decisions seem to me to have any necessary consequences for the regime of attribution of liability to judges. It is, however, worth highlighting three aspects that are of possible practical interest for our purposes:

1 The criminalization of special forms of contribution that are not particularly decisive or relevant (as is done by the common Chilean regime, which includes contributions such as 'providing lodgings or a hiding place' (*alojamiento o escondite*)) seems to offer a good argument for rejecting forms of complicity or external cooperation (*concorso esterno*) regarding the legal provision

of association (which would have already absorbed them, explicitly). That is, in such cases there is a good argument for not accepting the complementing or extension of punishability implied by the general rules of intervention (commission and participation). In other words, if the Italian legal provision over Mafia association had the same structure as art. 294 of the Chilean criminal code, the flanking of art. 110 of the Italian Penal Code would need to be rejected outright. Otherwise, we would be talking about 'complicity in complicity' or complicity in ex-post-facto cooperation.

2 Depending on the type of conduct that is criminalized under the modality of active participation, there will or will not be space to include the class of contribution expected from judges. In other words, to the extent that the legal provision of association punishes classic material contributions without any generic formula, an attribution to judges will be highly improbable[23] (except if one is ready to attribute affiliation, but that is another matter). A case in point is Article 294 of the Chilean criminal code, which limits its scope to very specific contributions, as "means or instruments to commit the [...] crimes; lodging, a hiding place, or a meeting place".

3 The more lax or soft the criteria for attribution of affiliation or membership, the less relevant, in practice, becomes the problem of liability for contributions by agents external to the association. Indeed, the trivialization of the requirement of affiliation can lead to any instance of contribution to the organization being counted as a form of perpetration of the crime of association. (This risk seems, for example, to have been understood in Chile in the case of special drug law offenses and the special offense of money laundering.) This relaxation of criteria is in line with the new criminological realities of criminal organizations,[24] which today operate in a less 'organized' (but no less assertive) manner. They increasingly take the form of fluid networks with 'cool' business patterns (utilizing outsourcing or interchangeable suppliers, etc.).[25]

18.2.2.2 Attribution Outside the Organization (Complicity, External Cooperation (Concorso Esterno))

Here, attribution is a matter of assigning a form of complicity or cooperation with the organization to agents who are external to the organization per se. This may be either because they are authentically outside agents (free, interchangeable providers) or because insufficient proof of affiliation has been produced. If what we are dealing with here is accessory intervention (*Teilnahme*), the central question is: accessory to what? In other words, what is the external act (that of the perpetrator, *Täter*) to which one contributes from outside the organization? The question concerns the subject of the wrong (*injusto* or *Unrecht*) of criminal association, a question that is not always clarified in comparative case law, as far as I can see. It goes without saying that the answer is decisive for our query. If the wrong done by the perpetrator of the crime of organization is of a purely individual or personal nature (her own affiliation or agreement to affiliate, her specific contribution to a particular plan, etc.), then complicity must be understood as a contribution to that person's individual act. The accomplice will accordingly be the one who promotes or induces the enrollment of a potential affiliate, the one who provides weapons to a qualified member, etc., but not necessarily the one who provides some services to the organization as a whole. The opposite applies if we conclude that the act attributed to the perpetrator is, strictly speaking, an act of the organization as a whole, a wrongful act of the collective as a source of danger (something that, on another level, poses problems in terms of the culpability principle).[26] Thus, to sum up in a few words: what is the nature of the wrong attributed through criminal association? Is it an individual wrong, or a collective one? This is a question relevant to the case of judges, at least at first glance. Preliminarily, contribution actions by judges more easily fit the second schema. Judges do not engage in enrolling members or providing supplies (and if they do, they are acting as mere citizens). On the other hand, this second schema is more demanding in terms of accreditation or proof, as will be discussed below.

Under the first schema (an individual wrongful act of association), judges should not risk punishment for complicity in the organization. At most – if the circumstances so determine – there may be a hypothesis of perpetrator cover-up (accessory after the fact; *favoreggiamento personale*). This may be autonomously or accessorily punishable,[27] depending on the legal system (a cover-up in relation to the goal crime or even the association crime). But in addition (as *Idealkonkurrenz*), the judge should be charged for judicial perversion of justice malfeasance (*Rechtsbeugung*) or corruption of public duty (*corruzione d'ufficio*), as the case may be.

If my reading is correct, Italian jurisprudence has opted to understand the wrongful act of organization – i.e., the problem of *concorso esterno* – under the second schema, as a collective wrongful act,[28] although without making this particularly explicit or clarifying it. The aim is, then, to seek a contribution (in this case from the judge) to the preservation (*conservazione*) or strengthening (*rafforzamento*) of the criminal organization itself. Put this way, however, the existence of one of two alternative sets of circumstances would seem necessary if a judge's contribution is to be considered a contribution to the organization as a whole.

Either we are dealing with:

1. A judge very high up in the judicial hierarchy: a 'quasi all-powerful' judge, with exalted powers of oversight over large portions of the territory, plus the capacity to peddle influence at different levels in order to shield the organization as a whole (but in such a case, how come this person is not considered a member?);

Or (more realistically):

2. A judge who is able to shield one or more particularly relevant members of the organization, i.e., one or more of those members without whom the organization runs the risk of dwindling or even dissolving (e.g., the leader or a key financier).

Is there no third possibility? Well, there is perhaps a third alternative, but it is much more debatable. This would be the case of a judge who regularly favors fungible members of an association, such as, for instance, by routinely favoring all the 'footsoldiers' of the association who happen to come before his or her court. Here we could speak of a contribution to the association within a very limited geographical-jurisdictional space (such as the jurisdiction of a court). Nonetheless, the stability or regularity of the contribution should most probably place the judge inside the association, rather than outside. Therefore, if the case is well investigated, such a judge should be facing charges as an affiliated or active participant (perpetrator).

The Italian jurisprudential discussion has been set within this playing field, and so the takeaway – or what ought to be the takeaway – is that a 'judicial service' that happens to favor a fungible member of the organization should not count as complicity in the crime of association. Accordingly, the judge should not risk more punishment than that which attaches to the crime of qualified corruption of public duty (*corruzione d'uffccio*: art. 319 ter, Italian criminal code).[29] Additionally, if the necessary assumptions of are met, he or she may be liable for the crime of personal cover-up (*favoreggiamento personale*: art. 378, Italian criminal code).[30] Of course, as has already been stated, if the abovementioned conditions of regularity or stability are (also) met, we should speak of affiliation, rather than complicity or external cooperation.

Owing to this schema of attribution of collective wrongdoing, Italian jurisprudence has faced difficulties in proving the causal contribution of the judge, according to the etiological parameter that art. 110 of the Italian criminal code entails. As noted above, in the final analysis, the court of cassation (*Cassazione)* declared a causality that strictly speaking was not such (being, at most, an *ex ante* suitability), punishing cases of failed complicity.

In closing, something more can be said. Two distinct moments in the Italian jurisprudence can be identified. In the first, the 'Carnevale 2002' case,[31] the *Cassazione* embraced an etiological (causal) approach in a kind of twin-track mode: more demanding in the case of episodic or sporadic judicial disposition to shield a member of the association (at least, a 'big boss' member), while relaxing this requirement in the case of repeated or constant disposition to shield (on the understanding that such permanent disposition would, by itself, reinforce the organization as such). In a second development, however, the *Cassazione* relaxed the causal parameter – exemplified by the cases *Mannino* 2005,[32] and *Maxi processo ter* 2006.[33] Here, the disposition of a single judge in a collegiate tribunal (e.g., a promise to vote in favor) was considered enough to satisfy the complicity requirements, without the need for that judge's conduct to be successful within the framework of the relevant collegiate decision.[34]

Notes

* This chapter is a revised version of a draft paper discussed at the International Colloquium 'Judicial Murder' (Santiago de Chile, 14–15 June 2023). The author is thankful to the organisers – all dear colleagues, and editors of this book – for such a wonderful

opportunity for academic discussion. Last but not least, the author is also thankful to Professor Cath Collins, also a colleague at Universidad Diego Portales, for her meticulous and generous language review of the English draft.

1 Chile's main dictatorship-era repressive agencies. The Dirección de Inteligencia Nacional, DINA, operated between 1973 and 1977, and the Central Nacional de Informaciones, CNI (1977–1990). Emblematic associated cases include that of DINA secret police chief Manuel Contreras. Other examples, however, exist, such as those of the notorious clandestine detention and torture centers Colonia Dignidad and Tejas Verdes: see Londoño, 'El "caso Manos Blancas": problemas de imputación en contextos de organización criminal a la luz del derecho penal chileno' in Couso/Werle (eds) 331, 336–337, note 8.

2 See Cancio, 'El "caso Manos Blancas": problemas de imputación en contextos de organización criminal a la luz del derecho penal español' in Couso/Werle (eds) 307, 309. Cancio identifies two patterns of organized crime: one that is common, or oriented to economic profit (drug trafficking and the like) and another that is politically oriented (terrorist organizations and 'political organized crime'). The same layout is followed here, but a subdivision is made explicit within the second group.

3 'State terrorism' or 'state terror' are terms often used to describe State criminality in South America during the 1970s and 1980s, an era when much of the region was under military dictatorship.

4 NMT, Judgment of 4 December 1947, 3 Trials of War Criminals Before the Nuremberg Military Tribunals Under Control Council Law No. 10, *USA v. Altstötter* 985.

5 See the chapter by Couso in this volume.

6 See Londoño (2017) (n 1).

7 Moreover, it goes without saying that there is no necessary relationship between the matter at hand (charges for criminal organization) and the fact that criminal cases over actions of the DINA or CNI have brought charges for co-perpetration drawing on the attribution theory known by some variant of 'dominion over an organised apparatus of power'. See Horvitz, 'El "caso Corvo y Moncada/Aislandia": Represión de protestas por una dictadura a la luz del derecho penal chileno' in Couso/Werle (eds) 155, 163 et seqq. This is because an organised apparatus of this kind can be constituted by the regular machinery of the State apparatus, without thereby necessarily giving rise to an 'apparatus within the apparatus', i.e., a criminal association within a criminal state.

8 See Article 223 No. 1 of the Chilean criminal code (Código Penal). On the other hand, the legal provision of *Rechtsbeugung* contained in § 339 of the German criminal code (StGB) is broader, as it covers not only the moment of decision (*Entscheidung*) in the case, but also the conduct of the case (*Leitung*).

9 See Article 224 No. 6 of the Chilean criminal code.

10 TOP Coyhaique, RIT 77-2022, Decision against *C.E.U.P.* Precisely because the judge did not act within her competence (*improper act*), she was not charged with prevarication under Article 224 No. 6 of the Chilean criminal code, which punishes disclosure of secrets regarding proceedings. The judge was charged – and eventually acquitted – under another hypothesis of prevarication (Article 224 No. 7), but that had nothing to do with the disclosure event. In the end, the judge was convicted in the same way as any other citizen would have been, for a common crime under the Chilean Law against Drug Dealing (Ley No. 20.000, Article 38). The article in question punishes the disclosure of secrets regarding drug dealing investigations and carries a more severe sanction than would have been available under the disclosure hypothesis of Article 224 No. 6.

11 For common (non-judicial) cases, see Viganò, 'El "caso Manos Blancas": problemas de imputación en contextos de organización criminal a la luz del derecho penal italiano'

in Couso/Werle (eds) 363, 375. Viganò is of a different opinion, although under a presupposition of regularity or stability in the 'outsourced' service: thus in the end there is agreement this issue, as will be seen from what follows.

12 Consider here the second part of Article 570 bis of the Spanish criminal code (where forms of co-operation are described disjunctively with respect to active participation). The same applies to Chilean law (Chilean criminal code Article 294).

13 See Article 110 of the Italian criminal code, according to the jurisprudential construction that gave rise to the *concorso esterno*. Viganò (2017) (n 11) 363, 365 et seqq.

14 Corrado Carnevale case, *Cassazione, Sezioni Unite*, 30 October 2002, n. 22327.

15 Maxi Processo ter case, *Cassazione, Sezione* V, 15 May 2006, n. 16493.

16 See Dubber/Hörnle, *Criminal Law. A Comparative Approach* (2016) 303 [5], 327 [9], for a comparison between German and US law with particular regard to attempted aiding or facilitation. Of course, causality also plays an important role in International Criminal Law, albeit downgraded to probability: see Werle/Jeßberger, *Tratado de Derecho Penal International* (2017) 375 et seqq [571–572], 401–402 [614].

17 The United Nations Convention against Transnational Organized Crime, known as the Palermo Convention.

18 See Barazzetta, 'Art. 416 bis' in Dolcini/Gatta (eds), *Codice Penale Commentato* 2148; as well as Caputo, 'Art. 416 bis' in Forti et al (eds), *Commentario breve al Codice Penale*, 1300.

19 See Couso, 'Art. 294' in Couso/Hernández (eds) 330.

20 See García del Blanco, 'Art. 570 bis' in *Memento Práctico* 1916 [18770 ff]; as well as Sánchez García de Paz, 'Art. 570bis' in Tomillo/Martín 553.

21 Article 28 of Law No. 19.913 and Article 16 of Law No. 20.000, respectively.

22 See Londoño (2017) (n 1) 331, 335.

23 In this sense, the Palermo Convention provisions do not, either, properly fit judicial contributions.

24 Consider the concept of organized criminal group as it appears in the Palermo Convention.

25 On this point, and with further bibliography, see Londoño (2017) (n 1) 331, 346 note 31.

26 The first schema for understanding wrongdoing seems to me to be the more accurate. Seen in this light, the attribution of accessory after the fact, or perpetrator's cover-up, should not be difficult and may set things in an adequate middle ground. Unless, of course, the conditions for attributing membership/perpetration are met. For more details on the alternative schemas, with some comparative and Chilean doctrinal discussion (Cancio/Silva/Mañalich) see Londoño (2017) (n 1) 331, 338 et seqq.

27 Chilean criminal law is an exception in the comparative field, insofar as it includes concealment as a form of accessory intervention and not as an autonomous offense against justice; see Articles 14 and 17 of the Chilean criminal code.

28 See, among many possible sources, Corvi, 'Il concorso esterno del magistrate nell'associazione di tipo mafioso' (2006) 9 *Dir pen proc* 1112, 1118 et seqq; Barazzetta, (2021) (n 18) 2148, 2187 et seqq [38 et seqq]; and Caputo (2017) (n 18) 1300, 1329.

29 See Caputo (2017) (n 18) 1300, 1329: only a crime under Article 319 ter of the Italian criminal code (corruption of public duty in judicial capacity) should be charged if the judicial involvement is intended to favor an isolated member of the association. If, on the other hand, the involvement is intended to favor the criminal association as a whole, then complicity (*concorso esterno*) with the association shall be considered.

30 Although I do not notice that this is raised in Italian jurisprudence (perhaps precisely because it ends up being claimed as complicity), the generic legal provision of abuse of public duty should favor a solution of *concorso formale* (Article 81 Italian Penal Code).

31 "Corrado Carnevale" case, *Cassazione, Sezioni Unite*, 30 October 2002, n. 22327.
32 "Calogero Mannino" case, *Cassazione, Sezioni Unite*, 12 July 2005, n. 33748.
33 "Maxi Processo ter" case, *Cassazione, Sez. Penale* V, 15 May 2006, n. 16493.
34 Among others, critical of this development, Corvi (2006) (n 28), 1112, 1118; see also Caputo (2017) (18) 1300, 1329.

Bibliography

Barazzetta A, 'Art. 416 bis' in Dolcini E/Gatta G L (eds), *Codice Penale Commentato, vol 2* (5th edn, Wolters Kluwer 2021), 2148.

Cancio M, 'El "caso Manos Blancas": problemas de imputación en contextos de organización criminal a la luz del derecho penal español' in Couso J/Werle G (eds), *Intervención delictiva en contextos organizados. Humboldt-Kolleg Santiago 2015* (Tirant Lo Blanch 2017) 307.

Caputo M, 'Art. 416 bis' in Forti et al (eds), *Commentario breve al Codice Penale* (6th edn, Wolters Kluwer – CEDAM 2017) 1300.

Corvi A, 'Il concorso esterno del magistrate nell'associazione di tipo mafioso' (2006) 9 *Diritto Penale e Processo*, 1112.

Couso J, 'Art. 294' in Couso J/Hernández H (eds), *Código Penal Comentado. Parte Especial. Libro Segundo. Título VI* (Thomson 2019) 330.

Dubber M D/Hörnle T, *Criminal Law. A Comparative Approach* (Oxford University Press 2016).

García de Blanco V, 'Art. 570 bis' in *Memento Práctico* (Francis Lefebvre 2016) 1916.

Horvitz M I, 'El "caso Corvo y Moncada/Aislandia": Represión de protestas por una dictadura a la luz del derecho penal chileno' in Couso J/Werle G (eds), *Intervención delictiva en contextos organizados. Humboldt-Kolleg Santiago 2015* (Tirant Lo Blanch 2017) 155.

Londoño F, 'El "caso Manos Blancas": problemas de imputación en contextos de organización criminal a la luz del derecho penal chileno' in Couso J/Werle G (eds), *Intervención delictiva en contextos organizados. Humboldt-Kolleg Santiago 2015* (Tirant Lo Blanch 2017) 331.

Sánchez García de Paz I, 'Art. 570bis' in Tomillo M/Martín A M (eds), *Comentarios Prácticos al Código Penal, vol 6* (Thomson Reuters – Aranzadi) 553.

Viganò F, 'El "caso Manos Blancas": problemas de imputación en contextos de organización criminal a la luz del derecho penal italiano' in Couso J/Werle G (eds), *Intervención delictiva en contextos organizados. Humboldt-Kolleg Santiago 2015* (Tirant Lo Blanch 2017) 363.

Werle G/Jeßberger F, *Tratado de Derecho Penal International* (Tirant Lo Blanch 2017).

19 Judges as Criminal Associates of Totalitarian Regimes

The Chilean Case under the Framework of International Law

Rocío Lorca

19.1 Introduction

Despite their tendency to dismantle the institutions that support democracy and the rule of law, authoritarian regimes often use the judiciary as an instrument of governance and sometimes of repression. Ways in which the judiciary contributes to state repression in authoritarian regimes include directly violating individual rights through the application of unjust laws, ensuring impunity by concealing crimes, validating evidence obtained through torture, creating an appearance of legitimacy, and so on. The many ways in which the judiciary has been instrumental to authoritarian regimes around the world have raised a variety of questions about what judges should do in these circumstances and how they themselves should subsequently be judged from a moral, political, or legal standpoint.

Perhaps the question that has been most widely explored in legal scholarship is how judges should resolve a conflict between their moral conscience and their 'rule-of-law duty' to apply the law regardless of its content and effect. Should judges in antebellum Massachusetts have applied fugitive slave laws to enslaved people who managed to escape from the U.S. South?[1] Should South African judges have resisted the application of apartheid laws?[2] Or, more generally, are there cases in which laws are so extremely unjust that they are not morally, politically, or legally binding on judges?[3] Radbruch famously argued, referring to the Nazi legal system, that extremely unjust law is not valid law, and that as a consequence judges are under no rule-of-law-duty to apply it.[4] These fascinating questions are widely debated, and the debate offers no easy answers: it requires us to consider the demands and limits of the rule of law; the limits of the democratic principle of separation of powers; the ethics of judging; and the nature of law. Even in the collective literary imagination – think for example, of Captain Vere in Melville's Billy Bud, or Creon in Antigone – it seems very clear that while excessive legalism carries moral and practical risks, so too does the overstepping of role boundaries by authority figures who choose to act according to their personal view of what is just.

The question addressed in this chapter is of a more concrete and bounded nature: the legal accountability of judges for atrocities committed under their watch. Inspired by the 2017 conviction, in Argentine courts, of four judges and prosecutors in what was known as the Mendoza 'megacase',[5] the chapter narrows

DOI: 10.4324/9781003470069-23

its focus of enquiry in two senses. First, using the Chilean case as an example, it attends to one particular kind of judicial contribution: namely, the failure of judges to investigate and impose sanctions in cases formally brought to their attention. Second, the chapter discusses whether this kind of contribution can trigger criminal responsibility of judges for the commission of the same crimes they fail to investigate by considering them to be members of a criminal organization within the normative framework of international criminal law.

19.2 Judges as Associates of a Repressive State: The Chilean Case (1973–1990)

During the 1973–1990 Pinochet dictatorship in Chile, most human rights violations committed by state agents of repression took place in extrajudicial or informal spaces. Although some of the regime's victims were formally convicted of political crimes, and some of the summary executions carried out were ordered by military courts (albeit sometimes after the fact), most torture, imprisonment, and executions of political opponents were carried out unofficially.[6] Despite this secrecy, Chile's regular judiciary played an important role in maintaining Pinochet's policies and repressive system by neutralizing the legal resistance that came from civil society. It is therefore not surprising that the judiciary was the only branch of government to survive the military coup, and subsequent seventeen years of dictatorship, unscathed.

According to evidence gathered by Chile's first official truth commission, the Chilean judiciary offered three main kinds of assistance to the systematic violations of human rights committed by Pinochet's regime.[7] First, the judiciary aided and abetted the illegal and illegitimate conduct of the military courts by refraining from exercising its own appellate jurisdiction and disciplinary powers over military trials and tribunals. In the Chilean legal system, the Supreme Court can review cases tried by military courts and supervise their overall functioning. However, during the dictatorship, the Court acted as if it were incapable of exercising these powers, severely limiting the due process rights of citizens and leaving the military courts free from control or oversight.[8] Second, the Chilean judiciary openly assumed an ideological position in favor of Pinochet's administration, making active efforts to legitimize it. The Chilean Supreme Court explicitly endorsed the narrative presented by the military.[9] In a discourse delivered by its President in 1975, the Supreme Court denied that people were being tortured or made to disappear. Instead, the Court insisted that the avalanche of *habeas corpus* writs with which it was being presented was interfering with the work of the court, to the detriment of individual rights.[10] A third mode of collaboration, and possibly the one that has cast the longest shadow over judicial legitimacy, was the creation of a context of impunity by judges' refusal to apply the law and fulfill their rule-of-law duties.[11] This dereliction of duty took various forms. For example, Chilean judges did not sanction or investigate crimes committed by state agents of repression, even though denunciations and evidence were formally brought to their attention. On the rare occasions when judges did open investigations into such crimes, they quickly declared themselves incompetent and referred cases to the military tribunals, knowing that they would be closed.[12] Chilean judges also applied the self-amnesty decree introduced by the Pinochet regime in 1978 in a way that favored impunity and fostered further human rights violations, going beyond the provisions of the law itself in order to do so.[13] The most salient and pervasive way in which Chilean judges failed to do their job, however, was by systematically rejecting the thousands of *habeas corpus* petitions that were presented to them in the name of people detained for political motives.[14]

By failing to process these petitions, the judiciary created a context that facilitated Pinochet's program of extermination of political opponents and allowed its scope to widen.[15] If we draw on the considerations that sustained guilty verdicts against the Argentine judges in the abovementioned Mendoza case, the creation of this context is relevant to the question of the criminal responsibility of judges. This is so not because of the intrinsic wrongfulness of impunity, but because a context of impunity may be considered a causal factor in the commission of human rights violations.[16] If Chilean judges had processed *habeas corpus* writs as required by law, visiting detention centers with the requisite promptness, the state's killing machine might have been less lethal, and more than a few lives might have been saved. This last observation raises the question of whether judges can be held responsible for the crimes committed in these detention centers, and if so, what kind of responsibility might be in play.

19.3 Judging Our Judges: Moral and Political Responsibility

While space does not allow for more detailed delving here into the complex issues surrounding the moral or political responsibility of Chilean judges, in assessing their legal responsibility, it is important to keep in mind that moral and political accounting has increasingly been undertaken. The Chilean judiciary's unwillingness to apply the law and hold state agents accountable continued after the end of the dictatorship, but when Pinochet was detained in London in 1998, judges began to reopen many cases against Pinochet himself and other state agents.[17] This change in judicial practice was partly due to a political compromise with the executive branch of the day. In order to create the conditions that would allow Pinochet to be brought home and protected from prosecution in Europe, the Chilean state had to show a willingness and capacity to prosecute him. Such a move also implied, however, a willingness on Chile's part to engage in a process of accountability over its own justice system. As Alexandra Huneeus has argued, the post-1998 effort to reopen cases offered the judiciary a way to 'atone' for its past complicity with the regime.[18]

The process of reopening cases and making amends for the past was accompanied by the judiciary's public acknowledgment of its political responsibility for human rights violations committed during the dictatorship. In September 2013, in stark contrast to the statement made by the President of the Supreme Court in 1975, the same court recognized that atrocities had occurred during the dictatorship and that this was partly due to the inaction of judges who did not investigate human rights violations.[19]

Assuming, then, that judges participated in omissions that contributed to the systematic violation of human rights by creating a context of impunity, and that this contribution makes them morally and politically accountable for such violations, I now turn to the question of whether a contribution of this nature satisfies the requirements for criminal liability under international criminal law.

19.4 Judging Our Judges as Criminal Associates under International Criminal Law

It has historically been difficult to hold judges criminally accountable under international criminal law.[20] International crimes, unlike ordinary ones, are collectively perpetrated by more or less organized power structures. These structures create a context in which human rights violations can be systematically committed through fragmented contributions.[21] As is well known, this leads to several complications in the attribution of criminal responsibility to a particular member of these collective agencies: individual contributions are often difficult to prove and, even when proven, often do not meet the classic conditions for individual criminal responsibility. However, it is precisely this collective, diffuse, and fragmented mode of execution that makes these crimes particularly serious. The international criminal law enterprise accordingly needs to uphold a form of individual responsibility that is reflexive and cognizant of these features.

Chilean judges were not commanders in the organizations that violated human rights in Chile. Nor were they the intellectual creators or final executors of the plan to exterminate political opponents. Instead, by using the powers of their office, they created a context of impunity that facilitated the commission of these crimes. Is their contribution one that could make them liable as perpetrators, co-perpetrators, or accomplices under the terms of international criminal law? Did they act with the kind of state of mind required by whatever mode of responsibility we deem most appropriate? International criminal law offers different answers to these questions. Since the general lineaments of the issue are explored by other authors in this volume,[22] here I will focus on whether the contribution made by Chilean judges – i.e., securing impunity for state agents of repression – can be criminalized under the normative framework of organizational liability in international criminal law.

19.4.1 Organizational Liability in International Criminal Law: The Nuremberg Precedent

The International Military Tribunal (IMT) at Nuremberg only had jurisdiction to establish *individual* criminal responsibility. However, it used the framework of organizational liability to facilitate the prosecution of a large number of defendants whose particular causal contributions were hard to prove.[23] In the way it was used by the IMT, organizational liability also provided a mode of addressing and describing the systematic, collective, and bureaucratic modes of Nazi criminality while avoiding disguising individual guilt or falling prey to the unfairness of collective punishment.[24]

The Charter of the Nuremberg Tribunal established a two-step model of organizational liability.[25] The first step, established in Article 9, allowed the Court to declare a certain group to have been a criminal organization in the process of convicting a member of this group for the commission of crimes that fell under IMT jurisdiction. Once such a declaration of criminality was made against an organization, Article 10 of the same Charter allowed for subsequent prosecution of individuals for membership in such organizations.[26]

Here, organizational liability was seemingly being prized not primarily as a way to establish the criminal nature of the organizations *per se* but rather for its instrumental value in facilitating prosecutions and convictions. While no repercussions (punishment) would accrue to an organization as a result of being declared criminal under Article 9, such a declaration did enable prosecution for membership under the terms of Article 10. In practice, however, this normative framework had a more modest effect than could have been expected. Perhaps due to the novelty of the concept of organizational criminality and/or its potential for expanding criminal liability in a way that could implicate the innocent, the Tribunal only issued three judgments declaring certain organizations to have been criminal. The organizations in question were the SS, the Gestapo, the SD, and the Leadership Corps of the Nazi Party. For the purposes of establishing membership in these organizations, the Tribunal required knowledge of the criminal nature and aims of the organization as well as voluntary participation in them.[27] Possibly due to the introduction of these subjective requirements, very few defendants were ultimately punished for having been members of one of the IMT-designated Nazi Criminal Organizations.[28] This seems to have been so in both the national and international criminal proceedings that were subsequently followed against German Nazi judges.[29]

The so-called 'Justice Case' at the Nuremberg Trials is one of those that demonstrates a rather limited reach of international criminal law where judges were concerned. In this case, sixteen judicial officers were prosecuted over different charges brought under the IMT Charter. Although seven of them were charged with being members of organizations previously declared criminal by the Tribunal, only four of them were finally convicted on this count.[30]

Could Chilean judges be convicted under this same legal and doctrinal framework? A definitive answer would require a more detailed exploration of the doctrine, as well as the specific facts pertaining to Germany and to Chile. It, nonetheless, seems unlikely that Chilean judges could be considered criminally liable as members of an organization in charge of the commission of international crimes. The main obstacle, in my view, does not lie in declaring that Chilean agencies in charge of exterminating political opponents can be considered 'criminal organizations' in the same way that the SS, Gestapo, etc. were. Nor would it be difficult to establish that these agencies benefited from the contribution made by the Chilean judiciary. The principal barrier would lie, rather, in satisfying the subjective requirements for establishing membership.

One could infer from Chilean judges' inaction, combined with the fact that evidence was persistently brought to their attention, that they were aware of the possibility that they were contributing to the criminal plans of repressive agencies.[31]

However, it would be difficult to affirm, based on this evidence, that in so acting they were also willingly participating in the actions of these organizations.

19.4.2 Organizational Liability in International Criminal Law: The Ad Hoc Tribunals and the ICC

Since 1993, with the establishment of the International Criminal Tribunal for the former Yugoslavia, ICTY, criminal organizational liability has been mostly absent from international criminal law. This is probably because the instrumental value of organizational liability became redundant with the development of new legal doctrines of participation and liability.[32] The ICTY developed the concept of joint criminal enterprise (JCE) to define three modes of commission of international crimes, each of which took into account the collective and fragmented manner in which these crimes were committed.[33] This theory allowed for a wide incriminatory reach, probably wider than the one that can be sustained by invoking organizational liability. However, in all three modes of JCE, what is being judged is how, by engaging with the actions of a group, defendants may have participated in the commission of an international crime. JCE was not, in other words, aimed at establishing membership in a criminal organization, nor at supporting a crime of membership.

The International Criminal Court (ICC) no longer relies on the doctrine of joint criminal enterprise. The Rome Statute of the ICC offers a much more detailed regulation of modes of perpetration than have previous statutes of international criminal law. These modes have generally been interpreted using German scholar Claus Roxin's theory of commission, often called 'control theory.'[34] Both the Rome Statute's provisions and control theory allow for the incrimination of organized criminal structures without the need to rely on criminal organizational liability.

According to Roxin's theory, there are three modes of perpetration. Direct perpetration requires that the accused perform all elements of the crime, in this way exercising full control over its commission. Direct co-perpetration requires that the accused perform elements of the crime jointly with others, or fulfill an essential task that gives him or her functional control over the crime. Indirect perpetration, or perpetration-by-means, requires either that the accused control the will of those who directly perform the elements of the crime, or that he or she control the actions of an organization.[35] While the adoption of control theory has been criticized by some,[36] it has facilitated attributing responsibility to those who, while far removed from the commission of crimes, still created the context that made those crimes possible. This may include, for example, political and military leaders.[37] However, while the figure of indirect perpetration through an organization would allow the ICC to reach all the members of an organization, it does not aim to reach them *qua* members, but as perpetrators of the actual crimes committed by the organization. The chain reaches from the direct trigger person, through middlemen, to the one who designs the plan. Consequently, membership liability would not serve a clear purpose in international criminal law today as a method of ensuring individual accountability.

19.5 Conclusion

The behavior of Chilean judges analyzed in this chapter, while not the most serious of all the possible forms of judicial collaboration with authoritarian regimes, is a pervasive one. It consists of a failure to apply the law equally to all members of the political community. This omission creates a context of impunity that favors the introduction and expansion of programs of repression. Such programs often entail the systematic commission of human rights violations, and international crimes such as genocide or crimes against humanity.

The purpose of this chapter has not been to question the usefulness of maintaining the judiciary in contexts of authoritarian rule. Even though judiciaries are usually complicit in the illegal actions of such regimes, on balance it is probably better, during a totalitarian government, to have a judiciary than not to have one. This is so even when judicial failings are as serious as those discussed in this volume.[38] Nor did the chapter primarily set out to judge whether international criminal law provides a good mechanism for justice, accountability, and peace in the wake of atrocity. The strategy of responding to atrocity through the pursuit of individual responsibility has been widely criticized, and the present author subscribes to the tenor of many of these criticisms.[39]

The chapter however simply identified a particular subset of judiciaries, namely those who assist state criminal organizations in their perpetration of human rights violations by creating a context of impunity. It then set about considering whether judges in such judiciaries are criminally responsible for their conduct under international criminal law, as members of a criminal organization aimed at committing international crimes. It seems that while the law and practice of the Nuremberg Trials offered some possibilities, contemporary international criminal law does not. This raises the question of whether international criminal law should refocus on organizations, reconsidering the possibility not only of penalizing membership crimes but also of holding the organizations themselves criminally responsible.[40] As Saira Mohamed has argued, organizational responsibility was expected to play an important role at Nuremberg. It was expected to operate not only as a structure of incrimination but also as a way of expressing that international crimes, unlike ordinary crimes, are committed in an organized, systematic, and diffuse manner, and that this determines not only how, but also why, they are committed.[41] These characteristics of international crimes must be kept in mind to ensure an accurate description of the facts that are being related and adjudicated.

Notes

1 See Cover, *Justice Accused: Antislavery and the Judicial Process* (1975).

2 Dyzenhaus, *Judging the Judges, Judging Ourselves: Truth, Reconciliation and the Apartheid Legal Order* (1998).

3 The so-called Radbruch Formula and the criticisms of it raised by H L A Hart gave rise to the ongoing controversy between legal positivists and non-positivists. For a general account, see Hart, 'Positivism and the Separation of Law and Morals' in Kenneth (ed)

63–99; Lon L Fuller, 'Positivism and Fidelity to Law: A Reply to Professor Hart' (1957) 71 *Harv L Rev* 630; Green, 'Positivism and the Inseparability of Law and Morals' (2008) 83 *NYU L Rev* 1035; Moore, 'Hart, Radbruch and the Necessary Connection Between Law and Morals' (2020) 39 *LaP* 691; Toharia 'Judicial Independence in an Authoritarian Regime: The Case of Contemporary Spain' (1974) 9 *Law Soc Rev* 475, 476.

4 Radbruch G, 'Statutory Lawlessness and Supra-statutory Law (1946)' (2006) 26 (1) *Oxf. J. Leg. Stud.* 1 et seqq.

5 '*Megacausa*', a term widely used in Argentina for any one of numerous large-scale domestic trials for dictatorship-era crimes against humanity. This particular one is now often referred to as the 'megacase-judges' trial' to differentiate it from a second megacase, currently ongoing, also in Mendoza ('megacase D2'). On the judges' trial, see the chapter in this volume by Omar Palermo.

6 CNVR, Informe de la Comisión Nacional de Verdad y Reconciliación (1991), I, Vol. 1, 116 et seqq.

7 Chile's National Truth and Reconciliation Commission, widely referred to as the 'Rettig Commission', was set up in 1990 and reported in 1991. For its observations about judicial failings, see CNVR (1991) (n 6) 95 et seqq. An English language summary translation of the report is available at: www.usip.org/sites/default/files/resources/collections/truth_commissions/Chile90-Report/Chile90-Report.pdf (accessed 1 August 2024).

8 See, on this point, Horvitz, 'La Jurisdicción Militar Hoy: Balance y Tareas Pendientes' in Couso et al (eds), 611, 614 et seqq; Couso, 'Responsabilidad Penal por la Intervención en Crímenes de la Dictadura en el Ejercicio de Roles Judiciales. Perspectivas Comparadas para una Exploración en Chile' in Couso et al (eds), 487–510.

9 Huneeus, 'Judging from a Guilty Conscience: The Chilean Judiciary's Human Rights Turn' (2010) 35 (1) *LSI* 99, 103–104.

10 CNVR (1991) (n 6) 96.

11 Given the hierarchical structure of the Chilean judiciary, this attitude was sometimes spontaneous and was sometimes imposed by internal pressures, as judges who were willing to abide by their legal duties were systematically harassed and sanctioned by higher courts. See Horvitz (2021) (n 8), Couso (n 8), and Huneeus (2010) (n 9) 103.

12 Aguilar, 'Jueces, represión y justicia transicional en España, Chile y Argentina' (2013) 71 (2) *RIS* 252, 281.

13 According to Chilean Decree Law 2.191 of 1978, amnesty had to be applied after the conclusion of a criminal investigation. However, whenever the amnesty was potentially applicable, Chilean judges would close the cases without pursuing any enquiry at all. See CNVR (1991) (n 6) 95–104.

14 According to a report by Chile's second official truth commission, the National Commission on Political Imprisonment and Torture (often referred to as the 'Valech Commission'), of around 9.000 *habeas corpus* petitions presented during the dictatorship, only about 28 were duly processed. See CNPPT, Informe de la Comisión Nacional sobre Prisión Política y Tortura (2005) 173.

15 See, on this, CNVR (1991) (n 6) 97 and 102–104, and CNPPT (2005) (n 14) 171 et seqq.

16 This was certainly the view expressed by both of Chile's truth commissions and has long been the view of international human rights organizations. For a more detailed account of this view, see Lorca, 'Should Feminist Worry About Impunity?' (2024) 37 (1) *HHRJ* 52–56, and Amnesty International, 'Policy Statement on Impunity' in Kritz (ed) 219.

17 See Huneeus (2010) (n 9) 105.

18 One piece of evidence suggesting that this shift was motivated by a sense of guilt and a search for atonement is the fact that the Chilean judiciary did not engage in a general

shift toward the protection of human rights. Instead, it made a limited effort to prosecute dictatorship-era human rights violations (see Huneeus (2010) (n 9) 128–130). Another piece of evidence is that, according to Huneeus, the government tried to contain the political tensions unleashed by trials by limiting the attention of the judiciary to certain cases and limiting the severity of punishment. Investigative magistrates, however, resisted pressure to limit their attention, rebelling against their hierarchical superiors. The new investigations came under intense public scrutiny, with judges who prosecuted Pinochet-era crimes being celebrated by some sectors of the media and civil society. This limited the ability of the hierarchy to control them, giving judges a unique opportunity to push the cases forward. Huneeus (2010) (n 9) 106 et seq and 111 et seq.

19 "We cannot fail to acknowledge that if these atrocities did indeed occur – which they did – this was due in part to omission of action on the part of the judges of the time, who did not do enough to investigate whether these crimes were in fact taking place". Author's translation. Full text of the original declaration available at: https://media.elmostrador.cl/2013/09/Declaraci%C3%B3n-Corte-Suprema.pdf (accessed 14 August 2024).

20 Graver, 'Judging without Impunity: On the Criminal Responsibility of Authoritarian Judges' (2016) 4 (1) *BJCLCJ* 125 et seqq.

21 See Smeulers, 'A Criminological Approach to the ICC's Control Theory' in Heller et al (eds) 379, 383.

22 See the contributions of Jaime Couso and Elies van Sliedregt in this volume.

23 Mohamed, 'From Machinery to Motivation: The Lost Legacy of Criminal Organizations Liability' in Heller et al (eds) 498; Bush, 'Nuremberg: The Modern Law of War and Its Limitations' (1993) 93 (8) *Colum. L. Rev.* 2076.

24 Mohamed, 'From Machinery to Motivation: The Lost Legacy of Criminal Organizations Liability' in Heller et al (eds) 498.

25 See Mohamed (2020) (n 23) 498 et seqq.

26 See the Charter of the International Military Tribunal (Annex to the Agreement for the Prosecution and Punishment of the Major War Criminals of the European Axis ("London Agreement"),) United Nations, 8 August 1945. www.refworld.org/legal/constinstr/un/1945/en/21123 (accessed 6 February 2024).

27 Mohamed (2020) (n 23) 501 et seqq. According to Mohamed, other salient organizations, such as the Reich Cabinet and the High Command of the German Armed Forces, were not declared criminal because they had few members and the process of using membership liability was not required regarding them.

28 From a total of 87 defendants charged with criminal membership, only 74 were finally convicted. See Mohamed (2020) (n 23) 503.

29 According to Graver, mens rea requirements proved to be a good shield against conviction, and gave rise to a doctrine of 'malicious motive' which would explain the lack of convictions in these cases. Mens rea requirements were coupled with a kind of judicial immunity created through a set of excuses for judges. The outcome was that no judges were convicted in post-Nazi trials, except for the ones convicted by the US Military Tribunal. Graver (2016) (n 20) 135–138. (See, however, Florian Jeßberger and Milan Kuhli's chapter in this volume, which claims that some judges – albeit only a handful – were indeed convicted in Germany's post-Nazi trials.)

30 Josef Altstotter and Günther Joël, for membership of the SS; and Rudolph Oeschey and Oswald Rothaug, for membership of the Leadership Corps of the Nazi Party. Due to the criticisms that followed the trials against Nazi judges, post-reunification (i.e., post-1990) German courts moved from the doctrine of malicious intent. They replaced it with a broad standard under which judges could be convicted for bending the law when the

outcomes had included "substantial and manifest human rights violations, intolerable disproportionate punishments, and substantial violations of the right to a fair trial". This allowed for a significant number of convictions of judges. The concept as described would certainly capture the behavior of Chilean judges, but since it has been largely considered too broad a standard for criminal conviction, it has not been endorsed in international criminal law. Graver (2016) (n 20) 138 et seq.

31 Namely, Pinochet's political or secret police, whose aim was to exterminate political opponents. The first such agency was the Dirección de Inteligencia Nacional, DINA (1973/4–1977); later replaced by the Central Nacional de Informaciones, CNI (1977–1990).

32 See Mohamed (2020) (n 23).

33 Cryer et al. (eds) *An Introduction to International Criminal Law and Procedure* (Cambridge University Press 2019) 344 et seqq. See also the chapter by Elise Van Sliedregt, in this volume.

34 Cryer et al. (eds) *An Introduction to International Criminal Law and Procedure* (Cambridge University Press 2019) 344 et seqq.

35 Cryer et al. (eds) *An Introduction to International Criminal Law and Procedure* (Cambridge University Press 2019) 344 et seqq.

36 SáCouto, 'Collective Criminality and Sexual Violence: Fixing a Failed Approach' (2020) 33 (1) *LJIL* 207, 223.

37 Smeulers (2020) (n 21) 389 et seqq.

38 Judges can only be instrumental *qua* judges if their actions embody some kind of rudimentary rule of law which can impose some limits, however modest, on the abuses committed by such regimes. See, in this line, Ginsburg/Moustafa, Rule by Law: The Politics of Courts in Authoritarian Regimes in Ginsburg/Moustafa (eds) 1, 21.

39 See, generally, Koskenniemi, 'Between Impunity and Show Trials' in Frowein/Wolfrum (eds) 1–32; Van der Wilt H, 'Selectivity in International Criminal Law: Asymmetrical Enforcement as a Problem for Theories of Punishment' in Jeßberger/Geneuss (eds) 305 et seqq. Drumbl, *Atrocity, Punishment and International Law* (2007) 149–180; Tallgren, 'The Sensibility and Sense of International Criminal Law' (2002) 13 (3) *EJIL* 561–595. Kiyan, 'Group-Based Differentiation and Local Repression: The Custom and Curse of Selectivity' (2016) 14 (4) *JICJ* 939–957; Lorca, 'Impunity Thick and Thin: The International Criminal Court in the Search for Equality' (2022) 35 (2) *LJIL* 421–431; Lorca, 'Castigar sin Estado: Consideraciones sobre la Corte Penal Internacional y la Naturaleza del Derecho Penal' (2020) 15 (29) *Polít. crim.* 290–309.

40 See Mohamed (2020) (n 23) and Stahn, *A Critical Introduction to International Criminal Law* (2018) 119–121 and 125–126 (claiming that despite the collective nature of international crime, international criminal law has been hostile to punishing organizations as such, to avoid coming closer to the idea that they are punishing the state). This, however, omits accountability not just of public institutions but also of corporations.

41 Mohamed (2020) (n 23).

Bibliography

Aguilar P, 'Jueces, represión y justicia transicional en España, Chile y Argentina' (2013) 71 (2) *Revista internacional de sociología* 281.

Amnesty International, 'Policy Statement on Impunity' in Kritz, *Transitional Justice: How Emerging Democracies Reckon with Former Regimes* (US Institute of Peace Press 1995) 219.

Bush J, 'Nuremberg: the modern law of war and its limitations' (1993) 93 (8) *Columbia Law Review* 2076.

Couso J, 'Responsabilidad Penal por la Intervención en Crímenes de la Dictadura en el Ejercicio de Roles Judiciales. Perspectivas Comparadas para una Exploración en Chile' in Couso J et al (eds), *Justicia Criminal y Dogmática Penal en la Era de los Derechos Humanos* (Thomson Reuters 2021) 487.

Cover R M, *Justice Accused: Antislavery and the Judicial Process* (Yale University Press 1975).

Cryer R et al, *An Introduction to International Criminal Law and Procedure* (Cambridge University Press 2019).

Drumbl M, *Atrocity, Punishment and International Law* (Cambridge University Press 2007).

Dyzenhaus D, *Judging the Judges, Judging Ourselves: Truth, Reconciliation and the Apartheid Legal Order* (Hart Publishing 1998).

Ginsburg T/Moustafa T, 'Rule by Law: The Politics of Courts in Authoritarian Regimes' in Ginsburg/Moustafa (eds), *Introduction: The Functions of Courts in Authoritarian Politics* (Cambridge University Press 2008) 1.

Graver H P, 'Judging without Impunity: On the Criminal Responsibility of Authoritarian Judges' (2016) 4 (1) *Bergen Journal of Criminal Law & Criminal Justice* 125.

Green L, 'Positivism and the Inseparability of Law and Morals' (2008) 83 *NYU Law Review* 1035.

Hart H L A, '*Positivism and the Separation of Law and Morals*' (first published 1958) in Kenneth E H (ed), *Law and Morality* (Routledge 2017) 63.

Horvitz M I, 'La Jurisdicción Militar Hoy: Balance y Tareas Pendientes' in Couso J et al (eds), *Justicia Criminal y Dogmática Penal en la Era de los Derechos Humanos* (Thomson Reuters 2021) 487.

Huneeus A, 'Judging from a Guilty Conscience: The Chilean Judiciary's Human Rights Turn' (2010) 35 (1) *Law & Social Inquiry* 99.

Kiyan A, 'Group-Based Differentiation and Local Repression: The Custom and Curse of Selectivity' (2016) 14 (4) *Journal of International Criminal Justice* 939.

Koskenniemi M, 'Between Impunity and Show Trials' in Frowein J A/Wolfrum R (eds), *Max Planck Yearbook of United Nations Law Online* (Kluwer Law International 2002) 1.

Kritz N (ed), *Transitional Justice: How Emerging Democracies Reckon with Former Regimes* (US Institute of Peace Press 1995).

Lon L F, 'Positivism and Fidelity to Law: A Reply to Professor Hart' (1957) 71 *Harvard Law Review* 630.

Lorca R, 'Castigar sin Estado: Consideraciones sobre la Corte Penal Internacional y la Naturaleza del Derecho Penal' (2020) 15 (29) *Politíca criminal* 290.

Lorca R, 'Impunity Thick and Thin: The International Criminal Court in the Search for Equality' (2022) 35 (2) *Leiden Journal of International Law* 421.

Lorca R, 'Should Feminist Worry About Impunity?' (2024) 37 (1) *Harvard Human Rights Journal* 47.

Mohamed S, 'From Machinery to Motivation: The Lost Legacy of Criminal Organizations Liability' in Heller K et al (eds), *The Oxford Handbook of International Criminal Law* (Oxford University Press 2020) 494.

Moore J G, 'Hart, Radbruch and the Necessary Connection Between Law and Morals' (2020) 39 *Law and Philosophy* 691.

Radbruch G, 'Statutory Lawlessness and Supra-statutory Law (1946)' (first published 1946) (2006) 26 (1) *Oxford Journal of Legal Studies* 1.

SáCouto S/Sadat L N/Sellers P V, 'Collective Criminality and Sexual Violence: Fixing a Failed Approach' (2020) 33 (1) *Leiden Journal of International Law* 207.

Smeulers A, 'A Criminological Approach to the ICC's Control Theory' in Heller K et al (eds), *The Oxford Handbook of International Criminal Law* (Oxford University Press 2020) 379.

Stahn C, *A Critical Introduction to International Criminal Law* (Cambridge University Press 2018).

Tallgren I, 'The Sensibility and Sense of International Criminal Law' (2002) 13 (3) *European Journal of International Law* 561.

Toharia J J, 'Judicial Independence in an Authoritarian Regime: The Case of Contemporary Spain' (1974) 9 *Law & Society Review* 475.

Van der Wilt H, 'Selectivity in International Criminal Law: Asymmetrical Enforcement as a Problem for Theories of Punishment' in Jeßberger F/Geneuss J (eds), *Why Punish Perpetrators of Mass Atrocities?: Purposes of Punishment in International Criminal Law* (Cambridge University Press 2020) 305.

20 A Judge's Participation in a Criminal or Terrorist Organization

From Nuremberg to Contemporary German Criminal Law

Julia Geneuss

20.1 Introduction

This chapter addresses the question of whether, under German criminal law, a judge can be held criminally responsible for membership in a criminal or terrorist organization on the basis of judicial activity they undertook under dictatorial rule. It should be made clear at the outset that the chapter does not deal with the attribution of liability for one or more specific crimes – such as crimes against humanity, murder, torture, and illegal detention – that a judge or any other member of the judiciary has committed or participated in as instigator or aider and abettor. Accordingly, forms or types of criminal responsibility, such as joint criminal enterprise or conspiracy – concepts that do not, moreover, feature as such in German criminal law – will not be discussed.[1] The chapter also omits discussion of the crime of judicial perversion of justice or other judiciary-specific or public official-specific crimes. Instead, the analysis focuses on the specifically organizational crime of a judge's membership in an association deemed criminal, or perhaps even terrorist, under German criminal law.

Currently, membership in a criminal or terrorist organization is a crime under sections 129 and 129a, respectively, of the German Criminal Code (*Strafgesetzbuch*). Organizational crimes of this sort offer the advantage, for prosecutors, of being able to overcome evidentiary obstacles that often arise when attempting to establish specific modes of participation, intent, or causality regarding a particular crime, obstacles that can loom particularly large in cases of judicial involvement in international core crimes. Although the category of organizational crimes is rightly criticized for various reasons, particularly in the 'ordinary criminal law'-context,[2] the other crimes like murder, etc. can be regarded as a useful instrument inasmuch as they offer at least some prospect of capturing the role of judges and other members of the judiciary in a dictatorial state. Since the judiciary is an essential part of the apparatus needed to maintain dictatorial regimes, judicial complicity should surely be addressed wherever there are post-conflict criminal prosecutions.

This chapter will first provide a historical perspective on whether participation in a criminal association played a role in prosecutions of members of the judiciary in the aftermath of the two most recent German dictatorships. The chapter will then enquire whether today's German criminal law could, at least in theory, hold judges

DOI: 10.4324/9781003470069-24

liable for the crime of membership in a criminal or terrorist organization on the basis of their exercise of judicial functions, concluding that this is unlikely on the basis of practice to date. Although, as we will see, organizational crimes are very broadly delineated in German criminal law, with the crime of membership in a terrorist organization moreover specifically covering situations where international crimes are committed, prevailing interpretation and practice do not seem to understand the provisions as including behavior by members of state organizations. Accordingly, judicial complicity in state crimes would not be covered.

20.2 Historical Perspective

Taking a historical perspective, the issue of liability for participation in a criminal organization does not seem to have arisen in post-Cold War prosecution of judicial figures for their involvement in the East German socialist regime of 1949 to 1989. Accordingly, only post-Second World War trials of members of the Nazi-era judiciary are relevant to the specific topic addressed by this chapter. Two such trials are particularly important for present purposes. The first is the trial of leading German political, military, and economic officials before the International Military Tribunal (IMT) at Nuremberg, during which a number of organizations were declared criminal. In the subsequent 'Justices Trial' before a US Military Tribunal, some members of the judiciary were convicted of membership in one of these organizations (alongside other crimes). Neither of these trials, of course, applied German criminal law, specifically. Nonetheless, they set an important precedent regarding the responsibility of judges – or, to be more precise, justice system officers – for the organizational crime of membership in a criminal organization in the context of international criminal law.

20.2.1 The International Military Tribunal: Charter and Trial

The IMT Charter contains two articles that relate to the crime of membership in a criminal organization, namely, Articles 9 and 10. Article 9 reads as follows:

> At the trial of any individual member of any group or organization the Tribunal may declare (in connection with any act of which the individual may be convicted) that the group or organization of which the individual was a member was a criminal organization.
> [...]

Article 10 reads:

> In cases where a group or organization is declared criminal by the Tribunal, the competent national authority of any Signatory shall have the right to bring individual *[sic.]* to trial for membership therein before national, military or occupation courts. In any such case the criminal nature of the group or organization is considered proved and shall not be questioned.

The purpose of both provisions was to be able to prosecute individuals for their membership in organizations that were declared criminal by the Military Tribunal, also in subsequent criminal proceedings before Allied courts.[3] The main Nuremberg Trial of 1945–1946, whose defendants were Nazi Germany's most important political and military leaders, ruled a number of organizations to be criminal under the terms of IMT Charter Article 9. These included the Leadership Corps of the NSDAP, that is, the Nazi Party (*Nationalsozialistische Deutsche Arbeiterpartei*); the SS (*Schutzstaffel*), a paramilitary security organization of the Nazi Party; the Gestapo (*Geheime Staatspolizei*), the secret police force of the Nazi state, notorious for its terrorism and brutality; and the SD (*Sicherheitsdienst*), that is, the intelligence agency of the SS and the Nazi Party itself.[4] The International Military Tribunal, however, expressly limited its declaration of group criminality to persons who became or remained members of such an organization with knowledge that the organization was being used for criminal acts or who were personally implicated as members of the organization in the commission of such crimes.[5] Membership alone was not sufficient for being held criminally accountable.

20.2.2 The US Military Tribunal: The Justices Trial

The year 1947 saw the Justices Trial – "The United States of America vs. Josef Altstötter, et al." – held before the US Military Tribunal at Nuremberg. There were fifteen defendants (one had previously died), three of whom were charged and eventually convicted for voluntary membership in a criminal organization with full knowledge of the criminal character of that organization.[6] The three defendants were Josef Altstötter, Günther Joël, and Rudolf Oeschey. Altstötter, who had been chief of the civil law and procedure division of the Ministry of Justice, was convicted of voluntary membership in the SS. Joël, former legal advisor and chief prosecutor at the Ministry of Justice, was found guilty of membership in the SS and SD. Oeschey, who had officiated during the war as Chief Justice of the Special Court at Nuremberg, was convicted for being a member of the Leadership Corps of the NSDAP at the district level in his wartime capacity as head of the Lawyers' League for the Bavarian administrative district of Gau Franconia.[7] All three of the defendants convicted on this particular charge, i.e., of membership in a criminal organization, were part of the judicial administration of the Nazi State. It was not their judicial activity as such that led to their convictions. Rather, they were each deemed to have made a career in judicial administration precisely because of their committed membership in organizations later declared criminal by the International Military Tribunal.

It should be noted that this approach to membership crimes has been discontinued and cannot be found in modern international criminal law. The 1998 Rome Statute of the International Criminal Court does not, for instance, contain a comparable membership crime. In particular, although its specific dogmatic structure is still unclear, Article 25(3)(d) of the Rome Statute, according to which a person's contribution to a group crime is punishable, sets out only a form of individual participation in a specific international crime. It does not establish a membership crime.[8]

20.3 The Applicable Legal Framework under German Criminal Law

In present-day German criminal law, in the German Criminal Code membership in a criminal or terrorist organization is a crime under sections 129 and 129a, respectively. The distinction that is drawn between a criminal organization (section 129) and a terrorist organization (section 129a) hinges around the crimes towards which the organization's objectives or activities are directed. In the case of a criminal organization, these objectives or activities are stipulated as being directed at the commission of offenses that incur a maximum penalty of two or more years' imprisonment. Where international core crimes are involved, however, the more serious offense of membership in a terrorist organization is the one that applies. According to section 129a of the German Criminal Code, entitled 'Forming Terrorist Organizations', an organization qualifies as terrorist if its objectives or activities are directed at the commission of certain grave crimes. When the German Code of Crimes Against International Law (*Völkerstrafgesetzbuch*) came into force in 2002, the international core crimes covered by the new Code were added to the existing list of grave crimes to which section 129a applies. Accordingly, under domestic law today, Germany's designation of a terrorist organization includes groups whose objectives or activities are directed at the commission of genocide, crimes against humanity, and war crimes (section 129a, para. 1, no. 1). Certain subtypes of murder and offenses against personal liberty are also contemplated (section 129a, para. 1, nos. 1 and 2). Note, however, the explicit absence of the crime of aggression, added to the German Code of Crimes Against International Law in 2017, which covers interstate violence.
Paragraph (1) of section 129a, 'Forming Terrorist Organizations', reads[9]:

> (1) Whoever forms an organization [defined according to] (section 129 (2)) whose objectives or activities are directed at the commission of:
> 1. murder under specific aggravating circumstances (section 211) or murder (section 212) or genocide (section 6 of the Code of Crimes against International Law) or a crime against humanity (section 7 of the Code of Crimes against International Law) or a war crime (sections 8, 9, 10, 11, or 12 of the Code of Crimes against International Law) or
> 2. offenses against personal liberty under section 239a or section 239b,
> 3. (repealed)
>
> or whoever participates as a member of such an organization incurs a penalty of imprisonment for a term of between one year and 10 years. [...]

Paragraph (5) of section 129a states that:

> (5) Whoever supports an organization as described in subsection (1), (2), or (3) incurs a penalty of imprisonment for a term of between six months and 10 years in the cases under subsections (1) and (2) and a penalty of imprisonment for a term not exceeding five years or a fine in the cases under subsection (3). Whoever recruits members or supporters for an organization as described in subsection (1) or (2) incurs a penalty of imprisonment for a term of between six months and five years. [...]

In contrast to paragraph (2) of section 129a, which lists a number of less serious crimes, paragraph (1) of the section does not contain an additional requirement of ideological intent. Paragraph (2), by contrast, follows the practice of the EU Framework Decision on Combating Terrorism, by additionally requiring that the crimes it lists must, if they are to merit the penalties associated with the 'terrorist' classification, be committed by an organization whose intention is or includes "to seriously intimidate the population, to unlawfully coerce an authority or an international organization by force or threat of force, or to destroy or significantly impair the fundamental political, constitutional, economic or social structures of a state or of an international organization and which, given the nature or consequences of such offences, may seriously damage a state or an international organization".[10] Given the inherent seriousness of the crimes listed in paragraph (1), the legislator deemed it unnecessary to include this additional, and restrictive, qualifying element regarding the perpetrating organization's intentions.[11]

20.3.1 Existence of an Organization

Paragraph (2) of section 129 is dedicated to a definition of the term 'organization', employing rather broad terms, which apply to both criminal and terrorist organizations:

> An organization is a structured association of more than two persons, established to exist for a longer period of time, regardless of whether it has formally defined roles for its members, continuous membership or a developed structure and whose purpose is the pursuit of an overriding common interest.[12]

According to this definition, the association must have a certain level of structure in order to be deemed an organization. However, the requirements are quite low: rudimentary organizational structures should suffice. Currently – since 2017 – the wording also includes hierarchical associations in which the members submit to the authoritarian will of a leader.[13] Above all, for section 129 to apply, it is necessary that the organization pursues an overarching common interest, such as is commonly in evidence in associations seeking to further ideological, ideological, religious, or political goals.[14]

To fit the definition, an institutionally organized criminal association is one that aims to commit certain crimes. This constituent element of the organization's objectives – criminality – is, however, also broadly defined. The commission of the crimes listed in the provision does not have to be the main or ultimate purpose of the organization, nor constitute the whole of its activity. It is sufficient that the crimes are committed in preparation of the actual aim of the organization. It is also not required that a specific crime of the ones listed in paragraphs one or two provision should already have been committed, nor even planned. The mere existence of an organization with emerging group dynamics that fit the definition is regarded as sufficient to create a risk to the protected legal good, thereby making it legitimate to criminalize the organization.[15]

20.3.2 Actus Reus: *Membership Activity*

While paragraph one of sections 129 and 129a each criminalize membership in a criminal or terrorist organization, they do not explain what constitutes membership as the *actus reus* of the crime. Most of the existing detail on this point was therefore established through case law, according to which anyone who submits to the overall will of a criminal or terrorist organization and its objectives and undertakes activities that promote it, is liable to be deemed to be a member.[16] From an objective point of view, this subordination is shown by participation in activities that further the criminal or terrorist objectives. This activity may consist of the commission of a crime, including one of the crimes listed in the text of the provision, but it can also take the form of non-criminal, i.e., legal, activity.[17]

An example can be drawn from recent German practice in international criminal law: female returnees from Syria were initially charged, by Germany's Federal Prosecutor General, with membership in a terrorist organization – namely, the so-called 'Islamic State' (IS). As regards the membership requirement, the prosecutor cited the raising of a child in the dominion of the 'Islamic State' and the carrying out of household chores while living with an IS fighter as active membership activities.[18] While the Federal Court of Justice, by contrast, held that these everyday activities could not be regarded as membership activity, the Court at the same time emphasized that activities that are legal in themselves can also constitute participatory acts within the meaning of paragraph (1) of sections 129 and 129a.[19]

If the *actus reus* of membership in a criminal or terrorist organization is to be interpreted in a broad manner, it could be argued that a judge's membership activity could likewise consist of a variety of judicial activities, some otherwise legal, some not. Drawing on the typology proposed by Robert Barros,[20] such judicial activity could range from 'extrajuridical repression' (e.g., unauthorized detention, torture, disappearance, and execution) to 'administrative repression', that is, activities that clearly violate the rule of law. Other judicial activity, where the violation of rule of law standards is less clear, could, however, also be regarded as membership activity. This seems true in particular for Barros's category of 'summary (quasi-) judicial repression', where some form of proceedings is undertaken, but the application of the law is flawed. This may consist, for example, of the use of retroactive, secret, or vague laws; limitation of the right to a defence or the application of dubious evidentiary standards. It can also describe legal repression of political opponents, where regular judicial mechanisms may be employed but there is a draconian application of the law.

What seems more difficult to argue is that omission could also constitute some sort of membership activity. A member of the organization, in order to be considered as such, must have submitted to the will of the organization and actively promoted the association's ends. This submission might be difficult to construe solely from the omission of a legally required conduct. Omission might, however, be regarded as constituting the crime of 'supporting' the organization, pursuant to section 129a paragraph five. This is a different and less severe crime when compared to the crime of membership, whereby the supporter furthers the organization without being part of its structures. In other words, the perpetrator does not specifically need to have fully submitted to the organization; it may suffice that their promotional act or omission is objectively useful to the association.

20.3.3 Mens Rea: Dolus Eventualis

The minimal mens rea standard required for the crime of membership in a terrorist organization is *dolus eventualis*,[21] i.e., the intent must relate to the existence of an organization. In addition, the perpetrator must at least consider it possible and accept with approval that the efforts and objectives of the organization include the commission of crimes that are catalogue offenses, that is, inter alia, crimes under international law.

20.3.4 Narrow Interpretation: Application to Non-state Organizations

In sum, under German criminal law, it is a crime to form an organization, participate in one as a member, supporter, or recruiter of other members or supporters when the organization's objectives or activities are directed at the commission of crimes under international law – genocide, crimes against humanity, and war crimes. So at least in theory, given this wording, the crime of membership in a terrorist organization could apply to state organizations that implement a policy of human rights violations amounting to international core crimes. In consequence, the crime could also encompass judges who are members of such organizations and who further such objectives or activities by their judicial activity.

There is, however, one major obstacle that would prevent a judge from being held criminally liable for their participation in a terrorist organization. Hitherto, the predominant interpretation and application of this provision by the German prosecution authorities has been to treat it as only applying to non-state groups (even though this is not explicitly stipulated in the text of the provision).[22] This interpretive practice is in evidence if we consider cases currently before German courts over crimes committed during the ongoing conflict in Syria. A look at these cases shows differential treatment of non-state and state agents, namely, members of the 'Islamic State', on the one hand, and members or former members of Syrian state intelligence agencies on the other. For example, in a large number of cases brought in Germany against 'fighters' or 'foreign fighters' – alleged members of IS or other non-state jihadist armed groups – individuals have been both charged with and convicted of membership in a terrorist organization, under section 129a, plus a specific crime under international law (usually a war crime, but in some cases a crime against humanity). In this set of cases, charges under international criminal law and under counter-terrorism criminal law are overlaid on one another. In contrast, Syrian state officials have been charged (only) with crimes under international law and perhaps other ordinary domestic crimes, but section 129a has not been invoked. For example, in what is commonly referred to as the 'Al-Khatib trial', two Syrian secret service officers were prosecuted before the Koblenz Higher Regional Court. The defendants were charged with crimes against humanity, pursuant to section 7 of the German Code of Crimes against International Law, as well as with a number of ordinary domestic crimes. This was in connection with the violent suppression of Syrian opposition figures through means including torture and killings.[23] The crime of membership in a terrorist organization did not play any role whatsoever in the proceedings. This despite the fact that a sound case could surely be made, first, that the Syrian secret service is an organization in the sense of section 129a of the German Criminal Code; second, that it systematically committed crimes against humanity during the relevant time period; and third, that the acts of the two defendants in arresting, kidnapping, interrogating, and torturing political opponents fall under the definition of membership activity.

To date, however, the predominant view has been that the concept of terrorism on which the relevant German criminal law provisions are based covers only 'private' violence, aimed directly or indirectly at states by groups that challenge state authority. Accordingly, state entities such as armed forces or intelligence services are being treated as not qualifying as terrorist organizations under section 129a paragraph 1 no. 1 of the German Criminal Code, even when their objectives and activities are directed at the commission of core international crimes. As mentioned above, this interpretation goes beyond the wording of the provision, which does not necessarily imply any such limitation to non-state actors. One might argue that this narrow interpretation enters into contradiction with the 'Nuremberg Law'. In broad-brush terms, it can be argued that the concept of 'state terrorism', deployed for the oppression of political opponents and one's own population, was brought into the realm of international criminal law by the time of the Nuremberg trials at the latest.[24] By today, excluding state-affiliated organizations from the organizational crime of membership in a terrorist organization that is part of international criminal law, the German courts' direction of travel moves away from attention on state-perpetrated, sponsored, or amplified crimes toward a focus on the criminalization of non-state actions.

20.4 Conclusion

In sum, the organizational crimes of membership in a criminal or terrorist organization are drawn very broadly under the letter of German criminal law. The crime of membership in a terrorist organization specifically covers situations where crimes under international law are being committed, and as we have seen, the required membership activity could in theory describe a variety of judicial activities, including activities that are legal in and of themselves. However, prevailing interpretation and practice do not seem to understand organizational crimes as applicable to state crimes, meaning that the figures are not being applied to judicial activity.

Notes

1 For a thorough discussion of similarities and differences, see Burghardt, 'Die Strafsache "Oskar Gröning" vor dem Bundesgerichtshof – Zugleich Überlegungen zum Begriff

der teilnahmefähigen Haupttat i.S.v. § 27 Abs. 1 StGB bei arbeitsteilig organisierten, systemischen Handlungszusammenhängen' (2019) 14 *ZIS* 32.

2 For this criticism, see, e.g., Weißer, 'Die Entwicklung des deutschen Terrorismusstrafrechts – Expansionen und notwendige Eingrenzungen' (2019) 20 *RW* 453; Hawickhorst K, *§ 129a StGB – Ein feindstrafrechtlicher Irrweg zur Terrorismusbekämpfung, Kritische Analyse einer prozessualen Schlüsselnorm im materiellen Recht* (Duncker & Humblot 2011).

3 See Werle/Jeßberger, *Principles of international Criminal Law* (2020), para 145.

4 IMT, Judgment of 1 October 1946, in The Trial of German Major War Criminals. Proceedings of the International Military Tribunal sitting at Nuremberg, Germany, Part 22 (22 August 1946 to 1 October 1946), 468 et seqq.

5 IMT, Judgment of 1 October 1946, in The Trial of German Major War Criminals. Proceedings of the International Military Tribunal sitting at Nuremberg, Germany, Part 22 (22 August 1946 to 1 October 1946), 468 et seqq, 469.

6 On this trial, see the contribution by Milan Kuhli and Florian Jeßberger in this volume.

7 US Military Tribunal, Nuremberg, Judgment of 4 December 1947 (Altstötter et al, the so-called Justice Trial), in Trials of War Criminals Before the Nuremberg Military Tribunals Under Control Council Law No 10, Vol. III, 1156, 1029, 1142 (Joël), 1168 (Oeschey), 1176 (Altstötter).

8 This notwithstanding the fact that the specific dogmatic structure of the Article is still unclear. See Ambos, 'The ICC and Common Purpose – What Contribution is Required under Article 25(3)(d)?' in Stahn (ed) 592, 593.

9 Translation published by the Federal Ministry of Justice and the Federal Office of Justice, provided by M. Bohlander, revised and regularly updated by U. Reusch'. See www.gesetze-im-internet.de/englisch_stgb (accessed 15 August 2024).

10 See n 9. See EU Framework Decision of 13 June 2002 on Combating Terrorism, implemented into German criminal law on 28 December 2002.

11 Explanatory Memorandum, 8 April 2003, BT-Drs. 15/813, 6. By waiving these additional restricting elements in regard to paragraph 1 offenses, the German legislature went beyond the requirements of the Framework Decision it was obliged to implement. The same is true as regards the extraterritorial application of the crime of membership in a terrorist organization.

12 See n 9. This definition was incorporated into German criminal law on 28 December 2002, in order to implement the EU Framework Decision of 13 June 2002 on Combating Terrorism.

13 See Explanatory Memorandum, 22 February 2017, BT-Drs. 18/11275, 11. According to the previous definition applied by the courts, a hierarchically structured organization of the sort described was generally not covered by the term association. See, e.g., BGH, Decision of 17 November 1981, 3 StR 221/81; BGH, Judgment of 1 October 1991, 5 StR 390/91; BGH, Judgment of 16 March 2004, 5 StR 364/03; BGH, Decision of 8 August 2006, 5 StR 273/06.

14 See BGH, Judgment of 2 June 202, 3 StR 21/21; BGH, Decision of 2 June 2021, 3 StR 33/21.

15 See BGH, Judgment of 21 October 2004, 3 StR 94/04.

16 Kuhli, '§ 129: Bildung krimineller Vereinigungen' in Matt/Renzikowski (eds), *Kommentar zum Strafgesetzbuch*, para 21; Eschelbach, '§ 129a: Bildung terroristischer Vereinigungen' in Kindhäuser et al (eds), *Kommentar zum Strafgesetzbuch*, para 77 et seqq.

17 See also Eschelbach, '§ 129a: Bildung terroristischer Vereinigungen' in Kindhäuser et al (eds), *Kommentar zum Strafgesetzbuch*, para 65.

18 On these cases, see Weißer, 'Zur strafrechtlichen Verantwortlichkeit sog. "IS-Heimkehrerinnen"' (2019) 12 *ZJS* 148. See also Sayatz, 'Kriegsverbrechen gegen Eigentum' in Jeßberger/Epik (eds) 199 and Sayatz, 'Shadows of Return: A Critical Assessment of Prosecuting Female IS Returnees for War Crimes Against Property under the German Code of Crimes Against International Law', *JICJ* 22 (2024) 445.
19 BGH, Decision of 22 March 2018, StB 32/17.
20 Barros, 'Courts Out of Context: Authoritarian Sources of Judicial Failure in Chile (1973–1990) and Argentina (1976–1983)' in Ginsburg/Moustafa (eds) 156, 167 et seqq. See also the chapter by Jaime Couso in this volume.
21 Kuhli, '§ 129: Bildung krimineller Vereinigungen' in Matt/Renzikowski (eds), *Kommentar zum Strafgesetzbuch*, para 37.
22 This is confirmed by a look at practice; see below, main text. See also the presentation by former Federal Public Prosecutor Christian Ritscher, 'Cumulative Prosecution – Combining Charges of Counterterrorism and International Crimes: Remarks from a National Prosecutor's Point of View', presented to the conference 'International Criminal Law before Domestic Courts', held at the University of Vienna, 14–16 October 2021, www.iclconference21.com/panel1 (accessed 1 October 2023; video on file with the author).
23 On this trial, see Kaleck/Kroker (eds), *Syrian State Torture on Trial* (2023).
24 On this argument, see Geneuss, 'On the Relationship Between German International Criminal Law and Counter-Terrorism Criminal Law', 21 *JICJ* (2023) 839.

Bibliography

Ambos K, 'The ICC and Common Purpose – What Contribution is Required under Article 25(3)(d)?' in Stahn C (ed), *The Law and Practice of the International Criminal Court* (Oxford University Press 2015) 592.

Barros R, 'Courts Out of Context: Authoritarian Sources of Judicial Failure in Chile (1973–1990) and Argentina (1976–1983)' in Ginsburg T/Moustafa T (eds), *Rule by Law – The Politics of Courts in Authoritarian Regimes* (Cambridge University Press 2008) 156.

Burghardt B 'Die Strafsache "Oskar Gröning" vor dem Bundesgerichtshof – Zugleich Überlegungen zum Begriff der teilnahmefähigen Haupttat i.S.v. § 27 Abs. 1 StGB bei arbeitsteilig organisierten, systemischen Handlungszusammenhängen' (2019) 14 *Zeitschrift für internationale Strafrechtsdogmatik* 32.

Eschelbach R, '§ 129a: Bildung terroristischer Vereinigungen' in Kindhäuser U et al (eds), *Nomos Kommentar zum Strafgesetzbuch* (6th edn, Nomos 2023).

Geneuss J, 'On the Relationship Between German International Criminal Law and Counter-Terrorism Criminal Law' (2023) 21 *Journal of International Criminal Justice* 839.

Hawickhorst K, *§ 129a StGB – Ein feindstrafrechtlicher Irrweg zur Terrorismusbekämpfung, Kritische Analyse einer prozessualen Schlüsselnorm im materiellen Recht* (Duncker & Humblot 2011).

Kaleck W/Kroker P (eds), *Syrian State Torture on Trial* (Bundeszentrale für politische Bildung 2023).

Kuhli M, '§ 129: Bildung krimineller Vereinigungen' in Matt H/Renzikowski J (eds), *Kommentar zum Strafgesetzbuch* (2nd edn, Vahlen 2020).

Sayatz N, 'Kriegsverbrechen gegen Eigentum' in Jeßberger F/Epik A (eds), *Zwanzig Jahre Völkerstrafgesetzbuch – Anwendungspraxis und Reformbedarf* (Nomos 2023) 199.

Sayatz N, 'Shadows of Return: A Critical Assessment of Prosecuting Female IS Returnees for War Crimes Against Property under the German Code of Crimes Against International Law', *Journal of International Criminal Justice* 22 (2024) 445.

Weißer B, 'Die Entwicklung des deutschen Terrorismusstrafrechts – Expansionen und notwendige Eingrenzungen' (2019) 20 *Rechtswissenschaft* 453.

Weißer B, 'Zur strafrechtlichen Verantwortlichkeit sog. "IS-Heimkehrerinnen" ' (2019) 12 *Zeitschrift für das Juristische Studium* 148.

Werle G/Jeßberger F, *Principles of International Criminal Law* (4th edn, Oxford University Press 2020).

Closing Remarks

Claudia Cárdenas and Milan Kuhli

1 Nuremberg, Mendoza, and Beyond: Analysis from Different Perspectives and Legal Cultures

This volume has been devoted to reflections concerning one specific issue within the field of criminal prosecutions as a tool for transitional justice. We normally think of judges as active players in this regard, deciding on the criminal responsibility of others in order to uphold the rule of law. This is indeed a key role that judges play, as it helps to individualize guilt and determine some relevant facts beyond reasonable doubt, among other features.[1] However, this key role of judges as guarantors of the application of the law makes it unavoidable to ask about their own possible responsibility for actions or omissions during the period of unfettered criminality that the people have suffered.

As is often the case where transitional justice is concerned, no general rule can be laid down regarding the responsibility of judges, given the multitude of potential factual scenarios. These range from suspension from office during the relevant period, through being allowed to continue their work during the regime (in a manner that could be described as "business as usual"), to having active involvement as a tool of the regime. A mixture of different cases could also be present within a given situation: one may – *inter alia* – think of judges applying legal provisions that violate human rights, omitting using their legal powers to prevent or avoid crimes or committing other offenses. In a broader sense, one could also think about the potential involvement of public prosecutors or of ministerial officials in such situations.

If it is determined that judges should be held responsible, the next question is whether this responsibility should be a criminal one. The answer to this question is sometimes called into doubt, and indeed our volume shows different approaches to it in both historical and contemporary settings (e.g., chapters by Combs; Wilenmann; Jeßberger and Kuhli; and Rojas).

In every case it is relevant to examine judges' own self-understanding and self-representation in the aftermath of such events, as Accatino does in this volume for the Chilean situation after the Pinochet dictatorship. Such an examination can reveal how judges perceive not only their own actions but also those of their colleagues. It can also show how this perception may vary over time.

DOI: 10.4324/9781003470069-25

One can, of course, imagine configurations in which issues such as lack of knowledge militate against criminal liability. Such considerations, however, deal with aspects of intent and guilt rather than with criminal liability in principle. So, if one is able to affirm that judges have criminal responsibility for the commission of murder, unlawful detention, etc., the next question is to determine for what deeds they should be held responsible and in what way(s). This volume addresses some key components of these problems. It does so from a variety of legal perspectives, taking it as given that transitional justice, by virtue of its very nature, has to navigate international law as well as different national legal systems.

The link to transitional justice additionally arises from the fact that the possibility of prosecuting judges for their involvement in killings, kidnapping, or torture has mainly been discussed, or has mainly arisen in practice, precisely in transitional justice contexts. This is particularly evident where state power has been misused, such as under dictatorships (what in German is called *Unrechtssysteme*). Here the role of judges often becomes that of a mere functional component of the system, with their key role reduced to lending a semblance of legitimacy to the actions undertaken.

The reflections in this volume could also, of course, be applicable to instances where one single judge has acted criminally in an environment that is generally governed by the rule of law and where existing legal remedies have not been enough to avoid the effects of that judge's decision. The questions addressed in this volume have, however, instead arisen when such a judge has acted as part of a system of mistreatment, thereby abandoning his/her very role within the juridical system, which is mainly to guarantee effective judicial protection of the rights of citizens.[2]

Experience shows that the criminal prosecution of judges has been rare (chapters by Jeßberger and Kuhli; Cornelius; Werle and Vormbaum; and Palermo). Among the cases discussed, one can identify two main scenarios. On the one hand, we have judges who decided to impose death penalties or imprisonment in conditions that would, in the ordinary course of events, involve mistreatment or disappearance. On the other hand, we have judges who were less than assiduous in attending to requests for protection (*habeas corpus*) in places where people in state custody were being mistreated and/or subjected to enforced disappearances. What both scenarios have in common is that they are not simple cases of miscarriage of justice – something which is, to a degree, inherent to and present in any and every juridical system. What distinguishes these cases is that an additional factor was present: these public servants did not use their powers to properly protect people. Instead, they permitted (or even ordered) the commission of crimes, even while themselves under an institutional obligation to prevent such things from occurring. The fact that a judge has ruled on a matter gives it the appearance of legality, thereby making it more difficult to prosecute.

In most situations where judges were involved in one of the aforementioned ways, they have not (yet) been prosecuted. The volume explores the potential implications and challenges of such an enterprise (chapters by Couso; Viganò; and Martins).

Once initial barriers are removed and one reaches the conclusion that judges might indeed be held criminally responsible, the next challenge would be how to determine what type(s) of criminal responsibility should be applied in efforts to hold them accountable for their involvement (chapters by van Sliedregt; Hernández; Lorca; Geneuss; and Londoño).

2 Key Issue: What Counts as a Judicial Act?

While dealing with the challenges involved in prosecuting judges for murder, kidnapping, or torture, certain main strands for the legal approach to the protection of judicial independence can be identified. These include judicial immunities in common law systems (chapter by Combs), procedural safeguards in civil law countries (chapter by Wilenmann), or the doctrine of the blocking effect of the judicial perversion of justice (*Rechtsbeugung*) in the German case (chapters by Jeßberger and Kuhli; Rojas).

Notwithstanding the differences that these doctrinal approaches reflect, one can identify, as a general rule for a functioning judiciary, that prosecution of judges for judicial acts should be allowable only in very exceptional cases. Therefore, the key issue is reducible, in essence, to a common one: what constitutes a judicial decision? It is widely accepted that judges do have the power to make decisions whose consequences will deprive persons of their liberty or even – in countries that admit the death penalty – lead to deaths. In such cases, judges may accordingly claim that they acted within the scope of their duty or powers. What should be determinant, however, is not the mere formal appearance of a judicial act, but rather whether the decision was taken according to the law and the merits of the case, using all the information and resources available. Of course, the issue of a possible mistake becomes an important one in such a scenario. This possibility is addressed from different perspectives in this volume (chapters by Castillo; Martins).

In addressing the question of what counts as a proper judicial act, the production of which should be protected, some cases may appear clearer than others. Where people who should exercise jurisdiction have misused this power to merely send people to be executed, tortured, and/or illegally detained, in such a way that it becomes doubtful whether these persons were exercising jurisdiction at all, the results might well fall under the label of farcical prosecutions. (Configurations of this sort are examined in the chapter by Abraham.) It is, however, interesting to note that the matter of what counts as a proper exercise of jurisdiction has also been addressed by international law, in a way that might be useful to different legal systems, by means of the fraudulent *res judicata* (chapters by Cárdenas; Mañalich).

3 Future Perspectives

Insofar as there is a legal response to judicial crimes, the question of whether or not the pursuit of the criminal responsibility of judges is justified is not the only one that arises. At least as important is the question of what purposes are to be achieved through the punishment of cases of judicial murder or other judicial crimes. The question of whether and to what extent criminal law can have a deterrent effect is certainly ubiquitous. It has been pointed out that there are reasons to doubt a far-reaching deterrent effect or a positive outcome in terms of rehabilitation. Similarly, skeptical views may also be found in the transitional justice field, where the question arises of whether to seek criminal sanctions for previous behavior after a system change. It has been suggested that international legal norms and international human rights standards are contradicted by the demands that dictatorships and totalitarian systems may place on judicial behavior.

This volume shows that there are compelling reasons to deny a fanatical judge the legal defense of a mistake of law. However, where fanatical blindness is present, it can render criminal liability for judicial conduct in dictatorships *de facto* irrelevant for the judge(s) concerned, as they will not be motivated by the law. Instead, they will act – or fail to act – under the mantle of a guarantee of impunity, at least for as long as the state or organization concerned retains the power to protect them. Moreover, aspects of group dynamics and neutralization techniques are likely to mean that even the punishment of one judge (for example, by an international court or by another state) could have little influence over the conduct of (other) judges whose decisions are functional to a totalitarian regime. Normally, even if prosecutions do arise, they will be delayed. Legal remedies in the form of appeals to other courts may help to overturn wrongful convictions in states in which the rule of law still applies. If, however, injustice becomes the norm in a dictatorship, legal remedies are of little value. The country-focused chapters contained in this collection (e.g., chapters by Cornelius; Palermo) are compelling evidence of this.

Skepticism as to the effectiveness of criminal law should not, however, be used as an argument against its application. Rather, it becomes important to rely on additional preventive measures drawn from other areas of endeavor, such as approaches to the strengthening of democracies. As far as a focus on the judiciary goes, the training given to would-be judges should also be shaped so as to contribute to prevention. In this respect, for example, recent German legislation is to be commended insofar as it requires the history of Nazi Germany to be given greater consideration in university-level legal studies.[3]

This latter example also makes it clear that the history of law and training in or toward its application should not be regarded as separate disciplines but as necessarily related and mutually intertwined. Historical knowledge can, for instance, make it clear why certain principles of criminal law are fundamental. It can also serve as an object lesson in the potential consequences of inaction in the face of emerging developments.

The interaction between past and present has also been central to this volume, with the history of law playing a key role alongside political science and the principles of criminal law. As is well known, however, we can learn not only from the past but also from other countries and legal cultures. Accordingly, this volume has not only provided a look at countries affected by judicial crimes in Latin America (chapters by Couso; Accatino; and Mañalich) and Europe (chapter by Viganò) but has also facilitated mutual exchange between and across cases.

We hope to have provided indicative answers to the questions of why and under what conditions judicial crimes should be punishable and in which contexts this seems more likely than in others. The aim of the volume is thereby to contribute to a number of relevant debates by exposing their complexity and showing some different approaches and relevant experiences, rather than seeking to offer definitive answers to all the questions that arise in the field of judicial crimes.

Notes

1 Werle G/Vormbaum M *Transitional Justice. Vergangenheitsbewältigung durch Recht* (Springer 2018), 43 et seq.

2 Articles 6 and 13 of the European Convention for the Protection of Human Rights, Article 25 of the American Convention on Human Rights and Article 2.3 of the International Covenant on Civil and Political Rights.

3 See Kuhli M, 'Vergangenes Unrecht und geltendes Strafrecht. Zur Reflexion des NS- und SED-Unrechts in der Juraausbildung' in Broemel R et al (eds), *Forschung als Handlungs- und Kommunikationszusammenhang. Beiträge zur Verarbeitung gesellschaftlichen Wandels im Recht. Festschrift für Hans-Heinrich Trute zum 70. Geburtstag* (Mohr Siebeck 2023), 265.

Index

Note: Page numbers in **bold** refer to tables.

For Product Safety Concerns and Information please contact our EU
representative GPSR@taylorandfrancis.com
Taylor & Francis Verlag GmbH, Kaufingerstraße 24, 80331 München, Germany

www.ingramcontent.com/pod-product-compliance
Ingram Content Group UK Ltd.
Pitfield, Milton Keynes, MK11 3LW, UK
UKHW021724240926
475702UK00030BA/2668
* 9 7 8 1 0 3 2 7 4 6 0 8 1 *